lonely planet

AUSTRALIA'S
BEST TRIPS

38 AMAZING
ROAD TRIPS

DISCARDED
From Nashville Public Library

This edition written and researched by
Anthony Ham

SYMBOLS IN THIS BOOK

✓ Top Tips 📖 History & Culture 📷 Essential Photo

⑤ Link Your Trips 👪 Family 🏃 Walking Tour

🗨 Tips from Locals 🍷 Food & Drink 🍴 Eating

↪ Trip Detour 🌳 Outdoors 🛏 Sleeping

☏ Telephone Number @ Internet Access 📋 English-Language Menu

🕑 Opening Hours 🛜 Wi-Fi Access 👪 Family-Friendly

P Parking 🥗 Vegetarian Selection 🐾 Pet-Friendly

🚭 Nonsmoking 🏊 Swimming Pool

❄ Air-Conditioning

MAP LEGEND

Routes

▬▬ Trip Route
▬▬ Trip Detour
▬▬ Linked Trip
▬▬ Walk Route
▬▬ Tollway
▬▬ Freeway
▬▬ Primary
▬▬ Secondary
▬▬ Tertiary
▬▬ Lane
▬▬ Unsealed Road
⁙⁙⁙ Plaza/Mall
┅┅┅ Steps
)= = Tunnel
═══ Pedestrian Overpass
--- Walk Track/Path

Boundaries

--- International
--- State
┬┬┬ Cliff
▬▬ Wall

Population

✪ Capital (National)
◉ Capital (State)
● City/Large Town
○ Town/Village

Transport

✈ Airport
⊕ Cable Car/Funicular
P Parking
⊕ Train/Railway
Ⓖ Tram
Ⓜ Underground Train Station

Trips

1️⃣ Trip Numbers
9️⃣ Trip Stop
🏃 Walking tour
↪ Trip Detour

Route Markers

M31 1 National Highway
A5 63 State Route

Hydrography

∿ River/Creek
∿ Intermittent River
▒ Swamp/Mangrove
⌒ Canal
⬭ Water
⬭ Dry/Salt/Intermittent Lake
▒ Glacier

Areas

▒ Beach
▦ Cemetery (Christian)
▦ Cemetery (Other)
▒ Park
▒ Forest
▒ Urban Area
▒ Sportsground

Note: Not all symbols shown here appear on the maps in this book

---

PLAN YOUR TRIP

ON THE ROAD

NEW SOUTH WALES & THE AUSTRALIAN CAPITAL TERRITORY 33

CONTENTS

Northern Territory
p267

Queensland
p159

Western Australia
p315

South Australia
p215

New South Wales & the Australian Capital Territory
p33

Victoria
p99

Tasmania
p371

Contents cont.

DRIVING IN AUSTRALIA 420

Classic Trips

Look out for the Classic Trips stamp on our favourite routes in this book.

Bay of Fires A string of beaches off Tasmania's east coast

JODIE GRIGGS/GETTY IMAGES ©

WELCOME TO
AUSTRALIA

Australia is custom-made for some of the best road trips on the planet. From the sea cliffs of southern Tasmania to the rainforests of the tropical north, from stirring coastal odysseys to the lonely outback, Australia's paved roads take you on journeys that showcase the extraordinary beauty of this vast continent.

The 38 trips in this book will take you within sight of Uluru and the Great Barrier Reef, deep into the heart of Kakadu, the rainforests of Tasmania and the wine country of South and Western Australia, and along winding and world-famous routes such as the Great Ocean Road or the pilgrimage north from Sydney to Byron Bay.

Whether your dream is a transcontinental epic or a more intimate loop along quiet country roads, we've got it covered. And if you've only got time for one trip, make it one of our eight Classic Trips, which take you to the very best of Australia. Turn the page for more.

→

AUSTRALIA'S
Classic Trips

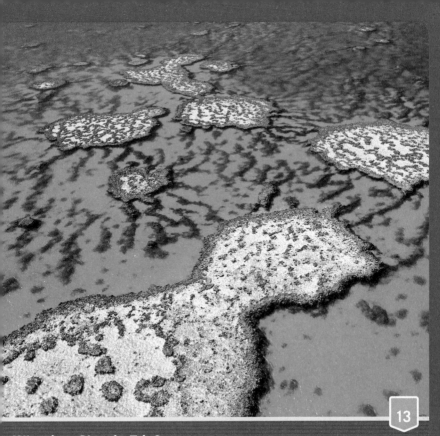

13

What is a Classic Trip?

All the trips in this book show you the best of Australia, but we've chosen eight as our all-time favourites. These are our Classic Trips – the ones that lead you to the best of the iconic sights, the top activities and the unique Australian experiences. Turn the page to see the map, and look out for the Classic Trip stamp throughout the book.

7 Great Ocean Road The forest meets the sea on this stunning coastal drive

13 Capricorn Coast Head north to the natural wonder of the Great Barrier Reef

19 Adelaide Hillls & the Barossa Sun-drenched vineyards and world-class wines

BENJAMIN GOODE/GETTY IMAGES ©

19

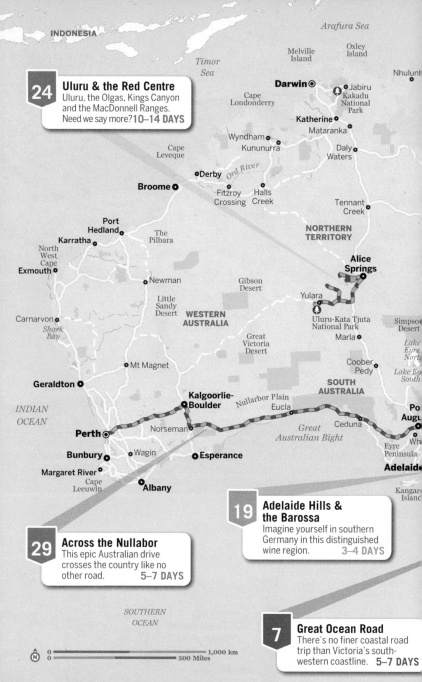

INDONESIA

Arafura Sea

Timor Sea

Melville Island

Oxley Island

Nhulunt

24 **Uluru & the Red Centre**
Uluru, the Olgas, Kings Canyon and the MacDonnell Ranges. Need we say more? **10–14 DAYS**

Darwin ⊙

Jabiru
Kakadu National Park

Cape Londonderry

Katherine ⊙
Mataranka ⊙

Wyndham ⊙
Kununurra

Daly Waters ⊙

Cape Leveque

⊙ Derby

Ord River

Broome ⊙

Fitzroy Crossing

Halls Creek

Tennant Creek ⊙

NORTHERN TERRITORY

Port Hedland ⊙
Karratha ⊙

The Pilbara

North West Cape
Exmouth ⊙

⊙ Newman

Gibson Desert

Alice Springs ⊙

Little Sandy Desert

WESTERN AUSTRALIA

Yulara

Carnarvon ⊙

Shark Bay

Great Victoria Desert

Uluru-Kata Tjuta National Park

Simpson Desert

Marla ⊙

Lake Eyre Nort

⊙ Mt Magnet

Coober Pedy ⊙

Lake Eyr South

Geraldton ⊙

SOUTH AUSTRALIA

Kalgoorlie-Boulder ⊙

Nullarbor Plain

Eucla

Po Augu

INDIAN OCEAN

Perth ⊙

Norseman ⊙

Ceduna ⊙

Great Australian Bight

Wh

Bunbury ⊙

⊙ Wagin

Esperance ⊙

Eyre Peninsula

Margaret River ⊙

Cape Leeuwin

Albany ⊙

Adelaide ⊙

19 **Adelaide Hills & the Barossa**
Imagine yourself in southern Germany in this distinguished wine region. **3–4 DAYS**

Kangar Islanc

29 **Across the Nullabor**
This epic Australian drive crosses the country like no other road. **5–7 DAYS**

SOUTHERN OCEAN

Ⓝ 0 ———— 1,000 km
0 ———— 500 Miles

7 **Great Ocean Road**
There's no finer coastal road trip than Victoria's south-western coastline. **5–7 DAYS**

AUSTRALIA'S
Classic Trips

13 **Capricorn Coast**
This brilliant road trip connects clamorous south with reef-fringed north. **10–14 DAYS**

1 **Sydney to Byron Bay**
The ultimate Aussie drive takes in surf beaches and breezy coastal towns. **7–10 DAYS**

2 **Sydney to Melbourne**
This coastal epic connects two dynamic cities via a string of beautiful towns. **5–7 DAYS**

34 **East Coast Tasmania**
Think of Tasmania and there's a fair chance you're thinking of the storied east coast. **3–5 DAYS**

Australia's best sights and experiences, and the road trips that will take you there.

AUSTRALIA
HIGHLIGHTS

Great Barrier Reef

The Great Barrier Reef is a jaw-droppingly beautiful underwater world rich in marine life and ripe for exploration. The reef extends almost 2000km along the Queensland coast, and you'll often find yourself within snorkelling, diving or scenic-flight distance of the reef and its extraordinary coral and colourful sea creatures. **Trip 13: Capricorn Coast** follows the reef pretty much all the way.

Trips

JEFF HUNTER/GETTY IMAGES ©

Great Barrier Reef Divers explore the reef's coral and sea life

Twelve Apostles Coastal Victoria's iconic landforms

Kakadu National Park

A prime candidate for the title of Australia's most remarkable wilderness, Kakadu National Park is a wild and elemental place. As you'll quickly discover on **Trip 27: Darwin & Kakadu**, Kakadu is a land of saltwater crocodiles lurking in postcard-pretty waterholes, of Indigenous rock art sheltering under jagged escarpments, and of utterly magnificent sunsets.

Trip 27

Twelve Apostles

The Twelve Apostles, craggy rock formations jutting out of wild waters, are one of Victoria's most vivid sights, and they've come to symbolise this stunning corner of the country with long and lonely Bass Strait beaches and dramatic rock formations. But it's the 'getting there' road trip on **Trip 7: Great Ocean Road**, one of the world's great coastal drives, that doubles their impact.

Trip 7

Byron Bay

Up there with kangaroos and Akubra hats, big-hearted Byron Bay (just Byron to its mates) is one of the enduring icons of Aussie culture and it's the main aim of **Trip 1: Sydney to Byron Bay**. Families, surfers and sun-seekers from across the globe gather by the foreshore at sunset, drawn by a chilled pace of life, an astonishing range of activities and, above all, an utterly splendid coastline.

Trip 1

Kakadu National Park Jim Jim Falls

BEST ROADS FOR DRIVING

Great Ocean Road Picturesque scenery and plenty of places to pull over. **Trip** 7

Route 1 (Pacific Highway) Iconic and spectacular road trip with numerous tempting detours. **Trip** 1

Stuart Highway Like traversing the outback soul of Australia. **Trip** 25

Tasman Highway Consistently Tasmania's most dramatic coastline. **Trip** 34

Indian Ocean Drive Long, but endlessly fascinating, between desert and sea. **Trip** 32

Daintree Rainforest

Lush green rainforests tumble down to a brilliant white-sand coastline in the ancient, World Heritage–listed Daintree Rainforest, and it's this meeting of reef and rainforest that dominates **Trip 16: Cairns & the Daintree**. This is an ancient world and there's no better way to explore it than in the company of the Kuku Yalanji who take you out into their traditional lands at Mossman Gorge.

Trip 16

15

HIGHLIGHTS ★

Uluru-Kata Tjuta National Park The Olgas (Kata Tjuta)

HOLGER LEUE/GETTY IMAGES ©

Uluru-Kata Tjuta National Park

Nothing prepares you for the burnished grandeur of Uluru as it first appears on the outback horizon. With its remote desert location, deep cultural significance and dazzling natural beauty, Uluru is a pilgrimage of sorts and the unforgettable centrepiece of **Trip 24: Uluru & the Red Centre**. Along with the equally captivating Kata Tjuta (the Olgas), it's an otherworldly terrain of mystical walks, sublime sunsets and ancient desert cultures.

Trip 24

BEST WINE REGIONS

Barossa Valley Old-school SA wineries with a Germanic feel. Trip 19

McLaren Vale SA reds that rival the best on earth. Trip 20

Clare Valley SA's quiet achiever on the outback cusp. Trip 23

Margaret River Beautiful WA gourmet landscape. Trip 31

Tamar Valley Developing cool-climate wine region of northern Tassie. Trip 37

TROYANA/GETTY IMAGES ©

Barossa Valley Vineyards in South Australian wine country

DAVID WALL PHOTO/GETTY IMAGES ©

Bungle Bungles Cathedral Gorge

Bungle Bungles

Harsh, remote and beautiful, Australia's final frontier is what **Trip 33: Kimberley Crossing** is all about. The soulful indigenous lands of the Kimberleys and the vast horizons of the outback come together in the Bungle Bungles, one of the most astonishing places anywhere in Australia. It's a place to switch off the engine and contemplate the spellbinding serenity.

Trip

South Australian Wine Regions

SA is home to three world-famous wine regions: the Barossa Valley, with its gutsy reds and German know-how (**Trip 19: Adelaide Hills & the Barossa**); McLaren Vale, a palette of sea, vines and shiraz (**Trip 20: McLaren Vale & Kangaroo Island**); and the Clare Valley, known for riesling and historic towns (**Trip 23: Clare Valley & the Flinders Ranges**).

Trips

Whale Watching

Wine and whales dominate **Trip 30: Western Australia's Southwest Coast**, one of Australia's most underrated coastlines, where it's not unusual to find yourself on a white-sand beach where the only footprints are your own. In late winter and early spring, spot whales migrating along the Humpback Highway, with Albany the ideal base for getting close to these giants.

Trips 30 31 32

Wilsons Prom

Mainland Australia's southernmost point and finest coastal national park, Wilsons Prom is heaven for bushwalkers, wildlife-watchers and surfers. The bushland and coastal scenery here is out of this world; even short walks from the main base at Tidal River will take you to beautiful beaches and bays. Drive **Trip 9: Gippsland & Wilsons Prom** for the best Prom views, then get out and walk if you're eager for more.

Trip 9

Kosciuszko National Park

The Australian alps may not reach great heights, but they're intensely beautiful nonetheless. **Trip 3: Snowy Mountains** weaves within Kosciuszko National Park where you'll see the classic and remote Bradleys and O'Briens Hut. Nearby is Permanent Creek, where there's a palpable sense of humanity's smallness amid the stunning natural surrounds.

Trip 3

PETER WALTON PHOTOGRAPHY/GETTY IMAGES ©

(left) **Wilsons Prom**
(below) **Cradle Mountain**

WWW.COLUMODWYER.COM/GETTY IMAGES ©

Cradle Mountain

A precipitous comb of rock carved out by millennia of ice and wind, crescent-shaped Cradle Mountain is the essence of wild Tasmania, a stirring mountain realm of extraordinary natural beauty. Wildlife here is abundant, there are numerous walks to all manner of beautiful corners and you can drive into the heart of the park as a stirring stop along **Trip 38: West Coast Wilderness Way**.

Trip 38

BEST OF THE OUTBACK

Red Centre Uluru, Kings Canyon, Olgas – need we say more? **Trip** 24

Mungo National Park Ancient, wind-sculpted land in southwest NSW. **Trip** 6

Outback Queensland Dry desert and the dense mangroves of the Gulf. **Trip** 18

Flinders Ranges Like a mini-Kimberleys in South Australia. **Trip** 23

Broome to Kununurra Kimberley to the north, deep desert to the south. **Trip** 33

IF YOU LIKE...

Architecture Oatlands, Tasmania

Wildlife

Australia is one of the world's leading wildlife-watching destinations. See koalas, kangaroos and all manner of world-famous Aussie creatures at numerous places around the country, while the bravest among you may want to cage-swim with great white sharks. Whales, too, are a possibility.

7 Great Ocean Road
Koalas at Kennett River, whales at Warrnambool and kangaroos at Anglesea.

20 McLaren Vale & Kangaroo Island Wildlife-rich Kangaroo Island has plenty of Aussie icons.

38 West Coast Wilderness Way Cradle Mountain is fabulous for wombats, pademelons, wallabies and echidnas.

21 Yorke & Eyre Peninsulas Swim with sea lions, great white sharks and tuna at Port Lincoln.

Historic Architecture

The early settlers to Australia built their structures to last, and 19th-century streetscapes are a feature of so many small towns across the country, although it's predominantly in the east and south that you're likely to find the richest pickings.

35 Heritage Trail Stone-built towns line the road from Hobart to Launceston.

38 West Coast Wilderness Way Georgian and Victorian landmarks line the streets of Tasmania's Deloraine.

10 Victoria's Goldfields
Castlemaine, Maldon, Ballarat and the Maryborough train station mark the gold-rush past.

11 Great Alpine Road
Almost uniformly sandstone Beechworth glows golden in late afternoon.

Wild Coastlines

With more than 35,000km of coastline, Australia has one of the longest coastlines on earth, and much of it is utterly spectacular, from remote beaches that seem to stretch into eternity to dramatic sea cliffs that ward off the great emptiness.

32 Coral Coast The Ningaloo Reef, Broome's Cable Beach, the Dampier Peninsula...

16 Cairns & the Daintree
Dense rainforest crowds the coast at idyllic beaches like Cape Tribulation.

38 West Coast Wilderness Way Western Tasmania's unspoiled beaches would be paradise if not for the weather.

36 Tasman Peninsula Cape Pillar's 300m-high sea cliffs are near Fortescue Bay.

30 Western Australia's Southwest Coast Whales in the vast Southern Ocean and a forested hinterland.

Food & Wine Lunch in Red Hill, Mornington Peninsula

Food & Wine

Australia's gourmet food trail just keeps on getting better, and southern Australia's main foodie focal points are far too numerous to mention here. In addition to what follows, there's the better-known Barossa Valley, McLaren Vale, Clare Valley and so much more.

31 Margaret River Wine Region Where food-lovers plan to spend their entire holidays.

8 Mornington Peninsula Wines, markets and cellar-door restaurants on Melbourne's doorstep.

11 Great Alpine Road The Milawa Gourmet Region has mustards, cheeses and wines.

6 Outback New South Wales Mudgee wines with a discerning foodie culture.

22 Coonawarra & the Coorong Southwestern SA's boutique wine region without the crowds.

Rainforest

Some of the oldest rainforests on earth inhabit Australia, but it's not just the preserve of the tropical north – cool temperate rainforests carpet much of Tasmania, while the Queensland and NSW coastal hinterlands also have vast stands of tall trees.

38 West Coast Wilderness Way Much of western Tasmania is dense rainforest, accessible from Strahan or Corinna.

16 Cairns & the Daintree Queensland's most celebrated rainforest right next to the sea.

5 New England A skywalk at Dorrigo National Park, part of the Gondwana Rainforests World Heritage Area.

14 Southern Queensland Loop Australia's largest remnant of subtropical rainforest.

Indigenous Culture

Australia's original inhabitants bring soul and personality to so many corners of the land, and these, the traditional owners, make wonderful companions for exploring many corners of the north. Elsewhere, rock art tells an ancient story of traditional ownership.

33 Kimberley Crossing Indigenous cultural tours, rock art and sacred places in the southern Kimberley.

16 Cairns & the Daintree The Indigenous rainforest tours at Mossman Gorge are outstanding.

24 Uluru & the Red Centre The Red Centre is Australia's Aboriginal heartland.

17 Cape York Prelude Eerily remote, 14,000-year-old rock art at Quinkan.

NEED ^{TO} KNOW

MOBILE PHONES

European phones work on Australia's network, but most American and Japanese phones won't. Use global roaming or a local SIM card and prepaid account. Telstra has the widest coverage.

INTERNET ACCESS

Wi-fi is widespread in urban areas, less so in remote Australia. For public wi-fi locations, visit www.freewifi.com.au. There are relatively few internet cafes; try public libraries.

FUEL

Unleaded and diesel fuel widely available. Prices vary from $1.20 in cities to $2.20 in the outback. Distances between fill-ups can be long in the outback.

RENTAL CARS

Avis (www.avis.com.au)

Budget (www.budget.com.au)

Europcar (www.europcar.com.au)

Hertz (www.hertz.com.au)

IMPORTANT NUMBERS

Emergencies ☏ 000

International Access Code ☏ 0011

Climate

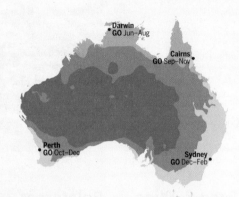

Darwin
GO Jun–Aug

Cairns
GO Sep–Nov

Perth
GO Oct–Dec

Sydney
GO Dec–Feb

Hobart
GO Jan–Mar

- Desert, dry climate
- Dry climate
- Tropical climate, wet/dry seasons
- Warm to hot summers, mild winters

When to Go

High Season (Dec–Feb)

» Summertime: local holidays, busy beaches and cricket.

» Prices rise 25% for big-city accommodation.

» Wet (and hence low) season in northern WA, NT and northern Queensland.

Shoulder Season (Mar–May & Sep–Nov)

» Warm sun, clear skies, shorter queues.

» Easter (late March or early April) is busy with Aussie families on the loose.

» Autumn leaves are atmospheric in Victoria, Tasmania and South Australia.

Low Season (Jun–Aug)

» Cool rainy days down south; mild days and sunny skies up north.

» Low tourist numbers; attractions keep slightly shorter hours.

» Head for the desert, the tropical north or the snow.

Daily Costs

Budget: Less than $100
» Hostel dorm bed: $25–$35 a night
» Simple pizza or pasta meal: $10–$15
» Short bus or tram ride: $4

Midrange: $100–$280
» Double room in a motel, B&B or hotel: $100–$200
» Breakfast or lunch in a cafe: $20–$40
» Short taxi ride: $25

Top End: More than $280
» Double room in a top-end hotel: from $200
» Three-course meal in a classy restaurant: $80
» Nightclub cover charge: $10–$20

Eating

Cafes Good for breakfasts and light lunches.

Restaurants International and mod-Oz cuisine.

Pubs Well-priced bistro food.

Roadhouses No-nonsense outback meals.

Vegetarians Wide choice in cities, less so elsewhere.

Eating price indicators represent the cost of a standard main course:

$	under $15
$$	$15–$32
$$$	more than $32

Sleeping

B&Bs Often in restored heritage buildings.

Campgrounds & Caravan Parks Most have sites and simple cabins.

Hostels Buzzing budget digs with dorm beds.

Hotels From simple to upmarket.

Motels No-frills but fine for a night.

Sleeping price indicators represent the cost of a double room with private bathroom in high season. Sydney, Perth and parts of northern Western Australia will cost more:

$	under $100
$$	$100–$200
$$$	more than $200

Arriving in Australia

Sydney Airport
Bus Pre-arranged shuttle buses service city hotels.

Train AirportLink trains run to the city centre every 10 minutes from around 5am to 1am (20 minutes).

Taxi A taxi into the city costs $40 to $50 (30 minutes).

Melbourne Airport
Bus SkyBus services (24-hour) run to the city (20 minutes), leaving every 10 to 30 minutes.

Taxi A taxi into the city costs around $40 (25 minutes).

Brisbane Airport
Bus Shuttle buses service city hotels (bookings required).

Train Airtrain run into the city centre (20 minutes) every 15 to 30 minutes from 5am (6am weekends) to 10pm.

Taxi A taxi into the city costs $35 to $45 (25 minutes).

Money

ATMs are widespread, but not off the beaten track or in some small towns. Visa and MasterCard are widely accepted, Diners Club and Amex less so.

Tipping

It's common (but not obligatory) to tip in restaurants if the service warrants it; 5% to 10% is the norm. Round up taxi fares.

Opening Hours

Banks 9.30am-4pm Monday to Thursday, until 5pm Friday

Cafes 7am-4pm or 5pm

Petrol stations & roadhouses 8am-10pm

Pubs noon-2pm and 6-9pm (food); drinking hours are longer and continue into the evening, especially from Thursday to Saturday

Restaurants noon-2pm and 6-9pm

Shops 10am-5pm or 6pm Monday to Friday, until either noon or 5pm on Saturday and (in major cities and tourist towns) Sunday

For more, see Driving in Australia (p420).

CITY GUIDE

Sydney Opera House

SYDNEY

Sydney is big, brash and spectacular, its unmistakeable glamour propelling it into the pantheon of the world's greatest cities. Its harbourside location speaks for itself, its culinary offering gets better with each passing year, and intimate, historic streets nicely complement the big-ticket attractions that won the city its fame.

Getting Around

Avoid driving in central Sydney if you can: there's a confusing one-way street system, parking's elusive and expensive, and parking inspectors, tolls and tow-away zones proliferate. Once you've ditched the car, the train system is the linchpin, with lines radiating out from Central station. Ferries head around the harbour.

Parking

Sydney's private car parks are expensive (around $15 per hour); public car parks are more affordable (sometimes under $10 per hour). Street parking devours coins (from $2.50 to $5 per hour), although some take credit cards.

Where to Eat

Circular Quay & The Rocks are home to Sydney's best and priciest fine-dining restaurants. In the City Centre, watch for all-hours dim sum. Atmospheric Paddington and Centennial Park are all gastropubs, chic cafes and white-linen restaurants.

Where to Stay

For the best transport links and possibly even a harbour view, Circular Quay, The Rocks and Sydney Harbour means most places are accessible on foot, but prices are sky high. Bondi to Coogee is all about sand, surf and sexy bods and a slow bus ride to the city.

Useful Websites

Destination NSW
(www.sydney.com) Official visitors' guide.

Urban Spoon
(www.urbanspoon.com) Restaurant ratings.

Lonely Planet
(www.lonelyplanet.com/sydney) Destination information.

Trips through Sydney:

DAVID HILL/GETTY IMAGES ©

Melbourne Centre Place

MELBOURNE

Melbourne is one cool city. The culinary and coffee scene is widely considered to be the best and most diverse in Australia, while its arts and sporting scenes lie at the heart of its appeal. Abundant greenery, a revitalised riverbank and laneways with attitude round out an irresistible package.

Getting Around

Some of the major free-ways have well-signposted toll sections. The City Loop train line runs under the city, and trams in the CBD are free. Buy a myki Visitor Pack ($14), which gets you one day's travel and discounts on various sights; available only from the airport, Skybus ter-minal or the PTV Hub at Southern Cross Station.

Parking

Most street parking is me-tered ($3.20 to $5.50 per hour); avoid the signposted Clearway zones. There are plenty of (expensive) park-ing garages in the city; rates vary and some have cheaper weekend deals.

Where to Eat

The city centre and South-bank areas are awash with fabulous restaurants to suit all budgets; yum cha for Sunday lunch in Chinatown is a city insti-tution. Carlton's Lygon St is famous for Italian restaurants, while Fitzroy and Brunswick have astonishing multicultural variety.

Where to Stay

Plenty of places in the city centre cover all price ranges and put you in the heart of the action. Other options are more far flung.

Useful Websites

Broadsheet Melbourne (www.broadsheet.com.au) The best eating, drinking and shopping spots.

That's Melbourne (www.thatsmelbourne.com.au) Downloadable maps, info and podcasts.

Trip through Melbourne:

Brisbane South Bank Parklands

BRISBANE

If you've never been to Brisbane, you'll love it, and if you haven't been here for a while, you'll be surprised. It's a diverse, happening and slightly eccentric city, a Queensland version of the sophisticated south but with nice weather and a refreshing lack of prentension.

Getting Around

A GPS unit could be your best friend: Brisbane's streets are convoluted. Thankfully, Brisbane has an excellent public-transport network (bus, train and ferry) run by TransLink. A single-trip fare in zone 1 costs $5.20.

Parking

There's ticketed two-hour parking on many streets in the CBD and the inner suburbs. During the day, parking is cheaper around South Bank and the West End than in the city centre, but it's free in the CBD during the evening.

Where to Eat

The city centre is the place for fine dining and coffee nooks. In Fortitude Valley you'll find cheap cafes and Chinatown. Nearby, New Farm has plenty of multi-cultural eateries, French-style cafes and award winners. Eclectic West End is littered with bohemian cafes and cheap multicultural diners. South Bank swings between mainstream and pricey eats.

Where to Stay

Head for Spring Hill for peace and quiet; Fortitude Valley for party nights; Paddington for cafes and boutiques; Petrie Terrace for hostels; gay-friendly New Farm for restaurants; and West End for bars and bookshops.

Useful Websites

Brisbane Visitor Information Centre (www.visitbrisbane.com.au) The low-down on the city's attractions.

Translink (www.translink.com. au) Brisbane transport info.

Trips Through Brisbane: `13` `14` `15`

Perth Kings Park

PERTH

Laid-back, liveable Perth has wonderful weather, beautiful beaches and an easygoing character. It's a sophisticated, cosmopolitan city with myriad bars, restaurants and cultural activities all vying for attention. When you want to chill out, it's easy to do so in the city's pristine parkland, bush and beaches.

Getting Around

Driving in the city takes practice as some streets are one way and many aren't signed. The metropolitan area is serviced by a wide network of Transperth buses (www.transperth.wa.gov.au) and three free Central Area Transit (CAT) services.

Parking

There are plenty of car-parking buildings in the central city, but no free parks. For unmetered street parking you'll need to look well away from the main commercial strips and check the signs carefully.

Where to Eat

The happening neighbourhoods for cafes and restaurants are Northbridge, Leederville and Mt Lawley, and the city centre has new options in the Brookfield Pl precinct on St George's Tce. Prices can be eye-watering, but it's still possible to eat cheaply, especially in the Little Asia section of William St, Northbridge.

Where to Stay

Perth is very spread out. Northbridge is backpacker/boozer central, and can be noisy. The CBD and Northbridge are close to public transport. If you love the beach, consider staying there as public transport can be time-consuming.

Useful Websites

Heat Seeker (www.heatseeker.com.au) Gig guide and ticketing.

Perth Now (www.perthnow.com.au) Perth and WA news and restaurant reviews.

Trips Through Perth:

AUSTRALIA
BY REGION

Vast in scale and astonishingly diverse, Australia is a road-tripper's dream, with a canvas of jagged coastline, soulful outback and epic rainforests. Here's your guide to what each Australian region has to offer.

Northern Territory
(p267)

There's a rougher edge, a frontier feel to the Top End (as the Territory's known), a place where crocs lurk in the shallows and wildly beautiful landmarks – Uluru, Kata Tjuta, Kings Canyon, Kakadu, Litchfield National Park – provide a canvas for Aboriginal artists and guides alike.

Watch an Uluru sunset on Trip `24`

Discover Aboriginal art on Trip `25`

Western Australia
(p315)

Australia's largest state has a suitably varied palette of ocean turquoise, vineyard green and outback red. The wine regions and forests of the southwest yield to world-class attractions – the Pinnacles, Ningaloo Reef, the Kimberley, the Bungle Bungles – with wildlife and Indigenous culture recurring themes.

Indulge your inner foodie on Trip `31`

Feed the dolphins on Trip `32`

South Australia
(p215)

Wines dominate much of the South Australian experience, with four premier wine regions providing a pleasurable focus for four road trips. Kangaroo island and Port Lincoln are fabulous for wildlife, while Coober Pedy and the Flinders Ranges are unforgettable tastes of the Outback.

Sample Barossa wines on Trip `19`

Swim with sharks on Trip `21`

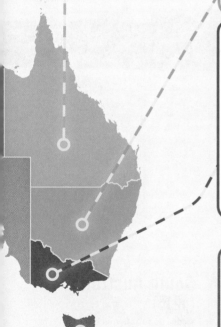

Queensland (p159)

The Great Barrier Reef shadows the coastline for more than 2000km, expansive rainforests are filled with wildlife and Indigenous stories, and the outback is a vast expanse of remote townships, dramatic landforms and big horizons. Down south, it's all about glitz, glamour and good times.

Snorkel the Great Barrier Reef on Trip 16

Admire the rock art on Trip 17

New South Wales & the Australian Capital Territory (p33)

Pretty seaside towns populate NSW's long and lovely coastline, then there are rainforests, world-class wine regions and Australia's highest peaks. Go a little further and you'll soon find yourself in the big-sky world of the outback.

Climb a mountain on Trip 3

Learn to surf on Trip  1

Victoria (p99)

Victoria's coastline rivals any on the continent, while its interior encompasses an exceptional portfolio of historic towns that struck it rich in the 19th century during the gold rush and riverboat trade. Throw in fine ski resorts and foodie towns and this is one of our favourite states.

Watch for whales on Trip 7

Pan for gold on Trip 10

Tasmania (p371)

Tasmania is one of the last great wilderness regions on earth. Drama-filled landscapes extend from the Cradle Mountain ramparts to the sea cliffs of the Tasman Peninsula. Historic towns, a gourmet wine region and wildlife you'll find nowhere else round out a small but fantastic package.

Return to the 19th century on Trip 35

Walk with wombats on Trip 38

New South Wales & the Australian Capital Territory Trips

SOME OF AUSTRALIA'S MOST MEMORABLE EXPERIENCES AWAIT YOU along the roads of its most populous state. Long the favourite of endearingly painted combis, NSW's coastline has always been one of the country's most popular road trips, connecting a string of quintessentially Aussie towns where the surfboard is king, from Batemans Bay to Byron. Leave the coast behind and a different world awaits, a land of hippie communities and the surprising stands of rainforest around New England, the stirring high country of Kosciuszko, and south to the wine region of Mudgee. And not far from Canberra, that underrated capital of a nation, the traffic thins and the colours turn to red and yellow in Bourke and Broken Hill and the profound silence of the outback reigns.

Byron Bay Main Beach (Trip 1)
PHOTO BY KARL LUNDHOLM/GETTY IMAGES ©

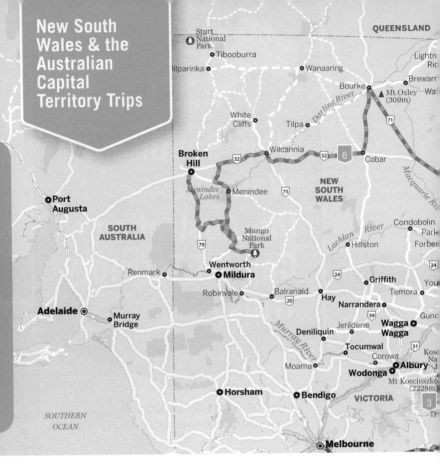

New South Wales & the Australian Capital Territory Trips

DON'T MISS

Wategos Beach

Leave the crowds of Byron Bay and seek the solitude of rainforest-fringed Wategos Beach. Visit on Trip **1**

Jervis Bay

Do everything it's possible to do above and below the water at wildly beautiful Jervis Bay. Go there on Trip **2**

Kangaroo Valley

Deviate from the coast for southern NSW's best-kept secret, utterly beautiful Kangaroo Valley. Explore it on Trip **4**

Roth's Wine Bar

Park your car and settle in for the night at NSW's oldest wine bar, Roth's, in the Mudgee wine region. Sidle up to the bar on Trip **6**

Permanent Creek

Soak up the poignant silence high above the treeline in Kosciuszko National Park. Make your way there on Trip **3**

Kangaroo Valley Fitzroy Falls (Trip 4)

Byron Bay Surf culture meets
hippie heartland

Classic Trip

Sydney to Byron Bay

1

One of the best-loved road trips anywhere on earth, this coastal odyssey connects two Aussie icons, with many a beautiful surf beach and wild coastal national park in between.

TRIP HIGHLIGHTS

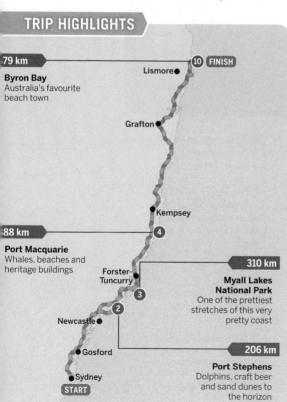

79 km

Byron Bay
Australia's favourite beach town

88 km

Port Macquarie
Whales, beaches and heritage buildings

310 km

Myall Lakes National Park
One of the prettiest stretches of this very pretty coast

206 km

Port Stephens
Dolphins, craft beer and sand dunes to the horizon

7–10 DAYS (OR A LIFETIME)
879KM / 546 MILES

GREAT FOR...

BEST TIME TO GO
November to March, when the weather's warm and the livin's good.

ESSENTIAL PHOTO
Sunset on the beach at Byron Bay.

BEST FOR FAMILIES
Port Stephens has wild dolphins, sand dunes and sheltered coves.

37

Classic Trip

1 Sydney to Byron Bay

Tearing yourself away from Sydney's singular charms is made easier by what lies ahead on this journey up the northern New South Wales coast. Classic beach resorts like Nambucca Heads and Coffs Harbour share the road with more family-oriented places like Ports Stephens and Macquarie, as well as national parks that protect some of the coast's more dramatic stretches. And don't miss the chance to go hippie in Nimbin!

- - - - - - - - - - - - - -

1 Sydney

Sydney is one of the greatest cities on earth, and its harbour is one of the most naturally beautiful settings for a city you can imagine. Scratch the surface and it only gets better. Compared to its Australian sister cities, Sydney is loud, uncompromising and in-your-face. Here the fireworks displays are more dazzling, heels are higher, bodies are more buffed, contact sports are more brutal, starlets are shinier, drag queens are glitzier and chefs are more adventurous. Australia's best musos, foodies, actors, stockbrokers, models, writers and architects flock to the city to make their mark, and the effect is dazzling: a hyperenergetic, ambitious marketplace of the soul, where anything goes and everything usually does. For a walking tour of Sydney, see p60.

The Drive » Rte 1 (Pacific Hwy) seems to take forever to leave the city's northern sprawl, but you're rewarded with some surprisingly wild country as the road cuts

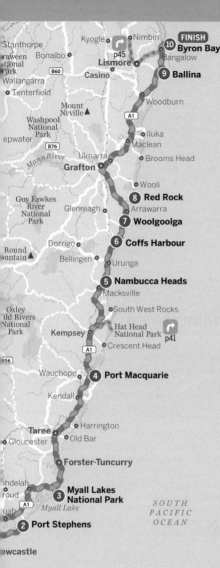

through Ku-ring-gai Chase National Park. Ignore turn-offs to Gosford, Wyong and Newcastle, but do no such thing when you see the Port Stephens sign (about an hour north of Newcastle).

TRIP HIGHLIGHT

② Port Stephens

Beloved by Sydney-siders looking for a slice of tranquil paradise without straying too far, Port Stephens inhabits a sheltered harbour along a submerged valley that stretches more than 20km inland. Framing its southern edge is the narrow Tomaree Peninsula, blessed with near-deserted beaches, national parks and an extraordinary sand-dune system. From the main centre, Nelson Bay, experience moving through a wild dolphin pod with **Dolphin Swim Australia** (☏1300 721 358;

LINK YOUR TRIP

2 Sydney to Melbourne

This drive along the coast to connect Australia's two largest cities begins in Sydney, perfect for when you finally come back from Byron.

4 Canberra & the South Coast

This route starts in Wollongong, just 84km south of Sydney's CBD.

Classic Trip

www.dolphinswimaustralia.com.au; 5hr trips $289; ⊗Sat & Sun Sep-May). Places in the vicinity to look out for include: **One Mile Beach**, a gorgeous semicircle of the softest sand and bluest water; the cult **Murray's Craft Brewing Co** (☎02-4982 6411; www.murraysbrewingco.com.au; 3443 Nelson Bay Rd, Bob's Farm; ⊗Tours at 2.15pm);

and the incredible **Worimi Conservation Lands** (www.worimiconservationlands.com; 3-day entry permits $10), the longest, moving sand dunes in the southern hemisphere, and where it's possible to become so surrounded by shimmering sand that you'll lose sight of the ocean or any sign of life.

✕ ⊨ p46

The Drive » Return to Rte 1 and at Bulahdelah turn east and follow the signs to Myall Lakes National Park.

TRIP HIGHLIGHT

❸ Myall Lakes National Park

On an extravagantly pretty section of the coast, the large **Myall Lakes National Park** (www.nationalparks.nsw.gov.au/myall-lakes-national-park; vehicle admission $7) incorporates a patchwork of lakes, islands, dense littoral rainforest and beaches. The lakes support an incredible

---

DETOUR: HUNTER VALLEY WINE REGION

Start: ❷ Port Stephens

Just south of the turn-off to Port Stephens, Rte 15 branches away to the northwest to Maitland, a nondescript regional centre that serves as a gateway to the Hunter Valley, one of Australia's favourite wine regions. Here, a skein of narrow lanes crisscrosses the verdant valley, and whichever road you take you'll encounter something to satisfy your inner foodie: fine wine, boutique beer, chocolate, cheese, olives... Bacchus would surely approve.

Home to some of the oldest vines (1860s) and biggest names in Australian wine, the Hunter is known for its semillon, shiraz and, increasingly, chardonnay. The valley's 150-plus wineries range from small-scale, family-run affairs to massive commercial operations. Most offer free tastings, although some charge a small fee.

There is a feeling in some circles that that the Hunter Valley has lost ground to producers in South and Western Australia. But a new generation of Hunter Valley winemakers has begun to exert greater influence over the local styles and is doing much to reinvigorate the local scene. These wineries are refreshingly attitude-free and welcoming of novices. Staff will rarely give you the evil eye if you swirl your glass once too often, or don't conspicuously savour the bouquet.

Most attractions lie in an area bordered to the north by the New England Hwy and to the south by Wollombi/Maitland Rd, with the main cluster of wineries and restaurants in Pokolbin. For spectacular views and a more chilled-out pace head to the vineyards northwest around Broke and Singleton. Grab a copy of the free *Hunter Valley Official Guide* from the visitor centre at Pokolbin and use its handy map to plot your course, or just follow your nose, hunting out the tucked-away small producers.

The Hunter Valley is exceedingly hot during summer so, like its shiraz, it's best enjoyed in the cooler months.

quantity and variety of bird life, and there are paths through coastal rainforest and past beach dunes at Mungo Brush in the south, perfect for spotting wildflowers and dingoes. The best beaches and surf are in the north around **Seal Rocks**, a bushy hamlet hugging Sugarloaf Bay. The beach has emerald-green rock pools and golden sand. Take the short walk to the **Sugarloaf Point Lighthouse** for epic ocean views. There's a detour to lonely **Lighthouse Beach**, a popular surfing spot. By the lighthouse is a lookout over the actual Seal Rocks – islets where Australian fur seals can sometimes be spotted. Humpback whales swim past during their annual migration.

🛏 p46

The Drive » Instead of returning to Rte 1, take the quieter coast road north through Tuncurry-Foster before rejoining Rte 1 just south of Taree. From there it's 80km to the Port Macquarie turn-off, then 10km more into the town itself.

TRIP HIGHLIGHT

❹ Port Macquarie

Making the most of its position at the entrance to the subtropical coast, Port, as it's commonly known, has a string of beautiful beaches within short driving distance from the centre of town. Surfing is particularly

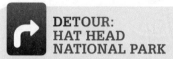

DETOUR: HAT HEAD NATIONAL PARK

Start: ❹ Port Macquarie

Covering almost the entire coast from Crescent Head to South West Rocks, this 74-sq-km national park (vehicle entry $7) protects scrubland, swamps and some amazing beaches, backed by one of the largest dune systems in NSW. The isolated beachside village of **Hat Head** (population 326) sits at its centre. At the far end of town, behind the holiday park, a picturesque wooden footbridge crosses the Korogoro Creek estuary. The water is so clear you can see fish darting around. The best views can be had from **Smoky Cape Lighthouse**, at the northern end of the park. During the annual whale migration it's a prime place from which to spot them. To get here, take the highway turn-off for South West Rocks, then follow the signs from Kinchela.

good at Town, Flynns and Lighthouse Beaches, all of which are patrolled in summer. The rainforest runs down to the sand at Shelly and Miners Beaches, the latter of which is an unofficial nudist beach. Whale season is May to November: there are numerous vantage points around town, or you can get a closer look on a whale-watching cruise with **Port Macquarie Cruise Adventures** (📞0414 897 444; www.cruiseadventures.com.au; Town Wharf; cruises from $15). While you're in town, don't miss the boutique and award-winning Little Brewing Company or the two-and-a-half-hour walking tours through Port's surprisingly rich historical heritage with **Port Macquarie Hastings**

Heritage (📞0447 429 016; www.pmheritage.com.au; per person $29; ⏱9.30am Wed-Sat).

🍴 🛏 p46

The Drive » The road is busy and runs just far enough inland that it's rare to catch a glimpse of the coast – hence the frequent detours east. For a scenic 17km detour from the Pacific Hwy, take Tourist Drive 14 through Stuarts Point and the eucalyptus forest to Grassy Head, then Yarriabini National Park and Scotts Head on your way back to the highway.

❺ Nambucca Heads

Nambucca Heads is languidly strewn over a dramatically curling headland interlaced with the estuaries of the glorious Nambucca River. It's a relatively quiet and unspoilt place, evoking

PETER HARRISON/GETTY IMAGES ©

JOERG HAUKE/GETTY IMAGES ©

WHY THIS IS A CLASSIC TRIP
ANTHONY HAM, AUTHOR

Sydney to Byron Bay is a rite of passage for Australians of all ages, from university students searching for the endless summer through middle-agers clinging to the surfing memories of their youth right up to grey nomads who call the road home. It's a coast I love for the reasons I love Australia – its wildlife, its soulful Indigenous story, and for beaches that never seem to end.

Top: Coffs Harbour
Left: Eastern grey kangaroo
Right: Byron Bay

PHOTO BY KARL LUNDHOLM/GETTY IMAGES ©

sun-soaked holidays of the '70s and '80s, when a fishing rod and zinc cream was all you needed. For decades residents and holidaymakers have decorated the rocks of Nambucca's breakwater with vivacious multicoloured artwork, and with notes to lovers, families and new-found friends. Visitors are encouraged to paint their own message, if they can find some space on the boulders. Long before such idle fun, Nambucca (pronounced nam-buk-a and which means 'many bends') was a river valley ruled by the Gumbainggir people until European timber cutters arrived in the 1840s. There are still strong Aboriginal communities in Nambucca Heads and up the valley in Bowraville.

✕ ⊨ p46

The Drive ≫ Rte 1 hugs the coastline pretty much all the way from Nambucca Heads to Coffs Harbour, save for the initial 10km and a stretch inhabited by Bongil Bongil National Park

- - - - - - - - - -

⑥ Coffs Harbour

Coffs captures the essence of this coastline, mingling the down-at-heel with the downright luxurious, and fine surf breaks and surf schools such as **East Coast Surf School** (✆02-6651 5515; www.eastcoastsurfschool.com. au; Diggers Beach; lessons from $55) with the sophisticated

Classic Trip

Crying Tiger Cooking School (☏02-6650 0195; 382 Harbour Dr; per person $110; ☺10am). And then there's **Muttonbird Island** (www.nationalparks.nsw.gov.au/Muttonbird-Island-Nature-Reserve). The Gumbainggir people knew it as Giidany Miirlarl, meaning Place of the Moon. It was joined to Coffs Harbour by the northern breakwater in 1935. The walk to the top (quite steep at the end) provides sweeping vistas. From late August to early April this eco treasure is occupied by some 12,000 pairs of wedge-tailed shearwaters, with their cute offspring visible in December and January. In other words, there's something for everyone in Coffs.

✕ 🛏 p46

The Drive 》 The road north of Coffs passes beneath tall, tall trees, within sight of the Big Banana, then almost as close to the coast as you can get. Before it sweeps inland, just after Sandy Beach, you'll hit Woolgoolga.

7 Woolgoolga

Woolgoolga is home to one of coastal Australia's more incongruous combinations – Woopi, as locals call it, is famous for its surf-and-Sikh community. If you're driving by on the highway you're sure to notice the impressive Guru Nanak Temple, a Sikh gurdwara (place of worship). There is a twice-monthly Saturday **Bollywood Beach Bazaar** (http://bollywoodmarkets.blogspot.com.au; ☺First and fourth Saturday of the month) here, while in September the town goes all out with the annual **Curryfest** (www.facebook.com/WoolgoolgaCurryfest) celebration. Somehow it all fits together and makes a refreshing change from some of the somewhat monocultural beach towns elsewhere along the coast.

✕ 🛏 p47

The Drive 》 A mere 7km north of Woopi, where Rte 1 again arcs inland, take the Red Rock turn-off along a much quieter road that sticks to the coast.

8 Red Rock

The village of Red Rock (population 310) is set between a beautiful beach and a glorious fish-filled river inlet. It takes its name from the red-tinged rock stack at the headland. The local Gumbainggir people know it by a more sombre name: Blood Rock. In the 1880s a detachment of armed police slaughtered the inhabitants of an Aboriginal camp, chasing the survivors to the headland, where they were driven off. The Blood Rock Massacres are commemorated by a simple plaque, and the area is considered sacred. The **Yarrawarra Aboriginal Cultural Centre** (☏02-6640 7100; www.yarrawarra.org; 170 Red Rock Rd, Corindi Beach; ☺9am-4pm Wed-Sun) has an interesting art gallery and a bush-tucker cafe, where you can try kangaroo and lemon-myrtle damper. It also holds bush-medicine tours and art classes; call ahead if you're interested in joining one.

The Drive 》 Return back down the road to Rte 1, turn right (northwest) and follow it all the way north through flat agricultural country, passing Grafton, Maclean and Woodburn en route.

9 Ballina

At the mouth of the Richmond River, Ballina is spoilt for white sandy beaches and crystal-clear waters. In the late 19th century it was a rich lumber town; a scattering of gracious historic buildings can still be found on its backstreets. For a good sampling of local history, stroll the length of **Norton Street**, which boasts a number of impressive late-19th-century buildings. For architecture (and intrigue) of a different kind, the **Big Prawn** (Ballina Bunnings, 507 River St) is 1km west of town; Ballina's big prawn was nearly thrown on the BBQ in 2009, but no one had the stomach to dispatch it. After a 5000-signature pro-prawn petition and a $400,000 restoration in 2013, the 9m, 35-tonne, 14-year-old crustacean is looking as tasty as ever.

 p47

The Drive » Ignore the main highway and hug the coast, drawing near to Lennox Head's picturesque coastline with some dramatic views from the road. Byron begins a long time before you arrive – ignore its sprawl and head for the centre.

TRIP HIGHLIGHT

⑩ Byron Bay

What makes Byron special is the singular vibe of the town itself. It's here that coastal surf culture flows into the hippie tide washing down from the hinterland, creating one great barefooted, alternative-lifestyle mash-up. The town centre is low-rise and relaxed, and its unique atmosphere has a way of converting even the most cynical with its long, balmy days, endless beaches, reliable surf breaks, fine food, raucous nightlife and ambling milieu. West of the town centre, wild **Belongil Beach** with its high dunes avoids the worst of the crowds.

Immediately in front of town, lifesaver-patrolled **Main Beach** is busy from sunrise to sunset with yoga classes, buskers and fire dancers. Around the rocks is gorgeous **Wategos Beach**, a wide crescent of white sand surrounded by rainforest. **Tallow Beach** is a deserted sandy stretch that extends for 7km south from Cape Byron. This is the place to flee the crowds, many of whom will have followed you all the way from Sydney.

 p47

↱ DETOUR: BANGALOW & NIMBIN

Start: ⑩ Byron Bay

Before you arrive in Byron (or as a detour from Byron itself), two hinterland communities make for a fascinating detour. First up, surrounded by subtropical forest and rolling green farmland, sophisticated **Bangalow** is home to a small, creative community, a dynamic, sustainable food scene and a range of urbane boutiques.

And then there's **Nimbin**, Australia's alternative-lifestyle capital, an intriguing little town that struggles under the weight of its own clichés. Nimbin was once an unremarkable Northern Rivers dairy village, but that changed forever in May 1973. Thousands of students, hippies and devotees of the back-to-earth movement descended on the town for the Aquarius Festival, with many staying on and creating new communities in the beautiful valleys in an attempt to live out the ideals expressed during the 10-day celebration.

Another landmark in Nimbin's history came in 1979 with the Terania Creek Battle, the first major conservation victory of its kind in Australia, which is often credited with ensuring the survival of NSW's vast tracts of rainforest. Protestor Falls, in what is now Nightcap National Park, is named in their honour.

Today the old psychedelic murals of the rainbow serpent dreaming and marijuana bliss that line Nimbin's main street are fading, the dreadlocked, beaded locals are weathered and, while genuine remnants of the peace-and-love generation remain, the town has changed a lot since the '80s. Even so, Nimbin is utterly unlike anywhere else in Australia, and a stroll down the main street will show you what we mean.

Classic Trip

Eating & Sleeping

Port Stephens ❷

✗ Little Beach Boathouse   Seafood $$

(☎02-4984 9420; www.littlebeachboathouse.
com.au; Little Beach Marina, 4 Victoria Pde;
lunch mains $20, dinner mains $32; ⊙12-3pm &
5.30-9pm Tue-Sat) In a cosy dining room right
on the water you can order fabulously fresh
salads and local seafood share plates. It's hard
to concentrate on the food with views of diving
dolphins and majestic pelicans coming in to
land.

⌂ Beaches Serviced Apartments   Apartments $$

(☎02-4984 3255; www.beachesportstephens.
com.au; 12 Gowrie Ave, Nelson Bay; apt from
$190; ❁❋☎⊞) You'll find all the comforts
of home in these beautifully kept apartments,
ranging from studio to three bedroom. There's a
pretty palm-lined pool, and a putting green too.

⌂ Bali at the Bay   Apartments $$$

(☎02-4981 5556; www.baliatthebay.com.au;
1 Achilles St, Shoal Bay; apt $260-300; ❋) Two
exceedingly beautiful self-contained apartments –
chock full of flower-garlanded Buddhas and carved
wood – do a good job of living up to the name here.
The bathrooms are exquisite and spa treatments
are available.

Myall Lakes National Park ❸

⌂ Sugarloaf Point Lighthouse   Cottage $$$

(☎02-4997 6590; www.sealrockslighthouse-
accommodation.com.au; cottages from $340;
☎) Watch the crashing waves and wildlife
from one of three fully renovated, heritage
lighthouse-keeper's cottages. Each is self-
contained and has two or three bedrooms and
a barbecue.

Port Macquarie ❹

✗ Stunned Mullet   Modern Australian $$$

(☎02-6584 7757; www.thestunnedmullet.com.
au; 24 William St; mains $36-39; ⊙noon-2.30pm &
6-10.00pm) This fresh, seaside spot is one serious
dining destination. The inspired contemporary
menu features classic dishes such as pork belly
with seared scallops, alongside exotic listings
such as Patagonian toothfish. The extensive
international wine list befits Port's best restaurant.

⌂ Northpoint Apartments   Apartments $$

(☎02-6583 8333; www.northpointapartments.
com.au; 2 Murray St; apt from $190; ❋☎⊞)
Some of these large, classy and contemporary
one- to three-bedroom apartments have
fabulous sea views, although you'll save quite a
bit if you're prepared to go without.

Nambucca Heads ❺

✗ Nambucca Boatshed & Cafe   Cafe $$

(☎02-6568 6511; www.nambuccaboatshed.com.
au; Riverside Dr; mains $12-18; ⊙7.30am-4pm
Mon-Sat, 8am-3pm Sun) Right on the river's edge,
the highlight of this low-key veranda cafe is the
sublime view. Work off a plentiful burger lunch
with a frolic in a kayak, on a paddleboard or in a
tinny hired from the **tackle shop** (☎02-6568
6432; www.nambuccacbd.com.au/beachcomber;
Riverside Dr; ⊙7am-5pm) next door.

⌂ Riverview Boutique Hotel   Guesthouse $$

(☎02-6568 6386; www.riverviewlodge-
nambucca.com.au; 4 Wellington Dr; s/d from
$139/179; ❂❁❋☎) Built in 1887 this former
pub is today a wooden, two-storey charmer with
eight stylish rooms (with fridges); some rooms
have views.

Coffs Harbour ⑥

✖ Fiasco
Italian $$$

(☎02-6651 2006; www.fiascorestaurant. com.au; 22 Orlando St; mains $38; ⊗5-9pm Tue-Sat) Classic Italian fare is prepared in an open kitchen using produce from the best local suppliers and herbs from its own garden. Expect earthy delights like bean soup, wood-fired pizza and home-made pasta. If you're not overly hungry, grab some antipasti at the bar.

⌖ Coffs Jetty BnB
B&B $$

(☎02-6651 4587; www.coffsjetty.com.au; 41a Collingwood St; d from $125; 🛜) A cut above your average B&B, this suburban town house has tastefully appointed rooms and terrific bathrooms. It's an easy walk to the beach and restaurants.

Woolgoolga ⑦

✖ Bluebottles Brasserie
Cafe $$

(☎02-6654 1962; www.bluebottlesbrasserie. com.au; 53 Beach St; mains breakfast $12-17, lunch $14-23, dinner $24-30; ⊗6.15am-4pm Mon-Thu, to 9pm Fri & Sat, 7am-3pm Sun) Starting with strong, early-morning presurf coffees and stacks of corn fritters, the all-day breakfast menu rolls on to generous salads and afternoon cakes.

⌖ Solitary Islands Lodge
B&B $$

(☎02-6654 1335; www.solitaryislandslodge. com.au; 3 Arthur St; r $160; 🛜) The three immaculate guest rooms in this modern hilltop house have impressive sea views. The charming hosts stock the rooms with ingredients for a Continental breakfast.

Ballina ⑨

✖ Lighthouse Beach Cafe
Cafe $$

(☎02-6686 4380; lighthousebeachcafe.com. au; 65 Lighthouse Pde; breakfast mains $13-20, lunch mains $18, dinner $18-27; ⊗7am-3pm Mon-Wed, to 9pm Thu-Sat, to 6pm Sun) With terrific views of East Ballina's Lighthouse Beach, this family-friendly cafe at the surf club turns out hearty breakfast platters and some tasty pasta and seafood dishes.

Byron Bay ⑩

✖ Fishheads
Seafood $

(www.www.restaurantbyronbay.com.au; 1 Jonson St; mains $9.50-22; ⊗7.30am-9pm; 🛜) Right on the beach, this fabulous takeaway shop sells traditional battered fish and chips ($12.50), or take it up a notch with grilled prawns and salad ($18). The restaurant is fine too, but why wouldn't you dine on the beach?

⌖ Atlantic
Hotel $$$

(☎02-6685 5118; www.atlanticbyronbay.com. au; 13 Marvell St; r from $180; ✳🛜) There are three fabulously decorated Caribbean-style plantation cottages at this chic enclave in the centre of town, all with private decks opening on to tropical gardens. If this wasn't cool enough, there's also the option of sleeping in a polished-aluminium Airstream caravan parked on the back lawn.

Pambula Beach Popular
with families and kangaroos alike

Classic Trip

Sydney to Melbourne

2

You could zip down the Hume Hwy from Sydney to Melbourne, but this longer, slower and infinitely more beautiful coastal route passes by some of the country's loveliest stretches of coastline.

TRIP HIGHLIGHTS

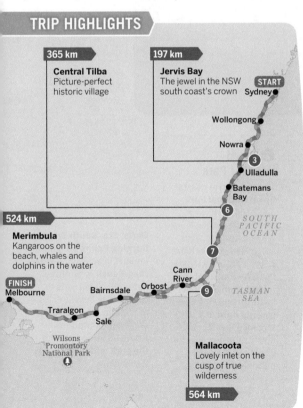

365 km

Central Tilba
Picture-perfect historic village

197 km

Jervis Bay
The jewel in the NSW south coast's crown

START
Sydney

Wollongong

Nowry

Ulladulla

Batemans Bay

SOUTH PACIFIC OCEAN

524 km

Merimbula
Kangaroos on the beach, whales and dolphins in the water

FINISH
Melbourne

Bairnsdale

Traralgon

Sale

Cann River

Orbost

TASMAN SEA

Wilsons Promontory National Park

Mallacoota
Lovely inlet on the cusp of true wilderness

564 km

5–7 DAYS
1032KM / 642 MILES

GREAT FOR...

BEST TIME TO GO
November to March promises warmer beach weather and a good chance of clear skies.

ESSENTIAL PHOTO
Empty beaches near Jervis Bay.

BEST FOR FAMILIES
Wildlife around Merimbula includes kangaroos on the beach and whales in the spring.

Classic Trip

2 Sydney to Melbourne

Australia's most popular stretch of its famous Rte 1 shadows a stunning coastline, passing en route some pristine stands of tall-trees forest. Jervis Bay, Mallacoota and Cape Conran provide the most spectacular stretches of coastal wilderness, while Central Tilba is easily the most charming of Rte 1's historic hamlets. For lovers of wildlife, there are koalas at Paynesville, seals and seabirds at Montague Island and kangaroos aplenty near Merimbula.

1 Sydney

Sydney may be one of the world's most beguiling cities, but for our purposes it's merely the starting point of this classic coastal route to Melbourne. For more on exploring Sydney on foot, turn to p60.

The Drive » Drive south of Sydney along Rte 1. Just after passing Heathcote, and not long after leaving Sydney's urban sprawl, take the turn-off for Bundeena and Royal National Park.

2 Royal National Park

The wonderful coastal **Royal National Park** (☎02-9542 0648; www.environment.nsw.gov.au; cars $11, pedestrians & cyclists free; ⏰ park gates locked at 8.30pm) protects 15,091 hectares and stretches inland from 32km of beautiful coast. Encompassing dramatic cliffs, secluded beaches and lush rainforest, it's the world's second-oldest national park (1879).

Garie, **Era**, **South Era** and **Burning Palms** are popular surf beaches and **Werrong Beach** is 'clothing optional'. Side roads to the smaller beaches close at 8.30pm. Even if you don't get out and walk, Route 68 loops through the park and is an utterly lovely drive.

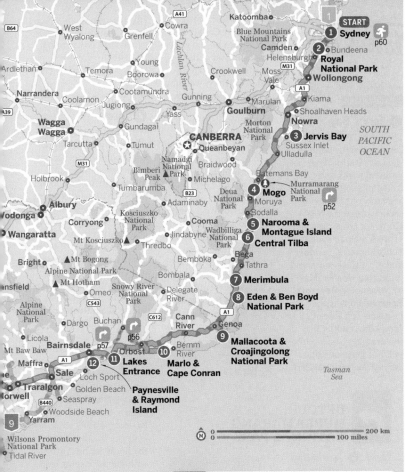

The Drive » Make sure you take the coast road along the Sea Cliffs Bridge that links Otford with Stanford Park – the cantilevered bridge hangs out over the water beneath high sea cliffs and is breathtaking. There are more dramatic views on the approach to Wollongong. Later, after Kiama, take the Jervis Bay turn-off.

LINK YOUR TRIP

1 Sydney to Byron Bay

If you've done Sydney–Melbourne in reverse, continue up the coast for 879km to Byron Bay.

9 Gippsland & Wilsons Prom

This route through Victoria's Gippsland region shares the Princes Hwy for part of the drive – detour to Phillip Island before arriving in Melbourne to get started.

Classic Trip

TRIP HIGHLIGHT

❸ Jervis Bay

This large, sheltered bay combines snow-white sand, crystalline waters, national parks and frolicking dolphins – it's arguably our favourite section along the NSW stretch of coast. Seasonal visitors include Sydney holidaymakers (summer and most weekends), and migrating whales (May to November). **Beecroft Peninsula** forms the northeastern side of Jervis Bay, ending in the dramatic sheer cliffs of Point Perpendicular. **Jervis Bay National Park**

(www.nationalparks.nsw.gov.au) begins near Callala Bay. Getting out on the water here is almost obligatory, from the dolphin-, seal- and whale-watching trips of **Dolphin Watch Cruises** (☎02-4441 6311; www.dolphinwatch.com.au; 50 Owen St; ☼dolphin-/whale-/seal-watching tour $35/65/80) or diving and snorkelling with **Dive Jervis Bay** (☎02-4441 5255; www.divejervisbay.com; 64 Owen St) to boat trips with **Jervis Bay Eco Adventures** (www.jervisbayecoadventures.com.au; 58 Owen St, Huskisson; per adult $55-85, per child $30-45; ☼tours 10.30am & 1pm) or sea kayak expeditions with **Jervis Bay Kayaks** (☎02-4441 7157; www.jervisbaykayaks.com; 13 Hawke St; kayak hire 3hr/day $49/69, tours $55-165).

🍴 🛏 p58

DETOUR: MURRAMARANG NATIONAL PARK

Start: ❸ Jervis Bay

The beautiful 12,386-hectare coastal Murramarang National Park is home to wild kangaroos, rich birdlife and the protected Murramarang Aboriginal Area, which contains ancient middens and Indigenous cultural treasures. Wasp Head, Depot, Pebbly and Merry Beaches are popular with surfers. Walking trails snake off from these beaches, and a steep but enjoyable walk is up Durras Mountain (283m). To get here, take Rte 1 from Jervis Bay all the way past Ulladulla. At Termeil, turn left (southeast) towards Bawley Point and then follow the roads along the coast to Durras. In the park, many of the roads are pretty rough, but those to Durras, Durras Lake, Depot Beach and Durras North are all sealed, as is Mt Agony Rd to Pebbly Beach (but not Pebbly Beach Rd).

The Drive ❭❭ Return to the main highway, then turn south, passing through towns like historic little Milton, beachy Ulladulla and rather lovely Batemans Bay on your way into Mogo.

❹ Mogo

While Batemans Bay is the more popular place to stay along this section of the coast, Mogo, a historic strip of wooden houses with cafes and souvenir shops, makes an interesting and much quieter alternative. It also has a couple of quite impressive attractions, one in keeping with its heritage, the other somewhat incongruous. The nearby **Gold Rush Colony** (☎02-4474 2123; www.goldrushcolony.com.au; 26 James St; adult/child $20/12; ☼10am-5pm) is a rambling re-creation of a pioneer village, while **Mogo Zoo** (☎02-4474 4855; www.mogozoo.com.au; 222 Tomakin Rd; adult/child $29.50/16; ☼9am-5pm), 2km east off the highway, has rare white lions, a snow leopard and an enthralling troop of gorillas, which you just don't expect to see in a small rural Australian town.

The Drive ❭❭ The road meanders along the contours of the coastline, passing through Moruya ('black swan') with Victorian buildings gathered around a broad river and a popular Saturday market. Dense woodlands line the roadside into Narooma.

⑤ Narooma & Montague Island

At the mouth of a tree-lined inlet and flanked by surf beaches, Narooma is a pretty seaside town with little to distinguish it from others in the area, although it does have some decent beaches – the best place for swimming is over the bridge at the south end of Bar Beach – and a pretty setting. But what really stands out here is **Montague Island (Barangu-ba)**. Nine kilometres offshore from Narooma, this small, pest-free island is home to seabirds and fur seals. Little penguins nest here, especially from September to February. Three-hour guided tours conducted by NSW National Parks & Wildlife Service rangers are dependent on numbers and weather conditions, so book ahead through the visitor centre. Diving with grey nurse sharks, snorkelling and whale-watching are all possible through **Island Charters Narooma** (✆02-4476 1047; www.islandchartersnarooma. com; Bluewater Dr; diving from $95, snorkelling from $75).

✖ p58

The Drive » The road stays close to the coastline south of Narooma, but take the turn-off for Central Tilba soon after the road turns inland and heads for the hills.

TRIP HIGHLIGHT

⑥ Central Tilba

This National Trust village feels like a toy town of heritage buildings. Central Tilba has remained virtually unchanged since it was a 19th-century gold-mining boomtown – it's one of Australia's best-preserved historic villages. Cafes and craft shops fill the heritage buildings along Bate St. Behind the pub, walk up to the water tower for terrific views. There's information and maps at **Bates Emporium** (Bate St; ⏰8am-5pm; 🛜), while gardening freaks will love the magical 1.4-hectare private garden at **Foxglove Spires** (www. foxglovespires.com.au; Corkhill Dr; admission $7.50; ⏰10am-4pm), with lots of hidden avenues and bowers.

✖ 🛏 p58

The Drive » From Central Tilba, take the coast road instead of Rte 1 wherever possible – via Bermagui, Mimosa Rocks, Tathra and Tura Beach – and stop regularly to take in the view.

TRIP HIGHLIGHT

⑦ Merimbula

Merimbula is one of those south coast beach resorts to which families have been returning for decades. Part of its appeal lies along a long, golden beach and a lovely inlet, but there are also plenty of activities and an above-average selection of eateries. But we love it especially for its range of wildlife experiences. Go dolphin-watching in the bay, or whale-watching from mid-September to November, with **True Blue** (www.merimbulamarina.com; Merimbula Marina; adult/child $30/20), while kangaroos and wallabies inhabit **Pambula-Merimbula Golf Course** and **Pambula Beach**; they're most visible at dusk. There's also a 1.75km **mangrove boardwalk** in town with birds particularly abundant.

✖ p58

The Drive » There's no mystery about the route to Eden – take Rte 1 for 26km and you're there.

⑧ Eden & Ben Boyd National Park

Eden's a sleepy place where often the only bustle is down at the wharf when the fishing boats come in. Migrating humpback whales and southern right whales pass so close to the coast that experts consider this to be one of Australia's best whale-watching locations. Often the whales can be seen feeding or resting in Twofold Bay during their southern migration back to Antarctic waters during October and November. There's even a **Whale Festival**

Classic Trip

LEE ROGERS/GETTY IMAGES ©

ALASTAIR POLLOCK PHOTOGRAPHY/GETTY IMAGES ©

WHY THIS IS A CLASSIC TRIP
ANTHONY HAM, AUTHOR

I've lived in both Melbourne and Sydney and have lost track of how many times I've chosen to take this longer, slower coastal route. It's a route beloved by locals of both states. I love the remote beaches of Jervis Bay, the chance to see penguins at Montague Island and whales off Eden, and the forests that line the roadside like a guard of honour into Victoria.

Top: White-sand cove, Jervis Bay
Left: Fur seal, Montague Island
Right: Luxury camping, Jervis Bay

KENT MATHEWS/GETTY IMAGES ©

(www.edenwhalefestival.com.au; ⊙Nov). The wilderness barely pauses for breath in 10,485-hectare **Ben Boyd National Park** ($7 per vehicle), which protects a dramatic coastline peppered with isolated beaches. The northern section of the park can be accessed from the Princes Hwy north of Eden, while the southern section is accessed by mainly gravel roads leading off sealed Edrom Rd, which leaves the Princes Hwy 19km south of Eden. At its southern tip, the elegant 1883 **Green Cape Lightstation** offers awesome views.

✗ ⊨ p59

The Drive » South of Eden, the Pacific Hwy leaves the coast and cuts inland, crossing into Victoria deep in forest. The traffic thins and settlements are tiny to nonexistent for much of the way. Soon after crossing the state border, at Genoa, take the Mallacoota turn-off.

TRIP HIGHLIGHT

❾ Mallacoota & Croajingolong National Park

One of Gippsland's, and indeed Victoria's, little gems, Mallacoota is the state's most easterly town, snuggled on the vast Mallacoota Inlet and surrounded by the tumbling hills and beachside dunes of beautiful Croajingolong National Park. Those prepared to come this far are

Classic Trip

treated to long, empty, ocean-surf beaches, tidal estuaries and swimming, fishing and boating on the inlet, which has more than 300km of shoreline. Croajingolong is one of Australia's finest coastal wilderness national parks and covers 87,500 hectares, stretching for about 100km from the town of Bemm River to the NSW border. Another option is the windswept 154-hectare Gabo Island, 14km offshore from Mallacoota, and home to seabirds and one of the world's largest colonies of little penguins. Whales, dolphins and fur seals are regularly sighted off shore. Get there by boat with **Wilderness Coast Ocean Charters** (☏03-5158 0701, 0417 398 068).

✕ ⊨ p59

The Drive » Return the 22km northwest back up the road to the Princes Hwy, turn left, then

---

DETOUR: BUCHAN CAVES

Start: ⑩ Marlo

The sleepy town of Buchan, in the foothills of the Snowy Mountains, is famous for the spectacular and intricate limestone cave system at the **Buchan Caves** (☏13 19 63; www.parks.vic.gov.au; tours adult/child/family $20.90/12.20/57.50, 2 caves $31.20/18.10/85.80; ☉tours 10am, 11.15am, 1pm, 2.15pm & 3.30pm, hours vary seasonally), open to visitors for almost a century. Underground rivers cutting through ancient limestone rock formed the caves and caverns, and they provided shelter for Aboriginal people as far back as 18,000 years ago. Parks Victoria runs guided caves tours daily, alternating between the equally impressive **Royal** and **Fairy Caves**. Royal has more colour, a higher chamber and extinct kangaroo remains; Fairy has more delicate decorations and potential fairy sightings. The rangers also offer hard-hat guided tours to the less-developed **Federal Cave** during the high season. The reserve itself is a pretty spot with shaded picnic areas, walking tracks and grazing kangaroos. Invigoration is guaranteed when taking a dip in the icy **rock pool**.

To get here from Marlo, return to Rte 1 (14km), then travel west for 34km. At Nowa Nowa, take the Buchan turn-off, from where it's 34km to the caves.

---

drive all the way down through Cann River. Just past Orbost, take the 15km road south to Marlo.

- - - - - - - - - - -

⑩ Marlo & Cape Conran

Marlo is a sleepy beach town at the mouth of the Snowy River. It's a lovely spot, popular with anglers, but we love it especially as the gateway to the **Cape Conran** (☏03-5154 8438; www.conran.net.au; camp sites $26.80, cabins up to 4 people $147, lodge $291, safari tents $165) section of what is known as the Wilderness Coast. This blissfully undeveloped part of the coast is one of Gippsland's most beautiful corners, with long stretches of remote white-sand beaches. The 19km coastal route from Marlo to Cape Conran is particularly pretty, bordered by banksia trees, grass plains, sand dunes and the ocean. Aside from the coast, the main attraction in Marlo is the **PS Curlip** (☏03-5154 1699; www.paddlesteamercurlip.com.au; adult/child/family $25/15/60; ☉10.30am Sat & Sun, longer hours Dec & Jan), a re-creation of an 1890 paddle steamer that once chugged up the Snowy River to Orbost. You can buy tickets at the general store in town.

⊨ p59

The Drive » Once again, it's back onto the Princes Hwy, then it's 59km from Orbost into Lakes Entrance.

NEW SOUTH WALES & THE AUSTRALIAN CAPITAL TERRITORY **2** SYDNEY TO MELBOURNE

⑪ Lakes Entrance

Lakes Entrance has a certain trashy charm, which we'll forgive because the setting is just lovely. A number of lookouts watch out over town from the neighbouring hilltops (ask at the Lakes Entrance Visitor Centre for directions), and a footbridge crosses the shallow Cunninghame Arm waterway separating the town from the crashing ocean beaches. On the other side, climb over the dunes covered with coastal heath and down onto peerless **Ninety Mile Beach** with its crashing waves and endless sand. There are also boat cruises and some terrific places to eat, with the freshest local seafood a specialty.

 p59

The Drive » Rte 1 loops up and out of town to the east – don't miss the Jemmys Point Lookout as you near the tip of the climb. The turn-off to Paynesville is at Lucknow on the Princes Hwy.

---

⑫ Paynesville

Paynesville is a relaxed little lake town that feels a million miles from the busy coast road. Down here, life is all about the water, and some residents have their luxury boats moored right outside their house

on purpose-built canals. A good reason to detour here is to take the ferry on the five-minute hop across to **Raymond Island** for some koala-spotting. There's a large colony of koalas here, mostly relocated from Phillip Island in the 1950s. The flat-bottom car and passenger ferry operates every half-hour from 7am to 11pm and is free for pedestrians and cyclists; cars and motorcycles cost $10. If you happen to be here on the last weekend in February, the popular **Paynesville Jazz Festival** is outstanding.

 p59

The Drive » Return to the main highway, then set your

DETOUR: METUNG

Start: ⑪ Lakes Entrance

Curling around Bancroft Bay, little Metung is one of the prettiest towns in the Lakes District and it has developed a niche appeal as the sophisticated alter ego to the plebby clamour of Lakes Entrance. Besotted locals even go so far as calling it the Gippsland Riviera, and with its absolute waterfront location and unhurried charm, it's hard to argue. Suitably, there are some excellent places to eat here, among them **Bancroft Bites** (☑ 03-5156 2854; www. bancroftbites.com.au; 2/57 Metung Rd; mains $15-36; ⏰ 8am-3pm & 6-8pm Thu-Tue) and **Metung Galley** (☑ 03-5156 2330; www.themetunggalley.com.au; 50 Metung Rd; lunch mains $10-22, dinner mains $19-35; ⏰ 8am-4pm Tue, to late Wed-Fri, 7.30am-late Sat, to 4pm Sun). To get here, take Rte 1 northwest out of Lakes Entrance for 16km. At Swan Reach, turn off south for the 8km into Metung.

sights on Melbourne, 298km away. The reason is simple – the best of the road lies behind you and the final crossing of Gippsland – through Bairnsdale, Sale, Traralgon, Moe and Warragul – has very little to recommend it.

---

⑬ Melbourne

The cosmopolitan charms of Melbourne await you at journey's end. This artsy city could be the starting point of a new journey but it's equally a fabulous destination in its own right, with ample attractions to satisfy architecture, foodie and sporting buffs. For more on exploring the city centre on foot, see p122.

Classic Trip

Eating & Sleeping

Jervis Bay ❸

🍴 Wild Ginger   Asian $$
(☎02-4441 5577; www.wild-ginger.com.au; 42
Owen St; mains $31.50; ⊘4.30pm-late Tue-Sun)
A relaxed showcase of flavours from across
Southeast Asia and Japan. Look forward to
tasty local seafood.

🍴 Gunyah
Restaurant   Modern Australian $$$
(☎02-4441 7299; 3-course meals $70; ⊘6.30-
9pm Sep-Jun) Sit under the canopy on the
forested balcony of this acclaimed restaurant
at Paperbark Camp. The focus is on local
ingredients, and booking is essential for outside
guests.

🛏 Huskisson B&B   B&B $$$
(☎02-4441 7551; www.huskissonbnb.com.au;
12 Tomerong St; r $225; ❄🛜) Bright, airy and
colourful rooms containing comfy beds and
fluffy towels.

🛏 Paperbark Camp   Campground $$$
(☎1300 668 167; www.paperbarkcamp.com.
au; 571 Woollamia Rd; d from $395; ⊘Sep-
Jun) Camp in ecofriendly style in 12 luxurious
solar-powered safari tents with en suites and
wraparound decks. It's set in dense bush 3.5km
from Huskisson; borrow kayaks to paddle up the
creek to the bay.

Narooma & Montague Island ❺

🍴 Inlet   Fish & Chips $$
(www.facebook.com/theinletnarooma; Riverside
Dr; mains $18-26; ⊘11.30am-2.30pm Tue-Sun,
5-10pm Tue-Sat) Formerly Taylor's Seafood, and
now gussied up as the Inlet. Don't worry: the
fresh seafood, fish and chips, and glorious inlet
views are all intact.

Central Tilba ❻

🍴 Rose & Sparrow Café   Cafe $
(3 Bate St; mains $5-15; ⊘breakfast &
lunch) Serves generous portions of healthy
food, including delicious lentil burgers with
homemade hot mango chutney.

🛏 Bryn at Tilba   B&B $$
(www.thebrynattilba.com.au; 91 Punkalla-Tilba
Rd; r $180-220) Beautiful rooms with dark wood
and white linen.

Merimbula ❼

🍴 Wheelers Oyster Farm   Seafood $$
(www.wheelersoysters.com.au; 162 Arthur
Kaine Dr, Pambula; mains $22-36; ⊘shop
10am-5pm daily, restaurant noon-2.30pm daily,
6pm-late Mon-Sat) Delicious fresh oysters –
either takeaway or from the shop or enjoyed in
Wheelers' spectacular restaurant. The menu
features oysters prepared loads of ways and
other great seafood and steak dishes. Tours
showcasing some people's favourite bivalve
depart at 11am daily.

🍴 Zanzibar   Modern Australian $$$
(☎02-6495 3636; http://zanzibarmerimbula.
com.au; cnr Main & Market Sts; two/three/five
courses $65/75/85; ⊘noon-2pm Thu & Fri,
6pm-late Tue-Sat) This culinary gem prides itself
on locally caught seafood and hand-picked
south coast produce. Intriguing menu options
include marinated yellowfin tuna, beetroot and
crème fraiche. The five-course 'Locavore' menu
is a well-spent $85.

Eden & Ben Boyd National Park

✗ Wharfside Café   Cafe $$

(Main Wharf; mains $15-28; ⊙8am-3pm daily, 6-10pm Fri & Sat) Decent breakfasts, strong coffee and harbour views make this a good way to start the day. Try the Asian prawn salad with a glass of wine for lunch, or ask if local oysters and mussels are available. The Main Wharf is downhill from town.

⊨ Seahorse Inn   Boutique Hotel $$

(📞02-6496 1361; www.seahorseinnhotel.com. au; Boydtown; d $175-349; ❋ 🛜) At Boydtown, 6km south of Eden, the Seahorse Inn overlooks Twofold Bay. It's a lavish boutique hotel with all the trimmings, and there's a good restaurant and garden bar open to nonguests.

Mallacoota & Croajingolong National Park ⑨

✗ Lucy's   Asian $$

(📞03-5158 466; 64 Maurice Ave; mains $10-23; ⊙8am-8pm) Lucy's is popular for delicious and great-value homemade rice noodles with chicken, prawn or abalone, as well as dumplings stuffed with ingredients from the garden. It's also good for breakfast.

⊨ Adobe Mudbrick Flats   Apartment $

(📞03-5158 0329, 0409 580 0329; www. adobeholidayflats.com.au; 17 Karbeethong Ave; d $80, q $95-180) A labour of love by Margaret and Peter Kurz, these unique mud-brick flats in Karbeethong are something special. With an emphasis on recycling and eco-friendliness, the flats have solar hot water and guests are encouraged to compost their kitchen scraps. The array of whimsical apartments are comfortable, well equipped and cheap.

Marlo & Cape Conran ⑩

⊨ Marlo Hotel   Hotel $$

(📞03-5154 8201; www.marlohotel.com.au; 17 Argyle Pde; d $140, with spa $130-160, mains $14-30) You can't beat an afternoon beer from the expansive wooden verandah of the **Marlo Hotel** with a sublime view of the Snowy River emptying into the sea. The boutique rooms here are above average for a pub – some with spa – and the restaurant serves local seafood such as gummy shark and king prawns (mains $14 to $30).

Lakes Entrance ⑪

✗ The Boathouse   Modern Australian $$$

(📞03-5155 3055; www.bellevuelakes.com; 201 The Esplanade; mains $38; ⊙6-9pm Tue-Sat) This much-awarded restaurant is Lakes Entrance's most celebrated kitchen. The atmosphere is refined and the emphasis is on creatively conceived seafood. Start with the Atlantic scallops with pea puree, pancetta and ocean foam.

⊨ Bellevue on the Lakes   Hotel $$

(📞03-5155 3055; www.bellevuelakes.com; 201 Esplanade; d from $179, 2-bedroom apt from $284; ❋ 🛜 ⊞) Right in the heart of the Esplanade, Bellevue brings a bit of style to the strip with neatly furnished rooms in earthy tones, most with water views. For extra luxury, go for the spacious spa suites or two-bedroom self-contained apartments.

Paynesville ⑫

✗ Fisherman's Wharf Pavilion   Cafe, Seafood $$

(📞03-5156 0366; 70 The Esplanade; lunch $8-24, dinner $22-43; ⊙8am-3pm & 6-8pm Tue-Sun) Perched over the water and with an alfresco deck, this airy cafe is a sublime place for a pancake breakfast or quiche for lunch on a sunny day. By night it's a fine-dining steak-and-seafood restaurant, using fresh, local produce.

⊨ Mariners Cove   Motel $$

(📞03-5156 7444; www.marinerscoveresort. com; d $100-165, f $165, apt $160-225; ❋) These bright, sunny waterside motel-style units are well located near the Raymond Island ferry. Boat hire is available.

STRETCH YOUR LEGS
SYDNEY

Start/Finish: Observatory Hill

Distance: 4km

Duration: 4 hours

Sydney is a city of ready superlatives and this walk traverses some of the centre's most spectacular terrain, from the Rocks to the Opera House and into the luxuriant harbourside greens of the Royal Botanic Garden.

Take this walk on Trips

Observatory Hill

High above the Rocks, Observatory Hill hosts the 1850s-era, copper-domed, Italianate Sydney Observatory, but we love it for the views and sense of peace high above the clamour. Bring a picnic and take it all in from the shade of one of the huge Moreton Bay fig trees. Bliss.

The Walk >> Head north down the hill to Argyle St, with Argyle Place just across the road.

Argyle Place

A quiet, English-style village green lined with terraced houses, Argyle Place offers the sacred appeal of the Garrison Church and the more secular delights of the Lord Nelson Brewery Hotel, which lays claim to being Sydney's oldest pub. It's said that any Australian has the legal right to graze livestock on the green, so bring a sheep if you'd like.

The Walk >> Walk down the hill along Argyle St to the southeast, pass through Argyle Cut, a canyonlike section of road cut by convicts through the sandstone ridge. Turn left into the Rocks and follow the signs to the museum.

Rocks Discovery Museum

Divided into four chronological displays – Warrane (pre-1788), Colony (1788–1820), Port (1820–1900) and Transformations (1900 to the present) – this excellent **museum** (☎02-9240 8680; www.rocksdiscoverymuseum.com; Kendall Lane; ⊙10am-5pm; ℝCircular Quay) digs deep into the Rocks' history and leads you on an artefact-rich tour. Sensitive attention is given to the Rocks' original inhabitants, the Gadigal people.

The Walk >> Take any Rocks thoroughfare heading east, then follow the waterfront south to the Museum of Contemporary Art.

Museum of Contemporary Art

One of the country's best and most challenging galleries, the **Museum of Contemporary Art** (☎02-9245 2400; www.mca. com.au; 140 George St; ⊙10am-5pm Fri-Wed,

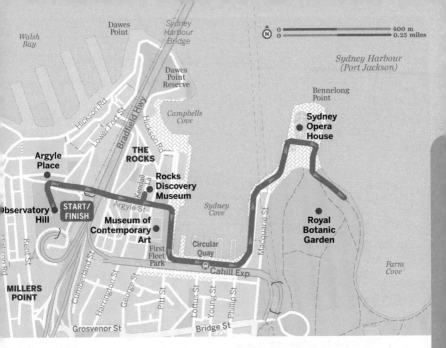

to 9pm Thu; Circular Quay) is a showcase for Australian and international contemporary art. Aboriginal art features prominently and the fab Gotham City–style art-deco building is another highlight, even despite the unfortunate architectural meddling of recent times.

The Walk ≫ There are few busier corners of Sydney – stroll at your leisure along slight junky Circular Quay with its didgeridoo buskers, people rushing to ferries and fast food outlets.

Sydney Opera House

It may be something of a Sydney cliche, but the **Sydney Opera House** (02-9250 7250; www.sydneyoperahouse.com; Bennelong Point; tours adult/child $37/20; tours 9am-5pm; Circular Quay) remains one of the most splendid architectural creations in the country. Visually referencing the billowing white sails of a seagoing yacht, the complex comprises five performance spaces where dances, concerts, opera and theatre are staged. The best way to experience the building is to attend a performance, but you can also take a one-hour guided tour.

The Walk ≫ Take the steps down away from the harbour and turn left (east) and follow the footpath that leads through the iron gates and into the Royal Botanic Garden.

Royal Botanic Garden

Bordering Farm Cove, east of the opera house, the **Royal Botanic Garden** (02-9231 8111; www.rbgsyd.nsw.gov.au; Mrs Macquaries Rd; 7am-8pm Oct-Feb, to 5.30pm Mar-Sep; Circular Quay) was established in 1816 and features plant life from Australia and around the world. Long before the convicts arrived, this was an initiation ground for the Gadigal people.

The Walk ≫ This is such a fabulous walk that it's worth taking twice – return to your car along the same route, perhaps at a more leisurely pace to take it all in.

Kosciuszko National Park
*On the way to the top of
Australia's highest peak*

DAVID WALL PHOTO/GETTY IMAGES ©

Snowy Mountains

3

Range across the high country from Cooma to Mt Kosciuszko, passing Australia's highest town, its highest mountain and some fabulous mountain scenery en route.

TRIP HIGHLIGHTS

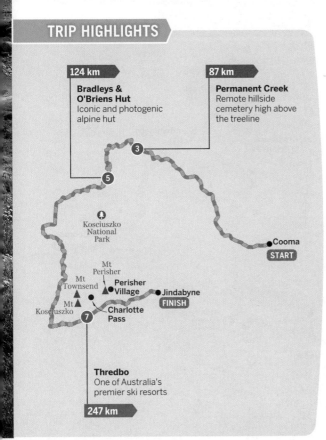

124 km

Bradleys & O'Briens Hut
Iconic and photogenic alpine hut

87 km

Permanent Creek
Remote hillside cemetery high above the treeline

5

Kosciuszko National Park

Mt Perisher

Mt Townsend

Perisher Village

Mt Kosciuszko

7

Charlotte Pass

●Jindabyne
FINISH

●Cooma
START

Thredbo
One of Australia's premier ski resorts

247 km

**2–3 DAYS
275KM / 171 MILES**

GREAT FOR...

BEST TIME TO GO

Spring and autumn. Roads may be impassable without chains in winter, when it's all about skiing.

ESSENTIAL PHOTO

Bradleys & O'Briens Hut, a classic high-country hut.

BEST FOR OUTDOORS

Permanent Creek for thrilling scenery with a soulful human story.

3 Snowy Mountains

From Cooma to Jindabyne (with a Mt Kosciuszko add-on for those with an urge to climb), this spectacular route through the Snowy Mountains traverses the wild uplands of southern New South Wales. Along the way, as wedge-tailed eagles soar high above on the thermals, the road passes dense alpine forests, lonely grasslands above the treeline and the kind of up-country views that you won't find anywhere else in Australia.

❶ Cooma

Cooma is a fine place to begin this crossing of Australia's highest terrain. But so much of your experience here will depend on when you come. You could 'coo-ee' down the main street in summer and not raise an eyebrow, yet proximity to the snowfields keeps this little town punching above its weight during winter. It imbues the best of country towns, with good places to hang out, an attractive centre and a laid-back vibe. On

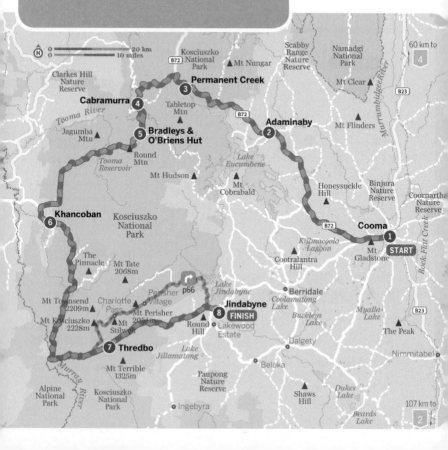

the Monaro Hwy, 2km north of the town centre, the Snowy Mountains Scheme Information Centre has fascinating information on the hydroelectric scheme that is one of Australia's finest feats of engineering; the dams and hydroelectric plant took 25 years and more than 100,000 people to build.

 p69

The Drive » To begin, take Sharp St in Cooma west then take the turn-off to Tumut 7km out of town. From there, it's 44km to Adaminaby, climbing gently through sub-alpine pastures as you go.

❷ Adaminaby

Gloriously named Adaminaby, at an elevation of 1017m, looks like any

LINK YOUR TRIP

2 Sydney to Melbourne

Drive south from Cooma for 45km then turn east towards the coast. You enter Trip 2 at Merimbula.

4 Canberra & the South Coast

Take the Monaro Hwy north from Cooma for 116km to Queanbeyan, which lies along Trip 4 between Canberra and Batemans Bay.

other sleepy Australian hamlet of widely spaced houses and shady parklands, but looks can be deceptive – old Adaminaby was drowned by the rising waters of Lake Eucumbene when dams were built in the 1950s. Many buildings you see today were actually transported here to beat the rising tide of water, but in times of drought, when the waters recede, old relics of the former town emerge like ghostly spectres. Snowfalls are common here in winter and the trout fishing in local waters is legendary. And this somnambulant place punches above its weight when it comes to name recognition: the town inspired Australia's Nobel Prize–winning author Patrick White's first novel, *Happy Valley*, while its racecourse has appeared in two Hollywood films: *The Sundowners* (1959), starring starring Robert Mitchum, Peter Ustinov, and Deborah Kerr; and *Phar Lap* (1983).

The Drive » Some 13km beyond Adaminaby, you leave behind rolling grazing country and enter the denser woodlands of Kosciuszko National Park. Soon enough, the landscape opens out a little and the first ghostly trunks (left by a 2003 fire) appear.

TRIP HIGHLIGHT

❸ Permanent Creek

Covering 673,492 hectares and stretching for 150km, Kosciuszko National Park is the jewel in NSW's considerable national-park crown. In spring and summer, walking trails and camp sites are framed by alpine flowers. It's less a single stop than a series of places where you'll be tempted to pull over, turn off the engine and take in the views in blissful silence. At the 86km mark out of Cooma, at the sign for Permanent Creek, leave the car by the roadside and climb to the poignant hillside graves of the Kiandra Cemetery – from 1891 to 1912, 47 people were buried at this remote gold-mining spot and only six died of old age. The scenery here has a wild and lonely aspect.

The Drive » After Permanent Creek, the road climbs past the ruins of Kiandra at 1400m above sea level, then take the turn-off for Cabramurra soon after at the 89km mark, with another turn-off for Cabramurra at 104km. Cabramurra itself is a further 4km on.

❹ Cabramurra

At a dizzying elevation of 1488m (by Australian standards at least), Cabramurra is Australia's highest town. It's a strange place in a stunning setting, its custom-built houses were first constructed in the 1950s to house workers on the Snowy Mountains Scheme, then left behind to house those who maintain it. There's little to see, but it's a curiously soulless place, a company town with a bare minimum of facilities. Stop briefly to see what we mean, before continuing on your way.

The Drive » The steep descent from Cabramurra is one of the prettiest on the whole route,

with a stunning honour guard of eerie white, fire-scarred trunks before the road drops down to the dam itself, then on through the alternating alpine woodlands and grasslands that are such a feature of this itinerary.

TRIP HIGHLIGHT

❺ Bradleys & O'Briens Hut

Surrounded by the chalk-white trunks left behind by the 2003 bushfires that ravaged the region, around 124km out of Cooma, Bradleys

& O'Briens Hut is a wonderful timber-framed mountain hut clad in corrugated iron. It's an evocative place, one of those isolated Aussie structures that somehow captures the loneliness of human settlements in this vast land. The hut itself, with its chimney recently restored, was first built by the O'Brien and Bradley families in 1952 (hence the name). It's still used by walkers and day-trippers to Kosciuszko National Park.

The Drive » As you continue southwest, you'll pass a number of rest areas and trail heads, always following the signs to Khancoban. The views open out along this section of the route, with Victoria's High Country visible across the state border to the south.

❻ Khancoban

Blissfully isolated, and quiet as a mouse outside the winter months, Khancoban is a tiny place that feels like an oasis after coming in from the long, lonely roads that lead here. The town's permanent population hovers just below 300 and its setting, hemmed in by the foothills of the Snowy Mountains, lends it an idyllic air, especially when the sun is shining. Stop long enough to pick up a snack or fill the tank with petrol (more expensive here than in Thredbo or Cooma), but push on towards Thredbo, especially if it's late in the day.

DETOUR: MT KOSCIUSZKO

Start: ❼ Thredbo or ❽ Jindabyne

It may be a mere hill when compared to mountains elsewhere around the world, but Mt Kosciuszko (2228m) is still the highest mountain on the Australian continent. As mountains go, it's relatively easy to climb, although getting to the top can still be strenuous. There are two possible trailheads and three available routes. The first is the **Mt Kosciuszko Track** – from Thredbo, take the **Kosciuszko Express Chairlift** (day pass adult/child return $34/18; ⊙year-round); from the top of the lift it's a steep 13km-return climb to the summit and back.

The other two trails require you to drive to the end of the paved road above Charlotte Pass (36km beyond Jindabyne). The easier of the two routes is the **Summit Walk**, which follows a wide gravel track along a 9km climb to the summit (18km return), including a steep final climb. The other option is the **Main Range Track**, a strenuous 20km loop that crosses minor creeks en route.

When choosing which route to take, remember that no park fees for Kosciuszko National Park are payable if you're just driving straight through. If, however, you're overnighting or driving beyond Jindabyne towards Charlotte Pass, the fee is $16 per vehicle per 24 hours.

GRAHAM MONRO/GM PHOTOGRAPHICS/GETTY IMAGES ©

Thredbo Snowboarder mid-flight

67

The Drive » With the trip clock at 192km, pause for fine views at Scammells Ridge Lookout. You'll pass a number of riverside rest areas, then after 243km you climb to one of the highest points of the road, a sign says 'Great Dividing Range 1580m', before dropping down the river valley into Thredbo.

TRIP HIGHLIGHT

❼ Thredbo

At 1370m, Thredbo is oft lauded as Australia's number-one ski resort, and its narrow valley setting is a dramatic sight as you descend in from the Khancoban road. If you're here in winter, it's all about skiing. Thredbo's skiing terrain is roughly 16% beginner, 67% intermediate and 17% advanced, with different snow 'parks' to suit each category. A smattering of worthwhile summer activities also feature, and summer is the time

when the **Thredbo Blues Festival** (www.thredbo.com. au/thredboblues/; ⊘ mid-Jan) wakes Thredbo from its off-season slumber.

✖ 🛏 p69

The Drive » Although you'll pass through plenty of alpine woodland on the first stretch out of Thredbo, the more picturesque sections of the route are now behind you and it's an easy run through open country for the last few kilometres into Jindabyne.

❽ Jindabyne

Jindabyne is the closest town to Kosciuszko National Park's major ski resorts, and more than 20,000 visitors pack in over winter. It lacks the natural drama and beauty of Thredbo – it's a feeder town rather than a destination in its own right – but in summer, the town assumes a more peaceful vibe and

fishing and mountain biking are the mainstay activities. Horse riding, too, is a popular summer pastime, with **Snowy River Horseback Adventure** (02-6457 8393; www.snowyriver horseback adventure.com.au; half-/1- /2-day rides $120/215/780; ⊘Oct-May) and **Reynella Kosciusko Rides** (✆02-6454 2386, 1800 029 909; www.reynellarides.com.au; 669 Kingston Rd, Adaminaby; three-/four-/five-day treks from $1200/1555/1870). But if it's exploring on four wheels that you love and you're still keen for more at journey's end, **Stone Bridge Tours** (✆02-6456 6745; www.stonebridgetours. com.au; half-/full-day tours $75/150) offers 4WD expeditions into the surrounding mountains and gorges.

✖ 🛏 p69

Eating & Sleeping

Cooma ❶

✖ Kettle & Seed   Cafe $

(📞02-6452 5882; 47 Vale St; mains from
$7.50; ⏰7am-4pm Mon-Fri, 8am-4pm Sat) A
coffee shop that wouldn't be out of place in an
upmarket Sydney suburb, this place roasts
its own beans and it shows. The light meals
(sandwiches and spinach pies) are good, but
almost incidental with coffee this great.

✖ Lott Food Store   Bakery, Cafe $$

(📞02-6452 1414; www.lott.com.au; 177 Sharp St;
mains $13.50-19; ⏰7.30am-4pm Mon-Fri, 8am-
5pm Sat-Sun) Cooma's light-and-airy foodie hub
has excellent coffee, hearty snacks and light
lunches, and lots of gourmet goodies perfect
for picnics.

🛏 Royal Hotel   Hotel $

(📞02-6452 2132; www.royalhotelcooma.com;
59 Sharp St; s/d $40/60) The oldest licensed
hotel in Cooma is a beautiful old sandstone
place with decent pub rooms, open fires, shared
bathrooms and a great verandah. Rooms are
simple but clean.

🛏 Alpine Hotel   Hotel $$

(📞02-6452 1466; www.alpinehotel.com.au; 170
Sharp St; s/d with shared bathroom $70/100,
d with private bathroom $145) This renovated
art-deco pub has comfortable budget rooms.
Downstairs is a cosy bistro with classic pub
meals and outdoor seating.

Thredbo ❼

✖ Gourmet 42   Cafe $

(100 Mowamba Pl, Village Sq; mains $12-19;
⏰7.30am-3pm) Hungover snowboarders and
sleepy bar staff rock up for coffee, soup and pasta.

✖ Knickerbocker   Modern Australian $$

(📞02-6457 6844; www.jeanmichelknicker-
bocker.com.au; Diggings Tce; mains $32-33;
⏰noon-2pm Sat & Sun, 6pm-late Wed-Sun)

Sit indoors for alpine cosiness, or rug up on the
deck with brilliant views. Seriously gourmet
meals go down well after drinks in the bar (from
4pm).

🛏 Candlelight Lodge   Lodge $$

(📞1800 020 900, 02-6457 6318; www.
candlelightlodge.com.au; 32 Diggings Tce; s/d
winter from $210/250, summer from $135/180;
📶) This Tyrolean lodge has great rooms, all
with views. The restaurant's fondue (winter
only) is fabulous.

🛏 Lake Crackenback
Resort   Resort, Lodge $$$

(📞1800 020 524; www.lakecrackenback.com.
au; 1650 Alpine Way; r from $255; ❄@📶🏊)
Apartments and chalets are classy at this
lakeside spa resort, the restaurants are
excellent, and plenty of activities are on offer
throughout winter and summer.

Jindabyne ❽

✖ Café Darya   Middle Eastern $$

(📞02-6457 1867; www.cafedarya.com.au; Snowy
Mountains Plaza; mezze $14, mains $29-32; ⏰6-
9pm Tue-Sat) Fill up on slow-cooked lamb shank
in Persian spices and rose petals or a rustic trio
of dips. BYO beer and wine. Cash only.

✖ Wild Brumby Mountain
Schnapps   Bistro $$

(www.wildbrumby.com; Alpine Way; mains $12-
30; ⏰10am-5pm) Located between Jindabyne
and Thredbo, this is the place to go for punchy
schnapps. Sit on the verandah and team a wheat
beer with a cheese and charcuterie platter.
Check online for occasional live music over
summer.

🛏 Banjo Paterson Inn   Hotel $$

(📞02-6456 2372; www.banjopatersoninn.com.
au; 1 Kosciuszko Rd; r summer $100-130, winter
$150-230) The best rooms have balconies and
lake views. Other facilities include a rowdy bar
and microbrewery. Come winter, it's extremely
popular.

STRETCH YOUR LEGS
CANBERRA

Start/Finish:
Parliament House

Distance: 3km

Duration: 3 hours
(longer for the museums)

Canberra is a serious-minded place, and this walk through a succession of national landmarks is a serious-minded walk. Contrary to what you've heard, Canberra can really buzz, but its gift to the nation is its role as guardian of the national memory.

Take this walk on Trip

Parliament House

Opened in 1988, Australia's Parliament House is dug into Capital Hill, and has a grass-topped roof topped by an 81m-high flagpole – it's one of the country's most distinguished modern architectural landmarks. The rooftop lawns encompass 23 hectares of gardens and provide superb 360-degree views. Underneath incorporates 17 courtyards, an entrance foyer, the Great Hall, the House of Representatives, the Senate and seemingly endless corridors.

The Walk >> Leave via Parliament House's front door and walk down the hill running down to the northeast, all the way to the white Old Parliament House building.

Museum of Australian Democracy

The seat of government from 1927 to 1988, the Museum of Australian Democracy offers visitors a whiff of bygone parliamentary activity. In addition to the museum's displays, you can also visit the old Senate and House of Representative chambers and the prime minister's office.

The Walk >> Walk around the north side of the museum and you'll come across the Aboriginal Tent Embassy.

Aboriginal Tent Embassy

The lawn in front of Old Parliament House is home to the Aboriginal Tent Embassy. On 26 January 1972, four Aboriginal men set up a beach umbrella on the lawn to protest the then government's refusal to acknowledge Aboriginal land rights. Since then, it has been a flashpoint for protests.

The Walk >> Head down through the grassland to the north. Cross King Edward Tce and Questacon is just on the other side of the road, at the corner with Parkes Pl.

Questacon

Now here's something to lighten the mood a little. **Questacon** (☏02-6270 2800; www.questacon.edu.au; King Edward Tce, Parkes; adult/child $20.50/15; ⊘9am-5pm)

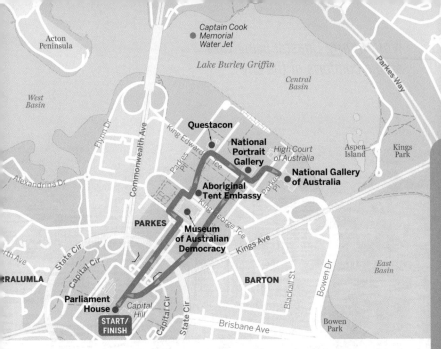

is a kid-friendly science centre with educational and fun interactive exhibits. Explore the physics of sport, athletics and fun parks, cause tsunamis, and take shelter from cyclones and earthquakes. It will appeal to all of those with a burning desire to press buttons and see what happens.

The Walk >> As you walk through the parks to the east, admire the Captain Cook Memorial Water Jet, away to the north on Lake Burley Griffin, the artwork of Reconciliation Pl, and the imposing High Court Building.

National Portrait Gallery

There's something special about the **National Portrait Gallery** (☏02-6102 7000; www.portrait.gov.au; King Edward Tce, Parkes; ⏰10am-5pm), which tells the story of Australia through its faces – from wax cameos of Aboriginal tribespeople to colonial portraits of the nation's founding families and contemporary works such as Howard Arkley's Day-Glo portrait of musician Nick Cave. There

is a good cafe for post-exhibition coffee and reflection.

The Walk >> Due east of the National Portrait Gallery, the National Gallery of Australia sits across the road on Parkes Pl.

National Gallery of Australia

Arguably Australia's premier art gallery, the **National Gallery of Australia** (☏02-6240 6502; www.nga.gov.au; Parkes Pl, Parkes; admission costs for special exhibitions; ⏰10am-5pm) includes an extraordinary Aboriginal Memorial from Central Arnhem Land. The work of 43 artists, this 'forest of souls' presents 200 hollow log coffins (one for every year of European settlement) and is part of an excellent collection of Aboriginal and Torres Strait Islander art.

The Walk >> To return to where you started, retrace your steps to the National Portrait Gallery and King Edward Tce, then climb back up through the greenery to the top of the hill and Parliament House.

Wollongong Coastal living with all the comforts of the city

Canberra & the South Coast

4

This inland foray picks the best from the hinterland of the New South Wales south coast, with fabulous scenery, historic highlights and even the nation's capital to enjoy en route.

TRIP HIGHLIGHTS

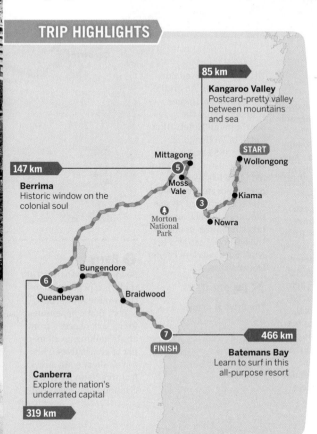

85 km

Kangaroo Valley
Postcard-pretty valley between mountains and sea

START
Wollongong

Mittagong
5

147 km

Berrima
Historic window on the colonial soul

Moss Vale
3

Kiama

Morton National Park

Nowra

Bungendore

6
Queanbeyan

Braidwood

7
FINISH

466 km

Batemans Bay
Learn to surf in this all-purpose resort

Canberra
Explore the nation's underrated capital

319 km

3–4 DAYS
466KM / 290 MILES

GREAT FOR...

BEST TIME TO GO

November to March for coastal areas, but year-round everywhere else.

ESSENTIAL PHOTO

Parliament House, Canberra.

BEST FOR OUTDOORS

Kangaroo Valley and the road up and over the Great Dividing Range are simply gorgeous.

73

PETER HARRISON/GETTY IMAGES ©

4

Canberra & the South Coast

While everyone else gets distracted by the big Pacific blue, this itinerary eases you away from the coast and within no time at all, the splendour of Kangaroo Valley will hold you in its thrall. Berrima and Bowral rank among inland NSW's most charming historic towns, while Canberra is Australia's cultural heartland. Then it's down through forests to rejoin the coast at Batemans Bay, where we'll even have you learning how to surf.

1 Wollongong

With its echoes of Sydney on a far more manageable scale, the 'Gong' is the envy of many cities, capturing as it does the Aussie ideal of coastal living yet with all the comforts of a big city on hand. Restaurants, bars, arts, culture and entertainment all combine with a laid-back beachy lifestyle, and the bright lights of Sydney are easily accessible by local rail. There are 17 patrolled beaches in the vicinity – North Beach generally has better surf than Wollongong City Beach, while further north are the surfer magnets of Bulli, Sandon Point, Thirroul (where DH Lawrence lived during his time in Australia) and pretty Austinmer. And don't miss the Scarborough Hotel, 21km north of Wollongong. Built in 1886 and now heritage-listed, this grand old place has recently been renovated, reopened and reinvigorated so that punters can once again take advantage of one of the best beer gardens in NSW with peerless Pacific Ocean views.

✗ 🛏 p79

The Drive » Forsake the truck-heavy Rte 1 for the quieter coastal road, passing Shellharbour, Kiama and Gerringong before rejoining Rte 1 all the way into Berry.

2 Berry

Berry, home to barely 1700 souls, is a popular inland stop on the south coast, a town that compensates for its lack of ocean frontage by talking up all manner of alternatives. The town's short main street features National Trust–classified buildings, and

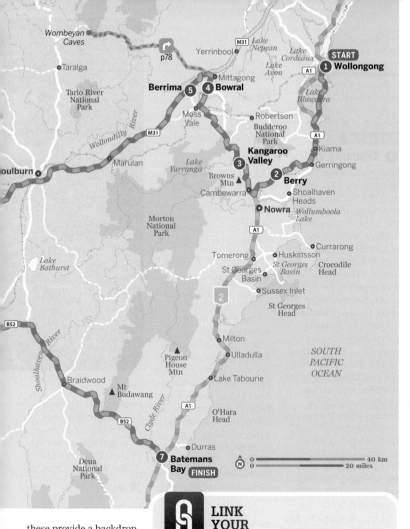

these provide a backdrop to a smattering of antique and design stores, not to mention an emerging foodie scene with good cafes and restaurants: the latter are complemented by some good-quality vineyards, such as Jasper Valley Wines, in the rolling countryside around the town.

LINK YOUR TRIP

2 Sydney to Melbourne

Wollongong lies close to the start of the Sydney to Melbourne Trip, while Batemans Bay is close to its midpoint.

3 Snowy Mountains

From Queanbeyan, drive 109km south along the Monaro Hwy to Cooma, where the 275km Snowy Mountain loop begins.

MIKE BERCEANU/GETTY IMAGES ©

The Drive » Follow Rte 1 for around 12km and, just when it seems like you have no choice but to pass through unlovely and sprawling Nowra, turn off away to the right and journey northwest into Kangaroo Valley.

TRIP HIGHLIGHT

❸ Kangaroo Valley

Now here's something special. Set back within a sea breeze of the coast, unbelievably picturesque Kangaroo Valley rises from the coastal littoral like an idyll of rural New South Wales. Arrayed against a fortress-like backdrop of rainforest-covered cliffs, its valley floor is carpeted by sweeping green pasturelands, river gums and gurgling creeks. The slow country town of Kangaroo Valley itself has an excellent pub, a bakery and a general store. It also has the odd feel-good shop and gallery to satiate wealthy Sydneysiders who populate the town at the weekend. The formal entry to the valley is the castellated sandstone-and-iron **Hamden Bridge** (1898), a few kilometres north of the town. The river beach just below the bridge is a good spot for a swim. If you've time to linger, consider a cooking class at **Flavours of the Valley** (☏02-4465 2010; www.flavoursofthevalley. com.au; per person from $130), while **Kangaroo Valley Adventure Co** (☏02-4465

1372; www.kvac.com.au; Glenmack Park Camp Site) can set you up for everything from hiking to kayaking.

🛏 p79

The Drive » The road northwest from Kangaroo Valley is a wonderfully winding ascent of the escarpment, with fine views of the coastal plains and Pacific beaches before you get lost in the dizzyingly tall trees of the upper montane forest; watch for colourful king parrots in the upper reaches. Pass through Fitzroy Falls and Moss Vale on your way into Bowral.

❹ Bowral

You could be forgiven for thinking you've taken a wrong turn in the southern highlands and ended up in the south of England when you reach Bowral, a pretty area that revels in its Englishness. That feeling will soon come to seem rather incongruous, however, when you learn that it was here that Sir Donald Bradman, that quintessential Aussie hero and nemesis of English cricket, spent his boyhood. Within the **International Cricket Hall of Fame** (☏02-4862 1247; www. internationalcrickethall.com. au; St Jude St, Bowral; adult/child $20/11; ⊗10am-5pm) complex, there's a pretty cricket oval, and fans pay homage to Bradman at the **Bradman Museum of Cricket** (www.bradman. com.au), which has an engrossing collection of Ashes and Don-centric

memorabilia. The ever-expanding collection showcasing the international game is a must for all sports fans, not just cricket buffs.

🗶 🛏 p79

The Drive » To reach Berrima, you'll need to loop north and then southwest onto the Hume Fwy ever so briefly. You should be there no more than 20 minutes after leaving Bowral.

TRIP HIGHLIGHT

❺ Berrima

Heritage-classified Berrima could just be the loveliest town along the Hume Hwy. Founded in 1829 with visions of a fu-

Wollongong Coastal drive

ture as a major metropolis, Berrima grew into an important inland waystation that was, during its 19th-century peak, home to 14 hotels. It later settled into quiet obscurity, but not before an appealing portfolio of sandstone buildings adorned the streets. These buildings – among them the **Berrima Courthouse** (1838), the **Old Berrima Gaol** (1839), the **Holy Trinity Anglican Church** (1849) and the **St Francis Xavier Catholic Church** (1849) – together speak volumes for the preoccupations of early settlement life. That other essential pillar of bijou rural Aussie towns, the second-hand bookshop, finds expression in **Berkelouw's Book Barn & Café** (☎02-4877 1370; www.berkelouw.com. au; Old Hume Hwy, Bendooley; ⏰9am-5pm), with over 200,000 second-hand tomes around 3km north of town.

✗ p79

The Drive » It's possible to avoid the Hume Fwy as far south as sleepy Bundanoon, a gateway to Morton National Park. But thereafter you might as well join the freeway, bypassing Goulburn, then following the signs down into Canberra.

TRIP HIGHLIGHT

6 Canberra

Canberra, Australia's custom-built capital, is a city built for the car, and having one allows you to explore its expansive open spaces and catch a sense of the city's seamless alignment of built and natural elements. Though Canberra seems big on architectural symbolism and low on spontaneity, the city's cultural institutions have lively visitor and social programs, and there's a cool urban energy emerging in Braddon, New

DETOUR:
WOMBEYAN CAVES

Start: ❹ Bowral

Southern New South Wales is riddled with fabulous limestone caves and there are none more spectacular than **Wombeyan Caves** (☎02-4843 5976; www.nationalparks.nsw.gov.au; Wombeyan Caves Rd; Figtree Cave adult/child $18/12, 2 caves & tour 'Discovery Pass' $30/23; ⏰9am-4pm). This convoluted network of extraordinary underground caverns lies up an unsealed mountain road (which is passable in a 2WD vehicle but adds a real sense of adventure to the excursion), 70km northwest of Bowral. Nearby are walking trails and plenty of wildlife.

Acton and the Kingston Foreshore. During parliamentary-sitting weeks the town hums with the buzz of national politics, but it can be a tad sleepy during university holidays, especially around Christmas and New Year. If you're here at such times, get out and explore its kangaroo-filled parks and its picturesque natural hinterland.

🛏 p79

The Drive » From Canberra's city centre, follow the signs to Queanbeyan, then take the Kings Hwy as it loops up and over the Great Dividing Range on a twisting forest road down to the coast. Although it's only 170km from Canberra to Batemans Bay, count on it taking three hours, and avoid Friday afternoon when Canberrans head for the coast.

- - - - - - - - - - - -

TRIP HIGHLIGHT

❼ Batemans Bay

Like any good south-coast beach town worth its salt, Batemans Bay promises a decent restaurant strip, good beaches and, in this case, a sparkling estuary. It all makes for some diverse water-borne activities, from family-friendly kayaking and fishing, to surf lessons amid the crashing surf; for the latter, try **Broulee Surf School** (☎02-4471 7370; www.brouleesurfschool.com. au; adult/child from $45/40), or **Surf the Bay Surf School** (☎0432 144 220; www.surfthebay.com.au; group/private lesson $40/90), which also offers paddleboarding. And there are plenty of beaches if all you need is somewhere to lay your towel. Closest to town is **Corrigans Beach**, and longer beaches north of the bridge lead into **Murramarang National Park**. Surfers flock to **Pink Rocks**, **Surf Beach**, **Malua Bay**, **McKenzies Beach** and **Bengello Beach**. **Broulee** has a wide crescent of sand, but there's a strong rip at the northern end. It should be scarcely surprising, therefore, that Batemans Bay is one of coastal NSW's most popular holiday centres, so book ahead if you're planning to arrive and stay in summer or on a weekend.

✕ 🛏 p79

Eating & Sleeping

Wollongong ❶

✕ Lee & Me   Cafe $

(www.leeandme.com.au; 87 Crown St; breakfast $11-16, lunch $11-16; ⏰7am-4pm Mon-Fri, 8am-4pm Sat & Sun) A cafe and art-and-clothing store in a two-storey, late-19th-century heritage building. Standout dishes include buttermilk-malt hotcakes or the classic beef burger.

🛏 Chifley   Hotel $$

(☎02-4201 2111; www.silverneedlehotels.com; 60-62 Harbour St; r from $152) Wollongong's newest hotel has ocean and golf-course views, tastefully designed rooms and shared public areas. Good beaches, pubs and restaurants are a short walk away.

Kangaroo Valley ❸

🛏 Cloud Song   B&B $$$

(☎02-4465 1194; www.cloudsonginkangaroo valley.com.au; 170 Moss Vale Rd; d from $220) Beautifully designed modern cabins with open fireplaces and some with balconies. It's just off the main road right in the centre of town.

Bowral ❹

✕ Biota Dining   Modern Australian $$$

(☎02-4862 2005; http://biotadining.com; 18 Kangaloon Rd, Bowral; brunch mains $19, degustation $105-165; ⏰9-11am Sat & Sun, noon-2.30pm Fri-Mon, 6-9.30pm daily) Innovative seasonal menus include interesting dishes like salted cucumber with oysters and beach plants, and the wine list is as good as the weekend brunch. Try the crab and creamed-egg sliders with a restorative pepperberry Bloody Mary.

🛏 Links Manor   Guesthouse $$$

(☎02-4861 1977; www.linkshouse.com.au; 17 Links Rd; r $190-340; ❄🔊) This boutique guesthouse has a drawing room and garden courtyard straight out of Remains of the Day. Prices are highest on Friday and Saturday.

Berrima ❺

✕ Bendooley Bar & Grill   Bistro $$

(☎02-4877 2235; www.bendooleyestate.com. au; pizza $22-25, mains $27-34; ⏰10am-3pm) A top spot for a leisurely lunch showcasing local and seasonal produce. Try the prawn and chilli pizza with a Aussie craft beer. Attached to Berkelouw's Book Barn & Café (p77).

✕ Eschalot   Modern Australian $$$

(☎02-4877 1977; www.eschalot.com.au; 24 Old Hume Hwy, Berrima; mains $36-40, 7-course degustation $110; ⏰noon-2.30pm Thu-Sun, 6-9pm Wed-Sat) This heritage sandstone cottage showcases superb modern Australian cooking. Flavours could include sesame-crusted alpaca tataki (seared and thinly sliced meat) with watermelon, kaffir cream and wild rice.

Canberra ❻

🛏 Peppers Gallery Hotel   Boutique Hotel $$

(☎1300 987 600; www.peppers.com.au/gallery; 15 Edinburgh Ave, Civic; r $159-344, apt $424-554; P❄🔊) In the hip New Acton precinct near Civic, Peppers Gallery has a sheen of cosmopolitan sophistication. Eight types of rooms and apartments occupy a renovated 1926 apartment block. Bicicletta Restaurant is also here.

Batemans Bay ❼

✕ Innes Boatshed   Fish & Chips $

(1 Clyde St; fish & chips $14, 6 oysters $9; ⏰9am-2.30pm Sun-Thu, to 8pm Fri & Sat) Since the 1950s, this has been one of the South Coast's best-loved fish-and-chip and oyster joints. Head out to the spacious deck but mind the pelicans. Cash only.

🛏 Lincoln Downs   Hotel $$

(☎1800 789 250; www.lincolndowns.com.au; Princes Hwy; r from $149; ❄🔊🐾) Excellent motel-style rooms, many of which overlook a private lake. There's also a resident peacock.

Dangar Falls Ancient rainforest
of World Heritage acclaim

New England **5**

While most visitors are obsessed with the beaches from Bondi to Byron, discerning travellers take a New England detour through national parks, historic towns and Australia's country-music capital.

TRIP HIGHLIGHTS

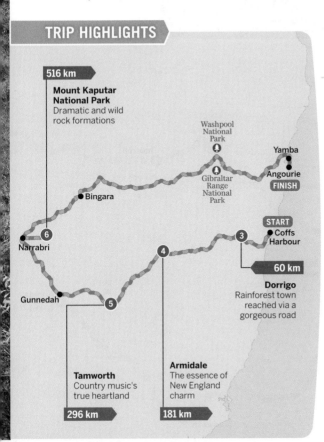

516 km

Mount Kaputar National Park
Dramatic and wild rock formations

Washpool National Park

Gibraltar Range National Park

Yamba
Angourie
FINISH

Bingara

START
Coffs Harbour

6

Narrabri

3

4

60 km

Dorrigo
Rainforest town reached via a gorgeous road

Gunnedah

5

Tamworth
Country music's true heartland

296 km

Armidale
The essence of New England charm

181 km

5–7 DAYS
884KM / 547 MILES

GREAT FOR...

BEST TIME TO GO
Tamworth's country music festival in mid-January; March to May best for autumnal colours.

ESSENTIAL PHOTO
Mount Kaputar National Park for dramatic land formations.

✓ BEST FOR HISTORY
Armidale is New England in a nutshell with fine heritage architecture.

YURY PROKOPENKO/GETTY IMAGES ©

5 New England

Leave the coast behind and head for the hills – the drive from Coffs to Armidale is one of New South Wales' prettiest. After Tamworth, that big-hat capital of all things country, the roads empty and a string of national parks and lovely little towns (where you can strike it rich in more ways than one) will keep you company all the way down to Yamba.

❶ Coffs Harbour

Coffs Harbour is one of the beach stalwarts of the Aussie coast, a popular if slightly ageing resort with surf schools, fish and chips, and long, unspoiled stretches of sand. It's the sort of place that's as popular with families as it is with backpackers and blue-rinse retirees. Of the beaches, try **Park Beach**, a long, lovely stretch of sand backed by dense shrubbery and sand dunes that conceal

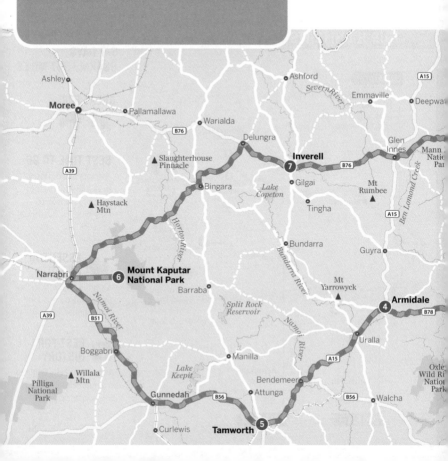

the buildings beyond. **Jetty Beach** is somewhat more sheltered. We also love Coffs for the chance to learn surfing at East Coast Surf School (p43), which is run by former pro surfer Helene Enevoldson. And then there's the Big Banana...

The Drive >> From Coffs, take Rte 1 south of town for around 20km, then bid farewell to the coast and head inland (west), bound for Bellingen. Almost immediately, the world becomes quieter and the hills of the Great Dividing Range rise up ahead of you.

❷ Bellingen

Buried in foliage on a hillside above the Bellinger River, this gorgeous town dances to the beat of its own bongo drum. Thick with gourmet, organic cuisine and accommodation, 'Bello' is hippie without the dippy. Partly it's the location that catches the eye, but it also has just the right mix of seasonal markets, quirky stores such as the Old Butter Factory, and its very own Bellingen Jazz Festival. Throw in river canoeing, a huge colony of

flying foxes on Bellingen Island and a quirky literary heritage – there's the Bellingen Book Nook, the **Bellingen Readers & Writers Festival** (◷Jun) and its fame as the setting of Peter Carey's Booker Prize–winning novel *Oscar and Lucinda* – and you'll soon be hooked.

✕ p87

The Drive >> The Waterfall Way (www.visitwaterfallway.com. au) road from Bellingen runs pancake-flat for a wee while, then climbs the eastern flank of the Great Dividing Range and barely stops doing so until you're in Dorrigo, 27km after leaving Bellingen. The views are splendid on the first half.

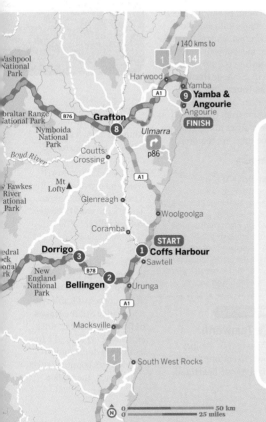

LINK YOUR TRIP

1 Sydney to Byron Bay

Coffs Harbour sits roughly on the midpoint between Sydney and Byron Bay, while Yamba is closer to Byron, where Trip 1 ends.

14 Southern Queensland Loop

Drive 180km north of Yamba and you'll end up nudging Coolangatta, part of a loop through the Queensland coast.

CAROL BUCHANAN/GETTY IMAGES ©

TRIP HIGHLIGHT

❸ Dorrigo

Amid so much natural beauty, Dorrigo can seem almost incidental, although it's a pretty little place arrayed around the T-junction of two wider-than-wide streets. The town's main attraction is the Dangar Falls, 1.2km north of town, which cascades over a series of rocky shelves before plummeting into a basin. But even more beautiful attractions await in the nearby **Dorrigo National Park**. Stretching for 119 sq km, this park is part of the Gondwana Rainforests World Heritage Area. The **Rainforest Centre** (☎02-9513 6617; www.nationalparks.nsw.gov.au/Dorrigo-National-Park; Dome Rd; adult/child $2/1; ⏱9am-4.30pm; 🛜), at the park entrance, has displays and can advise you on which walk to tackle. It's also home to the **Skywalk**, a viewing platform that juts over the rainforest and provides vistas over the valleys below.

🛏 p87

The Drive » It's a long, lovely drive through forests, light woodland and, increasingly the further west you go, the open farmlands of this lush corner of New England. There's barely a straight section, so count on taking longer than you planned.

TRIP HIGHLIGHT

❹ Armidale

Few places capture that graceful and refined New England air quite like Armidale, and it's here that the entire region's name makes the most sense. Armidale's heritage buildings, gardens and moss-covered churches look like the stage set for an English period drama, and it's these facades, coupled with spectacular autumn foliage (March to May), that will live longest in the memory. Armidale also has an appealing microclimate – set at an elevation of 980m, it enjoys mild summers and crisp winters. To make the most of your time here, take the free (and detail-rich) 2½-hour **Heritage Bus Tours** (☎02-6770 3888; ⏱10am) of Armidale that depart from the visitor centre daily at 10am; advance bookings are required.

🛏 p87

The Drive » Some of Australia's premier grazing country surrounds Armidale, and the green, rolling pasturelands through which you'll pass en route to Tamworth (125km) evoke the farms of southern England in places, although the colours turn Aussie yellow-and-brown the further you go.

TRIP HIGHLIGHT

❺ Tamworth

If you had to identify a town to epitomise the rural Aussie heartland, Tamworth would be close to the top of the list. Surrounded by rich farmlands, and a pilgrimage destination for country-music lovers, Tamworth wears its provinciality like a proud badge of honour. There's the world's biggest **golden guitar** (☎02-6765 2688; www.biggoldenguitar.com.au; New England Hwy; ⏱9am-5pm), the **Hands of Fame** (with over 200 hand prints of the stars at the corner of Kable Ave and Bridge St), the **Noses of Fame** at Joe Maguire's Hotel on Peel St, and a fine exhibition dedicated to Tamworth's country-music soundtrack, the **Walk a**

Sawn Rocks Mount Kaputar National Park

Country Mile Museum
(www.countrymusichalloffame.
com.au; cnr Peel & Murray Sts).
But it all pales in compari-
son to the truly awesome,
10-day **Country Music
Festival** (www.tcmf.com.au)
held in the second half of
January – the biggest mu-
sic festival in the southern
hemisphere. If you missed
it, get along to **Hats Off to
Country Music** in July.

🛏 p87

The Drive » From
Tamworth, Rte 34 crosses
yet more farmland on its
way to Gunnedah (75km), an
agricultural centre and the self-
proclaimed 'Koala Capital of the
World'. Then it's 95km northwest
to Narrabri, then on to Mount

Kaputar National Park, around
40km northeast.

- - - - - - - - - - - - - - - -

TRIP HIGHLIGHT

6 Mount Kaputar National Park

One of New England's
most spectacular corners,
Sawn Rocks, a pipe-organ
formation about 40km
northeast of Narrabri
(20km unsealed but fine in
a 2WD vehicle), is the most
accessible and popular
part of Mount Kapu-
tar National Park. The
southern part of the park
has dramatic lookouts,
rock climbing, bushwalk-
ing and camping, but it's
the organ pipes that most

people come here to see.
Ask at the **visitor centre**
(📞02-6799 6760; www.
narrabri.nsw.gov.au; Newell Hwy)
in Narrabri for directions.

The Drive » Return to
Narrabri, then take the quiet,
quiet road running northeast
107km to interesting little
Bingara (look for its art-deco
1930s theatre), then through
Myall Creek (24km). At the
Gwydir Hwy (Route 38), turn
right (southeast); it's 32km from
the turn-off to Inverell.

- - - - - - - - - - - - - - -

7 Inverell

Sapphires put Inverell on
the map – in the sapphire
boom of the 1970s the
town was supplying 80% of

the world's sapphire market, and there are those who believe that the supply has yet to be exhausted. Read the stories and, if you've sapphires in your eyes, pick up a fossicking map at the **visitor centre** (☎02-6728 8161; www.inverell.com.au; Campbell St; ☺9am-5pm Mon-Fri, to 2pm Sat & Sun) and go forth to search for sapphires. Even if you find nothing (which is likely), the looking is half the fun. Once you're done, then sample olive oil at **Olives of Beaulieu** (☎02-6722 1458; www.olivesofbeaulieu.com.au; 439 Copeton Dam Rd; ☺11am-4pm Wed-Sun).

 p87

The Drive » Inverell to Glen Innes covers just 49km along the Gwydir Hwy, and is one of the least-interesting sectors of the route – drive right on through. Later the Gwydir Hwy bucks and weaves up and over the forested hillsides of the Great Dividing Range, passing tempting national parks en route.

❽ Grafton

On the flat coastal plain but without the ocean frontage, Grafton's appeal is not immediately obvious. But it's a grand old place once you take a second look. Its grid of gracious streets are adorned with imposing old pubs and some splendid historic houses. In late October the town is awash with the soft lilac rain of jacaranda flowers – a simply wonderful sight – and for two weeks from late October, Australia's longest-running floral festival, the **Jacaranda Festival** (www.jacarandafestival.org.au; ☺Oct), paints the town a lovely shade of mauve. **Susan Island**, in the middle of the river, is home to a large colony of fruit bats; their evening fly-past is pretty impressive.

✖ 🛏 p87

DETOUR: ULMARRA

Start: ❽ Grafton

It's worth taking a small detour from the Pacific Hwy to Ulmarra (population 435), a heritage-listed town with a river port that few travellers know about. Its name comes from an old Aboriginal word that means 'bend in the river' and there's a lazy, sub-tropical feel to this enchanted little place. The **Ulmarra Hotel** (www.ulmarrahotel.com.au; 2 Coldstream St, Ulmarra) is a quaint old corner pub with a wrought-iron verandah and a greener-than-green beer garden that stretches down to the river – the perfect place to slow down to the decidedly laid-back Ulmarra pace of life.

The Drive » The delta between Grafton and the coast is a patchwork of farmland in which the now sinuous and spreading Clarence River forms more than 100 islands, some very large. Follow the Pacific Hwy northeast then drop down to the coast by following the signs into Yamba.

❾ Yamba & Angourie

At the mouth of the Clarence River, the fishing town of Yamba is rapidly growing in popularity thanks to its quasi-bohemian lifestyle, top beaches and excellent eateries. Oft-heard statements such as 'Byron Bay 20 years ago' are not unfounded. Its neighbour Angourie, 5km to the south, is a tiny, chilled-out place that has long been a draw for experienced surfers who were thrilled when it became one of Australia's first surf reserves. Choose whichever of the two appeals, use it as a base to explore the beaches, nature reserves and coastal walking trails in the area and then sit back to rest from the long and winding New England road.

Eating & Sleeping

Bellingen ❷

✖ Hearthfire Bakery   Bakery $

(📞02-6655 0767; www.hearthfire.com.au;
73 Hyde St; items $9-14; ⊙7am-5pm Mon-Fri,
7.30am-2pm Sat, 9am-2pm Sun) Follow the smell
of hot-out-of-the-woodfire organic sourdough
and you'll find this outstanding country bakery
and cafe. Try the famous macadamia fruit
loaf or settle in with a coffee and an incredibly
indulgent pie. There is a full breakfast menu.

✖ Oak Street Food
& Wine   Modern Australian $$$

(📞02-6655 9000; www.oakstreetfoodandwine.
com.au; 2 Oak St; lunch $12-18, dinner mains $34;
⊙midday-9.30pm Wed-Sat, 10am-3pm Sun)
This much loved restaurant continues to turn
out sophisticated, but accessible dishes that
make the most of the Bellinger Valley bounty.
There is a fabulous Sunday brunch menu.

Dorrigo ❸

🛏 Tallawarra Retreat B&B   B&B $$

(📞02-6657 2315; www.tallawalla.com; 113
Old Coramba Rd; s/d from $130/165; 🐾) This
peaceful B&B is set amid picturesque gardens
and forest around 1km from Dorrigo town
centre. Paul and Di are friendly hosts and the
rooms are comfortable and blissfully quiet.
There's also a beautiful summer-only tea house
and cafe.

Armidale ❹

🛏 Lindsay House   B&B $$

(📞02-6771 4554; www.lindsayhouse.com.au;
128 Faulkner St; s/d $130/180; 🛜) Immerse
yourself in a past when beds were four-poster,
ceilings were ornate, furniture was beautifully
crafted and port was served in the evening. This

lovely old home is as restful and recuperative
as it is grand.

Tamworth ❺

🛏 Retreat at Froog-Moore Park B&B $$$

(📞02-6766 3353; www.froogmoorepark.com.
au; 78 Bligh St; r incl breakfast from $225; 🛜)
Five individually styled suites (with names like
Moroccan Fantasy and The Dungeon) make this
avant-garde B&B one of Tamworth's quirkier
and more luxurious options. Rooms are large,
the gardens are delightful, and the breakfasts
could just be the best in town.

Inverell ❼

🛏 Blair Athol Estate   B&B $$

(📞02-6722 4288; www.babs.com.au/blairathol;
Warialda Rd; d $130-180) For a grand taste of
yesteryear, Blair Athol's estate dates from 1904
and has stunning grounds peppered with a rich
mix of flora. Breakfast is additional ($10/20 for
Continental/cooked).

Grafton ❽

✖ Heart & Soul Wholefood Cafe   Cafe $

(📞02-6642 2166; www.cafeheartandsoul.com.
au; 124a Prince St; $8-15; ⊙7.30am-3pm, to
2pm Sat, 8am-12pm Sun; 🍴) This beautifully
styled cafe is the work of two couples who love
plant-based foods. Expect ceramic bowls filled
with warming Asian numbers and bright salad
dishes. Sweet treats like the choc mint 'cheese-
fake' are worth sampling.

🛏 Annies B&B   B&B $$

(📞0421 914 295; www.anniesbnbgrafton.
com; 13 Mary St; s/d $145/160; ❄🛜🐾) This
beautiful Victorian house on a leafy corner has
private rooms with an old-fashioned ambience,
set apart from the rest of the family home. A
Continental breakfast is provided.

Broken Hill *A desert frontier town close to the end of the earth*

Outback New South Wales

6

From Bathurst to Broken Hill, this vast east–west New South Wales traverse takes you from the food-and-wine hinterland of Sydney to the profound silences and quirky towns of the outback.

MANFRED GOTTSCHALK/GETTY IMAGES © LINE OF LODE MINERS MEMORIAL, DESIGNED BY ANGUS BARRON, STEVE KELLY AND DARIO PALUMBO

TRIP HIGHLIGHTS

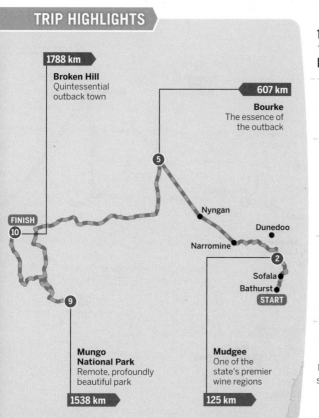

1788 km
Broken Hill Quintessential outback town

607 km
Bourke The essence of the outback

5

Nyngan

Dunedoo

FINISH 10

Narromine

2

Sofala
Bathurst **START**

9

Mungo National Park Remote, profoundly beautiful park
1538 km

Mudgee One of the state's premier wine regions
125 km

10–14 DAYS
1788KM / 1111 MILES

GREAT FOR...

BEST TIME TO GO
April to October has cold outback nights, but is better than searing daytime temperatures of summer.

ESSENTIAL PHOTO
Walls of China sand dunes in Mungo National Park.

BEST FOR WINE
Mudgee is one of the state's best wine regions.

89

Outback New South Wales

You've heard about the outback. The only way to get there is via long and empty roads that pass through fascinating, isolated communities whose very names – Bourke, Wilcannia and Broken Hill – carry a whiff of outback legend. Before heading for the 'Back of Bourke', however, take time to sample the culinary and architectural treasures of civilisation in Bathurst, Mudgee and Gulgong.

Australia's oldest inland settlement, Bathurst has historical references strewn across its old centre, especially in the beautiful, manicured central square where formidable Victorian buildings transport you to the past; the most impressive of these is the 1880 **Courthouse**, and don't miss the utterly fascinating **Australian Fossil & Mineral Museum** (www.somervillecollection.com. au; 224 Howick St; adult/child $12/6; ⊙10am-4pm Mon-Sat,

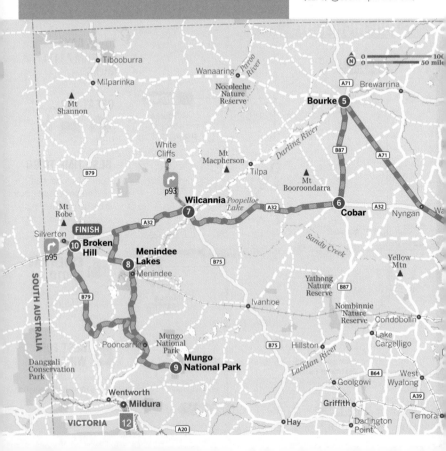

to 2pm Sun) with Australia's only complete skeleton of *Tyrannosaurus rex*. But this is no static open-air architectural museum. Instead, Bathurst displays a Sydney sensibility when it comes to enjoying good food and wines. And then, in a dramatic change of pace, it's also the bastion of Australian motorsport: if you're a devotee of motorsports, head to the **Mount Panorama Motor Racing Circuit** (www.mount-panorama.com.au), home to the epic Bathurst 1000 V8 race each October, as well

as the **National Motor Racing Museum** (www.nmrm.com.au; Murrays Corner, Mt Panorama; adult/child $12.50/5.50; ⊘9am-4.30pm).

 p96

The Drive » Follow the signs towards Lithgow from Bathurst city centre, then take the turn-off for Sofala, before joining the main road to Mudgee (209km from Bathurst).

- - - - - - - - - - - -

TRIP HIGHLIGHT

❷ Mudgee

The name Mudgee is an Aboriginal word for 'nest in the hills', a fitting name for this pretty town surrounded by vineyards and rolling hills. The wineries come hand-in-hand with excellent food, making Mudgee a popular weekend getaway (which is why we recommend visiting during the week). Mudgee's 35 cellar doors (all family-owned operations) are primarily clustered northeast of town – check out www.mudgeewine.com.au for further details. If wine's why you're here, consider

taking a guided excursion with **Mudgee Wine & Country Tours** (☏02-6372 2367; www.mudgeewinetours.com.au; half-/full-day wine tours $50/80) or **Mudgee Tourist Bus** (☏02-6372 4475; www.mudgeetouristbus.com.au; half-/full-day tours $45/70), stop by Mudgee's best (and NSW's oldest) wine bar, **Roth's** (www.rothswinebar.com.au; 30 Market St; ⊘5pm-midnight Wed-Sat), and consider dropping everything to be here in September for the three-week **Mudgee Wine Festival** (www.mudgeewine.com.au). And if you're visiting the wineries under your own steam, begin with **Lowe Wines** (☏03-6372 0800; www.lowewine.com.au; Tinja Lane; ⊘10am-5pm) and **Robert Stein Winery & Vineyard** (www.robertstein.com.au; Pipeclay Lane; ⊘10am-4.30pm).

 p96

The Drive » On the main Ulan Rd, around 29km after leaving Mudgee, follow the signs for Gulgong, which lies 24km away through dense, fire-scarred forest.

Moree

Walgett

76

Narrabri

A39

Coonamble

Coonabarabran

gandra

Munghorn Gap Nature Reserve

Dunedoo

Dubbo ❹

Gulgong ❸

omine

Peak Hill

Mudgee ❷

Molong

Sofala

Parkes

Orange ❶

bes

Bathurst ❶

START 183 kms to ❶

Cowra

renfell

Young

Crookwell

LINK YOUR TRIP

❶ Sydney to Byron Bay

It's 196km from Bathurst to Sydney to start this coastal odyssey, a mere blip on your speedo compared to outback distances.

12 Along the Murray

Although Mungo Park is actually closer to Mildura, the 299km paved road (Silver City Hwy) connects Mildura with Broken Hill.

SCENIC ROUTES: BATHURST-TO-MUDGEE

The region north of Bathurst is good driving territory with beautiful scenery, parks and reserves and a handful of quaint little towns. An easy drive through increasingly rolling country dips down into a valley 43km northeast of Bathurst. Just before crossing the bridge, detour along the charming, ramshackle main street of **Sofala**, a pretty hangover from the region's gold-mining days – it's such a perfect evocation of a semi-abandoned mining village that you'll wonder whether it's custom made. From Sofala continue for 28km to Ilford, where you join the main Lithgow–Mudgee road. As you head northwest, you'll pass pretty Lake Windamere before reaching Mudgee. Ignore the town's untidy outskirts and head for the centre, taking Church St which becomes Ulan Rd, which in turn heads northwest of town past some of the best wineries. Some 11km out of Mudgee, consider a detour to the **Munghorn Gap Nature Reserve**, where there's the popular 8km-return Castle Rock walking trail; the reserve is home to the endangered regent's honeyeater.

➌ Gulgong

To catch a glimpse of a small, rural, timbered Australian country town as it once was, there's nowhere better than Gulgong. And it's not just we who think so – this sweet, time-warped town once featured alongside author Henry Lawson on the $10 note. Australia's most famous poet, Henry Lawson spent part of his childhood in Gulgong and, suitably, the town celebrates a **Henry Lawson Heritage Festival** during the June long weekend, with concerts at the Opera House and other festivities, and there's the **Henry**

Lawson Centre (www.henrylawsongulgong.org.au; 147 Mayne St; adult/child $6/4; ⏰10am-3.30pm Mon-Sat, to 1pm Sun), which explores his life and works, as well as his early memories of the town. Today the narrow, rambling streets, classified by the National Trust, are not so done-up that they have lost their charm: we recommend a gentle wander up and down the main street to really see what we mean.

The Drive ›› From Gulgong, loop north along Rte 86 and pass through Birriwa before turning left (west) at Dunedoo. From there, it's 87 dry and dusty kilometres into Dubbo.

➍ Dubbo

It's at Dubbo that you get the first hint of what lies ahead – there's a dryness in the air in this big-sky country and to the west of here the outback really begins. With that in mind, Dubbo takes on the appearance of the last big city before the desert (and eternity) begins. Before venturing out in the void, there are three attractions that seem perfectly suited to this vast and barren land. With unfailingly clear skies to encourage you, Dubbo Observatory is a place to stargaze; advance bookings are essential. Then there's a glimpse of the wild at Taronga Western Plains Zoo, one of the best zoos in regional Australia. And finally, there's Dundullimal, about 2km beyond the zoo, a National Trust timber-slab homestead built in the 1840s and an exemplary example of the remote and rural homestead of Australian lore.

✖ 🛏 p96

The Drive ›› It's time to fill your tank with petrol and head for the outback. And the directions here are simple: take the Mitchell Hwy and stay on it all the way to Bourke (369km) via Narromine. It's dry country out here: the sand turns from yellow to orange and the foliage turns to scrub. Welcome to the outback fringe.

⑤ Bourke

Australian poet Henry Lawson once said, 'If you know Bourke, you know Australia.' Immortalised for Australians in the expression 'back of Bourke' (in the middle of nowhere), this town sits on the edge of the outback, miles from anywhere and sprawled along the Darling River. The Back O' Bourke Exhibition Centre is an excellent exhibition space that follows the legends of the back country (both Indigenous and settler) through interactive displays – ask about its packages that include a river cruise on the PV *Jandra*, an entertaining outback show, and a bus tour of the town and surrounds (note that the cruise and show operate April to October only). And then there's Bourke's Historic Cemetery, peppered with epitaphs like 'perished in the bush'; Professor Fred Hollows, the renowned eye surgeon, is buried here. If you're keen to explore on your own, ask for the leaflet called *Back O'Bourke Mud Map Tours*.

✗ ⊨ p96

The Drive ⟩⟩ Rte 87, lined with dull eucalyptus greens and scrubby horizons, runs due south of Bourke for 160km with not a single town to speak of en route.

⑥ Cobar

Out here, a town doesn't need to have much to have you dreaming of arriving. It might be just a petrol station, but occasionally a place has a little more to detain you. And on this score, Cobar fits the bill perfectly. It's a bustling mining town with a productive copper mine, and as something of regional centre down through the decades, it even boasts a handful of interesting buildings – true to old colonial form, these include the **old courthouse** and **cop station**. And even if you're not the museum type, don't miss the **Cobar Museum** (adult/child/family $8/6/18; ☺8.30am-5pm) at the Great Cobar Heritage Centre: it has sophisticated displays on the environment, local Aboriginal life and the early Europeans. Watch also for the Big Beer Can, Cobar's contribution to that strange provincial Australian need to erect oversized and decidedly kitsch monuments to the prosaic icons of Aussie life.

The Drive ⟩⟩ It's not quite the Nullarbor (Australia's straightest road), but the Barrier Hwy is very long and very straight, all 250km of it into Wilcannia. Long straw-coloured paddocks line the

DETOUR: WHITE CLIFFS

Start: ⑦ **Wilcannia**

There are few stranger places in Australia than the tiny pock-marked opal-mining town of White Cliffs (www.whitecliffsnsw.com.au), 93km northwest of Wilcannia along the sealed Opal Miners Way. Surrounded by pretty hostile country and enduring temperatures that soar well past 40°C in summer, many residents have moved underground, Coober Pedy–style, to escape the heat. You can visit opal showrooms where local miners sell their finds (these are well signed), or try fossicking around the old diggings, where you'll see interpretative signs. Watch your step as many of the shafts are open and unsigned. If you can't face the long haul back to civilisation, you can stay underground at the **White Cliffs Underground Motel** (☎08-8091 6677; www.undergroundmotel.com.au; s/d with shared bathroom incl breakfast $115/145; ✿) – custom-built with a tunnelling machine. It has a pool, a lively dining room and simple, cool, silent rooms. The motel's museum on local life is very good – it's free for guests, but a pricey $10 for nonguests.

roadside until, all of a sudden, you're crossing the Darling River and its tree-lined riverbanks at the entrance to town.

7 Wilcannia

In the old times, Wilcannia was one of the great river ports of inland Australia, and it still boasts a fine collection of old sandstone buildings dating from this prosperous heyday in the 1880s. In more recent times, the town and its large Indigenous population have become a poster child for Aboriginal disadvantage and hopelessness. With this modern history in mind, it should come as no surprise that Wilcannia (www.wilcannia-tourism.com.au) hasn't in the recent past had a lot of love from travellers. But it can be a fascinating, complicated place where the certainties and optimism of modern Australia seem a whole lot less clear. Make of it what you will.

🛏️ p97

The Drive » Dusty backcountry trails head southwest from Wilcannia, but continue southwest along the Barrier Hwy for 119km, then take one such trail south off the main highway towards Menindee Lakes. Along the 52 unpaved kilometres (fine for 2WD vehicles) you'll pass remote homesteads before turning left on the MR66 for the final 48km into Menindee.

8 Menindee Lakes

Out here, water can seem like a vision of paradise, and Menindee Lakes, which fan out from the scruffy town of Menindee, are no exception. This series of nine natural, ephemeral lakes adjacent to the Darling River are rich in birdlife, and the dead trees in the shallows make for some photogenic corners. If you've planned ahead, bring a picnic, visit the **visitor centre** (☎08-8091 4274; www.menindeelakes.com; Yartla St) in Menindee town for a map, and head out to soak up the miracle of water in the epic, otherwise empty land.

🛏️ p97

The Drive » Unless it has been raining, which is rare out here, take the unsealed gravel-and-sand road that heads south from Menindee for around 120km, then follow the signs east for 41km into Mungo National Park. This is dry, barren country, deliciously remote and filled with sparse desert flora and fauna.

TRIP HIGHLIGHT

9 Mungo National Park

One of Australia's most soulful places, this isolated, beautiful and important park covers 278.5 sq km of the Willandra Lakes Region World Heritage Area. It is one of Australia's most accessible slices of the true outback, where big red kangaroos and emus graze the plains and unimpeded winds shape the land into the strangest shapes. Lake Mungo is a dry lake and site of the oldest archaeological finds in Australia, as well as being the longest continual record of Aboriginal life (the world's oldest recorded cremation site has been found here), dating back more than 50,000 years, making the history of European settlement on this continent seem like the mere blink of an eye. The undoubted highlight here, aside from the blissful sense of utter remoteness, is the fabulous 33km semicircle ('lunette') of sand dunes known as **Walls of China**, created by the unceasing westerly wind. From the visitor centre a road leads across the dry lakebed to a car park, then it's a short walk to the viewing platform. For more information on the park, visit www.visitmungo.com.au.

🛏️ p97

The Drive » Numerous trails lead to Broken Hill, and none of them are paved (but nor do they require a 4WD unless the rains have been heavy). Return north to Menindee (from where it's 118 paved kilometres into Broken Hill), or cross the skein of tracks west to the paved Silver City Hwy which also leads to Broken Hill.

DETOUR: SILVERTON

Start: ❿ Broken Hill

If you think Broken Hill is remote, try visiting quirky Silverton (www.silverton.org.au), an old silver-mining town and now an almost-ghost town. Visiting is like walking into a Russell Drysdale painting. Silverton's fortunes peaked in 1885, when it had a population of 3000, but in 1889 the mines closed and the people (and some houses) moved to Broken Hill. It stirs into life every now and then – Silverton is the setting of films such as *Mad Max II* and *A Town Like Alice*. The town's heart and soul is the **Silverton Hotel** (☎08-8088 5313; Layard St; ☺9am-11pm), which displays film memorabilia and walls covered with miscellany typifying Australia's peculiar brand of larrikin humour. The 1889 **Silverton Gaol** (adult/child $4/1; ☺9.30am-4pm) once housed 14 cells; today the museum is a treasure trove: room after room is crammed full of a century of local life (wedding dresses, typewriters, mining equipment, photos). The **School Museum** (adult/child $2.50/1; ☺9.30am-3.30pm Mon, Wed, Fri-Sun) is another history pitstop, tracing the local school from its earliest incarnation in a tent in 1884. Considerably more offbeat is the **Mad Max 2 Museum** (Stirling St; adult/child $7.50/5; ☺10am-4pm), the culmination of Englishman Adrian Bennett's lifetime obsession with the theme.
To get here, take the A32 out of town (direction Adelaide). Almost immediately, the Silverton road branches off to the northwest – it's 25km from Broken Hill to Silverton. The road beyond Silverton becomes isolated and the horizons vast, but it's worth driving 5km to **Mundi Mundi Lookout** where the view over the plain is so extensive it reveals the curvature of the Earth.

`TRIP HIGHLIGHT`

❿ Broken Hill

The massive silver skimp dump that forms a backdrop for Broken Hill's town centre accentuates the unique character of this desert frontier town somewhere close to the end of the earth. Broken Hill's unique historic value was recognised in 2015, when it became the first Australian city to be included on the National Heritage List. It joins 102 other sites (including the Sydney Opera House and the Great Barrier Reef)

as examples of exceptional places that contribute to the national identity.

One of the most memorable experiences of Broken Hill is viewing the sunset from the **Sculpture Symposium** (Nine Mile Rd; admission to reserve adult/child $5/2) on the highest hilltop 12km from town. The sculptures are the work of 12 international artists who carved the huge sandstone blocks on site. Other highlights include: the **Palace Hotel** (☎08-8088 1699; www.the palacehotelbrokenhill.com.au; cnr Argent & Sulphide Sts), the astonishing star of the

hit Australian movie *The Adventures of Priscilla, Queen of the Desert*; the **Line of Lode Miners Memorial** (Federation Way; ☺6am-9pm), with its poignant stories and memorable views; the **Pro Hart Gallery** (www. prohart.com.au; 108 Wyman St; adult/child $5/3; ☺10am-5pm Mar-Nov, to 4pm Dec-Feb); and the **Royal Flying Doctor Service** (☎08-8080 3714; www.flyingdoctor. org.au/Broken-Hill-Base. html; Airport Rd; adult/child $8.50/4; ☺9am-5pm Mon-Fri, 10am-3pm Sat & Sun).

✕ ⊨ p97

Eating & Sleeping

Bathurst ❶

✖ Elie's Café   Modern Australian $$

(📞02-6332 1707; 108 William St; mains $28; ⏱7.30am-6pm Mon-Wed, to late Thu-Sat, to 4pm Sun) Set on the ground floor of the stunning heritage building of the old Royal Hotel, this engaging spot has some tables out on the street and an attractive indoor area. Service is friendly and the food is creative without going too far – modern Australian cooking as it should be.

🛏 Accommodation Warehouse   Apartments $$

(📞02-6332 2801; www.accomwarehouse. com.au; 121a Keppel St; s/d $100/130; ❄🛜) A three-level woollen mill dating from the 1870s has been cleverly converted into five self-contained apartments – they're not slick, they're sweet and homey and have considerably more character than a modern motel room. It's down a laneway, arrowed off Keppel St.

Mudgee ❷

✖ Butcher Shop Café   Cafe $

(49 Church St; mains $10-17; ⏱8am-5pm Mon-Fri, to 4pm Sat & Sun) A hip eatery in an old butchery with stained glass, vintage decor and contemporary artwork on the walls. The delicious fare is understated and includes salads and gourmet burgers, and the coffee is roasted in-house.

🛏 Perry Street Hotel   Boutique Hotel $$

(📞02-6372 7650; www.perrystreethotel.com. au; cnr Perry & Gladstone Sts; ste from $165; ❄🛜) Stunning apartment suites make a sophisticated choice in town. The attention to detail is outstanding, right down to the kimono bathrobes, Nespresso machine and free gourmet snacks.

Dubbo ❹

✖ Red Earth Estate Vineyard   Vineyard $

(www.redearthestate.com.au; 18 Camp Rd; ⏱11am-5pm Thu-Tue) Around 4.5km past the Western Plains Zoo, Red Earth offers 'adult time' with wine tastings and cheese platters ($11 per person) on the verandah.

✖ Two Doors Tapas & Wine Bar   Tapas $$

(📞02-6885 2333; www.twodoors.com.au; 215 Macquarie St; dishes $7-20; ⏱4pm-late Tue-Fri, from 10am Sat) Kick back in a leafy courtyard below street level, while munching on flavour-packed plates of halloumi skewers, soft-shell crab or slow-roasted pork belly.

🛏 Westbury Guesthouse   Guesthouse $$

(📞02-6881 6105; www.westburydubbo.com.au; cnr Brisbane & Wingewarra Sts; s/d $125/150; ❄🛜) This lovely old heritage home (1915) has six spacious, elegant rooms, and a delightful Thai restaurant attached.

Bourke ❺

✖ Poetry on a Plate   Australian $$

(www.poetryonaplate.com.au; Kidman's Camp; adult/child $25/10; ⏱6.30pm Tue, Thu, Sun Apr-Oct) A heartwarmingly unique offering: a well-priced night of bush ballads and storytelling around a campfire under the stars, with a simple, slow-cooked meal and dessert to boot. Dress warmly and bring your own drinks, camp chair and eating utensils (plate, cutlery and mug) – or pay an extra $5 to hire these.

🛏 Bourke Riverside Motel   Motel $$

(📞02-6872 2539; www.bourkeriversidemotel. com.au; 3-13 Mitchell St; s/d from $110/125; ❄🛜🏊) This rambling motel has riverside gardens and a range of well-appointed rooms and suites: some have heritage overtones and antique furniture, some have kitchen, some are family-sized. A fine choice.

Wilcannia 🟡7

🛏 Warrawong on
the Darling   Campground, Motel $$

(📞1300 688 225; www.warrawongonthedarling.
com.au; Barrier Hwy; camp sites $20-35, d
$120-140) Just east of town, this new riverside
property has lush green camp sites by a
billabong, or the opportunity for bush camping.
The self-contained motel units are excellent
value, each with kitchenette and barbecue.
Amenities are large and spotless. Cheerful
managers make the place sparkle – plus there's
a friendly emu named Rissole. Still to come: a
restaurant-bar, and waterfront cabins.

Menindee Lakes 🟡8

🛏 Bindara Station   Guesthouse $$

(📞08-8091 7412; www.bindarastation.com; d
half-board per person $95, cottage $110) Just
south of Kinchega National Park, glorious old
Bindara Station is an eco-conscious working
cattle property with B&B accommodation,
campsites, jillaroos' quarters and a cottage.

Mungo National Park 🟡9

🛏 Shearers' Quarters   Hostel $

(📞1300 072 757; www.visitmungo.com.au/
accommodation; adult/child $30/10; ❄) The
former shearers' quarters comprises five neat,
good-value rooms (each sleeping up to six in
various configurations; BYO bedding); rooms
share a communal kitchen and bathroom, and
barbecue area.

🛏 Mungo Lodge   Lodge $$$

(📞1300 663 748; www.mungolodge.com.au;
ste $199-269; ❄🤝) The plushest option is an
attractive (and pricey) deluxe cabin at Mungo
Lodge, on the Mildura road about 4km from
the park visitor centre. There are cheaper self-
catering budget cabins that are quite scruffy
but scheduled for an upgrade. There's also a
handful of unadvertised budget beds ($20)
in very basic quarters. The lodge houses an
inviting bar, lounge and restaurant area open
for breakfast, lunch and dinner (mains $22-32).
Bookings advised for meals.

Broken Hill 🟡10

✖ Silly Goat   Cafe $

(360 Argent St; dishes $8-16; ⏰7.30am-5pm
Tue-Fri, 8am-2pm Sat, to 1pm Sun) What's
this? Pour-overs and single origin coffee in the
outback? Nice work, Silly Goat. The menu here
would be at home in any big-city cafe, the array
of cakes is tempting, the coffee is great, and the
vibe is busy and cheerful.

✖ Royal Exchange
Hotel   Modern Australian $$

(320 Argent St; mains $28-36; ⏰6-9.30pm
Mon-Sat) For an upmarket dining experience,
the Royal Exchange Hotel does gourmet takes
on Australian staples, such as scallops wrapped
in pancetta. Servings are smaller than they
should be for this price.

🛏 Caledonian B&B   B&B $

(📞08-8087 1945; www.caledonianbnb.com.
au; 140 Chloride St; s/d with shared bathroom
incl breakfast $79/89, cottages from $130;
❄🤝) This fine B&B is in a refurbished pub
(1898) known as 'the Cally' – it also has three
self-contained cottages, each sleeping up to
six. Hugh and Barb are welcoming hosts and
the rooms are lovingly maintained. Wake up
and smell Hugh's espresso coffee and you'll be
hooked.

🛏 Red Earth Motel   Motel $$

(📞08-8088 5694; www.redearthmotel.com.au;
469 Argent St; studio apt $160, 2-/3-bedroom
apt $220/260; ❄🤝🖥) One of the best motels
in rural NSW, this outstanding family-run place
has large, stylish rooms – each has a separate
sitting area and kitchen facilities, making them
ideal for longer stays. There's a guest laundry
plus pool and barbecue area.

Victoria Trips

DRIVING THROUGH VICTORIA IS LIKE TAKING AN ELITE, SELF-GUIDED TOUR through the best that Australia has to offer. The coastline down here has nothing to envy when compared with the rest of Australia – the surf beaches and sea cliffs of the Great Ocean Road, the soaring majesty of Wilsons Prom, and the endless sands of Ninety Mile Beach. No state in Australia can match Victoria's set of historic towns, with Walhalla, Maldon, Castlemaine, Echuca, Ballarat and Beechworth merely the pick of a rather impressive bunch. River red gums along the Murray, the bijou wineries of the Mornington Peninsula, the penguins of Phillip Island, the gourmet offerings of Milewa and Myrtleford in the High Country: these are Victoria's calling cards and the signposts that mark the state's fabulous drives.

Alpine National Park Wallace Hut, near Falls Creek (Trip 11)
PHOTOSBYASH/GETTY IMAGES ©

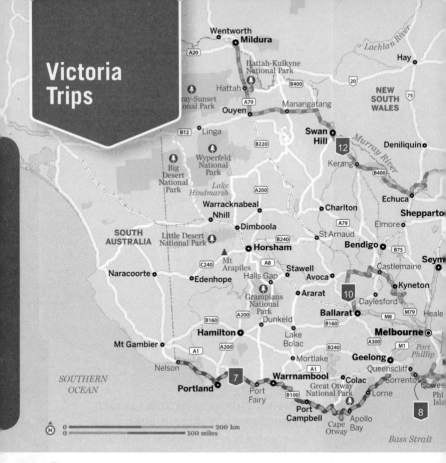

Victoria Trips

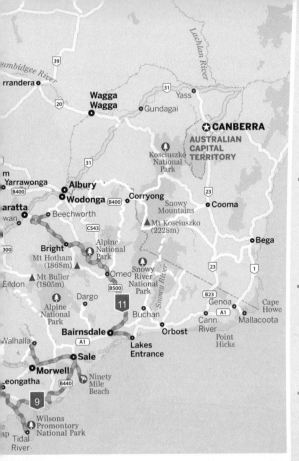

Twelve Apostles

It's a cliche, you've seen the photo, but these fine landforms still have the power to beguile. See them on Trip **7**

Mills Beach, Mornington

Little-known bathing boxes painted in bright colours capture the sedate charms of Trip **8**

Koonwarra Food & Wine Store

One of Victoria's best-kept secrets for food-lovers lies along the trail of Trip **9**

Coiltek Gold Centre, Maryborough

Act like the gold rush never ended and prospect for gold on the latter stages of Trip **10**

Kingfisher Cruises

Let a local guide you through the rarely visited Murray red gums of Barmah National Park on Trip **12**

Victoria A galah spreads its wings

Great Ocean Road Distractingly scenic
coastal driving

Classic Trip

Great Ocean Road

7

One of the most beautiful coastal road journeys on earth, this world-famous road hugs the western Victorian coast, passing world-class beaches, iconic landforms and fascinating seaside settlements.

TRIP HIGHLIGHTS

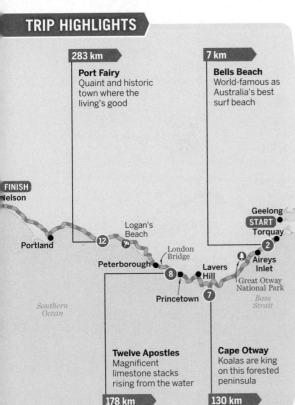

283 km

Port Fairy
Quaint and historic town where the living's good

7 km

Bells Beach
World-famous as Australia's best surf beach

FINISH
Nelson

Portland

12

Logan's Beach

London Bridge

Peterborough

8

Lavers Hill

Geelong
START
Torquay

2

Aireys Inlet

Great Otway National Park

Bass Strait

Southern Ocean

Princetown

7

Twelve Apostles
Magnificent limestone stacks rising from the water

178 km

Cape Otway
Koalas are king on this forested peninsula

130 km

5–7 DAYS
373KM / 232 MILES

GREAT FOR...

BEST TIME TO GO

Year-round, but October to March has the best weather.

ESSENTIAL PHOTO

The Twelve Apostles are one of Australia's most spectacular sights.

BEST FOR WILDLIFE

Koalas at Cape Otway, kangaroos at Anglesea and whales off Warrnambool.

Classic Trip

7 Great Ocean Road

The Great Ocean Road begins in Australia's surf capital Torquay, swings past Bells Beach, then winds its way along the coast to the wild and windswept koala heaven of Cape Otway. The Twelve Apostles and Loch Ard Gorge are obligatory stops before the road sweeps on towards Warrnambool with its whales, and Port Fairy with its fine buildings and folk festival, before the natural drama peaks again close to the South Australian border.

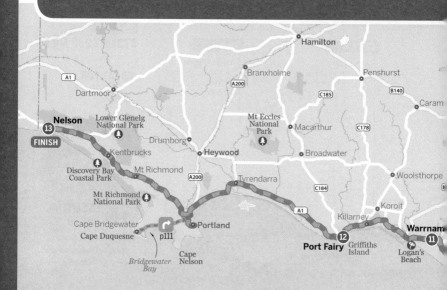

1 Torquay

The undisputed surfing capital of Australia is a brilliant place to start your journey. The town's proximity to world-famous Bells Beach, and status as home of two iconic surf brands – Rip Curl and Quicksilver – have assured Torquay's place at the pinnacle of mainstream surf culture. Torquay's beaches lure everyone from kids in floaties to backpacker surf-school pupils. **Fishermans Beach**, protected from ocean swells, is the family favourite. Ringed by shady pines and sloping lawns, the **Front Beach** beckons lazy bums, while surf lifesavers patrol the frothing **Back Beach** during summer. Famous surf beaches include nearby **Jan Juc** and **Winki Pop**. Visit the **Surf World Museum** (www.surfworld. com.au; Surf City Plaza; adult/child/family $12/8/30;

LINK YOUR TRIP

 Sydney to Melbourne

From Melbourne take the Princes Hwy (A1) towards Geelong, but bypass Geelong by following signs to Torquay.

 Victoria's Goldfields

Where Trip 10 ends in Ballarat, it's an 87km drive down the Midlands Hwy to the Geelong bypass, and from there it's around 30km into Torquay.

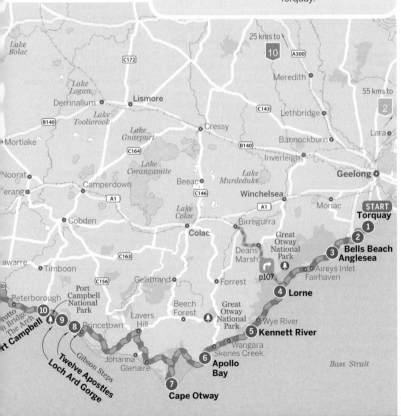

Classic Trip

⊙9am-5pm), home to the Australia's Surfing Hall of Fame, then start working on your legend by taking surf lessons with **Westcoast Surf School** (☏03-5261 2241; www.westcoastsurfschool.com; 2hr lesson $60) or **Torquay Surfing Academy** (☏03-5261 2022; www.torquaysurf.com.au; 34a Bell St; 2hr group/private lessons $60/180).

🍴 🛏 p112

The Drive » Pass the turn-off to Jan Juc, then take the next left (C132) and follow the signs to Bells Beach.

TRIP HIGHLIGHT

❷ Bells Beach

A slight detour off the Great Ocean Road takes you to famous Bells Beach, the powerful point break that is part of international surfing folklore (it was here, albeit in name only, that Keanu Reeves and Patrick Swayze had their ultimate showdown in the film *Point Break*). When the right-hander is working, it's one of the longest rides in the country. If you're here just to look, park in the car park and head for the lookout, from where stairs lead down to the beach (not for swimming).

The Drive » Return to the Great Ocean Road (B100), and soon after doing so consider taking the turn-off to spectacular Point Addis, a vast sweep of pristine beach. Anglesea is a further 10km down the Great Ocean Road, with dense woodland lining the road as you descend into town.

❸ Anglesea

Mix sheer orange cliffs falling into the ocean with hilly, tree-filled 'burbs and a population that booms in summer and you've got Anglesea, where sharing fish and chips with seagulls by the Anglesea River is a decades-long family tradition for many. **Main Beach** is good for surfers, while sheltered **Point Roadknight Beach** is for families. In addition to such quintessentially Australian summer pastimes, Anglesea is famous for those seeking to spy their first kangaroos – at **Anglesea Golf Club** (☏03-5263 1582; www.angleseagolfclub.com.au; Noble St; 9 holes from $25; ⊙clubhouse 8am-midnight) you can watch kangaroos graze on the fairways.

🍴 p112

The Drive » The B100 follows the coast (although it does sidestep attractive Point Roadknight) for 11km to Aireys Inlet, and then to Fairhaven, with a historic lighthouse and wonderful beaches. From Aireys it's 18km of glorious coast-hugging road into Lorne – stop for photos at the Great Ocean Road memorial archway.

❹ Lorne

There's something about Lorne... For a start, this is a place of incredible natural beauty, something you see vividly as you drive into town from Aireys Inlet: tall old gum trees line its hilly streets, and Loutit Bay gleams irresistibly. Kids will love the beachside swimming pool, trampolines and skate park, and there's more than 50km of bushwalking tracks around Lorne. Up in the hilly hinterland behind town, seek out the lovely **Erskine Falls** (Erskine Falls Access Rd); it's an easy walk to the viewing platform, or 250 (often slippery) steps down to its base. Back in town, the **Great Ocean Road National Heritage Centre** (15 Mountjoy Pde; ⊙9am-5pm) tells the story of the construction of the Great Ocean Road.

🍴 🛏 p112

The Drive » Although the winding nature of the road makes it feel longer – by now you know the deal: dense forests to your right, uninterrupted sea views to your left – it's just 20km from Lorne to Kennett River.

❺ Kennett River

Kennett River is one of the easiest places to see koalas in Australia. In the trees immediately west of the general store and around the excellent caravan park, koalas pose (well, they're often asleep) in the tree forks, sometimes at eye level. Local parrots and lorikeets are also known to swoop down and perch on heads and outstretched arms if you stay still enough.

The Drive » The road could hardly get closer to the coast for the 22km from Kennett River into Apollo Bay.

⑥ Apollo Bay

At Apollo Bay, one of the Great Ocean Road's largest towns, rolling hills provide a postcard backdrop to the town, while broad, white-sand beaches dominate the foreground. Local boy Mark Brack, son of the Cape Otway Lighthouse keeper, knows this stretch of coast better than anyone around – both his **Otway Shipwreck Tours** (☏0417 983 985; msbrack@ bigpond.com; 3hr tours adult/ child $50/15) and **Mark's Walking Tours** (☏0417 983 985; www.greatoceanwalk. asn.au/markstours; 2-3hr tour adult/child $50/15) are outstanding. Another worthwhile excursion is the kayak expedition out to an Australian fur seal colony in a double kayak with **Apollo Bay Surf & Kayak** (☏0405 495 909; www.apollobaysurfkayak. com.au; 157 Great Ocean Rd; 2hr kayak tours $65, 1½hr surf lessons $60).

 p112

DETOUR: BRAE AT BIRREGURRA

Start: ④ Lorne

Dan Hunter is one of Australia's most celebrated chefs and he singlehandedly put rural Dunkeld on the map with his fantastic Royal Mail Hotel. Thus the Birregurra tourism team must've been licking their lips when they heard he was moving to their town to open his new restaurant. **Brae** (☏03-5236 2226; www.braerestaurant.com; 4285 Cape Otway Rd, Birregurra; 8-course tasting plates per person $180, plus matched wines $120; ☉noon-3pm Fri-Mon, from 6pm Thu-Sun) takes over from the much-loved Sunnybrae, with its farmhouse getting a refit by renowned architects Six Degrees. The restaurant uses whatever is growing in its 12 hectares of organic gardens. Reservations are essential, well in advance. It all happens in the small historic town of Birregurra, 38km from Lorne on the way to Colac.

The Drive » The turn-off for Lighthouse Rd (ie Cape Otway), which leads 12km down to the lighthouse, is 21km from Apollo Bay. Those 12km are through dense woodland pretty much all the way.

TRIP HIGHLIGHT

⑦ Cape Otway

Cape Otway is the second most southerly point of mainland Australia (after Wilsons Promontory) and this coastline is particularly beautiful, rugged and historically treacherous for passing ships despite the best efforts of the **Cape Otway Lightstation** (☏03-5237 9240; www.lightstation.com; Lighthouse Rd; adult/child/ family $19.50/7.50/49.50; ☉9am-5pm). The oldest surviving lighthouse on mainland Australia, it

was built in 1848 by more than 40 stonemasons without mortar or cement. The forested road leading to Cape Otway is a terrific spot for koala sightings. Where are they? Look for the cars parked on the side of the road and tourists peering up into the trees.

🛏 p113

The Drive » The road levels out after leaving the Otways and enters narrow, flat scrubby escarpment lands that fall away to sheer, 70m-high cliffs along the coast between Princetown and Peterborough – a distinct change of scene. The Twelve Apostles are after Princetown.

TRIP HIGHLIGHT

⑧ Twelve Apostles

The most enduring image for most visitors to the Great Ocean Road, the

IGNACIO PALACIOS/GETTY IMAGES ©

YVA MOMATIUK & JOHN EASTCOTT/GETTY IMAGES ©

WHY THIS IS A CLASSIC TRIP
ANTHONY HAM, AUTHOR

Whenever I have visitors from overseas, the first place I take them is the Great Ocean Road. What makes it a classic is the winning combination of stunning natural beauty and world-famous attractions lined up along the roadside like a string of pearls – Bells Beach, koalas at Cape Otway, the Twelve Apostles, Loch Ard Gorge...and they're just the beginning.

Top: Loch Ard Gorge.
Left: Koala eating gum leaves, Cape Otway
Right: Great Otway National Park

SHAUN EGAN/GETTY IMAGES ©

Twelve Apostles jut from the ocean in spectacular fashion. There they stand, as if abandoned to the ocean by the retreating headland, all seven of them... Just for the record, there never were 12, and they were once called 'Sow and Piglets' until some bright spark in the 1960s thought they might attract tourists with a more venerable name. The two stacks on the eastern (Otway) side of the viewing platform are not technically Apostles – they're Gog and Magog. And the soft limestone cliffs are dynamic and changeable, with constant erosion from the waves: one 70m-high stack collapsed into the sea in July 2005 and the Island Archway lost its archway in June 2009. The best time to visit is sunset, partly to beat the tour buses, and to see little penguins returning ashore. For the best views, take a chopper tour with **12 Apostles Helicopters** (🖉03-5598 8283; www.12apostleshelicopters. com.au; 15min flights $145).

The Drive >> When you can finally tear yourself away, continue northwest along the Great Ocean Road and in no time at all you'll see the signpost to Loch Ard Gorge.

----

❾ Loch Ard Gorge
Close to the Twelve Apostles, Loch Ard Gorge is a gorgeous U-shaped

Classic Trip

canyon of high cliffs, a sandy beach and deep blue waters. It was here that the Shipwreck Coast's most famous and haunting tale unfolded: the iron-hulled clipper *Loch Ard* foundered off Mutton Bird Island at 4am on the final night of its long voyage from England in 1878. Of 37 crew and 19 passengers on board, only two survived. Eva Carmichael, a non-swimmer, clung to wreckage and was washed into a gorge – since renamed Loch Ard Gorge – where apprentice officer Tom Pearce rescued her. Despite rumours of a romance, they never saw each other again and Eva soon returned to Ireland. There are several walks in the area taking you down to the cave where the shipwreck survivors took shelter, plus a cemetery and rugged beach.

The Drive » It's around 6km along the B100 from Loch Ard Gorge into Port Campbell.

- - - - - - - - - - -

❿ Port Campbell

Strung out around a tiny bay, Port Campbell is a laid-back coastal town and the ideal base for the Twelve Apostles and Loch Ard Gorge. Its has a lovely, sandy, sheltered beach, one of few safe places for swimming along this tempestuous stretch of coast.

✖ 🛏 p113

The Drive » There is a feeling of crossing a high clifftop plateau on the first stretch out of Port Campbell. After the Bay of Islands, it turns inland through green agricultural lands.

- - - - - - - - - - -

⓫ Warrnambool

Warrnambool means whales, at least between May and September, when whales frolic off-shore on their migration. Southern right whales (named due to being the 'right' whales to hunt) are the most common visitors, heading from Antarctica to these more temperate waters. Undoubtedly the best place to see them is at Warrnambool's **Logans Beach whale-watching platform** – they use the waters here as a nursery. Call ahead to the visitor centre to check if whales are about, or see www.visitwarrnambool.com.au for latest sightings. Otherwise, take the time to visit top-notch **Flagstaff Hill Maritime Village** (📞03-5559 4600; www.flagstaffhill.com; 89 Merri St; adult/child/concession/family $16/6.50/12.50/39; ⊙9am-5pm) historic buildings, with its shipwreck museum, heritage-listed lighthouses and garrison, and its reproduction of a historical Victorian port town. It also has the nightly **Shipwrecked**, an engaging 70-minute sound-and-laser show telling the story of the *Loch Ard*'s plunge.

✖ p113

The Drive » The road – the Princes Hwy (A1), and no longer the Great Ocean Road – loops around to Port Fairy, just 29km from Warrnambool.

PORT CAMPBELL TO WARRNAMBOOL

The Great Ocean Road continues west from Port Campbell, passing **London Bridge**...fallen down. Now sometimes called London Arch, it was once linked to the mainland by a narrow natural bridge. In January 1990 the bridge collapsed, leaving two terrified tourists marooned on the world's newest island – they were eventually rescued by helicopter.

The **Bay of Islands** is 8km west of tiny **Peterborough**, where a short walk from the car park takes you to magnificent lookout points.

The Great Ocean Road officially ends near here, where it meets the Princess Hwy (A1).

TRIP HIGHLIGHT

12 Port Fairy

Settled in 1833 as a whaling and sealing station, Port Fairy retains its historic 19th-century charm with a relaxed, salty feel, heritage bluestone and sandstone buildings, whitewashed cottages, colourful fishing boats and wide, tree-lined streets; in 2012 it was voted the world's most liveable community. Across the bridge from the picturesque harbour, **Battery Hill** has cannons and fortifications. To guide your steps through the town's heritage, pick up a copy of the popular *Maritime & Shipwreck Heritage Walk* from the visitor centre. And there's a growing foodie scene here too – **Basalt Wines** (📞0429 682 251; www.basalt wines.com; 1131 Princes Hwy, Killarney; 🕑11am-4.30pm Sat & Sun), just outside Port Fairy in Killarney, is a family-run biodynamic winery that does tastings in its shed.

 p113

The Drive » The road hugs the coast into Portland (75km) and then the traffic lessens as you leave the main highway and drive northwest along the C192 for 67km into Nelson.

DETOUR:
CAPE BRIDGEWATER

Start: 12 Port Fairy

Cape Bridgewater is an essential 21km detour off the Portland–Nelson Rd. The stunning 4km arc of **Bridgewater Bay** is perhaps one of Australia's finest stretches of white-sand surf beach. The road continues on to **Cape Duquesne**, where walking tracks lead to a spectacular **Blowhole** and the eerie **Petrified Forest** on the clifftop. A longer two-hour return walk takes you to a **seal colony** where you can see dozens of fur seals sunning themselves on the rocks; to get a little closer, take the exhilarating **Seals by Sea tour** (📞03-5526 7247; www.sealsbyseatours.com. au; adult/child $35/20; 🕑Aug-Apr), a 45-minute zodiac cruise to see Australian fur seals.

13 Nelson

Tiny Nelson is the last vestige of civilisation before the South Australian border – just a general store, a pub and a handful of accommodation places. We like it especially for its proximity to the mouth of the **Glenelg River**, which flows through **Lower Glenelg National Park**. The leisurely 3½-hour trips run by **Nelson River Cruises** (📞0448 887 1225, 08-8738 4191; www. glenelgrivercruises.com.au; cruises adult/child $30/10; 🕑Sep-Jun) head along the Glenelg River and include the impressive **Princess Margaret Rose Cave** (📞08-8738 4171; www. princessmargaretrosecave. com; adult/child/family $17.50/11.50/40; 🕑hourly tours 11am to 4.30pm, reduced hours winter), with its gleaming underground formations – along this coastline of towering formations, these ones at journey's end are surely the most surprising. If you prefer to explore under your own steam, contact **Nelson Boat & Canoe Hire** (📞08-8738 4048; www.nelsonboatandcanoehire. com.au).

Eating & Sleeping

❶ Torquay

✕ Scorched
Modern Australian $$

(☎03-5261 6142; www.scorched.com.au; 17 The Esplanade; mains $26-36; ⏱3-9pm Mon-Thu, 10.30am-9pm Fri-Sun Dec & Jan; 3-9pm Wed-Thu, 10.30am-9pm Fri & Sat, to 3pm Sun Feb-Nov) This might be the swankiest restaurant in Torquay, overlooking the waterfront, with classy understated decor and windows that open right up to let the sea breeze in. Check out the seasonal grazing plate to share.

🛏 Woolshed B&B
B&B $$$

(☎0408 333 433; www.thewoolshedtorquay.com.au; 75 Aquarius Ave; apt incl breakfast $275; ❄ ❄) Set on a gorgeous farm on Torquay's outskirts, this century-old woolshed has been converted into a wonderful open and airy space with two bedrooms. It sleeps up to six, and guests can use the pool and tennis court. Book well in advance.

❸ Anglesea

✕ Uber Mama
Modern Australian $$

(☎03-5263 1717; www.ubermama.com.au; 113 Great Ocean Rd; mains $19-33; ⏱noon-3pm & 6-9pm Thu-Sat, 9am-3pm Sun) An example of the subtle revolution sweeping the kitchens of regional Australia, Uber Mama does modern Aussie cooking with Asian inflections that's creative without straying too far from local roots. Try the shared plates such as baked Otway brie or seared scallops with prosciutto, or classic fish and chips for main.

❹ Lorne

✕ Bottle of Milk
Burgers $

(☎03-5289 2005; www.thebottleofmilk.com; 52 Mountjoy Pde; burgers from $12; ⏱8am-3pm Mon-Fri, to 5pm Sat & Sun, 8am-9pm Nov-Feb) With a menu of 24 inventive burgers, all stacked with fresh ingredients, it's hard to go wrong at this popular hang-out on the main strip.

✕ Lorne Beach Pavilion
Modern Australian $$

(☎03-5289 2882; www.lornebeachpavilion.com.au; 81 Mountjoy Pde; breakfast & lunch mains $9-20, dinner $25-37; ⏱8am-9pm) With its unbeatable spot on the foreshore, life here is literally a beach, especially with a cold beer in hand. Come at happy hour for 1kg of mussels for $10 and two-for-one cocktails. Cafe-style breakfasts and lunches are tasty, while a more upmarket Modern Australian menu is on for dinner.

🛏 Qdos
Ryokan $$$

(☎03-5289 1989; www.qdosarts.com; 35 Allenvale Rd; r incl breakfast from $250; 🛜) The perfect choice for those seeking a romantic getaway or forest retreat, Qdos' luxury Zen treehouses are fitted with tatami mats, rice-paper screens and no TV. Two-night minimum; no kids.

❻ Apollo Bay

✕ Chris's Beacon Point Restaurant
Greek $$$

(☎03-5237 6411; www.chriss.com.au; 280 Skenes Creek Rd; mains from $38; ⏱8.30-10am & 6pm-late daily, plus noon-2pm Sat & Sun; 🛜) Feast on memorable ocean views, deliciously fresh seafood and Greek-influenced dishes at Chris's hilltop fine-dining sanctuary among the treetops. Reservations recommended. You can also stay in its wonderful stilted villas ($265 to $330). It's accessed via Skenes Creek.

🛏 Beacon Point Ocean View Villas
Villa $$

(☎03-5237 6196; www.beaconpoint.com.au; 270 Skenes Creek Rd; r from $165; ❄) With a commanding hill location among the trees, this wonderful collection of comfortable one- and two-bedroom villas is a luxurious yet affordable bush retreat. Most villas have sensational coast views, balcony and wood-fired heater.

7 Cape Otway

🛏 Great Ocean Ecolodge   Lodge $$$

(☎03-5237 9297; www.greatoceanecolodge. com; 635 Lighthouse Rd; r incl breakfast & activities from $380; 🐾) Reminiscent of a luxury African safari lodge, this mud-brick homestead stands in pastoral surrounds with plenty of wildlife. It's all solar-powered and rates go towards to the on-site **Centre for Conservation Ecology** (www. conservationecologycentre.org). It also serves as an animal hospital for local fauna, and it has a captive tiger quoll breeding program, which you'll visit on its dusk wildlife walk with an ecologist.

10 Port Campbell

🍴 12 Rocks Cafe Bar   Cafe $$

(19 Lord St; mains $21-37; 🕐9.30am-11pm) Watch flotsam wash up on the beach from this busy eatery, which has perfect beachfront views. Try a local Otways beer with a pasta or seafood main, or just duck in for a coffee.

🛏 Port Bayou   B&B $$

(☎03-5598 6009; www.portbayou. portcampbell.nu; 52 Lord St; d cottage from $185; ❄) Choose from the cosy in-house B&B or a rustic self-contained cottage fitted with exposed ceiling beams and corrugated-tin walls (we'd go for the cottage).

11 Warrnambool

🍴 Kermond's Hamburgers   Burgers $

(☎03-5562 4854; 151 Lava St; burgers $8; 🕐9am-9.30pm) Likely not much has changed at this burger joint since it opened in 1949, with Laminex tables, wood-panelled walls and classic milkshakes served in stainless-steel tumblers. Its burgers are an institution.

12 Port Fairy

🍴 Merrijig Kitchen   Modern Australian $$$

(☎03-5568 2324; www.merrijiginn.com; 1 Campbell St; mains $28-38; 🕐6-9pm Thu-Mon; 🛜) One of coastal Victoria's most atmospheric restaurants, warm yourself by the open fire and enjoy superb dining with a menu that changes according to what's seasonal. Delectable food with great service.

🛏 Douglas on River   B&B $$

(www.douglasonriver.com.au; 85 Gipps St; r incl breakfast from $160; 🛜) On the waterfront along the wharf, this 1852 heritage guesthouse lays claims to being the oldest in Port Fairy and is a great choice for those seeking boutique accommodation. The lovely front lawn and common area are both perfect for relaxing, and it does wonderful breakfasts using local produce.

Cape Schanck Beautiful and rugged ocean beaches

Mornington Peninsula

8

The Mornington Peninsula, southeast of Melbourne, is one of the city's favourite summer playgrounds, with exceptional beaches all along the shoreline and wonderful wineries in the interior.

TRIP HIGHLIGHTS

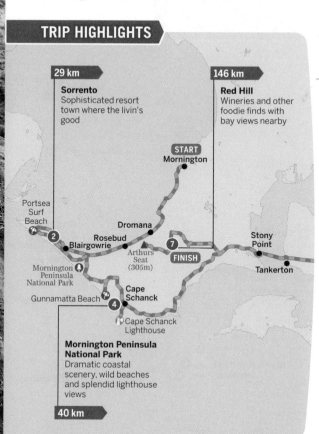

29 km

Sorrento
Sophisticated resort town where the livin's good

146 km

Red Hill
Wineries and other foodie finds with bay views nearby

START
Mornington

Portsea Surf Beach

2

Dromana

Rosebud
Blairgowrie

Arthurs Seat (305m)

7

FINISH

Stony Point

Tankerton

Mornington Peninsula National Park

Gunnamatta Beach

Cape Schanck

4

Cape Schanck Lighthouse

Mornington Peninsula National Park
Dramatic coastal scenery, wild beaches and splendid lighthouse views

40 km

3–4 DAYS
146KM / 91 MILES

GREAT FOR...

BEST TIME TO GO
October to March; winter months can be cold and the towns empty.

ESSENTIAL PHOTO
The view from Cape Schanck Lighthouse.

BEST FOR OUTDOORS
Swim with the dolphins off Sorrento then head for Portsea Back Beach.

FILEDIMAGE/GETTY IMAGES ©

8 Mornington Peninsula

To fully appreciate Melbourne's privileged bayside location, take the long drive south to where the bay meets the ocean, passing en route the lovely seaside towns of Mornington, Sorrento and Portsea. This fairly sedate coastline takes on a whole new personality in the wave-lashed Mornington Peninsula National Park, while Flinders is a quietly beautiful place. Finally, the area around Red Hill is one of Victoria's most important and pleasureable wine areas.

1 Mornington

Pretty Mornington, with its cute bathing boxes and swimming beaches, is the gateway to the peninsula's holiday coastal strip – just beyond the reaches of Melbourne's urban sprawl. Originally part of the lands of the Boonwurrung people, it was founded as a European township in 1854. Echoes of those days remain. Grand old buildings around Main St include the 1892 **Grand Hotel**, the 1860 **Old Court House**, on the corner of Main St

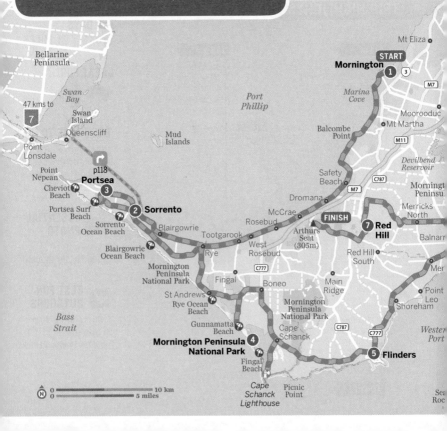

and the Esplanade, and the 1862 **Police Lock-Up** behind it. On the opposite corner is the 1863 **post office building**. For views over the harbour, take a walk along the 1850s **pier** and around the **Schnapper Point** foreshore boardwalk past the **Matthew Flinders monument** that commemorates his 1802 landing. **Mothers Beach** is the main swimming beach, while at **Fossil Beach** there are remains of a lime-burning kiln; fossils found here date back 25 million years! And it's at **Mills Beach** where you can see the colourful and photogenic bathing boxes.

 p121

The Drive ›› From Mornington, the Esplanade heads south for the gorgeous scenic drive towards Sorrento, skirting the rocky Port Phillip Bay foreshore. Inland, the Nepean Hwy (B110) takes a less-scenic route and again becomes the Mornington Peninsula Fwy.

TRIP HIGHLIGHT

② Sorrento

Historic Sorrento, the site of Victoria's first official European settlement in 1803, is the standout town on the Mornington Peninsula. The town has so much going for it – beautiful limestone buildings, ocean and bay beaches, and a buzzing seaside summer atmosphere – that it should come as no surprise that it has become one of Victoria's most refined resort towns. 'Twas ever thus here – some of the grandest old buildings, among them the **Sorrento Hotel** (1871), **Continental Hotel** (1875) and **Koonya Hotel** (1878), were built to serve well-to-do 19th-century visitors from Melbourne. These days, Sorrento also boasts some of the best cafes and restaurants on the peninsula, and the main street is lined with galleries, boutiques, and craft and antique shops. And on no account miss the chance to go swimming with the dolphins with **Polperro Dolphin Swims** (☏03-5988 8437; www.polperro.com.au; adult/child sightseeing $55/35, dolphin & seal swimming adult & child $135) or **Moonraker Charters** (☏03-5984 4211; www.moonrakercharters.com. au; 7 George St, Sorrento; adult/child sightseeing $55/44, dolphin & seal swimming $129/115).

p121

The Drive ›› The short, 4km hop from Sorrento to Portsea follows the coast – watch for fine bays views on the Portsea approach.

LINK YOUR TRIP

7 Great Ocean Road
Head north from Mornington or Red Hill to Melbourne, skip across town and down the A1, bypassing Geelong en route to Torquay.

9 Gippsland & Wilsons Prom
Phillip Island is a natural bedfellow for the Mornington Peninsula; take the back road to Koo Wee Rup and down to the island (127km).

③ Portsea

If you thought Sorrento was classy, wait until you see Portsea. The last village on the peninsula, wee Portsea is where many of Melbourne's wealthiest families have built seaside mansions. You can walk the **Farnsworth Track** (1.5km, 30 minutes) out to scenic London Bridge, a natural rock formation, and spot middens of the Boonwurrung people who once called this area home. Diving and snorkelling are both possible through **Dive Victoria** (☎03-5984 3155; www.divevictoria.com. au; 3752 Point Nepean Rd; snorkelling $85, s/d dive with gear $130/210), while

Portsea Surf Beach is where the ocean's sheer power never fails to impress. Back in town, Portsea's pulse is the iconic, sprawling, half-timber **Portsea Hotel**, an enormous pub with a great lawn and terrace area looking out over the bay.

🛏 p121

The Drive » Your next destination, Mornington Peninsula National Park, actually extends into the Portsea hinterland, and there are numerous access points – Portsea Surf Beach, along the back road between Portsea and Rye, at Gunnamatta Beach and, perhaps most memorably, at Cape Schanck.

DETOUR:
QUEENSCLIFF

Start: ② Sorrento

Historic Queenscliff, across the water from Sorrento on the Bellarine Peninsula, is one of coastal Victoria's lovelist towns. It's a place of heritage streetscapes, the formidable **Fort Queenscliff** (☎03-5258 1488, for midweek tours 0403 193 311; www.fortqueenscliff.com. au; cnr Gellibrand & King Sts; adult/child/family $10/5/25; ◷1pm & 3pm Sat & Sun, daily school holidays), fine cafes and restaurants, and parkland sweeping down to the beach. From some areas, particularly from the lookout at the southern end of Hesse St (next to the bowling club), the views across the Port Phillip Heads and Bass Strait are glorious. And getting here couldn't be easier – the **Queenscliff–Sorrento Ferry** (☎03-5258 3244; www.searoad.com.au; one way foot passenger adult/child $11/8, 2 adults & car $73; ◷hourly 7am-6pm) crosses the bay in 40 minutes throughout the day.

TRIP HIGHLIGHT

④ Mornington Peninsula National Park

Stretching from Portsea on the sliver of coastline to Cape Schanck and inland to the Greens Bush area, this national park showcases the peninsula's most beautiful and rugged ocean beaches. Along here are the cliffs, bluffs and crashing surf beaches of Portsea, Sorrento, Blairgowrie, Rye, St Andrews, Gunnamatta and Cape Schanck; swimming and surfing are dangerous at these beaches, so swim only between the flags at Gunnamatta and Portsea during summer. Built in 1859, Cape Schanck Lighthouse is a photogenic working lighthouse; from the lighthouse, descend the steps of the boardwalk that leads to the craggy cape for outstanding views. Longer walks are also possible.

🛏 p121

The Drive » From Cape Schanck Lighthouse, return to the C777 and follow it for 11km east along the coast to Flinders. Watch for sweeping ocean views, especially in the middle section of the route.

---

⑤ Flinders

Little Flinders, where the thrashing ocean beaches give way to Western Port Bay, has so far been largely

PETER WALTON PHOTOGRAPHY/GETTY IMAGES ©

Red Hill Summer vineyards

spared the development of the Port Phillip Bay towns. As a consequence, Flinders remains a delightful little community and is still home to a busy fishing fleet. Surfers have been coming to Flinders for decades, drawn by ocean-side breaks such as Gunnery, Big Left and Cyril's, and golfers know the clifftop **Flinders Golf Club** course as the most scenic and wind blown in Victoria. The historic **Flinders Hotel** has been a beacon on this sleepy street corner longer than anyone can remember. It's not that there's a lot to do here. It's more about sampling the Mornington Peninsula as it used to be before the crowds began arriving en masse.

✕ ⊨ p121

The Drive ❯❯ Follow the C777 along the Westernport Bay coast northeast to Balnarring. After a further 7km, turn off southeast to Stony Point (7km from the turn-off). Leave your car and take the ferry from Stony Point to French Island's Tankerton Jetty.

- - - - - - - - - - -

6 French Island

Exposed, windswept and wonderfully isolated, French Island is two-thirds national park and retains a real sense of tranquility – you can only get here by passenger ferry, so it's virtually traffic-free, and there's no mains water or electricity! The main attractions are bushwalking and cycling, taking in wetlands, checking out one of Australia's largest koala colonies and observing a huge variety of birds. Pick

up the *Parks Victoria* brochure at the Tankerton Jetty for a list of walks and cycling routes. All roads on the island are unsealed and some are quite sandy. From the jetty it's around 2km to the licensed **French Island General Store** (✆03-5980 1209; Tankerton Rd, Lot 1; bike hire $25; ⊙8am-6pm, from 9am Sun), which also serves as post office, tourist information and bike-hire centre.

The Drive ❯❯ Take the ferry back to Stony Point, return the 13km to Balnarring, then cut inland via Merricks North to Red Hill.

- - - - - - - - - - -

TRIP HIGHLIGHT

7 Red Hill

The undulating hills of the peninsula's interior around Red Hill and

Portsea Bathing boxes

Main Ridge is a lovely region of trees, where you can spend a sublime afternoon hopping around the winery cellar doors and restaurants. It can be difficult to choose (and pity the poor designated driver who'll be unable to drink), but we'd visit **Red Hill Brewery** (☑03-5989 2959; www.redhillbrewery.com.au; 88 Shoreham Rd; ⏲11am-6pm long weekends and by appointment), **Port Phillip** **Estate** and **Ten Minutes by Tractor**. If you happen upon Red Hill on the first Saturday of the month (except in winter), the **Red Hill Market** (www.craftmarkets.com.au; ⏲8am-1pm 1st Sat of month Sep-May) is well worth the effort. Whenever you're here, allow time to pick your own strawberries at **Sunny Ridge Strawberry Farm** (☑03-5989 4500; www.sunnyridge.com.au; cnr Shands & Mornington-Flinders Rds; adult/child $8/4; ⏲9am-5pm Nov-Apr, 11am-4pm Sat & Sun May-Oct) and take the 16km round-trip detour to **Arthurs Seat**, which, at 305m, is the highest point on the Port Phillip Bay coast. It's the ideal place to take it all in and contemplate just how far you've come.

✕ p121

NIGEL PAVITT/GETTY IMAGES ©

Eating & Sleeping

Mornington ❶

✕ The Rocks — Seafood $$

(☎03-5973 5599; www.therocksmornington.
com.au; 1 Snapper Point Dr; mains $18-36;
⊙8am-10pm) At the Mornington Yacht Club, this
restaurant, with an open-sided deck overlooking
the marina, is the perfect place for a drink or light
meal. The restaurant is strong on fresh seafood,
with oysters done every which way.

Sorrento ❷

✕ The Baths — Fish & Chips $

(☎03-5984 1500; www.thebaths.com.au; 3278
Point Nepean Rd, Sorrento; fish & chips $10,
restaurant mains $27-36; ⊙noon-8pm) The
waterfront deck of the former sea baths is the
perfect spot for lunch or a romantic sunset
dinner. The menu has some good seafood
choices and there's a popular takeaway fish and
chippery at the front.

🛏 Hotel Sorrento — Hotel $$$

(☎03-5984 2206; www.hotelsorrento.com.au;
5-15 Hotham Rd, Sorrento; motel r $195-280,
apt $220-320) The legendary Hotel Sorrento
trades on its famous name and has a swag
of accommodation. 'Sorrento on the Park'
offers standard and overpriced motel rooms,
but the lovely 'On the Hill' double and family
apartments have airy living spaces, spacious
bathrooms and private balconies.

Portsea ❸

🛏 Portsea Hotel — Hotel $$

(☎03-5984 2213; www.portseahotel.com.au;
Point Nepean Rd, Portsea; s/d without bathroom
from $75/105, s/d with bathroom from $135/175)
Something of a Portsea icon, the hotel's pub
and its rambling lawn and terrace offer lovely
views over the bay. There's an excellent bistro
and old-style accommodation (most rooms
have shared bathrooms) that increases in price
based on sea views (weekend rates are higher).

Mornington Peninsula National Park ❹

🛏 Cape Schanck B&B — B&B $$

(☎1300 885 259; www.capeschancklighthouse.
com.au; 420 Cape Schanck Rd; d from $130)
You can stay at **Cape Schanck B&B** in
the limestone Keeper's Cottage next to Cape
Schanck Lighthouse.

Flinders ❺

🛏 Flinders Hotel — Hotel $$$

(☎03-5989 0201; www.flindershotel.com.au; cnr
Cook & Wood Sts; d $225-500; ❄) Out back of
the historic hotel is a modern accommodation
wing with stylish en suite rooms. The real joy is
in the award-winning pub dining room, Terminus,
where pub grub goes gastronomic – nothing too
fussy, just staple dishes done really well.

Red Hill ❻

✕ Salix at Willow Creek Vineyard — Modern Australian $$$

(☎03-5989 7640; www.willow-creek.com.au;
166 Balnarring Rd/C784, Merricks North; mains
$36-38; ⊙noon-3pm daily, 6-10pm Fri & Sat)
Renowned for its sparkling wines, chardonnay
and pinot noir. Chef Bernard McCarthy's Salix
Restaurant is a serene place for a sophisticated
lunch on the deck or an intimate dinner.

✕ Ten Minutes By Tractor — Modern Australian $$$

(☎03-5989 6080; www.tenminutesbytractor.
com.au; 1333 Mornington-Flinders Rd, Main
Ridge; 5-/8-course tasting menu $109/139,
2-/3-course meal $69/89; ⊙cellar door 11am-
5pm, restaurant noon-3pm Wed-Sun, 6.30-9pm
Thu-Sat) This is one of regional Victoria's best
restaurants and you won't find a better wine list
on the Peninsula.

STRETCH YOUR LEGS
MELBOURNE

Start/Finish:
Queen Victoria Market

Distance: 5km

Duration: 3 hours

Melbourne is a vibrant, self-assured city known for its green open spaces, cosmopolitan food culture, grand gold-rush-era buildings and enticing laneways. This walk through the city centre introduces you to all of these personalities in the world's most liveable city.

Take this walk on Trip

Queen Victoria Market

So many Melbourne days begin at the 130-year-old **Queen Victoria Market** (www.qvm.com.au; 513 Elizabeth St; ⏰6am-2pm Tue & Thu, to 5pm Fri, to 3pm Sat, 9am-4pm Sun; 🚌Tourist Shuttle, 🚋19, 55, 57, 59), the largest open-air market in the southern hemisphere. Its 600-plus traders and laid-back atmosphere attract locals sniffing out fresh produce among the booming cries of spruiking fishmongers and fruit-and-veg vendors.

The Walk » Exit onto Elizabeth St, hurry south past the motorcycles and Asian grocery stores, then turn left up the hill on La Trobe St. At Swanston St, duck into Melbourne Central to see the iconic shot tower. Back on Swanston, the State Library is directly opposite.

State Library of Victoria

The **State Library of Victoria** (📞03-8664 7000; www.slv.vic.gov.au; 328 Swanston St; ⏰10am-9pm Mon-Thu, to 6pm Fri-Sun) has been the forefront of Melbourne's literary scene since 1854. There are over two million books in its collection. Don't miss its storied, octagonal La Trobe Reading Room (1913).

The Walk » Follow Swanston St south down the hill, passing Little Bourke St (Melbourne's Chinatown district), until you reach the Town Hall on your left, on the corner with Collins St.

Melbourne Town Hall

The 1870 **Melbourne Town Hall** (📞03-9658 9658; www.melbourne.vic.gov.au; cnr Collins & Swanston Sts; ⏰tours 11am & 1pm Mon-Fri) is an important Melbourne landmark. Queen Elizabeth II took tea here in 1954, and the Beatles waved to thousands of screaming fans from the balcony in 1964. Take the free one-hour tour to sit in the Lord Mayor's chair or tinker on the same piano Paul McCartney did.

The Walk » Admire the art-deco facade of the Manchester Unity Building (1932), then walk southwest down Collins St, one of Melbourne's most affluent thoroughfares. Before Elizabeth St, the Block Arcade is on your right.

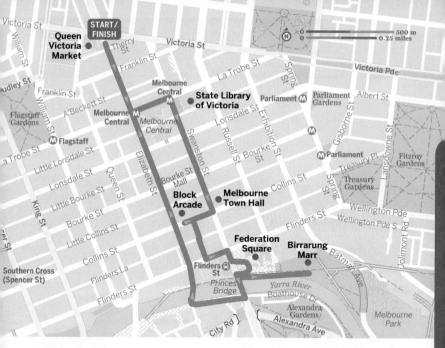

Block Arcade

The **Block Arcade** (www.theblockarcade. com.au; 282 Collins St; 🚋109) was built in 1891 – doing 'the Block' (walking around the block) was a popular pastime in 19th-century Melbourne – and features etched-glass ceilings and mosaic floors. Most of the shops and the extravagant Hopetoun Tea Rooms are pictures of elegance.

The Walk » Return to Collins St, cross the street, take the arcade at the pedestrian traffic lights, then follow the buzzing laneways out onto Flinders St. Pause to photograph Flinders Street Station (1854).

Federation Square

'Fed Square' is a favourite Melbourne meeting place. Its undulating and patterned forecourt is paved with 460,000 hand-laid cobblestones from the Kimberley region, with sight-lines to Melbourne's iconic landmarks. Down in the glass-roofed 'Atrium' the **Ian Potter Centre: NGV Australia** (📞03-8620 2222;

www.ngv.vic.gov.au; Federation Sq; exhibition costs vary; ⏰10am-5pm Tue-Sun; 🚋1, 3, 5, 6, 8, 16, 64, 67, 72, 🚃Flinders St) has an excellent permanent exhibition of Aboriginal art.

The Walk » Admire the river and Southbank views from Princes Bridge (cross over for some fine views back to the CBD), then drop down to the riverbank and walk east along Birrarung Mar.

Birrarung Marr

Riverside **Birrarung Marr** (btwn Federation Sq & the Yarra River; 🚋1, 3, 5, 6, 8, 16, 64, 67, 72, 🚃Flinders St) features grassy knolls, river promenades, a thoughtful planting of indigenous flora and symbols and great viewpoints of city and river. In the language of the Wurundjeri people, the traditional owners of the area, 'Birrarung Marr' means 'river of mists'.

The Walk » Cross the Yarra via Princes Bridge, walk west along the Southbank Promenade, then cross the first footbridge north, follow the tunnels below Flinders Street Station and then walk north all the way along Elizabeth St.

Wilsons Prom *Stirring coastal scenery and secluded beaches*

GLENN VAN DER KNUFF/GETTY IMAGES ©

Gippsland & Wilsons Prom

9

This loop through Victoria's southeast takes you from wild coastal landscapes to a semi-abandoned mining town hidden deep in the forest.

TRIP HIGHLIGHTS

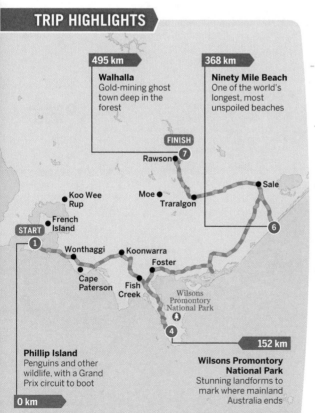

495 km
Walhalla
Gold-mining ghost
town deep in the
forest

368 km
Ninety Mile Beach
One of the world's
longest, most
unspoiled beaches

FINISH
Rawson **7**

Sale

Koo Wee
Rup

Moe
Traralgon

French
Island

START
1

Wonthaggi

Koonwarra

Foster

6

Cape
Paterson

Fish
Creek

Wilsons
Promontory
National Park

4

152 km

Phillip Island
Penguins and other
wildlife, with a Grand
Prix circuit to boot

**Wilsons Promontory
National Park**
Stunning landforms to
mark where mainland
Australia ends

0 km

**6–7 DAYS
495KM / 308 MILES**

GREAT FOR...

BEST TIME TO GO
October to April, when
the weather's warm.

 **ESSENTIAL
PHOTO**
Ninety Mile Beach
stretching out to
eternity.

 **BEST FOR
WILDLIFE**
Wilsons Prom's
wallabies are some of
Australia's tamest.

Gippsland & Wilsons Prom

Traversing one of Australia's most underrated corners, this journey southeast and east of Melbourne takes in the wildlife and wild landscapes of Phillip Island and Wilsons Prom, and engaging rural towns such as Inverloch, Koonwarra and Port Albert, before almost falling off the map in the ghost town of Walhalla on your way back to Melbourne.

TRIP HIGHLIGHT

1 Phillip Island

It may cover barely 100 sq km, but Phillip Island sure crams a lot in. For most visitors, Phillip Island means the nightly arrival of the penguins at the Penguin Parade, one of Australia's great wildlife spectacles. It doesn't happen until sunset, so wildlife-lovers will want to fill in the afternoon with a visit to Seal Rocks & the Nobbies, home to the country's largest colony of fur seals,

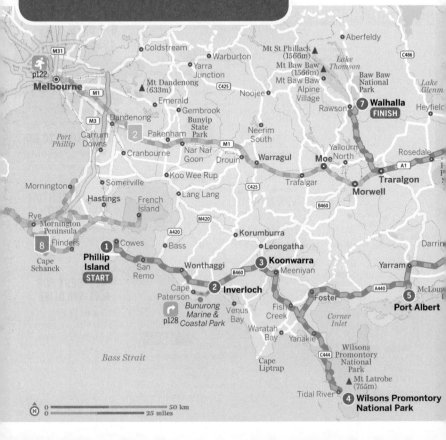

and the Koala Conservation Centre. The island's coast is the domain of swimmers and surfers, with world-class breaks at **Woolamai**, **Smiths Beach**, **Summerand Beach** and **Cat Bay**. And just to prove that there's something for everyone, Phillip Island has its **Motorcycle Grand Prix racing circuit** and attached History of Motorsport Museum.

 p131

The Drive » Leave the island via the causeway at Newhaven, then cruise along the pancake-flat B460, though Wonthaggi, and on to Inverloch just 50km from where your day's journey began.

- - - - - - - - - - - - -

❷ Inverloch

Inverloch is just far enough off main roads to feel like a secret – most visitors to Phillip Island are day-trippers who never make it this far, while those heading for the Prom cross Gippsland further north. And at the heart of this secret locals like to keep to themselves are fabulous surf, calm inlet beaches and outstanding diving and snorkelling; try **Offshore Surf School** (☏0407 374 743; www.offshoresurfschool.com.au; 32 Park St; 2hr lesson $60) if you feel inspired to learn how to catch a wave. Add in an eclectic place to stay and some good eating options and you, too, will soon want to keep the secret all to yourself.

 p131

The Drive » You could take the quiet and narrow back roads along the coast to Wilsons Prom, but we prefer to zip northeast

from Inverloch along the B460 for 10km before taking the turn-off to Koonwarra, a further 11km through rolling dairy country away to the northeast.

- - - - - - - - - - - - -

❸ Koonwarra

Blink and you could very easily miss Koonwarra, tucked away as it is in rolling dairy country along the South Gippsland Hwy. But this is one tiny township worth seeking out, having built itself a reputation as something of a niche foodie destination. Much of the appeal centres on two places. The first is the **Koonwarra Food & Wine Store** (☏03-5664 2285; www.koonwarrastore.com; cnr South Gippsland Hwy & Koala Dr; mains $12-26; ⊙8.30am-4pm), with its fresh produce and innovative menus in a gorgeous garden setting. Also worth lingering over is **Milly & Romeo's Artisan Bakery & Cooking School** (☏03-5664 2211; www.millyandromeos.com.au; 1 Koala Dr; adult/child from $90/50; ⊙9.30am-4.30pm Thu & Fri, 8.30am-4.30pm Sat

Lindenow

Fernbank ⊙　A1

Stratford　C106

Lake Wellington

Sale　Paradise Beach

Golden Beach

Gippsland Lake Coastal Park　C496

❻ Ninety Mile Beach

Ninety Mile Beach

odside ach

🔗 **LINK YOUR TRIP**

2　Sydney to Melbourne

If you were doing Trip 2 in reverse (ie from Melbourne), you'd miss nothing by driving from Walhalla to Paynesville and starting from there.

8　Mornington Peninsula

The road from Phillip Island to Red Hill (127km) connects you to the end point of the trip around the Mornington Peninsula.

DETOUR: BUNURONG MARINE & COASTAL PARK

Start: ❷ Inverloch

The inland route to Inverloch may be singularly lacking in drama, but the same can't be said for the 13km detour southwest to Cape Paterson. This stunning cliff-hugging drive looks out upon the **Bunurong Marine & Coastal Park**, and this surprising little park offers some of Australia's best snorkelling and diving – contact **SEAL Diving Services** (📞03-5174 3434; www.sealdivingservices. com.au; 7/27 Princes Hwy, Traralgon) to line up gear and guides. If you're going it alone and have the equipment to hand, **Eagles Nest**, **Shack Bay**, the **Caves** and **Twin Reefs** are great for snorkelling. **The Oaks** is the locals' favourite surf beach. The Caves took the archaeological world by storm in the early 1990s when dinosaur remains dating back 120 million years were discovered here; digs are still underway at the site.

& Sun, longer hr in summer), Victoria's first organic-certified cooking school and which offers short courses in making cakes, bread, traditional pastries, French classics and pasta, as well as running cooking classes for kids. But wait, there's more. If you happen upon Koonwarra on the first Saturday morning of the month, there'll be the **Farmers Market** (📞0408 619 182; www.kfm.org.au; Memorial Park, Koala Dr; ⏰8am-1pm 1st Sat of month) with organic everything (fruit, vegetables, berries, coffee), plus hormone-free beef and chemical-free cheeses. There's even a nearby winery where you can rest your head for the night...

🛏 p131

The Drive » From Koonwarra, the C444 sweeps down through Meeniyan, artsy Fish Creek and Yanakie, bound for the Prom. The further you go, the wilder the land becomes and the dramatic forested outcrops of the Prom's headlands soon come into view. By the time you reach the national park, slow down and watch for wildlife and, at regular intervals, fine little trails down to wonderful beaches.

- - - - - - - - - - - - -

TRIP HIGHLIGHT

❹ Wilsons Promontory National Park

The southernmost tip of mainland Australia, Wilsons Promontory (or 'The Prom' to its many friends) is a wild and wonderful place. Its dense woodland shelters a rich portfolio of native Australian wildlife and its combination of stirring coastal scenery and secluded white-sand beaches have made it one of the most popular national parks in Australia. The **Lilly Pilly Gully Nature Walk** (5km), **Mt Oberon Summit** (7km) and **Squeaky Beach Nature Walk** (5km) will give you a chance to stretch your legs and get a taste of the Prom's appeal. Even if you don't stray beyond Tidal River (where there's no fuel to be had), you'll catch a sense of the Prom's magic, with car-park access off the Tidal River road leading to gorgeous beaches and lookouts and with tame wildlife everywhere. Swimming is safe at the gorgeous beaches at **Norman Bay** (Tidal River) and around the headland at **Squeaky Beach** – the ultra-fine quartz sand here really does squeak beneath your feet!

🛏 p131

The Drive » Retrace your route northwest back up the C444 for 45km, then turn northeast towards Foster (a further 14km). From Foster, it's 48km to Port Albert along the A440, with a signed turn-off 5km before the town. En route, there are fine Prom views away to the south.

- - - - - - - - - - - - -

❺ Port Albert

Port Albert looks out over the water to a number of islands and has developed a reputation as a trendy stopover for boating, fishing and sampling the

CHRISTOPHER GROENHOUT/GETTY IMAGES ©

Wilsons Promontory National Park Tidal River

local seafood that's been a mainstay of this place for more than 150 years: the town proudly pronounces itself Gippsland's first established port, and the many historic timber buildings in the main street dating from its busy 1850s bear a brass plaque, detailing their age and previous use.

 p131

The Drive » Return to the A440, pass through Yarram, then wind down the window and breathe in the salty sea air. Around 64km from Yarram, take the C496 turn-off southeast to Seaspray (27km).

- - - - - - - - - - - - - - -
TRIP HIGHLIGHT

❻ Ninety Mile Beach

Quiet little Seaspray, a low-key, low-rise seaside village of prefab houses, feels stuck in a 1950s time warp, but the town itself plays second fiddle to what stretches out from its doorstep. To paraphrase the immortal words of Crocodile Dundee...that's not a beach, *this* is a beach. Isolated Ninety Mile Beach is a narrow strip of sand backed by dunes, featuring lagoons and stretching unbroken for more or less 90 miles

(150km) from near McLoughlins Beach to the channel at Lakes Entrance. Standing on the sand and watching the beach unfurl to the northeast while waves curl and crash along its length, and you'll likely be bid silent by the vast emptiness and sheer beauty of it all.

The Drive » With a last, longing look over your shoulder, steel yourself for the least interesting stretch of journey, the 127km to Walhalla that goes something like this: take the C496 for 27km, then the A440 for 6km into Sale. From there it's 55 downright dull kilometres to Traralgon, before the final 34km through rich forest to Walhalla.

- - - - - - - - - - - - - - -
TRIP HIGHLIGHT

❼ Walhalla

Welcome to Victoria's best-preserved and most charming historic town. Tiny Walhalla lies hidden high in the green hills and forests of west Gippsland. It's a postcard-pretty collection of sepia-toned period cottages and other timber buildings (some original, most reconstructed). The setting, too, is gorgeous, strung out along a deep, forested valley with Stringers Creek running through the centre of the township. In its gold-

mining heyday in the 1860s, Walhalla's population was 5000. It fell to just 10 people in 1998 (when mains electricity arrived in the town). Like all great ghost towns, the dead that are buried in the stunningly sited cemetery vastly outnumber the living. The best way to see the town is on foot – take the tramline walk (45 minutes), which begins from opposite the general store soon after you enter town. A tour of the **Long Tunnel Extended Gold Mine** (☎03-5165 6259; off Walhalla-Beardmore Rd; adult/child/family $19.50/13.50/49.50; ☻1.30pm daily, plus noon & 3pm Sat, Sun & holidays) offers insights into why Walhalla existed at all, while the **Walhalla Goldfields Railway** (☎03-5165 6280; www.walhallarail.com; adult/child/family return $20/15/50; ☻from Walhalla station 11am, 1pm & 3pm, from Thomson Station 11.40am, 1.40pm & 3.40pm Wed, Sat, Sun & public holidays) is a fine adjunct to your visit, snaking as it does along Stringers Creek Gorge, passing lovely, forested gorge country and crossing a number of trestle bridges en route.

🛏 p131

Eating & Sleeping

Phillip Island ❶

✗ Fig & Olive at Cowes
Modern Australian $$

(☎03-5952 2655; www.figandoliveatcowes.
com.au; 115 Thompson Ave, Cowes; mains
$24-38; ⊙9am-late Wed-Mon) A groovy mix of
timber, stone and lime-green decor makes this
a relaxing place to enjoy a beautifully presented
meal, or a late-night cocktail. The eclectic menu
is strong on seafood and moves from paella or
pork belly to wood-fired Tasmanian salmon.

🛏 Clifftop
Boutique Hotel $$$

(☎03-5952 1033; www.clifftop.com.au; 1 Marlin
St, Smiths Beach; d $235-300; ❄) It's hard
to imagine a better location for your island
stay than perched above Smiths Beach. Of the
seven luxurious suites here, the top four have
ocean views and private balconies, while the
downstairs rooms open onto gardens – all have
fluffy beds and slick contemporary decor.

Inverloch ❷

🛏 Moilong Express
Boutique Hotel $$

(☎0439 842 334; www.coastalstays.com/
moilongexpress; 405 Inverloch-Venus Bay Rd; d
$120) This quirky former railway train carriage,
on a hillside property about 3km from Inverloch,
has been converted into very comfortable
accommodation. There's a kitchen, queen-sized
bed, traditional wood panelling and an old
railway station clock.

Koonwarra ❸

🛏 Lyre Bird Hill Winery & Guest House
B&B $$

(☎03-5664 3204; www.lyrebirdhill.com.au; 370
Inverloch Rd; s/d $125/175; ⊙cellar door 10am-
5pm Wed-Mon Oct, Nov & Feb-Apr, daily Dec &
Jan, by appointment May-Sep; ❄) Stay among
the vines 4km southwest of Koonwarra. The
quaint, old-fashioned B&B has light-filled rooms

overlooking the garden, while the self-contained
country-style cottage is perfect for a family. The
vineyard is right next door.

Wilsons Promontory National Park ❹

🛏 Wilderness Retreat
Safari Tent $$$

(www.wildernessretreats.com.au; d $312, extra
person $25) Nestled in bushland at Tidal River,
these luxury safari tents, each with their own
deck, bathroom, queen-sized beds, heating
and a communal tent kitchen, sleep up to four
people and are pretty cool. It's like being on an
African safari with a kookaburra soundtrack.

Port Albert ❺

✗ Wildfish
Seafood $$

(☎03-5183 2002; www.wildfish-restaurant.com.
au; 40 Wharf St; lunch mains $8-17, dinner mains
$26-36; ⊙noon-3pm & 6-8pm Thu-Sun) With a
sublime harbour-side location and the freshest
local seafood, Wildfish is earning a well-
deserved reputation for serving good food. By
day it's a cafe offering coffee and sandwiches;
by night the menu turns to thoughtful seafood
dishes such as flake-and-scallop pie or tempura
garfish fillets.

Walhalla ❼

🛏 Walhalla Star Hotel
Historic Hotel $$

(☎03-5165 6262; www.starhotel.com.au; Main
St; d incl breakfast $189-249; ❄ @ 🛜) The
rebuilt historic Star offers stylish boutique
accommodation with king-sized beds and
simple but sophisticated designer decor,
making good use of local materials such as
corrugated-iron water tanks. Guests can
dine at the in-house restaurant; others need
to reserve in advance. Or you can get good
breakfasts, pies, coffee and cake at the
attached **Greyhorse Café** (mains from $5;
⊙10am-2pm).

Mt Macedon *A charming area – at its prettiest in autumn*

JOCHEN SCHLENKER/GETTY IMAGES ©

Victoria's Goldfields

10

Gold was what made Victoria great, and this lovely meander through old gold-mining towns and rolling hill country is one of the state's more agreeable and lesser-known drives.

TRIP HIGHLIGHTS

4–5 DAYS
201KM / 125 MILES

160 km

Clunes
Impeccable gold heritage and fabulous books

Bendigo●

81 km

Maldon
Storybook mining village, perfectly preserved

⑤

B180   C282   Chewton

Newstead

Malmsbury

⑦

Daylesford ●

②

●Macedon
START

⑧ FINISH

Ballarat
Victoria's premier gold-mining town

Woodend & Hanging Rock
Iconic volcanic outcrop swirling with mystery

201 km   **7 km**

GREAT FOR...

BEST TIME TO GO

Southern areas can be bitterly cold in winter. Autumn is wonderful around the Macedon Ranges.

Maldon's main street.

Castlemaine has fabulous gold-rush architecture and a palpable sense of history.

133

10 Victoria's Goldfields

The Macedon Ranges are the perfect place to begin, home as it is to haunting Hanging Rock and some lovely little towns that capture the essence of rural Victoria. From then on, it's stately, historic gold-mining towns all the way to Ballarat, which wears the region's gold-mining heritage like a glittering badge of honour. En route, stop by pretty little Kyneton, buzzing Castlemaine, timeworn Maryborough and Victoria's premier booktown, Clunes.

❶ Macedon

Less than an hour northwest of Melbourne and yet a world away, Macedon is a quiet unassuming town. It may lack the historical streetscapes of other towns along the route but its green parklands serve as an agreeable prelude to the Macedon Ranges, a beautiful area of low mountains, native forest, excellent regional produce and wineries. Charming at any time of the year, these hills can be enveloped in suggestive clouds in winter, but are at their best when bathed in golden autumnal shades. The scenic drive up **Mt Macedon**, a 1010m-high extinct volcano, passes grand mansions and gardens, taking you to picnic areas, walking trails, sweeping lookouts and the huge memorial cross near the summit car park. If you're keen to linger, there are some great wineries (www.macedonrangeswineries.com.au) in the area, while Wine Tours Victoria can arrange day tours.

✖ p140

The Drive » It's only 7km from Macedon north to Woodend, but forsake the M79 Calder Freeway and take the quieter back road that runs parallel.

TRIP HIGHLIGHT

❷ Woodend & Hanging Rock

Pleasant little Woodend has a certain bucolic appeal – the wide streets, the free-standing clock-tower, the smattering of heritage buildings with wide verandahs and

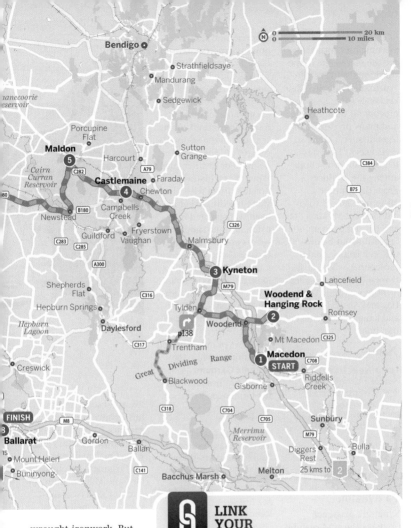

Macedon START
Woodend & Hanging Rock
Kyneton
Castlemaine
Maldon
FINISH Ballarat

wrought-ironwork. But it's the setting here that truly beguiles, amid rolling hills and expansive woodlands latticed by vineyards. East of town lies **Hanging Rock**, an ancient and captivating place made famous by the unsettling Joan Lindsay novel (and subsequent film by Peter Weir) *Picnic*

LINK YOUR TRIP

2 Sydney to Melbourne

Join this epic route in reverse by driving south along the Calder Hwy to Melbourne and then taking the Princes Hwy heading east.

7 Great Ocean Road

One of Australia's great road trips begins in Melbourne. From Macedon take the Calder Hwy south, then the Western Ring Rd to the Princes Hwy.

at Hanging Rock. The volcanic rock formations are the sacred site of the traditional owners, the Wurundjeri people. They also once served as a hideout for bushrangers, and many mysteries and legends surround it; an eerie energy is said to be felt by many who climb among the boulders. From the summit, a 20-minute climb, splendid views of Mt Macedon and beyond open up. Spreading out below the rock is its famous racecourse, which hosts two excellent picnic race meetings on New Year's Day and Australia Day, and kangaroos the rest of the time.

✕ p140

The Drive ≫ From Woodend, head west 12km to Tylden, from where the road branches southwest to your Trentham-Blackwood detour, or north to Kyneton. Whichever you choose, it's a pretty drive through sweeping farmlands and light eucalyptus woodlands.

- - - - - - - - - - - - -

❸ Kyneton

Kyneton's existence predates the gold rush by a year, and it's the first of the gold-mining towns you come to on this trip. It was the main coach stop between Melbourne and Bendigo, and the centre for the farmers who supplied the diggings with fresh produce. These days, Kyneton serves a similar purpose

as a regional centre set amid prosperous farming country, and it's filled with the kind of attractions that are a staple of the gold-era towns, but it's a whole lot quieter, too often overlooked on the rush to the regional centres of Daylesford, Bendigo or Castlemaine. Piper St is a historic precinct lined with bluestone buildings that have been transformed into cafes, antique shops, museums and restaurants. If you're keen to see what many of these buildings looked like on the inside, try the **Kyneton Historical Museum** (☎03-5422 1228; 67 Piper St; adult/child $6.50/3; ⏰11am-4pm Fri-Sun), decked out in period furnishings, while the **Botanic Gardens** (Clowes St) is a lovely spot beside the Campaspe River.

✕ 🛏 p140

The Drive ≫ The well-worn trail from Melbourne to Castlemaine passes right by Kyneton, but we recommend taking the quieter parallel roads that shadow the Calder Fwy. That way you'll get to see Malmsbury and lovely little Chewton on your way into Castlemaine.

- - - - - - - - - - - - -

❹ Castlemaine

In the heart of the central Victorian goldfields, Castlemaine is one of the most happening places in Victoria, where a growing community of artists and tree-changers

live amid some inspiring architecture and gardens. It all stems from the mid-19th century when Castlemaine was *the* thriving marketplace for the goldfields. Even after the gold rush subsided, Castlemaine built a reputation for industry and innovation – this was the birthplace of the Castlemaine XXXX beer-brewing company (now based in Queensland). Historic buildings littered around town include the Roman basilica facade of the old **Castlemaine Market** (1862) on Mostyn St; the **Theatre Royal** (1856) on Hargreaves St;

Ballarat Sovereign Hill

the **post office** (1894); and the original **courthouse building** (1851) on Goldsmith Cres. For a good view over town, head up to the **Burke & Wills Monument** on Wills St (follow Lyttleton St east of the centre). And to see why the buzz around Castlemaine never abates, stop by for a beer at the **Bridge Hotel** (☎03-5472 1161; http://bridgehotelcastlemaine.com; 21 Walker St; ⏰4-11pm Mon-Wed, to 1am Thu, noon-1pm Fri, noon-midnight Sat, to 11pm Sun), one of regional Victoria's best live-music venues.

✗ 🛏 p140

The Drive ❯❯ The C282 from Castlemaine to Maldon (16km) passes through the box-ironbark forests of Victoria's gold country. It's a lovely drive to a lovely place.

TRIP HIGHLIGHT

❺ Maldon

Like a pop-up folk museum, the whole of tiny Maldon is a well-preserved relic of the gold-rush era, with many fine buildings constructed from local stone. The population is significantly lower than the 20,000 who used to work the local goldfields, but this is still a living,

working town – packed with tourists on weekends but reverting to its sleepy self during the week. Evidence of those heady mining days can be seen around town – you can't miss the 24m-high **Beehive Chimney**, just east of Main St, while the **Old Post Office** (95 High St), built in 1870, was the childhood home of local author Henry Handel Richardson. A short trip south along High St reveals the remains of the **North British Mine**, once one of the world's richest mines.

✗ 🛏 p141

DETOUR: TRENTHAM & BLACKWOOD

Start: ❷ Woodend

The small historic township of **Trentham** (pop 630) sits at the top of the Great Dividing Range, midway between Woodend and Daylesford. At an elevation of 700m it's noticeably cooler than the surrounding areas, and is worth a visit to stroll its quaint streetscape with some excellent eateries. Although it's growing in popularity, visit on a weekday and you're likely to have the place all to yourself.

A mere 16km away to the south and surrounded by state forest, tiny **Blackwood** is a lesser-known, even-smaller version of the Trentham charm. On the main strip is **Blackwood Merchant** (p140), a cafe-general store with local produce and wines. Its back patio has lovely forest views. On the corner is the historic **Blackwood Hotel** (☑03-5368 6501; www.blackwoodpub. com; Martin St; r $90), established in 1868 with plenty of atmosphere, pub meals and basic accommodation. There's also the quaint **Garden of St Erth** (☑03-5368 6514; www.diggers.com.au/gardens-cafes/gardens/st-erth. aspx; Simmons Reef Rd, Blackwood; entry $10; ⊙garden 9am-5pm, cafe 10am-4pm Thu-Mon), a garden nursery that's centered around an 1860 sandstone cottage with a cafe serving produce grown onsite.

The Drive » On the way out of town, don't miss the 3km drive up to Mt Tarrengower for panoramic views from the poppet-head lookout. Once you're ready to leave, head due south towards Newstead, then west along the B180 through Joyces Creek and Carisbrook to Maryborough.

❻ Maryborough

Maryborough is an essential part of central Victoria's 'Golden Triangle' experience, but it's sufficiently far west to miss out on the day-trippers that flock to Castlemaine and Maldon. Those that do make it this far are rewarded with some splendid Victorian-era buildings, but **Maryborough Railway Station** (☑03-5461 4683; 38 Victoria St; ⊙10am-5pm) leaves them all for dead. Built in 1892, the inordinately large station, complete with clock tower, was described by Mark Twain as 'a train station with a town attached'. Today it houses a mammoth antique emporium, a regional wine centre and a cafe. Prospectors still turn up a nugget or two in the Maryborough

area. If you're interested in finding your own gold nuggets, **Coiltek Gold Centre** (☑03-5460 4700; www.maryboroughgoldcentre. com.au; 6 Drive-in Ct; ⊙9am-5pm) offers full-day prospecting courses with state-of-the-art metal detectors. It also sells and hires out prospecting gear.

🍴 p141

The Drive » The C287 runs south and then southeast for 32km to Clunes. It's an attractive, quiet road with stands of forest interspersed with open farmlands; watch for Mt Beckworth rising away to the southwest as you near Clunes.

❼ Clunes

Clunes may be small, but this is where it all began. It was here, roughly halfway between Maryborough and Ballarat, that a find in June 1851 sparked the gold rush that would transform Victoria's fortunes. These days, the small town is a quintessential gold-mining relic, with gorgeous 19th-century porticoed buildings whose grandeur seems way out of proportion to the town's current size. But Clunes has another claim to fame. The town hosts the annual **Booktown Book Fair** (www.clunesbooktown. com.au) in early May and is home to no fewer than (at last count) seven bookstores, with a focus on the second-hand trade.

The Drive >> There are two possible routes to Ballarat, although we prefer the quieter C287. All along its 24km, there's an growing sense of accumulating clamour as the flat yellow farmlands south of Clunes yield to the outskirts of Ballarat as you pass under the Western Hwy.

- - - - - - - - - - - -

TRIP HIGHLIGHT

❽ Ballarat

Ballarat is one of the greatest gold-mining towns on earth, a thriving testament to a mineral that continues to provide most of the town's major attractions, even long after the gold rush ended. Partly that heritage survives in the grand buildings scattered regally around the city centre. Take the time to walk along Lydiard St in particular, one of Australia's finest streetscapes for Victorian-era architecture. Impressive buildings include **Her Majesty's Theatre**, **Craig's Royal Hotel**, **George Hotel** and the **Art Gallery** (☎03-5320 5858; www.balgal.com; 40 Lydiard St Nth; ⊙10am-5pm), which also houses a wonderful collection of early colonial paintings with works

VICTORIA'S GOLD RUSH

When gold was discovered in New South Wales in May 1851, a reward was offered to anyone who could find gold within 300km of Melbourne, amid fears that Victoria would be left behind. They needn't have worried. By June a significant discovery was made at Clunes, 32km north of Ballarat, and prospectors flooded into central Victoria.

Over the next few months, fresh gold finds were made almost weekly around Victoria. Then in September 1851 the greatest gold discovery ever known (a 72kg nugget known as Welcome Stranger) was made at Moliagul, followed by others at Ballarat, Bendigo, Mt Alexander and many more. By the end of 1851 hopeful miners were coming from England, Ireland, Europe, China and the failing goldfields of California.

The gold rush ushered in a fantastic era of growth and prosperity for Victoria. Within 12 years the population had increased from 77,000 to 540,000. Mining companies invested heavily in the region, the development of roads and railways accelerated and huge shanty towns were replaced by Victoria's modern provincial cities, most notably Ballarat, Bendigo and Castlemaine, which reached the height of their splendour in the 1880s.

from noted Australian artists. But Ballarat's fine story is most stirringly told in two museums that hark back to the town's glory days: the fabulous, re-created gold-mining village at **Sovereign Hill** (☎03-5337 1100; www.sovereignhill.com.au; Bradshaw St; adult/student/child/family $49.50/39.60/22/122;

⊙10am-5pm, until 5.30pm during daylight saving) and the stunning new **Museum of Australian Democracy at Eureka** (MADE; ☎1800 287 113; www.made.org; cnr Eureka & Rodier Sts; adult/child/family $12/8/35; ⊙10am-5pm).

✕ ⮕ p141

Eating & Sleeping

Woodend ❷

Holgate Brewhouse   Pub $$

(📞03-5427 2510; www.holgatebrewhouse.
com; 79 High St; d $135-185; mains $19-29;
🕐noon-late) The excellent Holgate Brewhouse,
at Keatings Hotel, is a cracking brewery pub
producing a range of hand-pumped European-
style ales and lagers on site. Serves hearty Mod
Oz bistro food and has rooms upstairs.

✖ Blackwood Merchant   Cafe $$

(21 Martin St, Blackwood; mains $12-28; 🕐9am-
5pm Sun-Thu, to 11pm Fri & Sat) Southwest of
Woodend, in tiny Blackwood, this rustic general
store and cafe specialises in local produce and
wines. You can take in views of the forest from
out the back.

Kyneton ❸

✖ Flouch's   Australian $$

(📞03-5422 3683; 12-14 Piper St; mains $17-
36; 🕐11am-3pm & 6pm-midnight Wed-Fri,
10am-midnight Sat, to 3pm Sun) Celebrated
chef Michael Flouch presides over perfectly
prepared contemporary dishes; the focus is
on updated classic tastes without too many
frilly elaborations. Try the French-style potato
gnocchi with blue-cheese sauce and roasted
pear, or the more traditional chargrilled eye
fillet steak.

✖ Mr Carsisi   Middle Eastern $$$

(📞03-5422 3769; http://mrcarsisi.com; 37c
Piper St; mains $29-39; 🕐11.30am-late Fri-Tue)
Turkish tastes and Middle Eastern mezze
dominate this well-regarded place, which does
a faultless job of combining foreign flavours
with local produce – the honey-and-cardamom
Milawa duck breast is typical of the genre.

✖ Annie Smithers
Bistrot   Modern Australian $$$

(📞03-5422 2039; www.anniesmithers.
com.au; 72 Piper St; mains $36-40; 🕐noon-
2.30pm & 6-9pm Thu-Sat, noon-2.30pm Sun)
One of central Victoria's most exciting new
restaurants, this fine place has a menu that
changes with the seasons and dish descriptions
that read like a culinary short story about
regional produce and carefully conceived taste
combinations – such as hazelnut and fennel
seed crumbed cutlet of pork, apple and fennel
puree, spring slaw and pork with cider jus.

🛏 Airleigh-Rose Cottage   B&B $$$

(📞0402 783 489; www.airleigh-rosecottage.
com.au; 10 Begg St; r 2 nights $490, minimum
2-night stay) Attractive wood-and-brick rooms in
a Federation-era cottage.

Castlemaine ❹

✖ Public Inn   Modern Australian $$$

(📞03-5472 3568; www.publicinn.com.au; 165
Barker St; 2-course lunch $39, mains $19-45;
🕐noon-late Fri-Sun, 4pm-late Mon-Thu) The
former Criterion Hotel has been brilliantly
transformed into a slick bar and restaurant
that, with its plush tones and leather couches,
wouldn't look out of place in Manhattan. Food
is high-end 'gastropub'. Check out the 'barrel
wall', where local wines are dispensed.

✖ Naam Pla Thai Kitchen   Thai $$

(36 Hargreaves St; mains $13-24; 🕐noon-
2.30pm & 4-9pm Wed-Sun) A recent change of
locale has given space for this fine, fragrant den
of excellent Thai cooking to flourish. They don't
mess with unnecessary things like phones or a
website – the staff put all their energy into the
cooking instead, and it shows with dishes such
as fine roasted duck curry.

🛏 Apple Annie's   Apartments $$

(📞03-5472 5311; www.appleannies.com.au;
31 Templeton St; apt $120-160) Beautifully
appointed apartments with rustic wooden
floorboards, pastel shades, open fireplaces and
(in the front apartment) a lovely private patio.

🛏 Midland Private
Hotel   Guesthouse $$

(📞0487 198 931; www.themidland.com.au;
2 Templeton St; d $150) Opposite the train
station, this lace-decked 1879 hotel is mostly
original, so the rooms are old fashioned, but it

has plenty of charm, from the art deco entrance to the magnificent guest lounge and attached Maurocco Bar. No children.

Maldon ⑤

✖ Gold Exchange Cafe   Cafe $

(www.goldexchangecafe.com; 44 Main St; meals $7-15; ⊘9am-5pm Wed-Sun) This tiny licensed cafe is worth a visit for the yabby pies, made from locally farmed yabbies.

🛏 Maldon Miners Cottages   Cottage $$

(☎0413 541 941; www.heritagecottages.com.au; 41 High St; cottages from $150) Books accommodation in Maldon's 19th-century heritage cottages – a great choice.

Maryborough ⑥

✖ Station Cafe   Cafe, Restaurant $$

(☎03-5461 4683; www.stationantiques.com.au; 38c Victoria St; mains $14-31; ⊘10am-4pm Mon & Wed-Fri, 9.30am-4.30pm Sat & Sun) This excellent cafe is in a lovely light-filled room in the grand Maryborough train station. Stop in for a coffee or speciality crêpe. The evening menu features pasta and Black Angus steaks.

Ballarat ⑧

✖ The Lane   Cafe, Pizzeria $$

(☎03-5333 4866; 27 Lydiard St Nth; pizza $16-22, mains $23-39; ⊘7am-late) The laneway running beside the George Hotel buzzes with all-day diners. At the front is a bright cafe with breakfast, light meals and a bar; at the back is a great little pizzeria which doubles as an à la carte restaurant in the evenings.

✖ Catfish   Thai $$

(☎03-5331 5248; www.catfishthai.com.au; 42-44 Main Rd; mains $18-34; ⊘6pm-late Tue-Sat) Catfish is the newish kitchen of chef Damien Jones, who made the Lydiard Wine Bar such a treasured local secret. Thai cooking classes only add to what is an increasingly popular package.

🛏 Oscar's   Boutique Hotel $$

(☎03-5331 1451; www.oscarshotel.com.au; 18 Doveton St; d $150-200, spa room $225; ❄🖧) The 13 rooms in this attractive art deco hotel have been tastefully refurbished to include double showers and spas (watch TV from your spa).

🛏 Ansonia on Lydiard   B&B $$

(☎03-5332 4678; www.theansoniaonlydiard.com.au; 32 Lydiard St South; r $125-225; ❄🖧) One of Lydiard St's great hotels, the Ansonia exudes calm with its minimalist design, polished floors, dark-wood furnishings and light-filled atrium. Stylish rooms have large-screen TVs and range from studio apartments for two to family suites.

🛏 Comfort Inn
Sovereign Hill   Historic Hotel $$

(☎03-5337 1159; www.sovereignhill.com.au/comfort-inn-sovereign-hill; 39-41 Magpie St; r $175-195; ❄🖧) Formerly known as Sovereign Hill Lodge, this excellent place has bright, modern rooms that are located a stone's throw from Sovereign Hill itself. Ask about its accommodation-and-entertainment packages. Its 'Night in the Museum' package (s/d $425/695) lets you stay in the Steinfeld's building at the top of Main St within Sovereign Hill itself, where you'll be served by staff in period dress.

Mt Beauty Climb alpine roads by day, feast like a king by night

DANITA DELIMONT/GETTY IMAGES ©

Great Alpine Road

11

From Beechworth to Lakes Entrance, this spectacular traverse of Victoria's High Country and down to the coast is ideal for lovers of food and fine landscapes.

TRIP HIGHLIGHTS

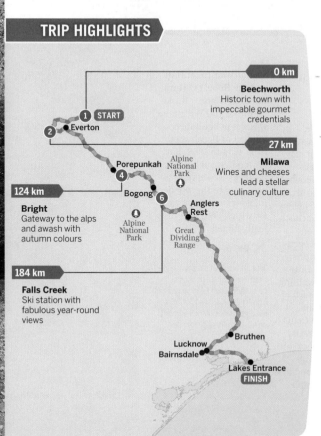

0 km

Beechworth
Historic town with impeccable gourmet credentials

1 START

Everton

2

Porepunkah
4

Alpine National Park

27 km

Milawa
Wines and cheeses lead a stellar culinary culture

124 km

Bright
Gateway to the alps and awash with autumn colours

Bogong **6**

Alpine National Park

Anglers Rest

Great Dividing Range

184 km

Falls Creek
Ski station with fabulous year-round views

Bruthen
Lucknow
Bairnsdale

Lakes Entrance
FINISH

7 DAYS
375KM / 233 MILES

GREAT FOR...

BEST TIME TO GO

October to April; the stunning autumnal colours around Bright often persist into May. Roads may close June to August.

 ESSENTIAL PHOTO

Bright in autumn.

 BEST FOR FOODIES

Milawa Gourmet Region has wine, cheese, mustard and more.

143

11 Great Alpine Road

The High Country of Victoria's northeast is one of the state's favourite playgrounds, from the foodie excursions to Beechworth (one of Victoria's best-preserved historic relics), Milawa and Myrtleford, to the ski slopes of Falls Creek. And either side of a stirring up-and-over mountain drive, Bright and Lakes Entrance are ideal getaways for putting your feet up surrounded by superb natural beauty.

225 kms to 12

START ❶ Beechwo

TRIP HIGHLIGHT

❶ Beechworth

There is a danger in beginning your journey in Beechworth: you may never want leave. Few regional Victorian towns have such a diverse array of disparate but somehow complementary charms. The most obvious of these is the town's open-air museum of historic, honey-coloured granite buildings. Take a walking tour that takes in such architectural luminaries as the Beechworth Courthouse, where the trials of many key historical figures took place (including Ned Kelly and his mother), the Telegraph Station, the Town Hall and the Robert O'Hara Burke Museum – Burke (of Burke and Wills fame) was the police superintendent at Beechworth from 1854 to 1858. But for foodies, such fine facades also serve as a backdrop to the wonderful gourmet temptations for which Beechworth is justly famed.

✕ ⫴ p149

The Drive >> It's a short hop from Beechworth to Milawa, passing through Everton and rich farmlands and stands of light eucalyptus woodlands – count on no more than 20 minutes.

TRIP HIGHLIGHT

2 Milawa Gourmet Region

If Beechworth is where the end product most often appears on restaurant tables, the Milawa Gourmet Region is where so much of the produce comes from. In Brown Brothers, Milawa boasts one of Victoria's best-known and most respected wineries, going strong since 1899. As well as the tasting room, there's the superb Epicurean Centre restaurant, a gorgeous garden, kids' play equipment and picnic and barbecue facilities. What Brown Brothers is to wine, the Milawa Cheese Company is to cheese. About 2km north of Milawa, it excels at soft farmhouse brie (from goat or cow) and pungent

LINK YOUR TRIP

2 Sydney to Melbourne

Lakes Entrance is Stop 11 on this classic route, but you could just as easily begin here and do it in reverse.

12 Along the Murray

Beechworth lies 203km southwest of the starting point of Echuca – drive via Wangaratta, Benalla and Shepparton.

washed-rind cheeses. There's a bakery here and an excellent restaurant where the speciality is a variety of pizzas using Milawa cheese. And on no account miss Milawa Mustard, offering up handmade seeded mustards, herbed vinegars and preserves along Milawa's main street.

 p149

The Drive » Return to Everton then drive southeast along the B500 until, barely half an hour after leaving Milawa, you reach Myrtleford. Depending on the season, mountains, possibly snow-capped, rise up ahead and red-orange leaves set fire to the landscape in autumn.

❸ Myrtleford

Near the foothills of Mt Buffalo, Myrtleford is noteworthy for two main reasons. First, this is the 'Gateway to the Alps', the first town of note along the Great Alpine Rd (B500). It's also home to the **Myrtleford Butter Factory** (☏03-5752 2300; www.thebutterfactory.com.au; Great Alpine Rd; ⏰10am-4pm Mon-Fri, 9am-5pm Sat & Sun), at once factory and produce store. Reassuringly you can still see butter being churned here and, if you happen to be here on a Thursday at 11am, don't miss the 45-minute guided tour of the factory. The produce store stocks a wide range of local products, including more uses for butter

than you could ever have imagined. Even if you don't like butter you'll want to find reasons to buy something here.

The Drive » One of the loveliest sections of the entire drive, the 31km from Myrtleford to Bright meanders through green farmlands with steeply forested hillsides lining the roadside and the Victorian alps away to the north and east.

TRIP HIGHLIGHT

❹ Bright

Ask many Victorians for their favourite country town, and the chances are that a significant proportion of them will say Bright. The town itself has little in the way of architectural appeal, but its location (spread across the valleys that preview the alps), glorious autumn colours, fine foods and a range of activities all add up to a real rural gem. Skiers tired of the off-piste scene up at Falls Creek or Mt Hotham use it as a quieter, more sophisticated base in winter. Thrill seekers love it for its adrenaline rush of activities, from paragliding (enthusiasts catch the thermals from nearby Mystic Mountain – try **Alpine Paragliding** (☏0428 352 048; www.alpineparagliding. com; ⏰Oct-Jun) to mountain biking. And then there's everything from bushwalking and kayaking to one of the state's most respected cook-

PETER WALTON PHOTOGRAPHY/GETTY IMAGES ©

ing schools at **Patrizia Simone Country Cooking School** (☏03-5755 2266; www.simonesbright.com.au; 98 Gavan St; per person $180).

 🛏 p149

The Drive » From Bright to Mt Beauty (30km), the road becomes lonelier, green fields rise gently into the Alpine foothills and there is the accumulating sense that very big mountains lie up ahead. As you draw near to Mt Beauty, the road becomes steeper with some lovely alpine views.

❺ Mt Beauty

The mountain air just feels cleaner in Mt

Milawa The historic flour mill

Beauty, a quiet pre-alpine village huddled at the foot of Victoria's highest mountain, Mt Bogong (1986m), on the Kiewa River. Mt Beauty and its twin villages of Tawonga and Tawonga South are the gateways to Falls Creek ski resort, but it's also a worthwhile stop in its own right, not least for the pleasing short walks in the vicinity: the 2km **Tree Fern Walk** and the longer **Peppermint Walk** both start from Mountain Creek Picnic and Camping Ground, on Mountain Creek Rd, off the Kiewa Valley Hwy

(C531). Located about 1km south of Bogong Village (towards Falls Creek), the 1.5km return **Fainter Falls Walk** takes you to a pretty cascade.

✖ p149

The Drive » From Mt Beauty the road *really* begins to climb, bucking and weaving along valley walls scarred by a devastating bushfire in 2013. In winter you'll need chains. For the rest of the year, count on pulling over often to take in the view.

- - - - - - - - - -

TRIP HIGHLIGHT

❻ Falls Creek

Part of the appeal of Falls Creek resides in its

deserved reputation as one of Australia's premier winter ski resorts. In that guise, Victoria's glitziest, most fashion-conscious resort combines a picturesque alpine setting with impressive skiing and infamous après-ski entertainment. The Summit chairlift also operates during the summer school holidays (per ride/day $15/25) and mountain biking is popular here in the green season. But for all this, we also love Falls for its location along one of the country's prettiest mountain traverses accessible by road.

147

DETOUR: MT BUFFALO NATIONAL PARK

Start: ❹ Bright

Beautiful Mt Buffalo is an easily accessible year-round destination – in winter it's a tiny, family-friendly ski resort with gentle runs, and in summer it's a great spot for bushwalking, mountain biking and rock climbing. This is a world of granite outcrops, lookouts, streams, waterfalls, wildflowers and wildlife. A road leads to just below the summit of the Horn (1723m), the highest point on the massif. En route, the views from the car park of the defunct Mt Buffalo Chalet are simply splendid, and activities are a year-round prospect, from 14km of groomed cross-country ski trails and tobogganing to summer hang-gliding and rock climbing. If a short stroll to a lookout is the most you can muster, **Mt Buffalo Olives** (🗹03-5756 2143; www.mtbuffaloolives.com.au; 307 Mt Buffalo Rd, Porepunkah; ⏲11am-5pm Fri-Mon & daily during school holidays), on the road up to Mt Buffalo from Porepunkah, might be more to your taste. To get here from Bright, return 6km northwest up the B500 to Porepunkah, from where the signposted road climbs steeply up Mt Buffalo.

The Drive ❯❯ With most of the ski action and ski-station approaches concentrated west of Falls Creek, the slow descent down to Omeo (first along the C531 then south along the C543) is every bit as beautiful but a whole lot quieter.

---

❼ Omeo

High in the hills, and not really on the road to anywhere, historic Omeo is the main town on the eastern section of the Great Alpine Rd; the road is sometimes snowbound in winter, so always check conditions before heading this way. There's not much to see here, although if you book ahead and are willing to stop in Anglers Rest, around 25km north of Omeo, you could relive *The Man from Snowy River* and go for a trail ride with **Packers High Country Horse Riding** (🗹03-5159 7241; www.horsetreks.com; Anglers Rest; 1½hr/half/full-day ride $80/150/250). Otherwise, Omeo is a place to simply enjoy the view, safe in the knowledge that a pretty road awaits in whichever direction you're travelling.

The Drive ❯❯ The descent from Omeo down the B500 to the coast is a really lovely drive. The first 95km twist and turn gently, following narrow river valleys and running alongside rushing rapids for at least part of the way. From Bruthen to Lakes Entrance go via Sarsfield, Lucknow and Swan Reach for the fine ocean views on the final approach.

---

❽ Lakes Entrance

Architecturally, Lakes Entrance is a graceless strip of motels, caravan parks, mini-golf courses and souvenir shops lining the Esplanade. But you're not here for the architecture. Instead it's about the fine vantage points such as **Jemmys Point Lookout** and **Kalimna Lookout**, where the drama of this watery prelude to the vast Tasman Sea becomes apparent. It's also about dining on some of Victoria's freshest seafood, all the while accompanied by a sea breeze. Or it's about cruising the lakes that sit just back from the marvellous Ninety Mile Beach – **Peels Cruises** (🗹03-5155 1246; Post Office Jetty; 2hr cruise adult/child $34/17, 4hr Metung cruise with/without lunch $44/12.50) is a respected operator of long standing. And behind it all, there's the satisfaction and sense of completion that comes from following mountain valleys down to the sea.

🍴 p149

Eating & Sleeping

Beechworth ❶

✗ Provenance   Modern Australian $$$

(☏03-5728 1786; www.theprovenance.com.
au; 86 Ford St; 2/3-course meals $63/80,
degustation menu without/with matching wines
$100/155; ☺6.30pm-late Wed-Sun) In an
1856 bank building, Provenance has elegant
but contemporary fine dining. Under the
guidance of acclaimed local chef Michael Ryan,
the innovative menu features dishes such as
Berkshire pork belly, tea-smoked duck breast
and some inspiring vegetarian choices. If you
can't decide, go for the degustation menu.
Bookings essential.

🛏 Freeman on Ford   B&B $$$

(☏03-5728 2371; www.freemanonford.com.
au; 97 Ford St; s/d incl breakfast from $255/275;
🐾) In the 1876 Oriental Bank, this sumptuous
but homely place offers Victorian luxury in six
beautifully renovated rooms, right in the heart
of town. The owner, Heidi, will make you feel
very special.

Milawa Gourmet Region ❷

✗ Milawa Gourmet
Hotel   Modern Australian $$

(☏03-5727 3208; www.milawagourmethotel.
com.au; cnr Snow & Factory Rds, Milawa;
mains $15-36; ☺noon-2.30pm & 6-8.30pm)
A traditional country pub serving meals with
gourmet flair and an emphasis on local produce.
Try the Milawa chicken stuffed with local
camembert, wrapped in bacon and served with
Milawa mustard.

Bright ❹

✗ Pepperleaf Bushtucker
Restaurant   Modern Australian $$

(☏03-5755 1537; 2a Anderson St; 1/10 tapas
$8/70, mains $18-30; ☺noon-2pm & 6pm-late

Fri-Tue, breakfast weekends) This place doesn't
look fancy but the philosophy and flavours –
using native ingredients such as wattleseed,
quandong, wild limes and lemon myrtle – are
something of a taste revelation. Tapas-style
plates give you an opportunity to sample the
goods. Mains range from salt-and-pepper
crocodile to wallaby and chorizo.

🛏 Odd Frog   Boutique Hotel $$

(☏0418 362 791; www.theoddfrog.com;
3 McFadyens Lane; d $150-195, q $250)
Designed and built by the young architect/
interior-designer owners, these contemporary,
ecofriendly studios feature light, breezy spaces
and fabulous outdoor decks with a telescope
for star gazing. The design features clever
use of the hilly site with sculptural steel-frame
foundations and flying balconies.

Mt Beauty ❺

✗ Å Skafferi   Swedish $$

(☏03-5754 4544; www.svarmisk.com.au; 84
Bogong High Plains Rd, Mt Beauty; mains $12-21;
☺8am-4pm Thu-Mon) This cool Swedish pantry
and foodstore is a fabulous place to stop.
Try the grilled Milawa cheese sandwiches for
breakfast and the Swedish meatballs or the
sampler of herring and knackebrod for lunch. It
sells a range of local and Scandinavian produce,
and has some excellent apartments, too.

Lakes Entrance ❽

✗ Ferryman's Seafood Cafe   Seafood $$

(☏03-5155 3000; www.ferrymans.com.au;
Middle Harbour, Esplanade; lunch mains $18-24,
dinner $21-45; ☺10am-late) It's hard to beat the
ambience of dining on the deck of this floating
cafe-restaurant, which will fill you to the gills
with fish and seafood dishes, including good
ol' fish and chips. The seafood platter is a great
order. It's child friendly and downstairs you
can buy fresh seafood, including prawns and
crayfish (from 8.30am to 5pm).

Murray River Follow the river
past glorious red gums

OLIVER STREWE/GETTY IMAGES ©

Along the Murray

12

This journey shadows one of Australia's most soulful inland waterways, mirroring the Murray River's journey from the densely populated heartland of southeastern Australia to the outback fringe.

TRIP HIGHLIGHTS

460 km

Mildura
Buzzing riverside town with restaurants, vineyards and river activities

FINISH
6

397 km

5
Hattah ●

Hattah-Kulkyne National Park
Rich birdlife and memorable Murray scenery

Ouyen ●

Lake Boga ●

Kerang ●
Cohuna ●
3

88 km

Gunbower National Park
River red gums at every turn

Barmah ●

0 km

1
START

Echuca
The Murray's most evocative old port

5 DAYS
460KM / 286 MILES

GREAT FOR...

BEST TIME TO GO
Spring (Sep-Nov) and autumn (Mar-May) have the mildest weather and clear skies.

 ESSENTIAL PHOTO

A riverboat setting out from Echuca's historic wharf.

 BEST FOR OUTDOORS

Hattah-Kulkyne National Park has stirring Murray River woodland and great birdwatching.

151

12 Along the Murray

The Murray has one of Australia's most evocative inland shores. River red gums, that icon of the Aussie bush, line the riverbank, drawing cockatoos, corellas and cormorants, while some of Victoria's older and more appealing towns – Echuca, Swan Hill and Mildura – watch over the water, harking back in architecture and atmosphere to the days when the Murray was the lifeblood for the river's remote hinterland.

TRIP HIGHLIGHT

❶ Echuca

Echuca is one of the grand old dames of inland Australia. While the modern town sprawls away from the water's edge, historic buildings cluster around the old wharf that climbs several storeys above the water level. Unpaved Murray Esplanade runs along behind the wharf, an appealing movie-set of facades and horse-drawn carriages, and from where access to

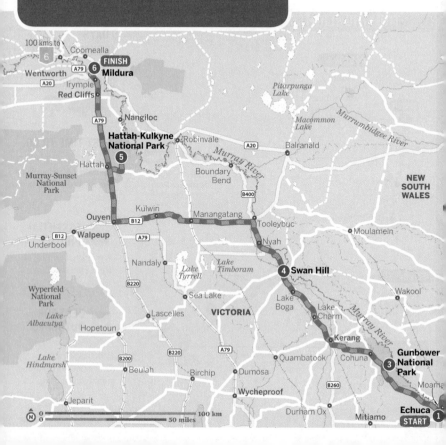

the wharf is via the outstanding Port of Echuca Discovery Centre, a swish new interpretation centre with museum-standard displays and boardwalks that lead you past old machinery and derelict riverboats, not to mention the best river views in town. This is also the place to arrange your excursion aboard one of Echuca's early-20th-century steam-powered riverboats; the PS *Pevensey* is one of the most atmospheric. A block back from the river, along Echuca's attractive

High St, covered verandahs shelter second-hand bookshops, stores selling local wines and cheeses, and fine restaurants.

 p157

The Drive » From Echuca, cross the Murray River, continue north through Moama and out onto the Cobb Hwy, passing through the vast wheat fields of southern NSW. Around 14km north of Moama, take the turn-off (east) for Barmah (14km), reached via another bridge across the Murray. The park entry is about 6km north of the tiny town of Barmah (turn at the pub).

- - - - - - - - - - - -

❷ Barmah National Park

Barmah is one of the prettiest corners of the Murray River floodplain and the largest remaining red gum forest in Australia. It's a place where the swampy understorey usually floods and the sight of these hardy gum trees half submerged in water is an

instantly recognisable emblem of the Australian bush – the red hued trunks, the muted eucalyptus greens, the slow-moving muddy brown of the Murray's waters. The area is also an important breeding area for many species of fish and birds: it's one of few places in Victoria to see the superb parrot. On your way into the park, stop off at the Barmah pub for a park map and head for the Barmah Lakes camping area, which has picnic tables, barbecue areas and tracks (mostly accessible by 2WD) that lead alongside the gums.

The Drive » Return to Echuca (40km) via the Cobb Hwy, then take the Murray Valley Hwy (B400) that shadows the Murray northwest of Echuca – aside from the occasional glimpse, the long line of trees to the north is all you'll see of the river. At Gunbower, 40km from Echuca, turn right (north); the road loops through Gunbower National Park and rejoins the B400 at Cohuna.

LINK YOUR TRIP

6 Outback New South Wales

The New South Wales trip swings south to Mungo National Park before heading north to Broken Hill – either is a few hours' drive from Mildura.

11 Great Alpine Road

Echuca lies 203km northwest of Beechworth, the starting point of this mountains-to-the-sea route – drive via Shepparton, Benalla and Wangaratta.

WAYNE FOGDEN/GETTY IMAGES ©

TRIP HIGHLIGHT

❸ Gunbower National Park

Gunbower Island, formed between the Murray River and Gunbower Creek, is one of the least-known highlights of the Murray traverse. In 2010 Parks Victoria created the 88 sq-km Gunbower National Park (previously a state forest) to protect its beautiful river red gum forests from logging; the result is one of Victoria's most accessible expanses of riverine woodland. Despite this, you may be lucky and have it all to yourself. As well as the glorious red gums, the park is home to abundant animals and birdlife: you might see kangaroos, possums, goannas, turtles and snakes, and more than 200 species of birds have been recorded here. A network of 'river tracks' criss-cross the island and lead to more than a hundred numbered bush-camping spots by the river bank on the Victorian side of the Murray. Some of the roads are dirt and a bit rough, but are passable to conventional vehicles when it's dry – after heavy rain it's 4WD-only. The main Gunbower–Cohuna road through the park is, however, sealed and accessible year-round in a 2WD.

The Drive » From Cohuna, the Murray Valley Hwy leaves the river behind for a time; although minor roads more closely follow the river's path, they rarely get close enough to render the slower journey worthwhile. From Kerang (32km from Cohuna), the B400 bisects vast agricultural fields, and passes turn-offs to the southern hemisphere's largest ibis rookery and Lake Boga en route to Swan Hill (59km from Kerang).

❹ Swan Hill

A classic Aussie provincial centre, Swan Hill possesses little obvious charm on first impressions – its long main street has the usual newsagent, porticoed pub and purveyors of gelato, fish and chips and cheap Asian food. But drop down to the riverbank and you'll find the terrific **Pioneer Settlement** (☏03-5036 2410; www.pioneersettlement. com.au; Monash Dr, Horseshoe Bend; adult/child/family $28/20.50/76.50; ⊙9.30am-4pm), an artful re-creation of a riverside port town from the paddle-steamer era. In the manner of such places, look for restored riverboats and old carriages, an old-time photographic parlour, an Aboriginal keeping place, a lolly shop and a school classroom. Every night at dusk the 45-minute **sound-and-light show** (adult/child/family $22/15/59) takes you on a dramatic

TOP TIP: KINGFISHER CRUISES

If you arrange it in advance and leave Echuca early enough, hook up with **Kingfisher Cruises** (☏03-5855 2855; www.kingfishercruises.com.au; 1hr cruise adult/child/family $32/17/80, 2hr cruise $37/21/100; ⊙10.30am Mon, Wed, Thu, Sat & Sun) in Barmah for a fascinating two-hour cruise. They're a mine of information on local plants and birdlife.

Echuca Steam-powered riverboats on the Murray

journey through the settlement in an open-air transporter. Swan Hill Regional Art Gallery, just across the road, has a fine portfolio of local art. For advice on how to get the most out of Swan Hill's riverside walks, visit the **Swan Hill Region Information Centre** (☏1800 625 373, 03-5032 3033; www. swanhillonline.com; cnr McCrae & Curlewis Sts; ⊗9am-5pm).

✕ 🛏 p157

The Drive ›› Some 46km northwest of Swan Hill, head due west along the Mallee Hwy, a long, lonely stretch of road where the land turns yellow and big horizons evoke the coming outback. After 100km on the Mallee Hwy, at Ouyen, turn north on the Calder Hwy, then follow the signs to the Hattah-Kulkyne National Park from the barely discernible hamlet of Hattah, 35km north of Ouyen.

TRIP HIGHLIGHT

⑤ Hattah-Kulkyne National Park

Northwestern Victoria has numerous big-sky national parks, but Hattah-Kulkyne may be the best of them, and is certainly the most easily reached. The park is classic Murray country and the vegetation here ranges from dry, sandy Mallee scrub to the fertile riverside areas closer to the Murray, which are lined with red gum, black box, wattle and bottlebrush. The Hattah Lakes system fills when the Murray floods, which is great for waterbirds. The many hollow trees here are perfect for nesting, and more than 200 species of birds have been recorded in the area – watch in particular for the rare and really rather beautiful regent parrot or the even rarer Mallee fowl. Even if you're not here to bushwalk or drive off-road, there are two nature drives, the Hattah and the Kulkyne, that are accessible in a

2WD vehicle. **Hattah-Kulkyne National Park Visitor Centre** (☎03-5029 3253) is a terrific place to begin exploring.

The Drive 》 Return to the Calder Hwy and it's 70 uncomplicated kilometres into Mildura. En route, the surrounding landscape turns greener by degrees, as the arid Mallee yields to the fertile floodplains that support vineyards and fruit orchards.

TRIP HIGHLIGHT

❻ Mildura

Sunny, sultry Mildura is something of an oasis amid some really dry country, a modern town with its roots firmly in the grand old pastoralist era. Its other calling cards include art-deco buildings and some of the best dining in provincial Victoria. In town, paddle-steamer cruises depart from historic Mildura Wharf, while the **Old Mildura Homestead** (Cureton Ave; admission by donation; ⊙9am-6pm) evokes the days of prosperous river-borne trade. The hinterland, too, is worth exploring with abundant Murray River activities that include fishing, swimming, canoeing, waterskiing, houseboating, taking a paddle-steamer cruise or playing on riverside golf courses. Mildura also just happens to be one of Australia's most prolific wine-producing areas: pick up a copy of the *Mildura Wines* brochure from the **visitor information centre** (☎1800 039 043, 03-5018 8380; www. visitmildura.com.au; cnr Deakin Ave & 12th St; ⊙9am-5.30pm Mon-Fri, to 5pm Sat & Sun) or visit www.mildurawines. com.au. If you can't make it out to the wineries themselves, the in-town **Sunraysia Cellar Door** (☎03-5021 0794; www. sunraysiacellardoor.com.au; 125 Lime Ave; ⊙9am-5pm Mon-Fri, 11am-5pm Sat & Sun) has tastings and sales for around 250 local wines from 22 different wineries, as well as a local craft beers.

✕ ⋐ p157

Eating & Sleeping

Echuca ❶

✖ Shebani's   Mediterranean $$

(☎03-5480 7075; 535 High St; mains $12-22; ☺8am-4pm) This wonderful addition to Echuca's eating scene is like taking a culinary tour of the Mediterranean – Greek, Lebanese, even North African all get a run with subtle flavours. The decor effortlessly brings together Mediterranean tilework, Moroccan lamps and a fresh Aussie cafe style.

🛏 Steampacket B&B   B&B $$

(☎03-5482 3411; www.steampacketinn.com. au; cnr Murray Esplanade & Leslie St; d $135-200; ❄) Staying in the old port area is all part of the Echuca experience. This 19th-century National Trust–classified B&B offers genteel rooms with all the old-fashioned charm, linen and lace, and brass bedstead you could want (but with air-con and flat-screen TVs, too). Ask for the large corner rooms for a view of the wharf. The lounge room is cosy and breakfast is served on fine china.

Swan Hill ❹

✖ Spoons Riverside Café   Modern Australian $$

(☎03-5032 2601; www.spoonsriverside.com. au; 125 Monash Dr, Horseshoe Bend; lunch mains $9.50-25, dinner $26-35; ☺8am-5pm Sun-Wed, to 11pm Thu-Sat) The riverside location alone is enough to lure you to this licensed cafe, which offers a big timber deck overlooking the Marraboor River and Pioneer Settlement. As well as light lunches and innovative dinners (in which fresh local ingredients take centre stage), there's a provedore deli selling fresh produce and gourmet hampers.

🛏 Travellers Rest Motor Inn   Motel $$

(☎03-5032 9644; www.bestwestern.com. au/travellersrest; 110 Curlewis St; d from $133; ❄🔊📶) Sitting in the shade of the Burke & Wills Tree, rooms here are spacious and comfortable with the usual motel accompaniments. There's a heated spa and outdoor pool.

Mildura ❻

✖ Jim McDougall in Stefano's Cellar   Italian $$$

(☎03-5023 0511; www.jimmcdougall.com. au; Quality Hotel Mildura Grand, Seventh St; 2/3-course lunch set menu $55/62, dinner set menu $130-175; ☺7-11pm Tue-Thu, noon-3pm & 7-11pm Fri & Sat) Stefano de Pieri may no longer run the kitchen but his protege, Jim McDougall is a fine heir to the Stefano throne. The food has broadened out beyond Stefano's Italian roots to a fresh, contemporary menu that sources most of its produce locally. The menu changes with the seasons, but expect kangaroo, yabbies, Murray cod and local fruits to feature.

🛏 Indulge Apartments   Apartment $$

(☎1300 539 559, 03-5018 4900; www. indulgeapartments.com.au; 150 Langtree Ave; studio $149, 1/2-bedroom apt $175/265; ❄) These stunning contemporary apartments in the centre of town could be Mildura's best, with polished floors, plenty of floor space and excellent facilities. They've a couple of other locations around town if the Langtree Avenue property is full.

🛏 Acacia Houseboats   Houseboat $$

(☎1800 085 500, 03-5022 1510; www. murrayriver.com.au/acacia-houseboats-949/ fleet; 3 nights $525-1800) Has five houseboats, ranging from four to 12 berths, with everything supplied except food and drink.

Queensland Trips

DISTANCES MAY BE GREAT UP HERE IN THE NORTHERN STATE OF QUEENSLAND, but the attractions are suitably big as well. For a start, the Great Barrier Reef is a constant presence along this splendid coast, surrounding idyllic archipelagos such as the Whitsundays, and is ideal for exploration, especially from Cairns to the Cape. Then there's the Daintree, a World Heritage–listed expanse of rainforest that carpets the interior and shadows pristine white-sand beaches. There are the crocs that lurk in northern rivers. And the rock art and remote roadhouses that inhabit the interior. And yet, when all's said and done, Queensland knows how to have a good time, and the southeastern coast has perfected the art of doing just that – and making sure the whole world knows about it.

Whitsunday Islands Whitehaven Beach (Trip 13)
ANDREW WATSON/GETTY IMAGES ©

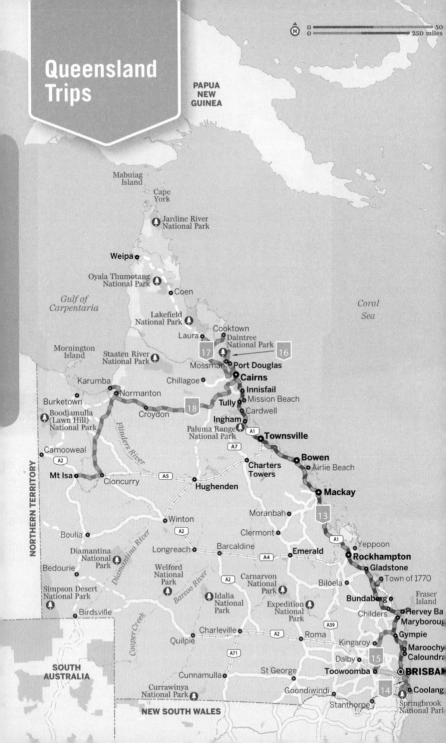

Queensland Rainbow lorikeet

13 **Capricorn Coast 10–14 Days**
This brilliant road trip connects the clamorous south with the reef-fringed north. (p163)

14 **Southern Queensland Loop 7 Days**
Busy beach resorts can't drown out wildlife sanctuaries and hinterland rainforests. (p175)

15 **Brisbane's Hinterland 3–4 Days**
The big city's alter ego includes Noosa, hippie markets and a terrific zoo. (p183)

16 **Cairns & the Daintree 7 Days**
Rainforests, reef, crocodiles and long, empty beaches are northern Queensland specialities. (p191)

17 **Cape York Prelude 5–7 Days**
Far North Queensland is Indigenous rock art and isolated settlements country. (p199)

18 **Outback Queensland 7–10 Days**
This road trip begins by the reef and ends up deep in the outback. (p207)

DON'T MISS

Whitehaven Beach
Kick off your shoes and walk along one of Australia's most beautiful beaches on Trip 13

Nerang–Murwillumbah Road
Drive one of Australia's best-kept secrets with gorges, rainforests and more on Trip 14

Spirit House
Book a meal at this otherworldly slice of Thailand on Trip 15

Kuku-Yalanji Dreamtime Walks
Explore Indigenous country with a local Aboriginal guide at Mossman Gorge on Trip 16

Split Rock Gallery
Surround yourself with rock art and profound silence at Quinkan on Trip 17

Fraser Island *Unspoilt natural beauty and abundant wildlife*

Classic Trip

Capricorn Coast

13

From Brisbane in southern Queensland to deep beyond the Tropic of Capricorn, this drive takes you within sight of some of the most magnificent coastal stretches on the planet.

TRIP HIGHLIGHTS

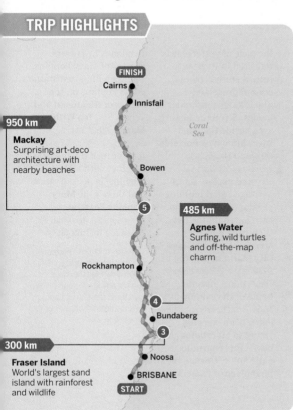

FINISH
Cairns
Innisfail

Coral Sea

950 km

Mackay
Surprising art-deco architecture with nearby beaches

Bowen

5

485 km

Agnes Water
Surfing, wild turtles and off-the-map charm

Rockhampton

4

Bundaberg

3

300 km

Fraser Island
World's largest sand island with rainforest and wildlife

Noosa

BRISBANE
START

10–14 DAYS
1680KM / 1044 MILES

GREAT FOR...

BEST TIME TO GO

April to September; the further north you go, the wetter it gets, especially from mid-December.

ESSENTIAL PHOTO

Whitehaven Beach, one of the most beautiful stretches of sand.

BEST FOR OUTDOORS

Snorkel the reef in all its technicolour glory.

163

Classic Trip

13 Capricorn Coast

Queensland's coastline is where so many happy legends of Australia's tropical paradise began. A string of islands – Great Keppel, Fraser, the Whitsundays – inhabit the 2000km-long Great Barrier Reef, one of the greatest natural wonders on earth, while the beaches here are long, white and fringed with forests. Rugged national parks and engaging seaside towns on both sides of the Tropic of Capricorn round out an unforgettable picture.

❶ Brisbane

Brisbane is a vibrant, artsy city, but for our purposes here, it's merely the beginning of a really long journey. If you have time to explore on foot before you set out, turn to p172.

The Drive ›› Take the A1 north of Brisbane, ignore the siren call of resorts from Moroochydore to Noosa, and you'll be in Maryborough in no time at all.

❷ Maryborough

You may be headed along an extraordinary coast, but it's well worth pulling into Maryborough, one of Queensland's oldest towns. Heritage and history are Maryborough's specialities; the pace of yesteryear is reflected in its beautifully restored colonial-era buildings and gracious Queenslander homes. Stroll the historic area beside the Mary River known as **Portside** (101 Wharf St; ⏱10am-4pm Mon-Fri, to 1pm Sat & Sun) and explore its 13 heritage-listed buildings, parkland and museum. On Thursdays the town is enlivened by the **Maryborough Heritage City Markets** (cnr Adelaide & Ellena Sts; ⏱8am-1.30pm Thu) – don't miss the firing of the cannon at 1pm. But there's another entirely unexpected string to Maryborough's bow – this charming old country town is the birthplace of Pamela Lyndon (PL) Travers, creator of Mary Poppins. There's a life-sized statue of Ms Poppins on the corner of Richmond and Wharf Sts, **Tea With Mary** (☎1800 214 789; per person $20; ⏱Thu & Fri) offers tours of the historic precinct with a Mary Poppins–bedecked guide, and there's the **Mary Poppins Festival** (www.marypoppinsfestival.com.au; ⏱Jun-Jul) in June/July.

The Drive ›› Drive northeast of Maryborough. After around 30km, you'll see the ocean straight ahead, whereupon the road turns sharply right and runs the final few kilometres into Hervey Bay.

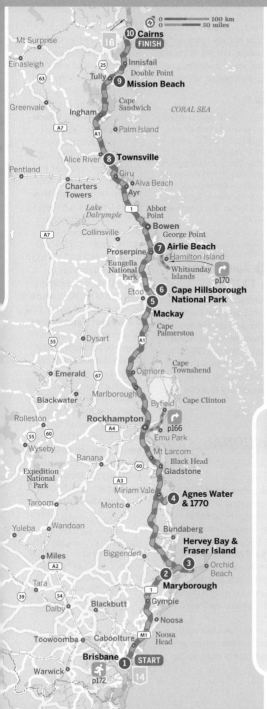

Map Legend

0	100 km
0	50 miles

Mt Surprise

Einasleigh

10 Cairns **FINISH**

Innisfail

Tully — Double Point

9 Mission Beach

Greenvale

Ingham — Cape Sandwich

CORAL SEA

Palm Island

Alice River — **8 Townsville**

Pentland — Giru

Charters Towers — Alva Beach

Ayr

Lake Dalrymple — Abbot Point

Collinsville — **Bowen**

George Point

Proserpine — **7 Airlie Beach**

Eungella National Park — Hamilton Island

Whitsunday Islands — p170

Eton — **6 Cape Hillsborough National Park**

5 Mackay

Cape Palmerston

Dysart

Cape Townshend

Emerald — Ogmore

Marlborough

Blackwater — Byfield — Cape Clinton

Rolleston — **Rockhampton** — p166

Wyseby — Emu Park

Banana — Mt Larcom

Expedition National Park — Black Head — **Gladstone**

Taroom — Miriam Vale

Monto — **4 Agnes Water & 1770**

Yuleba — Wandoan

Bundaberg

Miles — **Hervey Bay & Fraser Island**

Biggenden — **3**

Tara — Orchid Beach

2 Maryborough

Dalby — Blackbutt — Gympie

Toowoomba — Caboolture — Noosa

Noosa Head

Brisbane 1 START — p172

Warwick

TRIP HIGHLIGHT

3 Hervey Bay & Fraser Island

Hervey Bay would be worth a visit for its own sake thanks to its warm subtropical climate, long sandy beaches and calm blue ocean. But when you throw in the chance to see majestic humpback whales frolicking in the water and the town's convenient access to the World Heritage–listed Fraser Island, it changes the equation altogether. Whales pass by here from late July to early November, with sightings almost guaranteed from August to October. **MV Tasman Venture** (☑1800 620 322; www.tasmanventure. com.au; Urangan Harbour; ☺8.30am & 1.30pm),

QUEENSLAND **13** CAPRICORN COAST

LINK YOUR TRIP

14 Southern Queensland Loop

Like the Capricorn Coast, Trip 14 begins in Brisbane and is probably best driven before setting out on the long drive north.

16 Cairns & the Daintree

When you reach Cairns, this much-shorter add-on (195km) gets you out onto the reef and deep into the rainforest.

Classic Trip

famous dingo, while offshore waters teem with dugong, dolphins, manta rays, sharks and migrating humpback whales.

🛏 p171

The Drive » Head southwest then west and join the Bruce Hwy. Pass through Childers, and, unless you're a fan of Bundy rum, ignore the signs to Bundaberg. At Miriam Vale, turn east off the Bruce Hwy, from where it's 57km to Agnes Water and a further 6km to the Town of 1770.

TRIP HIGHLIGHT

❹ Agnes Water & 1770

Surrounded by national parks and the Pacific Ocean, the twin coastal towns of Agnes Water and Town of 1770 (which marks Captain Cook's first landing in the state) are among Queens-

Freedom Whale Watch (☎1300 879 960; www. freedomwhalewatch.com. au) and **Blue Dolphin Marine Tours** (☎07-4124 9600; www.bluedolphintours. com.au; Urangan Harbour) can all take you out in season, while the **Hervey Bay Whale Festival** (www. herveybaywhalefestival.com. au; ◷Aug) celebrates the return of the whales in August.

Fraser Island is the largest sand island in the world (measuring 120km by 15km), and the only known place where rainforest grows on sand. The island is home to a profusion of birdlife and wildlife, including the

land's loveliest. Tiny Agnes Water has the east coast's most northerly surf beach, and you can learn to surf on the gentle breaks of the main beach with the highly acclaimed **Reef 2 Beach Surf School** (☎07-4974 9072; www.reef2beachsurf. com; Agnes Water Shopping Centre, Agnes Water). If you hear the call of the reef, family-owned **Lady Musgrave Cruises** (☎07-4974 9077; www.1770reefcruises. com; Captain Cook Dr, Town of 1770; adult/child $190/90; ◷departs daily 8.30am) has excellent day trips to Lady Musgrave Island. Back on land, 8km south of Agnes Water you'll find **Deepwater National Park** (www.nprsr.qld.gov.au/parks/ deepwater), an unspoiled coastal landscape with long sandy beaches, walking trails, freshwater creeks and good fishing spots. It's also a major breeding ground for loggerhead turtles, which lay eggs on the beaches between November and February; hatchlings emerge at night between January and April.

The Drive » Northwest of Gladstone, just south of Rockhampton, you'll cross into the tropics by passing the Tropic of Capricorn – it's an obligatory photo stop, marked by a huge spire. Mackay is 334km northwest of Rockhampton, with the best sea views along a 20km stretch north of Clairview.

DETOUR:
BYFIELD NATIONAL PARK

Start: ❹ Agnes Water

When people driving this stretch of coast start seeing signs to Yeppoon, most start dreaming of Great Keppel Island, 13km offshore. While the island's charms are well known, we recommend taking the road north from Yeppoon, through Byfield to the staggeringly beautiful **Byfield National Park**, a diverse playground of mammoth sand dunes, thick semitropical rainforest, wetlands and rocky pinnacles. It's superb Sunday-arvo driving terrain, with enough hiking paths and isolated beaches to warrant a longer stay.

To get here, take the Yeppoon turn-off just north of Rockhampton. From Yeppoon (which was hit by a huge cyclone in 2015) Byfield town is 38km to the north.

⑤ Mackay

Attractive tropical streets, art-deco buildings, winding mangroves and welcoming populace aside, Mackay doesn't quite make the tourist hit list, which is precisely why we like it. It's a refreshing stop if you've been to one too many resort towns. Mackay's impressive art-deco architecture across the CBD owes much to a devastating cyclone in 1918, which flattened many of the town's buildings – most of the facades are at their finest on the 2nd storey. Noteworthy examples include the **Mackay Townhouse Motel**, the **Australian Hotel** and the **Ambassador Hotel**. If these have piqued your curiosity, pick up a copy of *Art Deco in Mackay* from the Mackay Visitor Centre. The redeveloped marina entices with al fresco restaurants and outdoor cafes along its picturesque promenade, and there are plenty of beaches, the best of which are 16km north of town: **Bucasia** is the most undeveloped and arguably the prettiest.

✕ ⊨ p171

The Drive » Cape Hillsborough National Park lies 50km north of Mackay, and is well signposted off the main highway.

⑥ Cape Hillsborough National Park

Despite being so easy to get to, this small coastal park feels like it's at the end of the earth. Ruggedly beautiful, it takes in the rocky, 300m-high Cape Hillsborough and Andrews Point and Wedge Island, which are joined by a causeway at low tide. The park features rough cliffs, a broad beach, rocky headlands, sand dunes, mangroves, hoop pines and rainforest. Kangaroos, wallabies, sugar gliders and turtles are common, and the roos are likely to be seen on the beach in the evening and early morning. There are also the remains of Aboriginal middens and stone fish traps, accessible by good walking tracks. On the approach to the foreshore area there's also an interesting boardwalk leading out through a tidal mangrove forest.

⊨ p171

The Drive » Return to the Bruce Hwy, which tracks relentlessly northwest. At Proserpine, take the Airlie Beach turn-off – Airlie is 34km off the highway with good Whitsunday views for much of the second half of the approach.

⑦ Airlie Beach

Unless you're a backpacker intent on tapping the party scene, Airlie Beach has little to recommend it, but there's one very important reason to come here – this is the jump-off point for the dreamy Whitsunday Islands. The Port of Airlie, from where the Cruise Whitsundays ferries depart and where many of the cruising yachts are moored, is about 750m east of the town centre along a pleasant boardwalk. Many other vessels leave from Abel Point Marina (1km west) or Shute Harbour (about 12km east); most cruise companies run courtesy buses into town.

⊨ p171

The Drive » Return to Proserpine, from where it's 65km to Bowen, a typical, old-style, small Queensland coastal town with wide streets, low-rise buildings and wooden Queenslander houses. From Bowen to Townsville it's 202km, via Ayr and the delta of the mighty Burdekin River, with rich sugar cane fields all around.

⑧ Townsville

Sprawling between a brooding red hill and a sparkling blue sea, Townsville is a tidy and relatively modern-feeling spot with a lot to offer: excellent museums, a huge aquarium, world-class diving, vibrant nightlife and an endless esplanade. It's a pedestrian-friendly city, and its grand, refurbished 19th-century buildings offer loads of landmarks. Townsville

SUSAN TRIGG/GETTY IMAGES ©

Classic Trip

ANDREW WATSON/GETTY IMAGES ©

WHY THIS IS A CLASSIC TRIP
ANTHONY HAM, AUTHOR

What could be more suited to a classic road trip than a highway that stays within sight of the Great Barrier Reef, Australia's top natural attraction, for almost 2000km? It's a drive that connects two worlds – the subtropical south with the steamy tropics of the Far North. It's the elemental combinations of land and sea, and the world famous and the little known, that most defines this wonderful, wonderful journey.

Top: Tropical resort, Whitsunday Islands
Left: Four-wheel drives on a beach, Fraser Island
Right: Dense tropical rainforest, Fraser Island

ANDREW WATSON/GETTY IMAGES ©

also has a lively, young populace, with thousands of students and members of the armed forces intermingling with old-school locals, fly-in-fly-out mine workers, and summer-seekers lapping up the average 320 days of sunshine per year. The **Reef HQ Aquarium** (www.reefhq. com.au; Flinders St E; adult/ child $28/14; ⏰9.30am-5pm) has 130 coral and 120 fish species, while kids will love seeing, feeding and touching turtles at the turtle hospital. Also of interest, the **Australian Institute of Marine Science** (AIMS; ☏07-4753 4444; www. aims.gov.au) runs free two-hour tours covering the institute's research (such as coral bleaching and management of the Great Barrier Reef) and how it relates to the community. In August, don't miss the internationally renowned **Australian Festival of Chamber Music** (www. afcm.com.au).

✕ ⛺ p171

The Drive » For all but a small stretch between Mutarnee and just after Ingham, the road hugs the coastline here and you'll want to pull over often to take in the view, or take a small side road leading down to the beach.

----

⑨ Mission Beach

Less than 30km east of the Bruce Hwy's rolling sugar-cane and banana plantations, the hamlets that make up greater Mission Beach are hidden

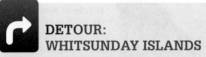

Classic Trip

among World Heritage rainforest. The rainforest extends right to the Coral Sea, giving this 14km-long palm-fringed stretch of secluded inlets and wide, empty beaches the castaway feel of a tropical island. Collectively referred to as Mission Beach, or just 'Mission', the area comprises a sequence of individual, very small and laid-back villages strung along the coast. **Bingil Bay** lies 4.8km north of **Mission Beach** proper (sometimes called North Mission). **Wongaling Beach** is 5km south; from here it's a further 5.5km south to **South Mission Beach**. While Mission's coastline seems to scream 'toe dip!', don't just fling yourself into the water any old where: stick to the swimming enclosures, lest you have a nasty encounter with a marine stinger...or croc. Walking tracks fan out around Mission Beach, with Australia's highest density of cassowaries (around 40) roaming the rainforest. Warning: the frightfully powerful Cyclone Yasi made landfall at Mission Beach in 2011, stripping much of the rainforest and vegetation bare, and the communities here are still recovering, making your visit all the more important.

The Drive >> The road north from Mission Beach rejoins the Bruce Hwy at El Arish, from where you can take the direct route north by continuing straight along the Bruce Hwy. Turn-offs lead to beach communities including exquisite Etty Bay, with its wandering cassowaries, rocky headlands and rainforest. Once you pass Innisfail, it's 102km to Cairns.

DETOUR: WHITSUNDAY ISLANDS

Start: ❼ Airlie Beach

Paradise may be an overused cliche, but here it might just be true. **Whitehaven Beach**, on Whitsunday Island, is a pristine 7km-long stretch of blinding sand (at 98% pure silica, said sand is some of the whitest in the world), bounded by lush tropical vegetation and a brilliant blue sea. From Hill Inlet at the northern end of the beach, the swirling pattern of dazzling sand through the turquoise and aquamarine water paints a magical picture. There's excellent snorkelling from its southern end. In other words, Whitehaven is up there in the elite of Australia's most beautiful beaches.

There are numerous ways to see the Whitsundays. Take a scenic helicopter flight with **HeliReef** (☏07-4946 9102; www.helireef.com.au), a scenic-flight-and-snorkel excursion with **Air Whitsunday** (☏07-4946 9111; www.airwhitsunday.com.au; Terminal 1, Whitsunday Airport), or sail the islands with **Illusions** (☏0455 142 021; www.illusion.net.au; day tours $125), a 12m catamaran that offers the least expensive, yet consistently good, sailing tours to the islands. As well as operating a ferry to the Whitsunday Islands, **Cruise Whitsundays** (☏07-4946 4662; www.cruisewhitsundays. com) offers trips to Hardy Reef, Whitehaven Beach and islands including Daydream and Long. Or grab a daily Island Hopper pass (adult/child $120/59) and make your own itinerary.

❿ Cairns

You've made it, and while Cairns is hardly the loveliest of the larger coastal towns, it does have all the choice that comes with arriving in a big city, from restaurants across a range of cuisines to a busy airport for onward connections. Cairns is also the starting point for at least three other really impressive road trips...

Eating & Sleeping

Hervey Bay ❸

🛏 Colonial Lodge   Hotel $

(📞07-4125 1073; www.herveybaycoloniallodge.
com.au; 94 Cypress St, Torquay; r $90-140;
❄🛜🏊) Hacienda-style, immaculate and
wonderfully friendly, these self-contained one-
and two-bedroom units are a steal. Hang out by
the pool or walk a block to the beach.

Mackay ❺

🍴 Burp Eat Drink   Modern Australian $$$

(📞07-4951 3546; www.burp.net.au; 86 Wood
St; mains from $33; 🕙11.30am-3pm & 6pm-late
Tue-Fri, 6pm-late Sat) A swish Melbourne-style
restaurant in the tropics, Burp has a small but
tantalising menu. Sophisticated selections
include pork belly with scallops, Kaffir-lime-
crusted soft shell crab, plus some serious
steaks.

🛏 Ocean Resort Village   Resort $$

(📞1800 075 144; www.oceanresortvillage.com.
au; 5 Bridge Rd; studio/family unit/2-bedroom
unit from $90/100/135; ❄🏊) This is a
good-value beachside resort set amid tropical
gardens. The cool, shady setting has two
pools, barbecue areas, half-court tennis and
the occasional possum drop-in. The village is
located 4km southeast of the town centre (take
Gordon to Goldsmith to Bridge).

Cape Hillsborough National Park ❻

🛏 Cape Hillsborough Nature Resort   Caravan Park $

(📞07-4959 0152; www.capehillsboroughresort.
com.au; 51 Risley Pde; unpowered/powered site

$29/34, fishing huts $65-75, cabins $65-135;
❄@🏊) This quiet spot sits on a long stretch
of beach. There's nothing fancy about the
joint, but once you see kangaroos on their
magical morning beach hops, things like shiny
surrounds somehow matter less.

Airlie Beach ❼

🛏 The Summit   Apartment $$

(📞1800 463 417; www.summitairliebeach.com.
au; 15 Flame Tree Court; 1-/2-bedroom apt from
$160/190; 🅿❄🛜🏊) Nestled high above
Airlie Beach are these exceptional apartments
with some of the best views of the Whitsundays
and hinterland. The fittings and furnishings are
equally top notch and the shaded recreation
area by the pool has free wifi and a spectacular
outlook. Management are brilliant.

Townsville ❽

🍴 Longboard Bar & Grill   Modern Australian $$

(📞07-4724 1234; The Strand, opposite Gregory
St; mains $15-37; 🕙11.30am-3pm & 5.30pm-
late) This waterfront eatery plies a lively crowd
with grill-house favourites such as sticky
barbecue pork ribs, steaks and buffalo wings.
Ignore the incongruous surf theme and be sure
to pack a bib.

🛏 Aquarius on the Beach   Hotel $$

(📞1800 622 474; www.aquariusonthebeach.com.
au; 75 The Strand; d $117-270; ❄@🛜🏊) The
spectacular balcony views impress almost as
much as the size of this place, the tallest building
on the Strand. Don't be put off by the dated
facade – this is one of the better places around,
and the service is faultless.

STRETCH YOUR LEGS
BRISBANE

Start/Finish:
South Bank Parklands

Distance: 5km

Duration: 3 hours

Brisbane is a terrific city to explore on foot (keep an eye on the weather, though – when it rains, it *really* rains), and so much of what's good about the city is found along the river that cuts through its heart.

Take this walk on Trips

South Bank Parklands

The beautiful green strip of **South Bank Parklands** (www.visitsouthbank.com. au; Grey St) is the perfect confluence of lovely open spaces and a city that knows how to enjoy them. Here you'll find performance spaces, sculptures, buskers, eateries, bars, pockets of rainforest, barbecue areas, bougainvillea-draped pergolas and hidden lawns. The big-ticket attractions here are Streets Beach and the London Eye–style Wheel of Brisbane.

The Walk >> Stroll through the parklands heading north, meandering as the mood takes you. After crossing Melbourne St, the Queensland Art Gallery is straight ahead.

Queensland Art Gallery

Duck into the **Queensland Art Gallery** (www.qagoma.qld.gov.au; Melbourne St; ◷10am-5pm) to see the fine permanent collection, with works by celebrated masters, including Sir Sydney Nolan, Arthur Boyd, William Dobell and George Lambert. Next door, the Queensland Museum has some fascinating historical exhibits and even a whale soundtrack. The attached **Sciencentre** has over 100 hands-on, interactive exhibits that delve into life science and technology.

The Walk >> Due north of the museum precinct, the Gallery of Modern Art is best reached from Stanley Pl, which runs off Grey St.

Gallery of Modern Art

All angular glass, concrete and black metal, the must-see **Gallery of Modern Art** (GOMA; www.qagoma.qld.gov.au; Stanley Pl; ◷10am-5pm) focuses on Australian art from the 1970s to today. Continually changing and often confronting, exhibits range from painting, sculpture and photography to video, installation and film. There's also an arty bookshop, kids' activity rooms, a cafe and free guided tours at 11am, 1pm and 2pm. Brilliant!

The Walk >> Spiky and striking Kurilpa Bridge crosses the Brisbane River and empties its foot

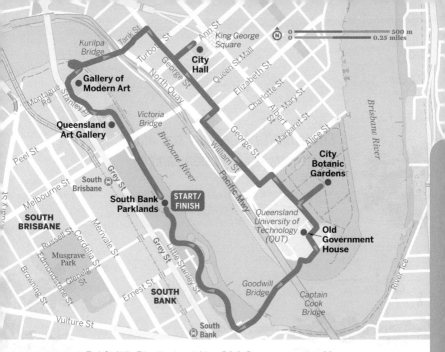

passengers onto Tank St. At the T-junction, turn right (south) along George St, then second left (east) on Ann St. City Hall is around 150m along on your right.

City Hall

Overlooking King George Sq, **City Hall** is a fine 1930s sandstone edifice fronted by a row of sequoia-sized Corinthian column. Its interior boasts vaulted ceilings, lavishly tiled lobbies and art-deco light fittings – the domed auditorium itself is truly magnificent (the Rolling Stones played their first-ever Australian gig here in 1965). It has an 85m-high clock tower with a fabulous lookout. Also here is the excellent **Museum of Brisbane** (☎07-3339 0800; www. museumofbrisbane.com.au; Level 3, Brisbane City Hall, King George Sq; ☺10am-5pm).

The Walk ≫ Return to George St, and walk past the stunning Treasury Building. Turn onto Elizabeth St, then William St, then Alice St and take the first right, past gorgeous Parliament House. Old Government House is around 500m further, on your right.

Old Government House

Built in 1862, **Old Government House** (☎07-3138 8005; www.ogh.qut.edu.au; 2 George St; ☺10am-4pm Sun-Fri) is a gem of a building, designed by estimable government architect Charles Tiffin as an appropriately plush residence for Sir George Bowen, Queensland's first governor.

The Walk ≫ You're almost surrounded to the east and south by the City Botanic Gardens. Take your pick of where to enter.

City Botanic Gardens

Brisbane's favourite green space descends gently from the Queensland University of Technology campus to the river: a mass of lawns, tangled Moreton Bay figs, bunya pines, macadamia trees and t'ai chi troupes.

The Walk ≫ To reach your car from the gardens, head west to the river, cross Goodwill Bridge and walk north through the South Bank Parklands.

Coolangatta *Legendary surf and wide stretches of golden sand*

PHOTO BY KARL LUNDHOLM/GETTY IMAGES ©

Southern Queensland Loop

14

The southern Queensland coast is one long beach playground, with two of the state's finest rainforest national parks not far away.

TRIP HIGHLIGHTS

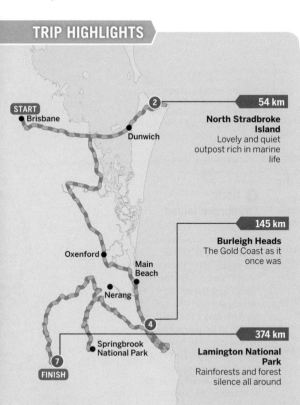

54 km
North Stradbroke Island
Lovely and quiet outpost rich in marine life

145 km
Burleigh Heads
The Gold Coast as it once was

374 km
Lamington National Park
Rainforests and forest silence all around

7 DAYS
374KM / 232 MILES

GREAT FOR...

BEST TIME TO GO
Year-round, although April to October is best; avoid the November schoolie season.

 ESSENTIAL PHOTO
Take a selfie with a rainbow lorikeet at Currumbin Wildlife Sanctuary.

 BEST FOR FAMILIES
Movie World is the pick of the many kid-friendly theme parks in the area.

175

14 Southern Queensland Loop

Brisbane to Lamington National Park is a fabulous journey and you'll quickly discover that there's more to southern Queensland than strangely appealing Surfers Paradise and its theme parks. The two Stradbroke islands and Burleigh Heads serve as reminders of why this coast is so coveted, while Springbrook and Lamington National Parks are worlds away with gorgeous, world-famous rainforests.

❶ Brisbane

Brisbane's charms are evident: the arts, the cafes, the bars, the weather, the old Queenslander houses, the go-get-'em attitude. But perhaps it's the Brisbane River itself that gives the city its edge. The river's organic convolutions carve the city into a patchwork of urban villages, each with a distinct style and topography: bohemian, low-lying West End; hip, hilltop Paddington; exclusive, peninsular New Farm; prim, pointy Kangaroo Point. To explore Brisbane on foot, see p172.

The Drive » Drive out through Brisbane's eastern suburbs, following the signs all the way to Cleveland. From Cleveland, the vehicle ferry sets out for an easy 30-minute chug across to North Stradbroke Island.

TRIP HIGHLIGHT

❷ North Stradbroke Island

This unpretentious holiday isle is the second-largest sand island in the world (after Fraser Island) and is a little like Noosa and Byron Bay rolled into one – imagine how lucky the good people of Brisbane are to have the best of both on their doorstep! There's a string of glorious powdery white beaches, great surf and some quality

places to stay and eat. It's also a hot-spot for spying dolphins, turtles, manta rays and, between June and November, hundreds of humpback whales. **Naree Budjong Djara National Park** (www.nprsr.qld.gov.au/parks/naree-budjong-djara) is the island's heartland, home to the glittering Blue Lake. Keep an eye out for forest birds, skittish lizards and swamp wallabies, and there's a wooden viewing platform at the lake, encircled by a forest of paperbarks, eucalyptuses and banksias. You can cool off in the water, if you don't mind the spooky unseen depths.

✕ p181

The Drive » You'll need to take the ferry back to Cleveland, then wind your way inland, and as long as you're heading west, you'll hit the M1 motorway to whisk you on your way south.

LINK YOUR TRIP

13 Capricorn Coast

This route along the length of the Queensland coast to Cairns (1680km) also begins in Brisbane.

15 Brisbane's Hinterland

Another road trip that begins in Brisbane: this 471km trip loops north, west then south as far as Toowoomba.

Just after Coomera, take Rte 4 to the east and loop up and around to Southport. At Main Beach, it's a short drive south to Surfers.

- - - - - - - - - -

❸ Surfers Paradise

Surfers Paradise. Its reputation precedes it, in the manner of overdeveloped beach resorts the world over – think Benidorm fused with Miami grafted onto the Aussie coast with a whole lot of tack thrown in for good measure. Some say the surfers prefer beaches elsewhere and that paradise has been tragically lost. And this wild and trashy party zone attracts a phenomenal number of visitors – 20,000 per day! And yet, and yet...the reason that

Surfers became famous is that its beach is one long line of damned impressive sand and surf, and for all its tarnished glitz, Surfers is a sexy place: lots of shirtless, tattooed backpackers and more cleavage than the Grand Canyon. And just to prove that there's something for everyone, Surfers is popular with families as well: there must be more amusement and theme parks in this corner of Queensland than almost anywhere else on earth. **Dreamworld** (📞1800 073 300, 07-5588 1111; www.dreamworld. com.au; Dreamworld Pkwy, Coomera; adult/child $95/75; ☺10am-5pm), in Coomera, touts itself as Australia's 'biggest' theme park

with thrill rides, Wiggles World and a range of interactive animal encounters. Also in Coomera, **WhiteWater World** (📞1800 073 300, 07-5588 1111; www.whitewaterworld. com.au; Dreamworld Pkwy, Coomera; adult/child $60/40; ☺10am-4pm Mon-Fri, to 5pm Sat & Sun) has more than 140 water activities and slides. In Oxenford, there's **Movie World** (📞07-5573 3999, 13 33 86; www.movieworld.com.au; Pacific Hwy, Oxenford; adult/child $83/50; ☺9.30am-5pm), with movie-themed shows, rides and life-sized cartoon characters wandering the grounds.

The Drive ❯❯ The high-rise hinterland of Surfers Paradise slowly spaces out on the short hop south along the Gold Coast Hwy to Burleigh Heads, with Currumbin barely separated from it a little further south.

- - - - - - - - -

DETOUR: SOUTH STRADBROKE ISLAND

Start: ❸ Surfers Paradise

North and South Stradbroke Islands used to be one single island, but a savage storm blew away the sand spit between the two in 1896. The result of being cast adrift is that this narrow, 21km-long sand island is largely undeveloped – the perfect antidote to the overdevelopment that blights so much of the Southern Queensland coast. At the northern end, the narrow channel separating it from North Stradbroke Island is a top fishing spot; at the southern end, the Spit is only 200m away. There's the luxury **Ramada Couran Cove Island Resort** (📞07-5597 9999; www. courancove.com.au; South Stradbroke Island; d/ste from $350/450; ❋❅) here, plus three campgrounds, lots of wallabies and plenty of bush, sand and sea. And no cars! That being the case, to get there, you'll need to rent a boat, take a water taxi or join an excursion from Main Beach or Surfers Paradise.

TRIP HIGHLIGHT

❹ Burleigh Heads & Currumbin

With its cheery cafes and beachfront restaurants, famous right-hand point break and beautiful beach, chilled-out surfie town Burleigh charms everyone – this must have been what Surfers looked like back before it went all bright lights and tall towers. A walk around the headland through **Burleigh Head National Park** (www.nprsr.qld.gov.au/ parks/burleigh-head; Goodwin Tce, Burleigh Heads; ☺24hr) is a must for any visitor –

TIM HESTER PHOTOGRAPHY/GETTY IMAGES ©

Stradbroke Island Beaches and surf

it's a 27-hectare rainforest reserve with plenty of bird life, and several walking trails with fine views of the surf en route. If wildlife is your thing, **David Fleay Wildlife Park** (☎07-5576 2411; www.nprsr. qld.gov.au/parks/david-fleay; cnr Loman La & West Burleigh Rd, West Burleigh; adult/child/ family $20.10/9.25/51.30; ☺9am-5pm), 3km inland from Burleigh Heads, has mangroves and rainforest, and plenty of informative native wildlife shows. Even better is **Currumbin Wildlife Sanctuary** (☎1300 886 511; 07-5534 1266; www.cws.org. au; 28 Tomewin St, Currumbin;

adult/child/family $49/35/133; ☺8am-5pm), with Australia's biggest rainforest aviary, kangaroo feeding, photo ops with koalas and crocodiles, reptile shows and Aboriginal dance displays.

✕ ⌷ p181

The Drive » The coast road arcs around to the southeast to Coolangatta, a mere 8km skip from Currumbin.

- - - - - - - - - - -

5 Coolangatta

A down-to-earth seaside town on Queensland's southern border, Coolangatta has quality surf beaches (including

the legendary 'Super-bank' break). Follow the boardwalk north around Kirra Point to the suburb of Kirra, with a beautiful long stretch of beach and challenging surf. The most difficult break here is Point Danger, but Kirra Point often goes off and there are gentler breaks down at Greenmount Beach and Rainbow Bay. At **Gold Coast Surfing Centre** (☎0417 191 629; www.goldcoastsurfingcentre. com/contact-us/; group lesson $45), former professional surfer and Australian surfing team coach Dave Davidson promises to get you up and surfing in your

179

first lesson. Alternatively, from June to the end of October, **Coolangatta Whale Watch** (☎5599 4104; www.coolangattawhalewatch.com.au; 3-10 Rivendell Dve, Tweed Heads South; 3hr cruise adult/child $95/75; ⏰9am-4pm) runs three-hour whale-watching cruises.

 p181

The Drive » Leave the coast behind, and follow the signs to Murwillumbah and Nerang. Narrow country lanes gradually become a climb through vertiginous mountain landscapes and deeply scooped valleys. Just after Rosins Lookout (44km from Murwillumbah), turn right and follow the signs to Springbrook.

---

❻ Springbrook National Park

This **national park** (www.nprsr.qld.gov.au/parks/springbrook) is a steep remnant of the huge Tweed Shield volcano that centred on nearby Mt Warning in NSW more than 20 million years ago. It's a treasured secret for hikers, with excellent trails through cool-temperate, subtropical and eucalypt forests offering a mosaic of gorges, cliffs and waterfalls. The park is divided into four sections. The 1000m-plus-high Spring-brook Plateau section houses the strung-out township of Springbrook along Springbrook Rd, and receives the most visitors: it's laced with waterfalls, trails and eye-popping lookouts. The scenic Natural Bridge section, off the Nerang–Murwillumbah road, has a 1km walking circuit leading to a huge rock arch spanning a water-formed cave – home to a luminous colony of glow-worms. The Mt Cougal section, accessed via Currumbin Creek Rd, has several waterfalls and swimming holes (watch out for submerged logs and slippery rocks); while the heavily forested Numinbah section to the north is the fourth section of the park.

The Drive » Return to Rosins Lookout (18km), then follow the signs along twisting mountain roads towards Nerang. Just before Nerang, loop north then west through Canungra and down south to Lamington National Park.

TRIP HIGHLIGHT

❼ Lamington National Park

Australia's largest remnant of subtropical rainforest cloaks the deep valleys and steep cliffs of the McPherson Range, reaching elevations of 1100m on the Lamington Plateau. Here, the 200-sq-km **Lamington National Park** (www.nprsr.qld.gov.au/parks/lamington) is a Unesco World Heritage site and has over 160km of walking trails. The two most accessible sections of the park are the **Binna Burra** and **Green Mountains** sections, both reached via long, narrow, winding roads from Canungra (not great for big campervans). Binna Burra can also be accessed from Nerang. Bushwalks within the park include everything from short jaunts to multiday epics. For experienced hikers, the **Gold Coast Hinterland Great Walk** is a three-day trip along a 54km path from the Green Mountains section to the Springbrook Plateau. Another favourite is the excellent **Tree Top Canopy Walk** along a series of rope-and-plank suspension bridges at Green Mountains. The splendidly remote lodges out here will soon have you wondering if all that coastal overdevelopment was just a bad dream.

🛏 p181

Eating & Sleeping

North Stradbroke Island ❷

✕ Island Fruit Barn   Cafe $

(📞07-3409 9125; www.stradbrokeholidays.com.
au; 16 Bingle Rd, Dunwich; mains $10-12; ⊙7am-
5pm Mon-Fri, to 4pm Sat & Sun; 🍴) On the main
road in Dunwich, Island Fruit Barn is a casual
little congregation of tables with excellent
breakfasts, smoothies, salads, soups, cakes
and sandwiches, all made using top-quality
ingredients. Order a spinach-and-feta roll, then
stock up in the gourmet grocery section.

Burleigh Heads & Currumbin ❹

✕ Barefoot Barista   Cafe $

(www.barefootbarista.com.au; 10 Palm Beach
Ave, Palm Beach; mains $11-18; ⊙5am-4pm
Mon-Fri, to 3pm Sat & Sun) One of the coolest
places on the coast, the Barefoot Barista, is
every bit as laid-back as the name implies. A
husband and wife team form the perfect duo;
she is a professional baker. And it shows. All
produce is local, down to the organic herbs. The
menu ranges from trendy twice-cooked pork
dishes to all-day breakfasts.

🛏 Hillhaven Holiday
Apartments   Apartment $$

(📞07-5535 1055; www.hillhaven.com.au;
2 Goodwin Tce, Burleigh Heads; 2-bedroom
apt from $170; @🛜) Right on the headland
adjacent to the national park, these 22
apartments have awesome views of Burleigh
Heads and the surf. It's ultra quiet and only
150m to the beach. Quality ranges from
'standard' to 'gold deluxe'.

Coolangatta ❺

✕ Cafe dbar   Modern Australian $$

(📞07-5599 2031; www.cafedbar.com.au;
275 Boundary St, Coolangatta; mains $14-26;
⊙11.15am-3pm Mon-Thu, to 8pm Fri-Sun) This
lovely spot is perched above the cliffs of Point

Danger, on the most easternpoint of two states,
almost on top of the NSW and Queensland border.
You can munch on any number of fabulous
breakfast options (our favourite meal here), fresh
salads or tapas, and sip on good coffee.

🛏 Hotel Komune   Hotel, Hostel $$

(📞07-5536 6764; www.komuneresorts.
com; 146 Marine Pde, Coolangatta; dm from
$35, 1-/2-bedroom apt from $105/145; 🛜🏊)
This spot offers a different take on the hostel
concept. With beach-funk decor, a palm-laden
pool area and an ultra laid-back vibe, this
10-storey converted apartment tower is the
ultimate surf retreat. There are budget dorms,
apartments and a hip penthouse begging for
a party.

Lamington National Park ❼

🛏 Binna Burra
Mountain Lodge   Guesthouse $$$

(📞1300 246 622, 07-5533 3622; www.
binnaburralodge.com.au; 1069 Binna Burra Rd,
Beechmont; unpowered/powered sites $28/35 d
incl breakfast with/without bathroom $300/190)
This wonderful spot is the nearest thing to a
ski lodge in the bush. You can stay in rustic
log cabins, superb flashy apartments ('sky
lodges'), or in a tent surrounded by forest in
this atmospheric mountain retreat. The central
restaurant serves a dinner buffet ($45) and
breakfast ($28).

🛏 O'Reilly's Rainforest
Retreat   Guesthouse $$$

(📞1800 688 722, 07-5502 4911; www.oreillys.
com.au; Lamington National Park Rd, Green
Mountains; r from $179, 1-/2-bedroom villas
from $330/360; @🛜🏊) This famous 1926
guesthouse has lost its original grandeur
but retains a rustic charm – and sensational
views! Newer luxury villas and doubles add
a contemporary sheen. There are plenty of
organised activities, plus a day spa, cafe, bar
and restaurant (mains $26 to $40), open for
breakfast, lunch and dinner.

Noosa Rainforests, crystal waters and a sophisticated beach scene

PATRICK OBEREM/GETTY IMAGES ©

Brisbane's Hinterland

15

Lovely coastline, an iconic zoo, a spirited Thai paradise and that's all before you even get to Noosa! On your way back down south, experience lovely inland towns.

TRIP HIGHLIGHTS

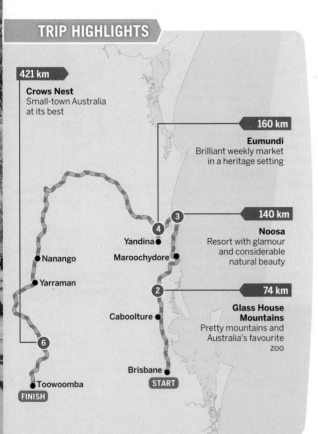

421 km

Crows Nest
Small-town Australia at its best

160 km

Eumundi
Brilliant weekly market in a heritage setting

3 **140 km**

Yandina
Maroochydore

Noosa
Resort with glamour and considerable natural beauty

2 **74 km**

Caboolture

Glass House Mountains
Pretty mountains and Australia's favourite zoo

• Nanango
• Yarraman

6

Brisbane
START

• Toowoomba
FINISH

3–4 DAYS
471KM / 293 MILES

GREAT FOR...

BEST TIME TO GO
Year-round is fine but fine weather is more likely May to October.

 ESSENTIAL PHOTO
Sweeping view over Noosa from Laguna Lookout.

 BEST FOR FAMILIES
See the crocs in action at Australia Zoo.

183

15 Brisbane's Hinterland

While you could visit most of these places as day trips from Brisbane, you'd lose that dual sense of the open road and the escape from the big city. The Glass House Mountains seem otherworldly this close to the big smoke, as does the extraordinary Spirit House experience. Throw in quiet Eumundi, nicer-than-you-expect Noosa, Crows Nest and Toowoomba and you'll very quickly see what we mean.

❶ Brisbane

Brissie may be the main event for so many visitors, and you should indeed explore what has become one of Australia's most vibrant and confident cities. – to see how to do so, turn to p172. But for this road trip it's the launching pad for a journey out into some of the much-loved playgrounds and weekend escapes for locals. Before you check out of your accommodation, it might be worth holding on to it for your day trip to Moreton Island.

The Drive ⟫ Follow any of the busy motorways that funnel north out of the city, but stay on them only as far as the turn-off;

once the signs starting point to Caboolture, start moving over towards the left-hand lane in readiness.

TRIP HIGHLIGHT

❷ Glass House Mountains

The volcanic plugs of the Glass House Mountains rise abruptly from the subtropical plains 20km northwest of Caboolture. In Aboriginal Dreaming legend, these rocky peaks belong to a family of mountain spirits. Rather less prosaically, the explorer James Cook thought the shapes resembled the industrial conical (glass-making) furnaces of his native Yorkshire, hence the name. It's worth

diverting off the Bruce Hwy onto the slower Steve Irwin Way and into the **Glass House Mountains National Park**, where you can snake your way through dense pine forests and green pastureland for a close-up view of these spectacular magma intrusions. For maps and directions, visit the extremely helpful **Glass House Mountains Visitor and Interpretive Centre** (☏07-5438 7220; www.visitsunshinecoast.com.au; Cnr Bruce Pde & Reed St; ⏱9am-4pm). And just north of Beerwah is the outstanding **Australia Zoo** (☏07-5436 2000; www.australiazoo.com.au; Steve Irwin Way, Beerwah; adult/child/family $59/35/172; ⏱9am-5pm), a fitting homage to its founder, zany wildlife enthusiast Steve Irwin.

🛏 p189

LINK YOUR TRIP

13 Capricorn Coast

Trip 13 runs the length of the Queensland coast, beginning in Brisbane and finishing in Cairns a mere 1680km later.

14 Southern Queensland Loop

This trip begins and ends in Brisbane, taking in the clamour of south coast Queensland and the tranquil rainforest hinterland.

The Drive >> Drive east, follow the signs to Caloundra and then turn north through a string of coastal resorts – Maroochydore, Mudjimba and Coolum Beach. Find out which part of Noosa you're headed to: Noosa Heads (around Laguna Bay and Hastings St), Noosaville (along the Noosa River) or Noosa Junction (the administrative centre).

TRIP HIGHLIGHT

③ Noosa

One of the most famous beach towns in Australia, Noosa is a swanky resort town with a stunning natural landscape of crystalline beaches and tropical rainforests. Designer boutiques and smart restaurants draw beach-elite sophisticates, but the beach and bush are still free, so fashionistas share the beat with thongs, board shorts and bronzed bikini bods. There's also a refreshing lack of high-rise, Gold Coast–style tourist developments. All manner of activities and tours are possible from Noosa, from kayaking and surf schools to 4WD adventures on Fraser Island – the **Noosa Visitor Centre** (☏07-5430 5000; www.visitnoosa.com.au; 61 Hastings St, Noosa Heads; ⊙9am-5pm) has a full list. But one of the best attractions is best explored under your own steam –

Noosa National Park (www. noosanationalpark.com) covers the headland, and has fine walks, great coastal scenery and a string of bays with great surfing. The most scenic way to access the national park is to follow the boardwalk along the coast from town. **Laguna Lookout** has fabulous views – walk or drive up to Laguna Lookout from Viewland Dr in Noosa Junction.

✕ ⊨ p189

The Drive >> Follow the signs from Noosa to the Bruce Hwy and turn south – Eumundi is right next to the motorway exit. It's also close enough to Noosa that many people visit as a day trip.

↱ DETOUR: MORETON ISLAND

Start: ❶ Brisbane

Queensland's islands are world famous, each painted in rich primary colours and seen to represent a slice of tropical paradise. If you're not going any further north in Queensland (and perhaps even if you are), slip over to blissful Moreton Island. Separated from the mainland by Moreton Bay (famous for its Moreton Bay bugs, which are beloved by those who value strange-looking-and-found-nowhere-else seafood), Moreton Island has a cache of sandy shores, bushland, bird life, dunes and glorious lagoons. A remarkable 95% of the island is protected as part of the **Moreton Island National Park & Recreation Area** (www.nprsr.qld.gov.au/parks/moreton-island). Apart from a few rocky headlands, it's all sand, with Mt Tempest, the highest coastal sand hill in the world, towering high at a lofty 280m. To go exploring both on land and sea, try **Moreton Bay Escapes** (☏1300 559 355; www.moretonbayescapes. au; 1-day tours adult/child from $189/139, 2-day camping tours $309/179).

PETER WALTON PHOTOGRAPHY/GETTY IMAGES ©

Glass House Mountains Grass trees amid the volcanic landscape

TRIP HIGHLIGHT

❹ Eumundi

Sweet little Eumundi, a quaint highland village, is the sort of place people remember. The town itself is attractive and wonderfully timeworn. Its historic streetscape is lined with fig trees and blends well with modern cafes, artsy boutiques and crafty folk. But Eumundi is best known for its **Eumundi Markets** (www.eumundimarkets.com. au; 80 Memorial Dr; ⊙8am-1.30pm Wed, 7am-2pm Sat), which attract over 1.6 million visitors a year

to their 600-plus stalls, selling everything from hand-crafted furniture and jewellery to homemade clothes and alternative healing. It's on market days that the town's quirky New Age vibe is greatly amplified and, once you've breathed Eumundi air, don't be surprised if you feel a sudden urge to take up beading or body painting.

🍴 p189

The Drive » Return to the Bruce Hwy for 11km, then take the turn-off for (and follow the signs to) Yandina. At the first roundabout, take the Coulson Rd exit. After about 500m, the

road ends at a t-junction with Ninderry Rd. Turn right and Spirit House is around 50m along on the right.

❺ Yandina

One of the great culinary excursions anywhere in the state, Yandina's **Spirit House** (✆07-5446 8977; www.spirithouse.com. au; 20 Ninderry Rd, Yandina; share plates $12-53; ⊙lunch daily, dinner Wed-Sat) is as much an experience as a restaurant. A path winds from the car park amid flowering greenery, past lily ponds and discreet Buddhist shrines. Almost immediately, it's as if

187

the outside world has ceased to exist and you've been transported into a world of Southeast Asian peace and sophistication. The first buildings you pass are for the **cooking school**, while the path continues to the main open-sided restaurant with tables arranged around a tranquil pool; watch for very Australian forest dragons scuttering through the underbrush and up the trees. The service is impeccable and the restaurant's kitchen produces some spectacular Thai-infused innovations – its signature dish is the whole crispy fish, perhaps with a tamarind chilli sauce, and always utterly divine.

The Drive » Return to the Bruce Hwy, follow the signs north to Gympie, then loop up and over the Coast Range of green hills, travelling via Kilkivan, Nanango, Yarraman and Wutul to Crows Nest.

- - - - - - - - - -

TRIP HIGHLIGHT

⑥ Crows Nest

Arrayed across a broad green valley on the gentle downslopes of the Great Dividing Range, cute Crows Nest (population 1450) surrounds a village green and otherwise bears all the hallmarks of a rural Australian settlement:

its porticoed pub, antique shops, increasingly artsy feel and strange local festival – Crows Nest hosts the **World Worm Races** (www.crowsnestfestival.com.au) as part of the Crows Nest Festival every October – whisper 'small-town Australia' at seemingly every turn. Getting the best from Crows Nest means slowing down to the pace of rural life and allowing it to infuse your soul. If such infusions take the form of artistic inspiration, there's the **Crows Nest Regional Art Gallery** (☑07-4698 1687; www.toowoombarc.qld.gov.au; New England Hwy; ◷10.30am-3.30pm Tue-Sat, 11.30am-3.30pm Sun), while on offer on the first Sunday of every month are the crafty **Crows Nest Village Markets** (☑0429 678 120; www. crowsnestvillagemarkets.com; Centenary Park; ◷7am-noon 1st Sun of the month).

The Drive » The sense of accumulating civilisation comes gently but unmistakenly on the 50km run south via Highfields to Toowoomba.

- - - - - - - - - -

⑦ Toowoomba

Squatting on the edge of the Great Dividing Range, 700m above sea level, Toowoomba is a sprawling country hub

with wide tree-lined streets, stately homes and down-to-earth locals. There's not a whole lot going on here from the travellers' perspective, but it's not a bad spot to stop and chill out for a day or two. The air is distinctly crisper up here on the range, and in spring the town's gardens blaze with colour; Toowoomba's **Carnival of Flowers** (www.tcof.com. au) is held during the last week in September. Not only is the 'Garden City' Queensland's largest and oldest inland city, it is also the birthplace of two national icons: the archetypal Aussie cake, the lamington, and Oscar-winner Geoffrey Rush. Take a walk through downtown Toowoomba and check out the stately late-19th-century sandstone buildings, but there's no better preparation for your return to busy Brisbane than a retreat to **Ju Raku En Japanese Garden** (www. toowoombarc.qld.gov.au; West St; ◷7am-dusk), a beautiful, Zen-like spot about 4km south of the centre at the University of Southern Queensland.

✕ ⊨ p189

Eating & Sleeping

Glass House Mountains ➋

🛏 Glass House Mountains Ecolodge
Lodge $$

(📞07-5493 0008; www.glasshouseecolodge. com; 198 Barrs Rd; r $120-220; P ❄ 📶) This novel retreat, overseen by a keen environmentalist, is close to Australia Zoo and offers a range of good-value, tranquil sleeping options, including cosy Orchard Rooms ($120), the converted Church Loft ($220), and converted railway carriages. Mt Tibrogargan can be seen from the gorgeous garden. Pick-ups available from Glass House Mountains station.

Noosa ➌

🍴 Little Humid
Modern Australian $$

(📞07-5449 9755; www.humid.com.au; 2/235 Gympie Tce, Noosaville; mains from $25; ⏲noon-2pm Wed-Sun & from 6pm Tue-Sun) Fine dining without pretensions. This extremely popular eatery is, according to locals, one of the best in town. It lives up to the hype, with toothsome treats including superb fillet steaks, sticky pork belly, and a large range of creative veggie options. Definitely book ahead.

🛏 Hotel Laguna
Apartment $$

(www.hotellaguna.com.au; 6 Hastings St, Noosa Heads; studios/ste from $155/210; ❄ 📶 🐾) One of the area's best-value accommodation options in this price range, and neatly wedged between the river and Hastings St, La Laguna has self-contained apartments and smaller studios. Given that all apartments are privately owned, each is individually decorated, but all are clean and smart. The location is a plus: a roll-out-of-bed away from the beach, and a coffee whiff from great cafes.

Eumundi ➍

🍴 Bohemian Bungalow
International $$

(📞07-5442 8679; www.bohemianbungalow. com.au; 69 Memorial Dr; lunch/mains $13-28, dinner $26-34; ⏲breakfast Wed, Sat & Sun, lunch Wed & Sun, dinner Thu-Sat) The fare in this gorgeous white Queenslander is outdone only by its whimsical interiors – postmodern Bohemian with peacocks, candles and ceramic horses on every ledge and corner. The food is just as satisfying: lovely coffees, gourmet pizzas, scrumptious salads and fine brekkies. Check ahead for opening hours.

Toowoomba ➐

🍴 Park House Cafe
Modern Australian $$

(📞07-4638 2211; www.parkhousecafe.com.au; 92 Margaret St; cafe/mains $11-28, restaurant $26-35; ⏲7am-late) Facing Queens Park, this chic cafe has a sunny streetside patio and a cosy dining room. Gourmet sandwiches, hefty salads (try the seared lamb with feta and roasted pumpkin), pastas, grilled meats and seafood lure pram-pushing mums from the park. At night the cafe vibe mutates into an upmarket restaurant scene, with generous pours of wine by the glass.

🛏 Vacy Hall
Guesthouse $$

(📞07-4639 2055; www.vacyhall.com.au; 135 Russell St; d $125-245; 📶) Uphill from the town centre, this magnificent 1873 mansion (originally a wedding gift from a cashed-up squatter to his daughter) offers 12 heritage-style rooms with loads of authentic charm. A wide verandah wraps around the house, all rooms have en suites or private bathrooms; and most have working fireplaces. Super-high ceilings make some rooms higher than they are wide. Free wi-fi.

The Daintree Retreat into an isolated piece of paradise

ANDREW WATSON/GETTY IMAGES ©

Cairns & the Daintree

16

Capturing the essence of Queensland's tropical Far North, this road trip from Cairns to Cape Trib takes you from the reef to the rainforest and most places in between.

TRIP HIGHLIGHTS

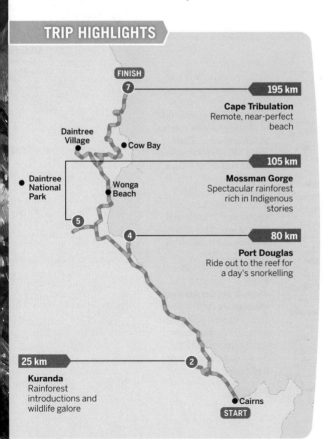

FINISH

7

195 km

Cape Tribulation
Remote, near-perfect beach

Daintree Village ● Cow Bay

105 km

Mossman Gorge
Spectacular rainforest rich in Indigenous stories

● **Daintree National Park**

Wonga Beach

5

4

80 km

Port Douglas
Ride out to the reef for a day's snorkelling

25 km

2

Kuranda
Rainforest introductions and wildlife galore

● Cairns
START

7 DAYS
195KM / 121 MILES

GREAT FOR...

BEST TIME TO GO
April to early December; summer is wet and cyclones are an ever-present danger.

 ESSENTIAL PHOTO

Cape Tribulation Beach is long, lovely and remote.

 BEST FOR CULTURE

Walk the rainforest with the original inhabitants at Mossman Gorge.

Cairns & the Daintree

Languid Cairns is a gateway to some of the best bits of tropical Far North Queensland — snorkelling the Great Barrier Reef is possible from Cairns to Port Douglas, there's fabulous rainforest and crocs along the river in the Daintree, the beaches from Palm Cove to Cape Trib have the unmistakeable whiff of paradise. Better still, distances are short, meaning there's ample energy left over for all manner of adventures.

❶ Cairns

Gateway to the Great Barrier Reef and Daintree Rainforest Unesco World Heritage sites, and starting point for serious 4WD treks into Cape York Peninsula's vast wilderness, Cairns (pronounced 'Cans') is an important regional centre, but it's more boardshorts than briefcases. Sun- and fun-lovers flock to the spectacular, lifeguard-patrolled, artificial, sandy-edged, 4800-square-metre pool at **Cairns Esplanade** (www.cairnsesplanade.com.au; 🕑 lagoon 6am-9pm Thu-Tue, noon-9pm Wed) on the city's reclaimed foreshore. If you're heading for the reef, marine experts at **Reef Teach** (📞07-4031 7794; www.

reefteach.com.au; 2nd fl, Main Street Arcade, 85 Lake St; adult/child $18/9; 🕑 lectures 6.30-8.30pm Tue-Sat) explain how to identify specific species of fish and coral. Then again, there's no substitute for the real thing – **Tusa Dive** (📞07-4047 9100; www.tusadive.com; cnr Shields St & The Esplanade; adult/child day trips from $185/110) and **Reef Magic** (📞07-4031 1588; www.reefmagiccruises.com; 1 Spence St; adult/child day trips from $195/95) both offer forays out onto the reef, while **Great Barrier Reef Helicopters** (📞07-4081 8888; www.gbrhelicopters.com.au; Bush Pilots Ave, Aeroglen; flights per person from $165) does wonderfully scenic flights.

🛏 p197

Bloomfield Falls

Wujal W

Da Na

Thorn Pe

Daintree Village ❻

Daintree National Park

Mossman Gorge ❺

Mossman

Ju

Mt Moll

17

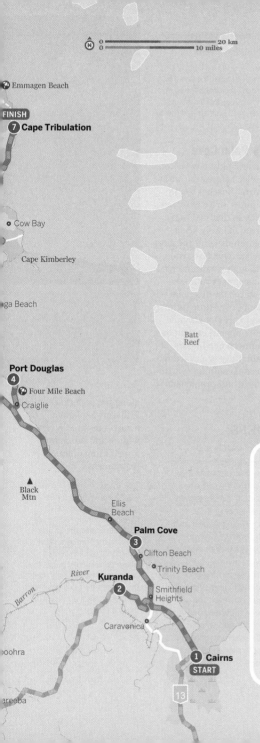

The Drive ›› Drive for 13km north of Cairns, past the airport turn-off, and then take the left-branching road, following the signs all the way into Kuranda.

TRIP HIGHLIGHT

❷ Kuranda

Nestled in the rainforest, arty Kuranda is one of Cairns' most popular day trips. Even this close to Cairns, it's rainforest at every turn up in this neck of the woods, and if you're finding it hard to find your entry point, begin at **Rainforestation** (☎07-4085 5008; www.rainforest.com.au; Kennedy Hwy; adult/child $44/23; ⊙9am-4pm), with a wildlife section, rainforest/river tours and interactive Aboriginal experience. Not surprisingly, wildlife is a recurring theme here, with **Kuranda Koala Gardens** (☎07-4093 9953; www.koalagardens.com; Rob Veivers Dr; adult/child

LINK YOUR TRIP

13 **Capricorn Coast**
Cairns is where the classic route ends after having traversed the length of the Queensland coast north from Brisbane.

17 **Cape York Prelude**
If this isn't far enough north for you, go a little further – our journey to Cooktown via the Cape York fringe begins in Cairns.

$17/8.50, koala photos extra; ⊗9.45am-4pm), **Birdworld** (☏07-4093 9188; www.birdworldkuranda.com; Rob Veivers Dr; adult/child $17/8.50; ⊗9am-4pm) and the **Australian Butterfly Sanctuary** (☏07-4093 7575; www.australianbutterflies.com; Rob Veivers Dr; adult/child/family $19/9.50/47.50; ⊗9.45am-4pm) all in the vicinity. But our favourite attraction of all is the **Tjapukai Aboriginal Cultural Park** (☏07-4042 9999; www.tjapukai.com.au; Cairns Western Arterial Rd, Caravonica; adult/child $40/25; ⊗9am-5pm). Managed by the area's original custodians, this award-winning cultural extravaganza tells the story of creation using giant holograms and actors. There's a dance theatre, a gallery, boomerang- and spear-throwing demonstrations and turtle-spotting canoe rides.

The Drive » It's 12km back down the road to the Cook Hwy. Turn left, then follow the signs to Palm Cove, located around a dozen or so kilometres further on.

PETER ADAMS/GETTY IMAGES ©

❸ Palm Cove

Surprisingly, few visitors realise before arrival that Cairns' beaches are 15 minutes' drive from the CBD, so that makes the string of lovely beach communities all the more special. Our favourite – although we recommend you conduct your own research on this point – is Palm Cove. More intimate than Port Douglas and more upmarket than its southern neighbours, Palm Cove is a cloistered coastal community with a beautiful promenade along the paperbark-lined Williams Esplanade, a gorgeous stretch of white-sand beach and a sprinkling of fancy restaurants.

The Drive » Head back onto the Cook Hwy, drive north, and then sit back and enjoy the ride. Dramatic sections of coastline open up at various points along the way and the region's boast of this being where the rainforest meets the sea is frequently evident along this stretch. Port Douglas is well signposted, 5km northeast of the Cook Hwy.

BEWARE OF STINGERS!

Australia's formidable portfolio of deadly and otherwise dangerous creatures can seem endless. The risks in most cases are way overblown, but you should definitely be careful of venturing out into the ocean here. Jellyfish – including the potentially deadly box jellyfish and Irukandji – occur in Australia's tropical waters. It's unwise to swim north of Agnes Water (which lies well south of Cairns) between November and May unless there's a stinger net. 'Stinger suits' (full-body Lycra swimsuits) prevent stinging, as do wetsuits. Swimming and snorkelling are usually safe around Queensland's reef islands throughout the year; however, the rare (and tiny) Irukandji has been recorded on the outer reef and islands. Wash stings with vinegar to prevent further discharge of remaining stinging cells, followed by rapid transfer to a hospital. Don't attempt to remove the tentacles.

Cape Tribulation Rainforest meets the sea in Daintree National Park

TRIP HIGHLIGHT

④ Port Douglas

From its humble origins as a sleepy 1960s fishing village, Port Douglas has grown into a sophisticated alternative to Cairns' hectic tourist scene. With the outer Great Barrier Reef less than an hour offshore, the Daintree Rainforest practically in the backyard, and more resorts than you can poke a stick at, Port Douglas has so much going for it that many visitors choose it as their Far North base, leaving Cairns at the airport. The town's main attraction is **Four Mile Beach**, a pristine strip of palm-fringed, white sand that begins at the eastern end of Macrossan St, the main drag for shopping, and wining and dining. There's not much you can't do from Port Douglas, but we reckon your first priority should be to get out on the reef. **Quicksilver** (☎07-4087 2100; www.quicksilver-cruises. com; Reef Marina; adult/child $225/113) runs well-regarded fast cruises out to its own pontoon on Agincourt Reef and 10-minute scenic helicopter flights.

🗡️ 🛏️ p197

The Drive ≫ Return to the Cook Hwy, then follow it away to the northwest into Mossman, 14km after rejoining the highway.

TRIP HIGHLIGHT

⑤ Mossman Gorge

Around 5km west of Mossman, in the southeast corner of Daintree National Park, **Mossman Gorge** (www.mossmangorge. com.au) forms part of the traditional lands of the Kuku Yalanji people. Carved by the Mossman River, the gorge is a boulder-strewn valley where sparkling water washes over ancient rocks. From the fantastic **Mossman Gorge Centre** (☎07-4099 7000; www.mossmangorge.com.au; Dreamtime walk adult/child $50/25; ⏰8am-6pm), which houses an art gallery and a bush-tucker restaurant, walking tracks loop along the river to a refreshing swimming hole – take care, as the currents can be swift. The complete circuit takes over an hour, or you can get a shuttle bus into the heart of the gorge. Better still, book through the Mossman Gorge Centre for the unforgettable 1½-hour Indigenous-guided **Kuku-Yalanji Dreamtime Walks** (adult/child $50/25; ⏰9am, 11am & 3pm) – it's an intimate experience getting to know the forest in this way, and you'll come away with a head full of anecdotes and soulful stories that centre on the traditional Kuku Yalanji relationship to the land.

The Drive ›› Travelling north from Mossman, it's 26km through cane fields and farmland before the crossroads to either Daintree village or the Daintree river ferry. It's a lovely drive through lush country, with the final stretch into Daintree village offering a hint of the forests that lie up ahead. No fuel is available in Daintree village.

- - - - - - - - - - -

❻ Daintree Village

Ease to a stop along Daintree's tiny main street, switch off the engine and listen to the silence in this, one of those deliciously remote, end-of-the-road places where just being here has an allure all its own. We love its sense of isolation and recommend that you linger long enough to absorb a little of the village's singular peace and quiet. That aside, most people come here because the Daintree River is one of the best places in Australia to catch a glimpse of wild crocs without swimming within sight of one. Croc-spotting cruises are big business here. Try **Crocodile Express** (☎07-4098 6120; www.crocodileexpress.com; 1hr cruises adult/child $23/12; ⏰from 8.30am), the original Daintree River cruise operator, or **Daintree River Wild Watch** (☎0447 734 933; www.daintreeriverwildwatch.com.au; 2hr cruises adult/child $60/35), which has informative sunrise birdwatching cruises and sunset photography nature cruises.

🍴 🛏 p197

The Drive ›› Return 10km back down the (only) road, take the ferry turn-off and make your way to the riverbank and the Daintree River Ferry (www.douglas.qld.gov.au/community/daintree-ferry; car/motorcycle $13.50/5, bicycle & pedestrian $1; ⏰6am-midnight, no bookings). From the other side, it's 40 wonderful, rainforested kilometres to the beach at Cape Tribulation, where the paved road, and this journey, ends. Watch out for cassowaries en route.

TRIP HIGHLIGHT

❼ Cape Tribulation

Part of the Wet Tropics World Heritage Area, the spectacular region from the Daintree River north to Cape Tribulation features ancient rainforest, sandy beaches and rugged mountains. This isolated piece of paradise retains a frontier quality, with road signs alerting drivers to cassowary crossings, croc warnings along the beaches and a tangible sense of having left civilisation, such as it was, back on the other side of Daintree River. The rainforest tumbles right down to magnificent **Myall** and **Cape Tribulation** beaches, which are separated by a knobby cape, and there are numerous ways to explore: **Ocean Safari** (☎07-4098 0006; www.oceansafari.com.au; Cape Tribulation Rd; adult/child $128/82) leads small groups on snorkelling cruises to the Great Barrier Reef, just half an hour offshore, while **Cape Trib Horse Rides** (☎07-4098 0043; www.capetribhorserides.com.au; from $99; ⏰8am & 2.30pm) organises blissful rides along the beach and into the forest. But for all that, our favourite activity up here is to simply walk barefoot on the beach at Cape Trib, heading slowly north...

🍴 p197

Eating & Sleeping

Cairns ❶

🛏 Cairns Plaza Hotel   Hotel $$

(📞07-4051 4688; www.cairnsplaza.com.au; 145 The Esplanade; d from $129; 🅿 ❋ @ 🛜 🐾) One of Cairns' original high-rise hotels, the triumphant Plaza is freshly refurbished and under new ownership. Rooms have crisp, clean decor, and functional kitchenettes and balconies; many enjoy stunning views over Trinity Bay. A guest laundry, friendly round-the-clock reception staff, the quiet Esplanade location and great rates make it an excellent midrange choice.

Port Douglas ❹

🍴 Port 'O Call   Australian $$

(📞07-4099 5422; www.portocall.com.au; cnr Port St & Craven Close; mains from $16; ⏲6-9.30pm Tue-Sun) The kitchen of this equally regarded hostel turns out some seriously good grub at reasonable prices, in a cheery casual environment. Standard staples of fish, steak, pastas and salads are anything but ordinary, and the talented chef's daily specials (including Mexican nights!) are well worth a look-see. Fettuccine carbonara, which can so often be *way* too creamy, is just right.

🛏 Pink Flamingo   Boutique Hotel $$

(📞07-4099 6622; www.pinkflamingo.com.au; 115 Davidson St; d from $135; ❋ @ 🛜 🐾 🐾) Flamboyantly painted rooms, private walled courtyards (with hammocks, outdoor baths and outdoor showers) and a groovy al fresco bar make the Pink Flamingo Port Douglas' hippest digs. Outdoor movie nights, gym and bike rental are also on offer.

Daintree Village ❻

🍴 Croc Eye Cafe   Cafe $$

(📞07-4098 6229; 3 Stewart St; mains $17-40; ⏲8am-3pm) Serves fish and chips, delicately prepared barramundi and a tasting platter with crocodile wontons and sugar-cane prawns.

🍴 Julaymba Restaurant   Indigenous $$$

(📞07-4098 6100; www.daintree-ecolodge.com. au; 20 Daintree Rd; mains $27-40; ⏲breakfast, lunch & dinner) The superb Julaymba Restaurant features local produce, including indigenous berries, nuts, leaves and flowers. It's located at Daintree Eco Lodge & Spa (p197); nonguests are welcome.

🛏 Daintree Eco Lodge & Spa   Resort $$$

(📞07-4098 6100; www.daintree-ecolodge. com.au; 20 Daintree Rd; treehouses from $215; ❋ @ 🛜 🐾) The 15 boutique 'banyans' (pole cabins; 10 with private spas) here sit high in the rainforest canopy a few kilometres south of Daintree Village. Even the day spa is eco-minded, with its own range of organic, Indigenous-inspired products and treatments. Nonguests are welcome at its superb Julaymba Restaurant (p197), which uses local produce, including indigenous berries, nuts, leaves and flowers.

Cape Tribulation ❼

🍴 Mason's Store & Cafe   Cafe $$

(📞07-4098 0016; 3781 Cape Tribulation Rd; mains from $15; ⏲10am-4pm Sun-Thu, to 7pm Fri & Sat) This laid-back local does good fish and chips and huge steak sarnies. There's a small general and liquor store, a tourist information counter and, best of all, a crystal-clear, croc-free swimming hole (admission by gold coin donation) out the back.

Cooktown Indigenous history and unforgettable cultural experiences

Cape York Prelude

17

This is where the paved road ends and you flirt with Cape York, but just being here is what it's all about.

TRIP HIGHLIGHTS

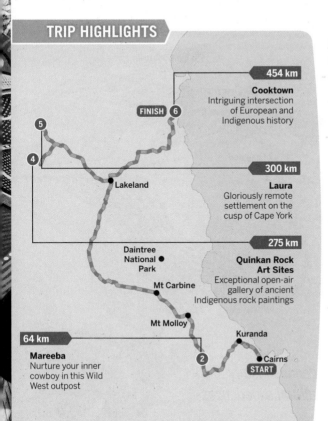

454 km
Cooktown
Intriguing intersection of European and Indigenous history

FINISH **6**

5

4

Lakeland

300 km
Laura
Gloriously remote settlement on the cusp of Cape York

Daintree National Park

275 km
Quinkan Rock Art Sites
Exceptional open-air gallery of ancient Indigenous rock paintings

Mt Carbine

Mt Molloy

Kuranda

64 km

Mareeba
Nurture your inner cowboy in this Wild West outpost

2

Cairns
START

5–7 DAYS
454KM / 282 MILES

GREAT FOR...

BEST TIME TO GO
The Dry (April to October), otherwise it's impossibly humid or raining.

ESSENTIAL PHOTO
The end of the paved road in Laura captures the remote location.

BEST FOR CULTURE
Quinkan Rock Art Sites are one of Australia's premier Indigenous rock art sites.

199

ANDREW WATSON/GETTY IMAGES ©

Cape York Prelude

From Cairns to Cooktown, this trip transports you to the very cusp of Cape York, as close as you can safely get in a 2WD vehicle. Cairns and Mareeba provide a gentle introduction, but from then on it's remote settlements such as Lakefield and Laura, fabulous Indigenous rock art at Quinkan, and the frontier charm of Cooktown.

❶ Cairns

Cairns, where so many journeys in Far North Queensland begin and end, is where you leave the coast behind. Enjoy its choice of restaurants before entering the realm of one-restaurant towns, go for a swim at the pool along the Esplanade (p192), take a lazy 3km walk along the foreshore **boardwalk**, and tell everyone you may be offline for the next week.

✕ 🛏 p205

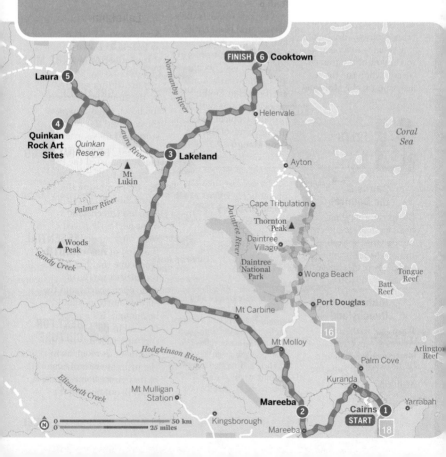

The Drive » Take the Cook Hwy north for 13km, take the left fork towards Kuranda then follow the Kennedy Hwy southwest all the way into Mareeba for a total trip clock of 64km for the day. Watch for rolling, rainforested hills along the way, especially close to Kuranda.

Cape York Peninsula Dance performance by indigenous school children

TRIP HIGHLIGHT

❷ Mareeba

You're still in the Cairns hinterland in Mareeba, but Mareeba revels in an unashamed Wild West atmosphere, with local merchants selling leather saddles, handcrafted bush hats and the over-sized belt buckle of your bronco-bustin' dreams. It all comes to a head at the height of the tourist season when the town gears up for the **Mareeba Rodeo** (www.mareebarodeo. com.au), one of Australia's biggest and best, with bull riding, a 'beaut ute' muster and boot-scootin' country music. Locals look somewhat askance at city-slicker foodie preoccupations with the proudly tropical sweet mango wine of **Golden Drop Mango** (📞07-4093 2750; www.goldendrop.com. au; 227 Bilwon Rd; ⏰8am-6.30pm daily) or the banana or mulberry spirits at **Mt Uncle Distillery** (📞07-4086 8008; www.mtuncle.com; 1819 Chewko Rd, Walkamin; ⏰10am-4.30pm daily).

🛏 p205

The Drive » Some 42km north of Mareeba, just after tiny Mt Molloy, the road arcs away to the northwest and then north, passing Mt Carbine and Maitland Downs en route. This is empty, drab-green country out here and the road is quiet. Arriving in tiny Lakeland feels like coming in out of the wild.

❸ Lakeland

Also known by locals as Lakeland Downs, this small settlement of barely 220 souls is prime farming country. By the time you survey the hotel, the roadhouse, the cafe and the small store, and fill your tank with petrol, you've pretty much exhausted the list of things to do out here. But that's missing the point. Just being out here, on Queensland's most northerly paved road, surrounded by the kind of Australian landscape that has fed its outback myths of wide open spaces and the endless horizon, should be enough. It's a place to revel in the almost dizzying vastness of this continent as much as in the intimate reassurance of its remote homesteads. So walk out beyond the

LINK YOUR TRIP

 Cairns & the Daintree

Cairns is the starting point for many journeys through the Far North – this one heads north and offshore in search of rainforest and reef.

 Outback Queensland

From Cairns, this route makes a foray from tropical coast deep into the Gulf Country and the outback.

last building, turn your back on human settlement and take it all in.

📖 p205

The Drive » From Lakeland take the Peninsula Developmental Rd (known as the PDR) as it leads northwest. It's paved as far as Laura. About 50km north of Lakeland and 12km south of Laura, you'll find the turn-off to the Split Rock Gallery.

- - - - - - - - - - - -

❹ Quinkan Rock Art Sites

Leaving Lakeland you enter Quinkan Country, so named for the Aboriginal spirits depicted at the rock-art sites scattered throughout this area. Unesco lists Quinkan Country in the world's top 10 rock-art regions. The **Split Rock Gallery** (Peninsula Development Rd; by donation) is the only rock-art site open to the public without a guide. Entrance is by donation at the car park. The sandstone escarpments here are covered with paintings dating back 14,000 years! Depending on when you come, it can be quite a surreal experience to walk the path up the hillside in silence, solitude and isolation, before coming upon the various other-worldly 'galleries' in the rock faces. There's a real sense of the sacred at Split Rock: it's both eerie and breathtaking. We recommend coming here alone to get a sense of place, and then returning on a tour from Laura – ask at the Quinkan & Regional Cultural Centre.

The Drive » From Quinkan, return to the PDR and skip on in to Laura. Along the way, soak up the palette of true Aussie colours – the red earth where the tarmac ends and the bush begins, the eucalyptus green of the dry woodlands, and the parched yellow of the sandstone escarpments nearby.

BEYOND TO CAPE YORK

Rugged, remote Cape York Peninsula has one of the wildest tropical environments on the planet. The Great Dividing Range forms the spine of the Cape: tropical rainforests and palm-fringed beaches flank its eastern side; sweeping savannah woodlands, eucalyptus forests and coastal mangroves its west. This untamed landscape undergoes a spectacular transformation each year when the torrential rains of the monsoonal wet season set in: rough, dry earth turns to rich, red, mud; quenched, the tinder-dry bush awakens in vibrant greens, and trickling creek-beds swell to raging rivers teeming with barramundi.

Generally impossible in the Wet, the overland pilgrimage to the Tip is a 4WD-trek into one of Australia's last great frontiers, and not for the uninitiated. Rough, corrugated roads numb your bum, and challenging croc-infested river crossings are par for the course. For 4WD journeys beyond Laura, the end of the sealed road, you must carry spare tyres, tools, winching equipment, food and plenty of water, which is scarce along the main track. Roadhouses can be hundreds of kilometres apart and stock only basic supplies. Be sure to check **RACQ road reports** (☏13 19 40; www.racq.com.au) before you depart. Mobile-phone service is limited to the Telstra network and is sketchy at best – take a satellite phone. Do not attempt the journey alone.

Permits (☏13 74 68; www.nprsr.qld.gov.au; $5.75) are required to camp on Aboriginal land, which includes most land north of the Dulhunty River. The Injinoo Aboriginal Community, which runs the ferry across the mighty Jardine River, includes a camping permit in the ferry fee. Travelling across Aboriginal land elsewhere on the Cape may require an additional permit, which you can obtain by contacting the relevant community council. See the Cape York Sustainable Futures website (www.cysf.com.au) for details. Permits can take up to six weeks.

Cooktown James Cook Museum

TRIP HIGHLIGHT

5 Laura

Perhaps more than anywhere else in Australia, Laura is a place to stand where the paved road ends and dream of what lies up the red-earth track. In 2013 the PDR was sealed as far as Laura, but beyond that the 'road', a true Australian epic, meanders through hard country all the way to Cape York. If this is as far as you're going, dream on, and then enjoy what sleepy little Laura has to offer. The **Quinkan & Regional**

Cultural Centre (☎07-4060 3457; www.quinkancc.com. au; admission by donation; ☺8.30am-5pm Mon-Fri, 9am-3.30pm Sat & Sun) covers the history of the region from Indigenous rock art to European settlement. It's also the place to organise one of its insightful tours of Quinkan Country rock-art sites with an Indigenous guide. If it's at all possible, be here in June of odd-numbered years for the simply wonderful three-day **Laura Aboriginal Dance Festival** (www. laurafestival.tv), the largest traditional Indigenous gathering in Australia.

Otherwise, you've been out here long enough to know the deal – there's a roadhouse, a general store with a few basic groceries and good honest tucker.

✗ ⌷ p205

The Drive ≫ Don't forget to fuel up at the Laura Roadhouse before retreating back down the road. At Lakeland, turn left (north) and from here it's 80km into Cooktown; on the final run into town, watch for the Coral Sea glittering away to the east.

TRIP HIGHLIGHT

6 Cooktown

You're as far north as you can get in Queensland on

203

a paved road by the time you reach rough-and-tumble Cooktown, but this vast land demands a sense of rather humbling perspective – you're still only at the southeastern edge of Cape York Peninsula. Dwarfed it may be by its surroundings, but this is a small place with a big history: for thousands of years, Waymbuurr was a meeting ground for Indigenous communities, and it was here on 17 June 1770 that Lieutenant (later Captain) Cook beached the *Endeavour*, which had earlier struck a reef offshore from Cape Tribulation. Cook's crew spent 48 days here repairing the damage, making Cooktown Australia's first (albeit transient) non-Indigenous settlement. While here, Cook climbed 162m-high **Grassy Hill** looking for a passage through the reefs; at dusk and dawn the 360-degree views of the town, river and ocean are truly spectacular. Cooktown's main street, Charlotte St, has some beautiful 19th-century buildings, among them the **James Cook Museum** (🖉07-4069 5386; www.nationaltrust.org.au/qld/JamesCookMuseum; cnr Helen & Furneaux Sts; adult/child $10/3; 🕙9.30am-4pm),with well-preserved relics from the *Endeavour*. For an Indigenous perspective on the land to take home with you, **Guurrbi Tours** (🖉07 40345020; guurrbitours.blogspot.com.au; tours 2/4hr from $95/120, self-drive from $65/85; 🕙Mon-Sat) is an unforgettable experience.

✗ 🛏 p205

Eating & Sleeping

Cairns ❶

✖ Fetta's Greek Taverna   Greek $$

(📞07-4051 6966; www.fettasgreektaverna.com.
au; 99 Grafton St; dishes $13-25; 🕙11.30am-
3pm Mon-Fri, 5.30pm-late daily) The white walls
and blue-accented windows do a great job
evoking Santorini. But it's the classic Greek
dishes that are the star of the show here.
The $35 set menu goes the whole hog – dip,
saganaki, mousakka, salad, grilled meats,
calamari, baklava and coffee. Yes, you can break
your plate.

🛏 201 Lake Street   Hotel $$$

(📞07-4053 0100, 1800 628 929;
www.201lakestreet.com.au; 201 Lake St;
r $120-260, apt $215-260) Lifted from the pages
of a trendy magazine, this new apartment
complex has a stellar pool and a whiff of
exclusivity. Grecian white predominates and
guests can choose from a smooth hotel
room or contemporary apartments with an
entertainment area, a plasma-screen TV and a
balcony.

Mareeba ❷

🛏 Jabiru Safari Lodge   Cabin $$

(📞07-4093 2514; www.jabirusafarilodge.com.
au; cabins per person incl breakfast $109-179,
all inclusive $215-285) The Jabiru Safari Lodge,
at the Mareeba Wetlands, has solar-powered
tented cabins and a spa. Take the Pickford Rd
turn-off from Biboohra, 7km north of Mareeba.
Accommodation is in fantastic luxury tents
(expect corrugated iron bathrooms, privacy
and access to an outdoor spa) or solar-powered
ecotents.

Lakeland ❸

🛏 Lakeland Hotel Motel   Motel $

(📞07-4060 2142; Peninsula Development
Rd; d from $90) The last watering-hole and
meal stop before Laura also has very basic
accommodation.

Laura ❺

✖ Laura Roadhouse   Roadhouse $

(📞07-4060 3440; Peninsular Development
Rd; meals from $10) You can fuel up at the
roadhouse, which sells gas, ice and basic
groceries.

🛏 Quinkan Hotel   Hotel $

(📞07-4060 3393; Deighton Rd; unpowered/
powered sites $25/32) The historic, corrugated-
iron Quinkan Hotel burnt down in 2002.
Although the rebuilt and refurbished pub
is clean and functional, it lacks the rustic
character of the original.

🛏 Laura Motel   Motel $$

(📞07-4060 3238; Deighton Rd; d from $120;
❄) The spick-n-span Laura Motel has 11
comfortable en-suite rooms with compact flat-
screen TVs and air-conditioning. Enquire at the
General Store.

Cooktown ❻

✖ Gill'd & Gutt'd   Fish & Chips $

(📞07-4069 5863; Fisherman's Wharf, Webber
Esplanade; mains $7-12; 🕙11.30am-9pm) Fish
and chips the way it should be – fresh and
smack on the waterside wharf.

✖ Restaurant 1770   Modern Australian $$$

(📞07-4069 5440; 3/7 Webber Esplanade; mains
from $28; 🕙7.30-9.30am, 11.30am-2pm &
6-9.30pm Tue-Sat; 🅿) Opening onto a romantic
waterside deck, Restaurant 1770 gives fresh
local fish top billing. Save space for mouth-
watering desserts.

🛏 Sovereign Resort Hotel   Hotel $$$

(📞07-4043 0500; www.sovereign-resort.
com.au; cnr Charlotte & Green Sts; d from $180;
❄@🛜🏊) Cooktown's swishest digs have
tropical-style rooms, gorgeous gardens, the
biggest pool in town and on-site wining and
dining.

The Savannah Way *Gateway to Queensland's lonely outback*

MANFRED GOTTSCHALK/GETTY IMAGES ©

Outback Queensland

18

From the tropical coast of Far North Queensland to the deepest outback, this odyssey is all possible in a 2WD.

TRIP HIGHLIGHTS

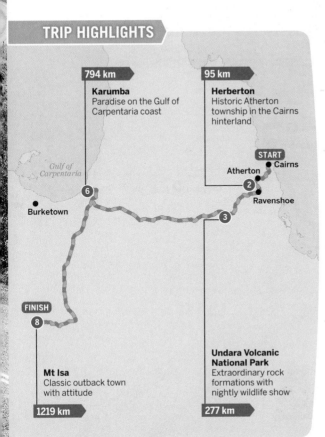

794 km

Karumba
Paradise on the Gulf of Carpentaria coast

95 km

Herberton
Historic Atherton township in the Cairns hinterland

FINISH

8

Mt Isa
Classic outback town with attitude

1219 km

Undara Volcanic National Park
Extraordinary rock formations with nightly wildlife show

277 km

7–10 DAYS
1219KM / 758 MILES

GREAT FOR...

BEST TIME TO GO

April to October – the rest of the year is wet, wet, wet.

ESSENTIAL PHOTO

The sunset from City Lookout, Mt Isa, for its mine lights and smokestacks.

BEST FOR OUTDOORS

Karumba is the most accessible corner of the Gulf of Carpentaria.

207

18 Outback Queensland

The outback may seem like the preserve of hardened 4WD adventurers, but this 2WD traverse crosses stirring outback country and has all the ingredients for a fine adventure without leaving the tarmac. It all begins in the lush, tropical surroundings of Cairns and the Atherton Tablelands, with dramatic Undara Volcanic National Park offering a parched preview, to Croydon, Normanton, Cloncurry and Mt Isa, each getting remoter by degrees.

① Cairns

Cairns is an unlikely gateway to the outback, but therein lies its charm. Above all else, swim in the ocean (you won't see it again for a while), stock up on your favourite snacks for the long drive ahead (most shops from here on will only stock the basics), and dive into the culinary scene (it's pub food and not much else until Mt Isa).

The Drive » Follow the coastal Bruce Hwy for 24km

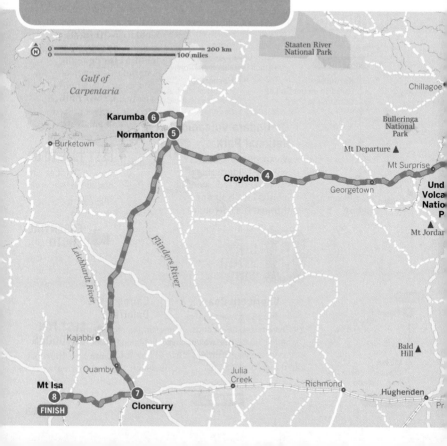

south to Gordonvale, then veer inland at the Gillies Hwy. The road bucks and weaves southwest through rainforested hillsides and rocky outcrops to Yungaburra close to the shores of Lake Tinaroo, 12km before reaching Atherton. It's then 18km southwest to Herberton.

TRIP HIGHLIGHT

② Herberton

A must-see on any comprehensive trip into the Tableland is the fascinating, fun and unique **Historic Village Herberton** (☎07-4097 2002; www.herbertonhistoricvillage. com.au; 6 Broadway; adult/

child $25/12; ☺9am-5pm, last entry 3.30pm), which comprises over 50 heritage buildings, restored and relocated to the sweet, sleepy Tableland town of Herberton. Exhibits range from the school to the sawmill, the bank to the bishop's house, the coachhouse to the camera store and everything in between. It all feels like a rather cutesy museum, but that's the point and there's nothing quite like it anywhere else in Australia.

The Drive » It's 18km back to the Kennedy Hwy, a further 19km south to Ravenshoe, then 142km to Undara Volcanic National Park, with the views either side of the road getting drier with each passing kilometre. Undara is 15km south off the Gulf Developmental Road on a sealed road.

TRIP HIGHLIGHT

③ Undara Volcanic National Park

About 190,000 years ago, the Undara shield volcano erupted, sending molten lava coursing through the surround-

ing landscape. While the surface of the lava cooled and hardened, hot lava continued to race through the centre of the flows, eventually leaving the world's longest continuous lava tubes from a single vent. There are over 160km of tubes here, but only a fraction can be visited as part of a guided tour. Most of these are operated by **Undara Experience** (☎07-4097 1900, 1800 990 992; www.undara.com.au; 2-4hr tours adult/child/family from $55/27.50/165), which runs daily two-hour tours, including 'Wildlife at Sunset', where you'll see tiny microbats swarm out of a cave entrance and provide dinner for lightning-fast hanging tree snakes, known as night tigers. Under your own steam, a worthwhile detour is the signposted drive to **Kalkani Crater**. The crater rim walk is an easy 2.5km circuit from the day-use car park.

🛏 p213

The Drive » Return to the Gulf Developmental Road

🔗 LINK YOUR TRIP

13 Capricorn Coast
Trip 13's traverse of the Queensland coast ends (or begins) in Cairns, which is also where your journey into the outback begins.

16 Cairns & the Daintree
Reef and rainforest are the highlights on this journey from Cairns to Cape Tribulation.

QUEENSLAND **18** OUTBACK QUEENSLAND

DETOUR: ATHERTON TABLELAND WATERFALLS

Start: ❷ Herberton

Climbing back from the coast between Innisfail and Cairns is the fertile food bowl of the far north, the Atherton Tableland. Quaint country towns, eco-wilderness lodges and luxurious B&Bs dot greener-than-green hills between patchwork fields, pockets of rainforest, spectacular lakes and waterfalls, and Queensland's highest mountains, Bartle Frere (1622m) and Bellenden Ker (1593m).

From Herberton it's 39km to Millaa Millaa, which lies along the Palmerston Highway; 1km east of Millaa Millaa, turn north onto Theresa Creek Rd. Surrounded by tree ferns and flowers, the Millaa Millaa Falls, 1.5km along, are easily the best for swimming and have a grassy picnic area. Almost ridiculously picturesque, the spectacular 12m falls are reputed to be the most photographed in Australia. Zillie Falls, 8km further on, are reached by a short walking trail that leads to a lookout peering down (with some vertigo) on the falls from above, while Ellinjaa Falls have a 200m walking trail down to a rocky swimming hole at the base of the falls.

(Savannah Way) and then tick off the tiny settlements that loom like mirages from time to time in this empty land – such as Georgetown after 127km – before pulling into dusty Croyon, a further 149km on.

- - - - - - - - - - - -

❹ Croydon

If you haven't already felt it on the road in here, Croydon is where that sense of having fallen off the map and emerged into the outback really takes hold. It's a dusty, red-earth kind of place that was, incredibly, once the biggest town in the Gulf of Carpentaria thanks to a short but lucrative gold rush. Gold was discov-

ered here in 1885, and in its heyday there were 30 pubs – just one, the Club Hotel, built in 1887, survives. Croydon's **visitor information centre** (📞07-4748 7152; Samwell St; ⊗9am-4.30pm daily Apr-Sep, 9am-4.30pm Mon-Fri Oct-Mar) has details of the historic precinct and shows a short film (free) about the gold-rush days. At the timber **Croydon General Store** (📞07-4745 6163; Sircom St; ⊗7am-6.30pm Mon-Fri, 9am-7.30pm Sat & Sun) the sign declares this the 'oldest store in Australia, established 1894'.

🛏 p213

The Drive » The Savannah Way (which continues, much of it unsealed, beyond Normanton into the Northern Territory) carries you across the red-and-yellow countryside for 148km into Normanton.

- - - - - - - - - - - -

❺ Normanton

The port for Croydon's gold rush, Normanton boasts a broad and rather long main street lined with some colourful old buildings. These days it's a quiet old place that occasionally springs into life: every Easter the **Barra Bash** lures big crowds, as do the **Normanton Rodeo & Show** (mid-June) and the **Normanton Races** (September). In the historic Burns Philp building, Normanton's excellent **visitor information and heritage centre** (📞07-4745 8444; www.carpentaria.qld.gov.au; cnr Caroline & Landsborough Sts; ⊗9am-4pm Mon-Fri, to noon Sat & Sun Apr-Sep, closed Sun Oct-Mar) has a library, historical displays and lots of regional information. Everyone stops to take a photo of **Krys the Crocodile** on Landsborough St. It's a supposedly life-sized statue of an 8.64m saltie shot by croc hunter Krystina Pawloski on the Norman River in 1958 – the largest recorded croc in the world.

The Drive » As the crow flies, Karumba is a short distance across the Mutton Wetlands, but by road you'll need to travel 37km north to Maggieville, then 42km west to Karumba on the shores of the Gulf.

AUSCAPE/UIG/GETTY IMAGES ©

Karumba Recreational fishing on the Gulf coast

TRIP HIGHLIGHT

6 Karumba

When the sun sinks into the Gulf of Carpentaria in a fiery ball of burnt ochre, Karumba is transformed into a little piece of outback paradise. Karumba is the only town accessible by sealed road on the entire Gulf coast, and it's a great place to kick back for a few days. The actual town is on the Norman River, while Karumba Point is about 6km away by road on the beach. Karumba's **visitor information centre** (☎07-4745 9582; www.carpentaria. qld.gov.au; Walker St, Karumba

Town; ☺9am-4.30pm Mon-Fri, to noon Sat & Sun Apr-Sep, closed Sun Oct-Mar; ☎) **has** details of fishing charters and cruises, **Ferryman** (☎07-4745 9155; www.ferryman. net.au; cruises $45, croc-spotting $60) operates regular sunset cruises and fishing charters in the Dry, while **Croc & Crab Tours** (☎0428-496 026; www.crocandcrab. com.au; half-day tours adult/ child $119/60, cruises adult/child $65/30) runs excellent half-day tours include crab-catching and croc-spotting on the Norman River.

✕ p213

The Drive » When you can bring yourself to leave the Gulf behind, the Burke

Developmental Road is a seriously quiet outback road, crossing the dry Gulf hinterland. After 192km, pause for some company at the Burke & Wills Roadhouse, and then it's 181 lonely kilometres south to Cloncurry.

7 Cloncurry

Compared with where you're coming from, Cloncurry (population 2313) will seem like the heights of civilisation. Known to its friends as 'the Curry', Cloncurry is renowned as the birthplace of the Royal Flying Doctor Service (RFDS) and today it's a busy pastoral centre with a reinvigorated mining industry. The outstanding **John Flynn Place** (📞07-4742 4125; www.johnflynnplace.com.au; cnr Daintree & King Sts; adult/child $10.50/5; ⏰8am-4.30pm Mon-Fri year round, 9am-3pm Sat & Sun May-Sep) celebrates Dr John Flynn's work setting up the invaluable and groundbreaking RFDS, which gave hope, help and health services to people across the remote outback.

🛏 p213

The Drive ≫ You're almost there and, having come so far, you'll barely notice the final 122km along the more heavily trafficked Barkly Hwy.

TRIP HIGHLIGHT

❽ Mt Isa

You can't miss the smokestacks as you drive into Mt Isa, one of Queensland's longest-running mining towns and a travel and lifestyle hub for central Queensland. The sunset view from the **City Lookout** of the twinkling mine lights and silhouetted smokestacks is strangely pretty and very Mt Isa. Strange rock formations – padded with olive-green spinifex – line the perimeter of town, and deep-blue sunsets eclipse all unnatural light. Try to visit in mid-August for Australia's largest **rodeo** (www.isarodeo.com.au; ⏰2nd weekend in Aug). Don't miss the award-winning

Outback at Isa (📞1300 659 660; www.outbackatisa.com.au; 19 Marian St; ⏰8.30am-5pm), which includes the **Hard Times Mine** (📞1300 659 660; www.outbackatisa.com.au; 19 Marian St; adult/child $49/30; ⏰daily), an authentic underground trip to give you the full Isa mining experience; the **Isa Experience & Outback Park** (📞1300 659 6601300 659 660; www.outbackatisa.com.au; 19 Marian St; adult/child $12/7.50; ⏰8.30am-5pm), a hands-on museum providing a colourful and articulate overview of local history; and the fascinating **Riversleigh Fossil Centre** (📞1300 659 660; www.outbackatisa.com.au; 19 Marian St; adult/child $12/7.50; ⏰8.30am-5pm).

 🛏 p213

Eating & Sleeping

Undara Volcanic National Park ❸

🛏 Undara Experience   Resort $$

(☏1800 990 992; www.undara.com.au; unpowered/powered sites per person $12.50/18, railway carriages s/d from $90/170; ❄ ⛟) Just outside the national park, Undara Experience has a great range of accommodation, from a shady campground to nifty little swag tents on raised platforms and modern en-suite rooms. Pride of place goes to the restored railway carriages, charmingly fitted out, some with en suite. Staying here puts you close to the caves and surrounding bushwalks, and there's a good restaurant, a bar and barbecue areas. There's a small shop on site and pricey fuel.

Croydon ❹

🛏 Club Hotel   Pub $

(☏07-4745 6184; www.clubhotelcroydon.com.au; cnr Brown & Sircom Sts; d $80, units $115; ❄ ⛟) The 1887 Club Hotel is the only pub left from Croydon's mining heyday, and has the best range of accommodation in town, including self-contained units and poolside rooms. The bar and bistro serve up huge meals ($18 to $32), ice-cold beer, and sunset views from the verandah.

Karumba ❻

🍴 Sunset Tavern   Pub $$

(☏07-4745 9183; www.sunsettavern.com.au; The Esplanade, Karumba Point; mains $15-35; ⊙10am-10pm) This big open-sided place is the hub of Karumba Point at sunset. It's *the* place to watch the sun sink into the Gulf over a glass of wine and a seafood platter. The food is

reasonably good but the view is better – arrive early for a seat at an outdoor table for the sweetest sunset experience.

Cloncurry ❼

🛏 Wagon Wheel Motel   Motel $$

(☏07-4742 1866; 54 Ramsay St; s/d $90/101, deluxe s/d $105/116; ❄ 🛜 ⛟) The historic main building at the Wagon Wheel Motel, with a restaurant and bar, is said to the oldest licensed premises in northwest Queensland. At the back, the motel rooms are clean and comfortable with TV and fridge. It's worth paying the few extra dollars for the larger and newer deluxe rooms. The restaurant (mains $22 to $36) is one of the better places to eat in town and is open for breakfast and dinner.

Mt Isa ❽

🍴 Rodeo Bar & Grill   Pub Food $$

(☏07-4749 8888; cnr Miles St & Rodeo Dr; mains $15-40; ⊙6.30-11.30am, noon-3pm & 6-9pm) Booth seating brings a touch of intimacy to this cavernous bar-restaurant inside the renovated Isa Hotel. The menu offers something for everyone, from pizzas ($16) and tapas-style snacks to outback-sized steaks. Breakfast (from 6.30am) in a booth is surprisingly good, too.

🛏 Red Earth Hotel   Hotel $$$

(☏1800 603 488; www.redearth-hotel.com.au; Rodeo Dr; d $189-229; ❄ @) The boutique Red Earth is undoubtedly Mt Isa's top address, with period-style furniture and claw-foot bathtubs. It's worth paying the little extra for a private balcony, spa and huge TV. There's a cocktail bar, and an excellent but pricey restaurant in the lobby. In the same block, the Mt Isa Hotel is part of the same hotel complex, with cheaper rooms.

South Australia Trips

SOUTH AUSTRALIA IS LIKE VICTORIA'S BASHFUL COUSIN, but this wonderful state has nothing at all to be shy about. For a start, the state's wine regions are Australia's finest, with the collective weight of the Barossa Valley, McLaren Vale, the Clare Valley and Coonawarra enough to secure Australia's reputation among the elite of the world's wine producers.

Whales and other wildlife are coastal specialities, with Kangaroo Island, in particular, filled with furry creatures, and Port Lincoln offering unique opportunities to swim with great whites, sea lions and some really big tuna.

Add the Flinders Ranges, truly one of our favourite outback playgrounds, and Australia's best oysters, and you have one of Australia's most rewarding road-tripping destinations.

Quorn River gums line the road (Trip 23)
MANFRED GOTTSCHALK/GETTY IMAGES ©

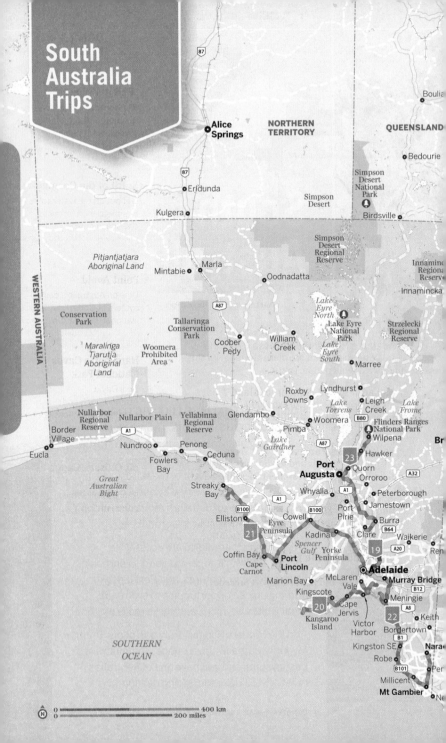

South Australia Trips

Port Lincoln Lincoln National Park

Classic Trip

19 **Adelaide Hills & the Barossa 3–4 Days**
Imagine yourself in southern Germany in this distinguished wine region. (p219)

20 **McLaren Vale & Kangaroo Island 7 Days**
McLaren Vale wines go especially well with the everywhere-you-look wildlife of Kangaroo Island. (p233)

21 **Yorke & Eyre Peninsulas 5–7 Days**
Historic townships and a wild, serrated coastline make these long promontories stand out. (p241)

22 **Coonawarra & the Coorong 5–7 Days**
The Murray meets the sea here, with wines, gorgeous towns and even a Unesco site. (p251)

23 **Clare Valley & the Flinders Ranges 7–10 Days**
World-class wines and historic towns precede red-rocked outback. (p259)

DON'T MISS

Barossa Wineries
Go from one cellar door to another through the lovely country along Trip **19**

Spirit of the Coorong
Get out on the water to shepherd the Murray to the ocean on Trip **22**

Oysters at Point Avoid
Dine on Australia's best oysters at Coffin Bay National Park on Trip **21**

Naracoorte Caves National Park
Do a David Attenborough and search for giant fossils at the end of Trip **22**

Mt Ohlssen Bagge
Our pick of the Flinders Ranges walks that dominate Trip **23**

Barossa Valley *Fine wines, blue skies and rolling hills*

Classic Trip

Adelaide Hills & the Barossa

19

The Barossa is like a quaint European world of historic villages settled comfortably in the pretty valleys lined with vineyards. It's hard to believe Adelaide is just over the hills.

TRIP HIGHLIGHTS

148 km

Tanunda
Classic Barossa town with classic Barossa wines

FINISH 10

9

139 km

Nuriootpa
Visit the iconic Penfolds winery

Eden Valley

Mount Pleasant

144 km

Lobethal
Come for the spectacular Christmas lights

Athelstone

Birdwood

START
Adelaide

6

125 km

Hahndorf
Beautiful Germanic village high in the Adelaide Hills

Bridgewater 3

3–4 DAYS
148KM / 92 MILES

GREAT FOR...

BEST TIME TO GO
October to April, but festivals are worth visiting at other times.

ESSENTIAL PHOTO
Don't miss Hahndorf, looking for all the world like Germany.

BEST FOR WINE
Tanunda lies in the heart of Barossa Wine Country.

Classic Trip

19 Adelaide Hills & the Barossa

When the Adelaide plains are desert-hot in the summer months, the Adelaide Hills (technically the Mt Lofty Ranges) are always a few degrees cooler, with crisp air, woodland shade and labyrinthine valleys. Early colonists built stately summer houses around Stirling and Aldgate, and German settlers escaping religious persecution also arrived, infusing towns like Hahndorf and Lobethal with European values and architecture. Further north, the Barossa's wineries are world class.

① Adelaide

Every time you visit Adelaide, there's a new side of the city to explore and, considering where you're heading on this trip, beachside Glenelg fits the bill perfectly. Glenelg, or 'the Bay' – the site of SA's colonial landing – is Adelaide at its most LA. Glenelg's beach faces towards the west, and as the sun sinks into the sea, the pubs and bars burgeon with surfies, backpackers and sun-damaged sexagenarians. The tram

rumbles in from the city, past the Jetty Rd shopping strip to the al fresco cafes around Moseley Sq. The Glenelg Visitor Information Centre has the local low-down, including information on diving and sailing opportunities. For more on exploring Adelaide, see p230.

The Drive » From the city centre, take Glen Osmond Rd running southeast and, soon enough, it becomes the M1. It winds up through the hills all the way to Stirling.

② Stirling

The photogenic little village of old-school **Stirling** (population 2870) is famed for its bedazzling autumn colours, thanks to the deciduous trees the early residents saw fit to seed – it's one of the most spectacular autumnal shows in the country. The architecture is mostly local but the scattered Germanic inflections set you up for what lies ahead. Nearby, and really rather oddly, one-horse **Aldgate** (population 3350) has been home to both Bon Scott and Mel Gibson over the years. Go figure.

✕ p229

The Drive ›› From Aldgate, forsake the M1 and follow the quieter, prettier Mt Barker Rd through Bridgewater and down into Hahndorf.

⑤ LINK YOUR TRIP

21 Yorke & Eyre Peninsulas

The 701km to Streaky Bay begins in Adelaide and crosses two peninsulas joined by a ferry.

26 Alice Springs to Adelaide

From the outback to South Australia's urbane capital (1500km), this trip couldn't be more different.

MANFRED GOTTSCHALK/GETTY IMAGES ©

Classic Trip

SOUTH AUSTRALIA **19** ADELAIDE HILLS & THE BAROSSA

TRIP HIGHLIGHT

3 Hahndorf

Hahndorf may be a cliche of the Adelaide Hills' Germanic past, but that's because it's absurdly pretty, with Teutonic sandstone architecture, European trees, and flowers overflowing from half wine barrels. And it's also interesting: Australia's oldest surviving German settlement (1839), founded by 50 Lutheran families fleeing religious persecution in Prussia. It's slowly becoming less kitsch and more cool; to get an informed taste of what it's all about, try **Hahndorf Walking Tours** (☏0477 288 011; www.facebook. com/hahndorfwalkingtours; 45/90min tours per person

$18/25; ⊘45min tour noon & 1pm Sat & Sun, 90min tour 2pm Sat & Sat plus 6pm daily Oct-Mar), while Hahndorf's history takes shape at **Hahndorf Academy** (www. hahndorfacademy.org.au; 68 Main St, Hahndorf; ⊘10am-5pm). But if this journey is all about the food for you, you can pick your own strawberries between November and May from the famous, family-run **Beerenberg Strawberry Farm** (☏08-8388 7272; www.beerenberg.com.au; Mount Barker Rd, Hahndorf; strawberry picking per adult/child $4/free, strawberries per kg from $9.50; ⊘9am-5pm).

✕ ⌂ p229

The Drive » Return northwest along Mt Barker Rd, then turn north (right) along Ambleside Rd. Where it ends, take Onkaparinga Valley Rd through Balhannah and on into Oakbank.

4 Oakbank

Strung-out Oakbank (population 450) lives

BAROSSA FESTIVALS

A Day on the Green (www.adayonthegreen.com.au) Mature-age moshpit at Peter Lehmann Wines, with mature-age acts (Jimmy Barnes, Cheap Trick, Dragon). Held in December.

Barossa Gourmet Weekend (www.barossagourmet. com) Fab food matched with winning wines at select wineries; happens in late winter or early spring.

Barossa Vintage Festival (www.barossavintagefestival. com.au) A week-long festival with music, maypole dancing, tug-of-war contests etc; it's held around Easter in odd-numbered years.

for the annual **Oakbank Easter Racing Carnival** (www.oakbankracingclub.com. au), said to be the greatest picnic horse-race meeting in the world – that's no small claim but we're yet to hear any convincing evidence to the contrary. It's a two-day festival of equine splendour, risqué dresses and 18-year-olds who can't hold their liquor.

Hahndorf Al fresco dining

The Drive » Continue northeast from Oakbank along Onkaparinga Valley Rd (B34); Woodside is just 7km up the road.

❺ Woodside

Agricultural **Woodside** (population 1830) has a few enticements for galloping gourmands, and it's here that the foodie character of the trip really begins to dominate, although you still have to wait for the wineries. Woodside Cheese Wrights is a passionate and unpretentious gem producing classic, artisan and experimental cheeses (soft styles a speciality) from locally grazed sheep and cows. Stock up on rocky road, scorched almonds and appallingly realistic chocolate cow pats at Melba's Chocolate & Confectionery Factory.

The Drive » Continue northeast along the B34 for 3km, then take the Lobethal turn-off. You'll be in Lobethal after 3km more.

TRIP HIGHLIGHT

❻ Lobethal

In the 'Valley of Praise', Lobethal was established by Lutheran Pastor

Classic Trip

MILTON WORDLEY/GETTY IMAGES ©

PETER WALTON PHOTOGRAPHY/GETTY IMAGES ©

WHY THIS IS A CLASSIC TRIP
ANTHONY HAM, AUTHOR

Classic wines and the lovely hill country that surround Adelaide make for a classic and suitably sedate side trip from the South Australian capital. Like all classic trips, it's a well-worn trail, one that takes in Hahndorf and the Barossa wineries as well-loved focal points. It's about the establishment, about old-school Adelaide and its weekend escapes, and about all the hallmarks of European wine touring.

Top: Harvest time, Barossa Valley
Left: Wine grapes, Barossa Valley
Right: Vineyards, Gumeracha

WALTER BIBIKOW/GETTY IMAGES ©

Fritzsche and his followers in 1842. The church opened for business in 1843. The town lacks the hype and uniformity of style of Hahndorf, but many visitors like it all the more for that. The main street has the usual complement of soporific pubs and hardware stores, but the town really hits its straps during December's **Lights of Lobethal festival** (www.lightsoflobethal.com.au), a blaze of Christmas lights bringing sightseers from the city. Check out the town, then repair to the streetside terrace at the **Lobethal Bierhaus** (🕿08-8389 5570; www.bierhaus.com.au; 3a Main St, Lobethal; ⊙noon-10pm Fri & Sat, to 6pm Sun) for some serious microbrewed concoctions. The Red Truck Porter will put hairs on your chest.

The Drive » Gumeracha is just 10km north of Lobethal, via Kenton Valley. Watch for good views of Mt Torrens and the Mt Lofty Ranges away to the east along the way.

❼ Gumeracha

While Gumeracha (population 400) is not the hottest item on the Barossa Valley ticket, it's worth a stop nonetheless. It's a hardy hillside town with a pub at the bottom (making it hard to roll home) and the main lure here is climbing the 18.3m-high **Big Rocking Horse** (www.thetoyfactory.

Classic Trip

com.au; Birdwood Rd, Gumeracha; admission $2; ⊘9am-5pm), which doesn't actually rock, but is unusually tasteful as far as Australia's 'big' tourist attractions go.

The Drive » While it takes you in the wrong direction, we recommend taking the stirringly scenic road west and then southwest through the Torrens River Gorge for around 24km as far as Athelstone, before turning around and returning to Gumeracha. Then it's east through Birdwood and Mt Pleasant, then north through to Angaston.

- - - - - - - - - - - -

❽ Angaston

In photo-worthy Angaston, an agricultural vibe persists as there are relatively few wineries on the town doorstep: cows graze in paddocks at the end of the town's streets. Along the main drag are two pubs, some terrific eateries and a few B&Bs in old stone cottages (check for double glazing and ghosts – we had a sleepless night!). Don't miss the hearty Germanic offerings, local produce and questionable buskers at the weekly **Barossa Farmers Market**

BAROSSA WINES

With hot, dry summers and cool, moderate winters, the Barossa is one of the world's great wine regions – an absolute must for anyone with even the slightest interest in a good drop. It's a compact valley – just 25km long – yet it produces 21% of Australia's wine.

The local towns have a distinctly German heritage, dating back to 1842. Fleeing religious persecution in Prussia and Silesia, settlers (bringing their vine cuttings with them) created a Lutheran heartland where German traditions persist today. The physical remnants of colonisation – Gothic church steeples and stone cottages – are everywhere. Cultural legacies of the early days include a dubious passion for oom-pah bands, and an appetite for wurst, pretzels and sauerkraut.

The Barossa is best known for shiraz, with riesling the dominant white. There are around 80 vineyards here and 60 cellar doors. Although there are a few boutique wineries, the long-established 'Barossa Barons' – big, ballsy and brassy – hold sway.

The following offer recommended tours of Barossa Valley wineries.

Barossa Epicurean Tours (☑0457 101 487; www.barossatours.com.au; half-/full-day tours from $150/160) Good-value, small-group tours visiting the wineries of your choice and Mengler Hill Lookout. From Adelaide or Barossa.

Barossa Wine Lovers Tours (☑08-8270 5500; www.wineloverstours.com.au; tours incl lunch from $75) Minibus tours to wineries, lookouts, shops and heritage buildings…a good blend. Good for groups; minimum numbers apply.

Barossa Experience Tours (☑08-8563 3248; www.barossavalleytours.com; half-/full-day tours from $90/150) Local small-group operator whisking you around the major sites. The Wine, Food & Heritage Tour ($150) includes lunch and lots of history. From Barossa.

Groovy Grape (☑1800 661 177; www.groovygrape.com.au; full-day tours $90) Backpacker-centric day tours from Adelaide with a BBQ lunch: good value, good fun. November to April only.

Taste the Barossa (☑08-8357 1594; www.winetoursbarossa.com; full-day tours $99) Great-value minibus tours from Adelaide visiting a fistful of top wineries, with lunch at Peter Lehmann.

Hahndorf Sandstone building on Main St

(www.barossafarmersmarket.com; cnr Stockwell & Nuriootpa Rds; ⏰7.30-11.30am Sat), or the **Barossa Valley Cheese Company** (www.barossacheese.com.au; 67b Murray St; ⏰10am-5pm Mon-Fri, 10am-4pm Sat, 11am-3pm Sun); it's unlikely you'll leave the latter without buying a wedge of the Washington Washed Rind. To get the whole wine thing happening, about 10km southeast of Angaston in the Eden Valley, old-school **Henschke** (www.henschke.com.au; Henschke Rd, Keyneton; ⏰9am-4.30pm Mon-Fri, to noon Sat) is known for its iconic Hill

of Grace red, but most of the wines here are classics.

✕ ⏍ p229

The Drive » Nuriootpa lies just 7km northwest of Angaston. You're now in the deep heart of the Barossa Valley.

- - - - - - - - - -

TRIP HIGHLIGHT

❾ Nuriootpa

Along an endless main street at the northern end of the valley, Nuriootpa is the Barossa's commercial centre. It's not as endearing as Tanunda or Angaston, but has a certain agrarian appeal. Lutheran spirit runs deep in Nuri: a sign says, 'God

has invested in you – are you showing any interest?' Don't miss a drive along **Seppeltsfield Road** (www.seppeltsfieldroad.com), an incongruous avenue of huge palm trees meandering through the vineyards behind Nuri. Beyond Marananga the palm rows veer off the roadside and track up a hill to the **Seppelt Family Mausoleum** – a Grecian shrine fronted by chunky Doric columns. But if wines are why you're here, **Penfolds** (www.penfolds.com.au; 30 Tanunda Rd, Nuriootpa; ⏰10am-5pm) is a Barossa institution and one Australia's best-

Classic Trip

known wineries. Book ahead for the 'Make Your Own Blend' tour ($65), or the 'Taste of Grange' tour ($150), which allows you to slide some Grange Hermitage across your lips.

 p229

The Drive » Take the B19 southwest from Nuri and after 7km you find yourself in Tanunda.

- - - - - - - - - -

TRIP HIGHLIGHT

⑩ Tanunda

At the centre of the valley both geographically and socially, Tanunda is the Barossa's main tourist town. Tanunda manages to morph the practicality of Nuriootpa with the charm of Angaston without a sniff of self-importance. The wineries are what you're here for and it's very much worth

the wait. Tanunda is flush with historic buildings, including the cottages around **Goat Square** (cnr John & Maria Sts). This was the *ziegenmarkt*, a meeting and market place, laid out in 1842 as Tanunda's original town centre. Then watch

honest-to-goodness coopers make and repair wine barrels, 4km south of town at the **Keg Factory** (www.thekegfactory.com.au; 25 St Hallett Rd; ⊙10am-4pm). That done, get down to the seriously pleasurable business of indulging in the region's wines.

TANUNDA WINES

Peter Lehmann Wines (www.peterlehmannwines.com.au; Para Rd, Tanunda; ⊙9.30am-5pm Mon-Fri, 10.30am-4.30pm Sat & Sun) The shiraz and riesling vintages here (oh, and semillon) are probably the most consistent, affordable and widely distributed wines in the Barossa. Peter Lehmann passed away in 2013: pay your respects with a cellar door visit!

St Hallett (www.sthallett.com.au; St Hallett Rd, Tanunda; ⊙10am-5pm) Using only Barossa grapes, improving St Hallet produces reasonably priced but consistently good whites (try the Poacher's Blend) and the excellent Old Block Shiraz. Unpretentious and great value for money.

Rockford Wines (www.rockfordwines.com.au; Krondorf Rd, Tanunda; ⊙11am-5pm) One of our favourite boutique Barossa wineries, this 1850s cellar door sells traditionally made, small-range wines, including sparkling reds. The Black Shiraz is a sparkling, spicy killer.

Eating & Sleeping

Stirling ②

✕ Stirling Hotel — Pub Food $$

(📞08-8339 2345; www.stirlinghotel.com.au; 52 Mt Barker Rd, Stirling; mains $16-32; ⏱noon-3pm & 6-9pm Mon-Fri, 8am-9pm Sat & Sun) The owners spent so much money tarting up this gorgeous old dame, it's a wonder they can pay the staff. A runaway success, the free-flowing bistro (classy pub grub and pizzas) and romantic restaurant (upmarket regional cuisine) are always packed.

Hahndorf ③

✕ Haus — Cafe $$

(📞08-8388 7555; www.haushahndorf.com.au; 38 Main St; breakfast mains $8-22, lunch & dinner $20-55; ⏱7.30am-11pm) Haus brings some urban hip to the Hills. Rustic-style pizzas are laden with local smallgoods, and the wine list is huge (lots of Hills drops). Also on offer are baguettes, pasta, burgers, salads and quiches. Good coffee, too.

✕ German Arms Hotel — Pub Food $$

(📞08-8388 7013; www.germanarmshotel.com.au; 69 Main St; mains $16-30; ⏱8.30am-10pm) Packed on weekends (with 18-to-25-year-olds, oddly enough), the bratwursts and schnitzels here are legendary.

▭ Manna — Motel, Apartments $$

(📞08-8388 1000; www.themanna.com.au; 25 & 35a Main St; d with/without spa from $225/150, 1-/2-bedroom apt from $159/318; ❄🛜🏊) The Manna is a stylish, contemporary maze of motel suites on the main street, spread over several buildings. The older (more affordable) units occupy a refurbished, exposed-brick motel complex set back from the street. Free wi-fi.

Angaston ⑧

✕ Vintners Bar & Grill — Modern Australian $$$

(📞08-8564 2488; www.vintners.com.au; cnr Stockwell & Nuriootpa Rds; lunch mains $16-36, dinner $34-39; ⏱noon-2.30pm daily, 6.30-9pm Mon-Sat) One of the Barossa's landmark restaurants, Vintners stresses simple elegance in both food and atmosphere. The dining room has an open fire, vineyard views and bolts of crisp white linen; menus concentrate on local produce (pray the cider-baked pork belly is on the menu when you visit).

▭ Marble Lodge — B&B $$$

(📞08-8564 2478; www.marblelodge.com.au; 21 Dean St; d $225; ❄🛜) A grandiose 1915 Federation-style villa on the hill behind the town, built from local pink-and-white granite. Accommodation is in two plush suites behind the house (high-colonial or high-kitsch, depending on your world view). Breakfast is served in the main house.

Nuriootpa ⑨

✕ Maggie Beer's Farm Shop — Deli $

(www.maggiebeer.com.au; 50 Pheasant Farm Rd; snacks $5-20, picnic baskets from $16; ⏱10.30am-5pm) Celebrity SA gourmet Maggie Beer has been hugely successful with her range of condiments, preserves and pâtés (and TV appearances!). The vibe here isn't as relaxed as it used to be, but stop by for some gourmet tastings, an ice cream, a cooking demo or a takeaway hamper of delicious bites. Off Samuel Rd.

STRETCH YOUR LEGS
ADELAIDE

Start/Finish: Central Market

Distance: 5km

Duration: 2-3 hours

Adelaide is one of Australia's most underrated capital cities and its downtown areas are eminently walkable, showcasing the city's vibrancy and rich architectural heritage, not to mention the state's Aboriginal history and impressive wine-growing areas.

Take this walk on Trips

Central Market

Adelaide's **Central Market** (www. adelaidecentralmarket.com.au; Gouger St; ⊙7am-5.30pm Tue, 9am-5.30pm Wed & Thu, 7am-9pm Fri, to 3pm Sat) is a terrific place to begin with 250-odd stalls. A sliver of salami from the Mettwurst Shop, a crumb of English Stilton from the Smelly Cheese Shop, a tub of blueberry yogurt from the Yoghurt Shop – there's so much here to enjoy. **Adelaide's Top Food & Wine Tours** (www.topfoodandwinetours.com.au) offers guided tours.

The Walk » Walk east along Grote St to the greenery of Victoria Sq, one of the lovelier open spaces in any Australian capital. Head north along King William St, then right on Grenfell.

Tandanya National Aboriginal Cultural Institute

Tandanya (☑08-8224 3200 www.tandanya. com.au; 253 Grenfell St; ⊙ 9am-4pm Mon-Sat) is an impressive space that offers an insight into the culture of the local Kaurna people, whose territory extends south to Cape Jervis and north to Port Wakefield. It's a good place to get an insight into Aboriginal South Australia before heading out of the city. Inside are interactive visual-arts gallery spaces, plus a gift shop and a cafe.

The Walk » Walk around 50m east, then north on East Terrace, cross Rundle St, then cross Rymill Park. The wine centre backs onto the park along the north side of Botanic Rd.

National Wine Centre of Australia

Given the importance of wine in so many SA trips, you'd do well to check out the **National Wine Centre of Australia** (www.wineaustralia.com.au; cnr Botanic & Hackney Rds; ⊙8am-9pm Mon-Fri, 9am-9pm Sat, 9am-7pm Sun, tours & tastings 10am-5pm), with its free self-guided, interactive Wine Discovery Journey exhibition, paired with tastings of Australian wines (from $10). Friday-evening 'uncorked' drinks happen at 4.30pm.

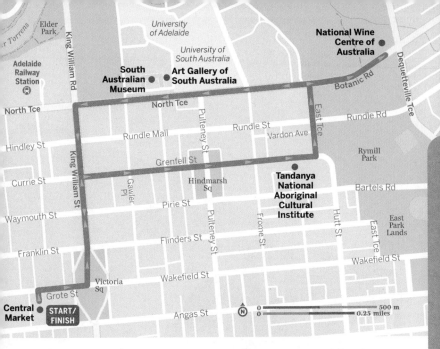

The Walk

The Walk » Return back along Botanic Rd (or through the park if you prefer). Just after Pulteney St branches off to the left, you'll see the Art Gallery of South Australia on your right.

Art Gallery of South Australia

Spend a few hushed hours in the vaulted, parquetry-floored **Art Gallery of South Australia** (www.artgallery.sa.gov.au; North Tce; ⏱10am-5pm) that represents the big names in Australian art. Permanent exhibitions include Australian, Aboriginal and Torres Strait Islander, Asian, European and North American art (20 bronze Rodins!). Progressive visiting exhibitions occupy the basement.

The Walk » You won't even have time to work up a sweat: the South Australian Museum is right next door.

South Australian Museum

At the **South Australian Museum** (www.samuseum.sa.gov.au; North Tce; ⏱10am-5pm), dig into Australia's natural history with the museum's special exhibits on whales and Antarctic explorer Sir Douglas Mawson. An Aboriginal Cultures Gallery displays artefacts of the Ngarrindjeri people of the Coorong and lower Murray – great if you're taking Trip 22. Free tours depart 11am weekdays and 2pm and 3pm weekends.

The Walk » Walk around 200m west along North Tce, turn left (south) along King William Street, enjoy Victoria Sq a second time, then turn right (west) along Grote St to return to where you started at the Central Market.

Remarkable Rocks *Astounding colours in an iconic Australian landscape*

McLaren Vale & Kangaroo Island

From the world-class wineries of McLaren Vale to the wonders of Kangaroo Island, this route combines two great Aussie obsessions.

TRIP HIGHLIGHTS

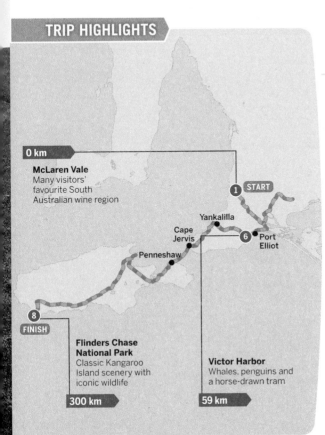

0 km

McLaren Vale
Many visitors' favourite South Australian wine region

① START

Yankalilla

Cape Jervis

⑥ Port Elliot

Penneshaw

⑧
FINISH

Flinders Chase National Park
Classic Kangaroo Island scenery with iconic wildlife

300 km

Victor Harbor
Whales, penguins and a horse-drawn tram

59 km

7 DAYS
382KM / 237 MILES

GREAT FOR...

BEST TIME TO GO
Year-round.

ESSENTIAL PHOTO

Vineyards of McLaren Vale at sunset.

BEST FOR WINES

McLaren Vale is known for its sophisticated reds.

GRANT DIXON/GETTY IMAGES ©

McLaren Vale & Kangaroo Island

20

Patterned with vineyards running down to the sea, the Fleurieu is home to the world-renowned McLaren Vale Wine Region which is known for its sophisticated reds. Further east, the Fleurieu's Encounter Coast is an engaging mix of surf beaches, historic towns and whales cavorting offshore, while wildlife-rich Kangaroo Island is a simply wonderful place to rest at journey's end.

TRIP HIGHLIGHT

❶ McLaren Vale

Flanked by the wheat-coloured Willunga Scarp and encircled by vines, McLaren Vale is an energetic, utilitarian town that's not much to look at, but it does have some great eateries and easy access to some excellent winery cellar doors. To make the most of your time here, consider taking one of the many tours that visit a number of wineries in a single day, among

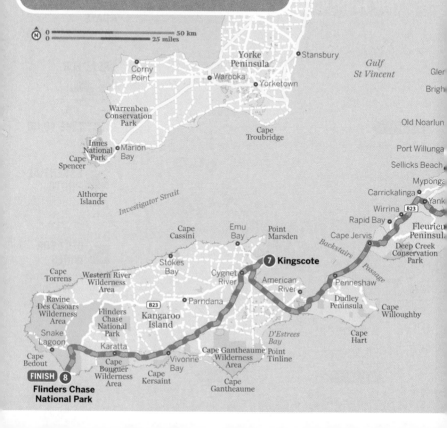

them **McLaren Vale Wine Tours** (☏0414 784 666; www.mclarenvaletours.com.au), **Chook's Little Winery Tours** (☏0414 922 200; www.chookslittlewinerytours.com.au; tours per person from $90) or **Wine Diva Tours** (☏08-8323 9806; www.winedivatours.com.au; tours per person from $150). And to mix it all up a little without straying too close to sobriety, family-run **Goodieson Brewery** (www.goodiesonbrewery.com.au; 194 Sand Rd; tastings $5; ⊙11am-5.30pm) brews a pale ale, pilsner, wheat beer and brown ale, plus brilliant seasonal beers.

✕ p239

The Drive 》 Willunga is a mere 4km south of McLaren Vale township, but a worthy destination in its own right nonetheless.

- - - - - - - -

❷ Willunga

A one-horse town with three pubs (a winning combo!), arty Willunga took off in 1840 when high-quality slate was discovered nearby and exported across Australia. Today, the town's early buildings along sloping High St are occupied by some terrific eateries, B&B accommodation and galleries, and it may work out as a far more appealing base for touring those wineries. **Willunga Farmers Market** (www.willungafarmersmarket.com; Willunga Town Sq; ⊙8am-12.30pm Sat) is heavy on the organic, the bespoke and the locally sourced.

✕ ⛱ p239

The Drive 》 The drive from Willunga to Currency Creek (28km) rises up and over the Mt Lofty Ranges, an attractive range that runs like a spine up through the peninsula, alternating between densely forested slopes and rolling farm country.

- - - - - - - -

❸ Currency Creek

If the McLaren Vale Wine region is too much of a scene, this smaller wine region close to Goolwa may appeal. Once slated as the capital of SA (strange but true), Currency Creek (www.currencycreekwineregion.com.au) is now content with producing award-winning wines. **Currency Creek Winery** (☏08-8555 4069; www.currencycreekwinery.com.au; Winery Rd, Currency Creek; ⊙10am-5pm) has 160 acres under vine (brilliant cabernet sauvignon) plus a fab restaurant, and is a fine place to get a sense of what goes on around here.

The Drive 》 Drive north from Currency Creek to Strathalbyn, then turn east for the final 16km into Langhorne Creek.

Map

p230
Adelaide
Woodside
Mt Barker
RT [B34] Callington
[M1]
aren Vale
Strathalbyn **Langhorne Creek** ❹
Villunga
Mt Compass
Currency ❸ **Creek**
[A13]
[B37] ❺ Goolwa
❻ Port Elliot
ctor
rbor
Younghusband Peninsula

SOUTHERN OCEAN

⑧ LINK YOUR TRIP

19 Adelaide Hills & the Barossa

This trip into the Mt Lofty Ranges and up into the Barossa begins in Adelaide.

26 Alice Springs to Adelaide

Head for Australia's Red Centre – our journey may begin in Alice Springs, but there's no reason you can't drive it in reverse.

❹ Langhorne Creek

Langhorne Creek (www.langhornecreek.com) is one of Australia's oldest wine-growing regions and is home to 20-plus wineries, producing shiraz, cabernet sauvignon and chardonnay. **Bleasdale Winery** (www.bleasdale.com.au; Wellington Rd, Langhorne Creek; ⊙10am-5pm) was the district's first, and has a large range, historic cellars and an old red-gum lever press, while **Bremerton** (www.bremerton.com.au; Strathalbyn Rd, Langhorne Creek; ⊙10am-5pm) is an innovative operator producing top chardonnay and shiraz in an old-school region.

The Drive » Return the way you came through Strathalbyn and Currency Creek. From the latter it's 10km into Goolwa.

❺ Goolwa

Goolwa is an unassuming town where the rejuvenated Murray River empties into the sea, and we reckon this meeting of sea and Australia's longest river is reason enough to come here. The town has far greater river than sea frontage (and is therefore somewhat sheltered from the wilds of the Southern Ocean), but beyond the dunes is a fantastic beach with ranks of breakers rolling in from the ocean, same as it ever was... Learn to surf with **Ocean**

Living Surf School (☎0487 921 232; www.olsurfschool.com.au; 2/4hr lessons $35/65), head down to the wharf and **Steam Exchange Brewery** (☎08-8555 3406; www.steamexchange.com.au; Goolwa Wharf; tastings $3.20; ⊙10am-5pm Wed-Sun) for stouts, ales and even SA's only single malt whiskey distillery, then take an eco-cruise on the Murray and into the Coorong National Park with **Spirit of the Coorong** (☎08-8555 2203, 1800 442 203; www.coorongcruises.com.au; Goolwa Wharf).

📖 p239

The Drive » Goolwa to its kissing cousin, Victor Harbor, is just 17 coastal kilometres, with views of Encounter Bay away to the south for much of the trip.

TRIP HIGHLIGHT

❻ Victor Harbor

The biggest town on the Encounter Coast, Victor Harbor is a raggedy, brawling holiday destination – avoid November when schoolies arrive en masse. At other times, Victor Harbor is excellent for wildlife. Just offshore is the boulder-strewn **Granite Island Nature Park & Penguin Centre** (☎08-8552 7555; www.graniteisland.com.au; Granite Island Nature Park; adult/child $8/6; ⊙11am-4pm Tues-Sun & holidays), connected to the mainland by an 1875 causeway. Ride out there on the 1894 double-decker horse-drawn tram, then take a sunset **penguin**

tour (☎08-8552 7555; www.graniteisland.com.au; adult/child/family $12.50/7.50/36; ⊙sunset). And best of all, Victor Harbor is on the migratory path of southern right whales (May to October). The multilevel **South Australian Whale Centre** (☎08-8551 0750; www.sawhalecentre.com; 2 Railway Tce; adult/child/family $9/4.50/24; ⊙10.30am-5pm) has impressive displays and can give you the low-down on where to see them. For whale sightings info, call the **Whale Information Hotline** (☎1900 942 537).

🍴 p239

PANORAMIC IMAGES/GETTY IMAGES ©

Kangaroo Island Fur seals

MCLAREN VALE WINERIES

If the Barossa Valley is SA wine's old school, then McLaren Vale is the upstart teenager smoking cigarettes behind the shed and stealing nips from dad's port bottle. The gorgeous vineyards around here have a Tuscan haze in summer, rippling down to a calm coastline that's almost Ligurian. This is shiraz country – solid, punchy and seriously good with a reputation in wine circles that, for many, now surpasses the Barossa.

Alpha Box & Dice (www.alphaboxdice.com; Lot 8 Olivers Rd; ☉11am-4pm Mon-Thu, 10am-5pm Fri-Sun) One out of the box, this refreshing little gambler wins top billing for interesting blends, funky retro furnishings, quirky labels and laid-back staff.

Samuel's Gorge (☎08-8323 8651; www.gorge.com.au; Chaffeys Rd; ☉11am-5pm) On a hill behind McLaren Vale township is this understated winner, inside an 1853 stone barn and with valley views that are bordering on English. Great grenache; BYO picnic.

Wirra Wirra (www.wirrawirra.com; McMurtrie Rd; ☉10am-5pm Mon-Sat, 11am-5pm Sun) Fancy some pétanque with your plonk? This barnlike, 1894 cellar door has a grassy picnic area, and there's a roaring fire inside in winter. Sample reasonably priced stickies (dessert wines) and the super-popular Church Block blend. Whites include a citrusy viognier and an aromatic riesling.

The Drive » Climb back up and over Mt Lofty as you cross the southern end of the Fleurieu Peninsula via Inman Valley and Yankalilla. Just west of the latter, stop at Carrickalinga for a gorgeous arc of white sandy beach, then make for Cape Jervis and the Kangaroo Island ferry terminal. Once on the island, Kingscote is 61km further on.

➐ Kingscote

The main appeal of Kangaroo Island (KI) rarely resides in its towns, but snoozy seaside Kingscote (pronounced kings-coat) is the main settlement on KI, and the hub of island life. It's a photogenic town with swaying Norfolk Island pines, a couple of pubs, some decent eateries and all manner of activities from the foodie-oriented to feeding the **pelicans** (📞08-8553 3112; Kingscote Wharf, Kingscote; adult/child $5/3; ⊙feeding 5pm) at Kingscote Wharf. Nurture your inner beekeeper at **Island Beehive** (www. island-beehive.com.au; 59 Playford Hwy, Kingscote; tours adult/child/family $4.50/3/13;

⊙9am-5pm, tours every 30min 9.30am-3.30pm), pass by Island Pure Sheep Dairy then sample the small-batch gin with KI native juniper berries, plus vodka, brandy and liqueurs and pray the organic honey-and-walnut version hasn't sold out at **Kangaroo Island Spirits** (KIS; www.kispirits.com.au; 856 Playford Hwy, Cygnet River; tastings free, bottles from $42; ⊙11am-5pm Wed-Mon, daily during school holidays).

🍴🛏 p239

The Drive » It's only 115km from Kingscote to the outer reaches of Flinders Chase National Park, but it's a drive to linger over as you take in the magnificence and many detours that come with crossing the island from one end to the other.

TRIP HIGHLIGHT

➑ Flinders Chase National Park

Occupying the south-western corner of the island, **Flinders Chase National Park** (www. environment.sa.gov.au; adult/child/family $10/6/27) is one of SA's top national parks. Wildlife is a

feature here: kangaroos, wallabies, bandicoots, echidnas and possums inhabit the wilderness, while koalas and platypuses were introduced to Flinders Chase in the 1920s when it was feared they would become extinct on the mainland. Much of the park is mallee scrub, and there are also some beautiful, tall sugar-gum forests, particularly around **Rocky River** and the **Ravine des Casoars**, 5km south of Cape Borda. Rocky River is especially good for wildlife, and a road runs south from here to a remote 1906 **lighthouse** atop wild **Cape du Couedic**. A boardwalk weaves down to **Admirals Arch**, a huge archway ground out by heavy seas, and passes a colony of New Zealand fur seals. At Kirkpatrick Point, a few kilometres east of Cape du Couedic, the much-photographed **Remarkable Rocks** are a cluster of hefty, weather-gouged granite boulders atop a rocky dome that arcs 75m down to the sea. Remarkable indeed!

Eating & Sleeping

McLaren Vale ❶

✗ Blessed Cheese   Cafe $

(www.blessedcheese.com.au; 150 Main Rd; breakfast mains $6-16, lunch $11-28; ☺8am-4.30pm Mon-Thu, to 5pm Fri-Sun) The cute staff at this blessed cafe crank out great coffee, croissants, wraps, salads, tarts, burgers, cheese platters, murderous cakes and funky sausage rolls. The menu changes every couple of days, always with an emphasis on local produce. The aromas emanating from the cheese counter are deliciously stinky.

Willunga ❷

✗ Fino   Modern Australian $$

(☎08-8556 4488; www.fino.net.au; 8 Hill St; mains $28-33; ☺noon-3pm Tue-Sun, 6.30-9pm Fri & Sat) A regular on 'Australia's Top 100 Restaurants' lists and with a cabinet full of regional awards for both food and wine, Fino is fine indeed. It's a low-key conversion of a slate-floored stone cottage, with a small, simple menu of small, simple dishes, sourced locally as much as possible. The Coorong Angus rib with mustard leaves is a winner.

⛏ Willunga House B&B   B&B $$$

(☎08-8556 2467; www.willungahouse.com.au; 1 St Peters Tce; d incl breakfast $210-280; ❋ 🛜 🏊) If you're looking for a real treat, this graceful, two-storey 1850 mansion off the main street is for you: Baltic-pine floorboards, Italian cherrywood beds, open fires, Indigenous art and a swimming pool. Breakfast is a feast of organic muesli, fruit salad and poached pears, followed by cooked delights.

Goolwa ❺

⛏ Australasian   Boutique Hotel $$$

(☎08-8555 1088; www.australasian1858.com; 1 Porter St; d incl breakfast from $395; ❋ 🛜) This gorgeous 1858 stone hotel, at the head of Goolwa's main street, has been reborn as a sassy B&B, with a sequence of Japanese-inspired decks and glazed extensions, and an upmarket dining room. All five plush suites have views, and the breakfast will make you want to wake up here again. There's a two-night minimum.

Victor Harbor ❻

✗ Anchorage Cafe   Modern Australian $$

(☎08-8552 5970; www.anchorageseafronthotel.com; 21 Flinders Pde; tapas $4-17, mains $16-34; ☺8-11am, noon-2.30pm & 5.30-8.30pm) This salty sea cave at the Anchorage hotel has an old whaling boat for a bar and a Mediterranean-Mod Oz menu (baguettes, pizzas, souvlaki) peppered with plenty of seafood. There's great coffee, tapas and cakes, plus Euro beers and a breezy terrace on which to drink too many of them.

Kingscote ❼

✗ Kangaroo Island
Fresh Seafoods   Seafood $

(www.goodfoodkangarooisland.com/eatingout/kifreshseafood.asp; 26 Telegraph Rd, Kingscote; meals $8-16; ☺8am-8pm Mon-Sat) This unassuming place attached to a petrol station has some of the best seafood you're ever likely to taste. Fat oysters go for around a dollar each, then there are all manner of cooked and fresh KI seafood packs and combos. Superb!

⛏ Aurora Ozone Hotel   Hotel $$

(☎08-8553 2011, 1800 083 133; www.auroraresorts.com.au; cnr Commercial St & Kingscote Tce, Kingscote; pub/motel d from $162/248, 1-/2-/3-bed apt from $270/482/543; ❋ @ 🛜 🏊) Opposite the foreshore and with killer views, the 100-year-old Ozone pub has quality pub rooms upstairs, motel rooms, and stylish deluxe apartments in a new wing across the street. The eternally busy bistro (mains $20 to $48) serves meaty grills and seafood, and you can pickle yourself on KI wines at the bar.

Moonta mines Classic outback scenery in historic mining towns

Yorke & Eyre Peninsulas

21

With old mining towns, swimming with sharks, world-famous oysters and a sea breeze your constant companion, it's hard to resist this fine traverse of South Australia's southern coast.

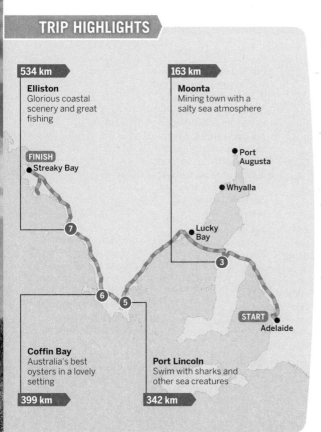

TRIP HIGHLIGHTS

534 km

Elliston
Glorious coastal scenery and great fishing

FINISH
● Streaky Bay

7

163 km

Moonta
Mining town with a salty sea atmosphere

● Port Augusta

● Whyalla

● Lucky Bay

3

6

5

Coffin Bay
Australia's best oysters in a lovely setting

399 km

Port Lincoln
Swim with sharks and other sea creatures

342 km

START
● Adelaide

5–7 DAYS
701KM / 436 MILES

GREAT FOR...

BEST TIME TO GO

Year-round, but June to August can be cold and wet.

ESSENTIAL PHOTO

Face-to-face with a great white shark.

BEST FOR OUTDOORS

Swimming with sea lions off Port Lincoln.

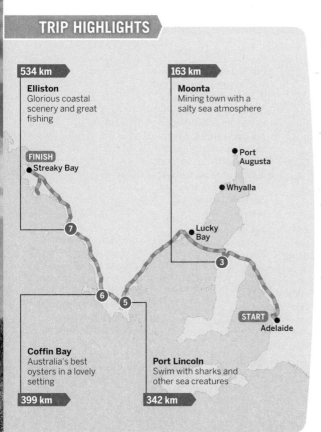

IAN WOOLCOCK/GETTY IMAGES ©

241

21 Yorke & Eyre Peninsulas

For history buffs, the northwestern end of 'Yorkes' has a trio of towns called the Copper Triangle: Moonta (the mine), Wallaroo (the smelter) and Kadina (the service town). Innes National Park is remote and definitely worth the detour before you loop up through a string of necessary if unappealing towns on your way to the dramatic Eyre Peninsula coastline that runs from Port Lincoln to Streaky Bay.

❶ Adelaide

If you've been in Adelaide any length of time, you may be looking for a new corner of the city to explore, and considering that you're heading north from the city, Port Adelaide might just be that place. Mired in the economic doldrums for decades, Port Adelaide, 15km northwest of the city, is slowly gentrifying, morphing its warehouses into art spaces and museums, and its brawl-house pubs into boutique beer emporia. There's even an organic food market here now: things are on the up! The helpful Port Adelaide Visitor Information Centre stocks brochures on self-guided history, heritage-pub and dolphin-spotting walks and drives, plus the enticements of neighbouring **Semaphore**, a very bohemian beach 'burb where activities include dolphin cruises and kayaking. If it's downtown Adelaide that appeals, turn to p230.

The Drive » You've a long road ahead of you so take the A1 motorway northwest out of the city to get some miles under your belt. After Port Wakefield, at the head of Gulf St Vincent, the traffic thins as you continue northwest on the B85 for the 51km to Kadina.

❷ Kadina

The largest of the three towns that make up the Yorke Peninsula's 'Copper Triangle', Kadina bakes without the benefit of a sea breeze. If you can stand the heat, it's worth exploring the town's impressive copper-era civic buildings a little on foot, as long as you remember to pause for some liquid refreshments at the town's slew

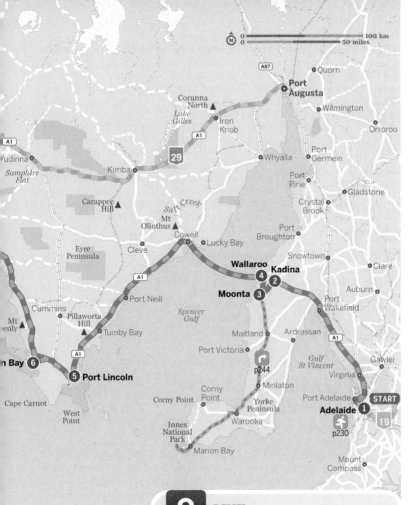

of massive old pubs. The
**Copper Coast Visitor
Information Centre**
(☎08-8821 2333, 1800 654
991; www.yorkepeninsula.com.
au; 50 Moonta Rd; ☺9am-
5pm Mon-Fri, 10am-4pm Sat &
Sun) isn't just any tourist
office – it's the peninsula's main visitor centre,
which makes it an es-
sential stop for planning

LINK YOUR TRIP

29 Across the Nullarbor

From where Trip 21 ends
at Streaky Bay, it's just
110km to Ceduna, which
is Stop 2 on the 2493km
Nullarbor Crossing.

19 Adelaide Hills & the Barossa

Both trips begin in
Adelaide, but the
Barossa journey is a
shorter, more intimate
journey.

ahead. Behind the centre is an amazing collection of old farming, mining and domestic bits and pieces at the **Farm Shed Museum** (www.nationaltrust. org.au/sa; 50 Moonta Rd; adult/child/family $8/3/20; ☺9am-5pm Mon-Fri, 10am-3.30pm Sat & Sun).

The Drive ›› Moonta lies 17km southwest of Kadina – watch for ocean views of Spencer Gulf on the final approach.

 TRIP HIGHLIGHT

❸ Moonta

In the late 19th century the Moonta copper mine was the richest in Australia. The legacy of those boom years bequeathed Moonta its fine streetscapes. The town, which calls itself 'Australia's Little Cornwall', maintains a faded glory and a couple of decent pubs. **Moonta Visitor Information Centre** (☎08-8825 1891; www.moontatourism.org. au; Blanche Tce, Old Railway Station; ☺9am-5pm) has a smattering of history pamphlets, and details on the **Moonta Heritage Site** 1.5km east of town. The site includes the excellent **Moonta Mines Museum** (www.nationaltrust. org.au/sa; Verran Tce; adult/child $8/4; ☺1-4pm), once a grand school with 1100 pupils; the **Old Sweet Shop** (Verran Tce; ☺10am-4pm) across the

road (built 1846); and a fully restored **Miner's Cottage** (Verco St; adult/child $4/2; ☺1.30-4pm Wed, Sat & Sun, daily during school holidays). But for all that history, Moonta's a pretty sleepy place, where fishing seems to be one of the main preoccupations – shallow Moonta Bay is 1km west of the town centre, with good fishing from the jetty and a netted swimming area.

🛏 p249

The Drive ›› It's a short, 17km hop up the road from Moonta to Wallaroo, with fine views of Wallaroo Bay on the last few kilometres into town.

↱ DETOUR: INNES NATIONAL PARK

Start: ❸ Moonta

The Yorke Peninsula has a shape that vaguely resembles Italy's famous boot, and the peninsula's south coast is largely sheltered from the Southern Ocean's fury by Kangaroo Island, so there are some great **swimming** beaches along here. The surf finds its way through and around Troubridge Point and Cape Spencer. The latter, at the extreme southwest of the peninsula, in the toe, forms a part of one of South Australia's least-visited national parks, **Innes National Park** (☎08-8854 3200; www.environment.sa.gov.au; Stenhouse Bay Rd, Stenhouse Bay; per car $10; ☺visitor centre 10.30am-3pm Wed-Sun), where sheer cliffs plunge into indigo waters and rocky offshore islands hide small coves and sandy beaches. **Marion Bay** (www.marionbay.com.au), just outside the park, and **Stenhouse Bay** and **Pondalowie Bay**, both within the park, are the main local settlements. Pondalowie Bay has a bobbing lobster-fishing fleet and a gnarly surf beach. The rusty ribs of the 711-tonne steel barque *Ethel*, which foundered in 1904, arc forlornly from the sands just south of Pondalowie Bay. Follow the sign past the Cape Spencer turn-off to the ghost-town ruins of **Inneston**, a gypsum-mining community abandoned in 1930. For more information on the park, there's the **Innes National Park Visitor Information Centre** (☎08-8854 3200; ☺10.30am-3pm Wed-Sat). It's 82km south from Moonta to Minlaton, then a further 72km southwest to Innes National Park.

ROBIN SMITH/GETTY IMAGES ©

Moonta Historic miner's cottage

4 Wallaroo

Still a major wheat port, Wallaroo is a town on the way up: the Eyre Peninsula ferry is running, there are plenty of pubs and the pubs are full of folks. There's a huge new subdivision north of town, and the shiny new **Copper Cove Marina** (www. coppercoastproperty.com.au/ marina) is full of expensive boats, adding an air of sophistication to what was once an industrial town that could have gone the way of unappealing Port Pirie, Port Augusta or Whyalla; fortunately

the ferry means that you can miss all three of these towns as you head to the Eyre Peninsula. Before you leave, don't miss the stoic 1865 post office, which now houses the **Heritage & Nautical Museum** (www.nationaltrust. org.au; cnr Jetty Rd & Emu St; adult/child $6/3; ⊗10am-4pm), with tales of square-rigged English ships and George the pickled giant squid. For more on local history, pick up the *Discovering Historic Wallaroo* walk or drive brochures from the Copper Coast Visitor Information Centre (p243).

The Drive » There's a daily vehicle ferry between Wallaroo (Yorke Peninsula) and Lucky Bay (Eyre Peninsula), a shortcut that shaves 350km and several hours off the drive via Port Augusta. The voyage takes around 1¾ hours one way and is run by SEASA (☎08-8823 0777; www.seasa. com.au; one-way per adult/child/car $35/10/140). There are good views of both peninsulas en route. From Lucky Bay it's 162km down to Port Lincoln.

TRIP HIGHLIGHT

5 Port Lincoln

Port Lincoln overlooks broad Boston Bay at the southern end of Eyre Peninsula. It is that rare place that lies a long way from well-travelled trails and yet somehow maintains a real buzz about it. It's a prosperous place, the 'Tuna Capital of the World' no less – if not for a lack of fresh water, Port Lincoln might also have become the South Australian capital, although we suspect that locals are secretly glad to have avoided such a fate. The grassy foreshore is a busy promenade, and there are some good pubs, eateries and aquatic activities here to keep you out of trouble. To get a feel for the place as told through its anecdotes – did you

know, for example, that local tuna fisherman Dean Lukin won the Super Heavyweight weightlifting gold medal at the 1984 Olympics? – tag along on a 90-minute **Port Lincoln Walk & Talk History Tour** (☏0474 222 020; www.facebook.com/portlincolnwalkandtalktours; adult/child $12/10) along the Port Lincoln foreshore with a fifth-generation local who knows the town backwards.

✗ ⊨ p249

The Drive >> Coffin Bay is barely 50km across the southern tip of the Eyre

Peninsula from Port Lincoln – you'll be there in less than an hour. The road continues beyond Coffin Bay town to Point Avoid, a wild and wind-blown vantage point for the Southern Ocean in all its cold fury.

- - - - - - - - -

TRIP HIGHLIGHT

❻ Coffin Bay

Deathly sounding Coffin Bay (named by Matthew Flinders after his buddy Sir Isaac Coffin) is a snoozy fishing village that just happens to be the oyster capital of Australia – salty Coffin Bay oysters from the nearby beds are exported worldwide, but you

PORT LINCOLN EXCURSIONS

When it comes to getting up close and personal with Australia's most charismatic marine wildlife, Port Lincoln has few peers. Eyre Peninsula's photogenic wild western flank is an important breeding ground for southern right whales, while this side of the peninsula sees Australian sea lions, tuna and great white sharks (the scariest scenes of *Jaws* were shot not far from here) so close you could almost reach out and touch them – now there's an experience you'll be telling your friends about for years to come.

Swim with the Tuna (☏1300 788 378, 08-8682 6010; www.swimwiththetuna.com.au; adult/child $90/60) Three-hour boat tours out to a floating tuna enclosure, where you can check out the big fish from an underwater observatory or jump into the brine with them.

Calypso Star Charters (☏08-8682 3939, 1300 788 378; www.sharkcagediving.com.au; 1-day dive adult/child $495/345) Runs cage dives with great white sharks around the Neptune Islands. Book in advance; it's cheaper if you're just watching nervously from the boat. Also runs four-hour swimming with sea lion trips (adult/child $150/105).

Adventure Bay Charters (☏08-8682 2979; www.adventurebaycharters.com.au) Carbon-neutral Adventure Bay Charters takes you swimming with sea lions (adult/child $195/135) and cage diving with great white sharks ($345/245). Multiday ocean safaris are also available, plus more laid-back 90-minute cruises around the Port Lincoln marina ($45/25).

Goin' Off Safaris (☏0427 755 065; www.goinoffsafaris.com.au; tours from $150) Check the big-ticket items off your Eyre Peninsula 'to-do' list – sharks, tuna, sea lions and seafood – with local guides. Day trips around Port Lincoln and Coffin Bay, plus overnight jaunts, seafood-focused trips and fishing expeditions.

shouldn't pay more than $1 per oyster around town. Otherwise, Coffin Bay basks languidly in the warm sun...until a 4000-strong holiday horde arrives every January. But restrict yourself to the town and you'll miss some of the best bits. Along the ocean side of Coffin Bay there's some wild coastal scenery, most of which is part of **Coffin Bay National Park** (www.environment.sa.gov. au; per car $10), overrun with roos, emus and fat goannas. In a 2WD you can get to picturesque **Point Avoid** (coastal lookouts, rocky cliffs, good surf and whales passing between May and October) and **Yangie Bay** (arid-looking rocky landscapes and walking trails). **Coffin Bay Explorer** (☏0428 880 621; www.coffinbayexplorer.com; adult/child $85/45) runs half-day wildlife and seafood tours with plenty of dolphins and oysters, or you can go kayaking with **Earth Adventure** (☏08-8165 2024; www. earthadventure.com.au; 3hr kayaking per person from $75). There's reliable surf at Greenly Beach just south of Coulta, 40km north of Coffin Bay.

🛏 p249

The Drive ≫ The Flinders Hwy (A1) plays hide-and-seek with this fabulous, wild coast for 135km northwest to Elliston.

THE PENINSULA FINGER

Something strange happens below a certain latitude on both the Yorke and Eyre Peninsulas: drivers in oncoming vehicles begin raising their index fingers off their steering wheels in cheery acknowledgement of your passing. It's a country courtesy, as if to say, 'Hello! Good to see you driving along this same sunny road today!' Stew in your city-side cynicism and ignore them, or respond in kind and see who can deliver the Peninsula Finger first!

TRIP HIGHLIGHT

❼ Elliston

Tiny Elliston is a small fishing town on soporific Waterloo Bay, with a beautiful swimming beach and a fishing jetty (hope the whiting are biting). **Elliston Visitor Information Centre** (☏08-8687 9200; www.elliston.com.au; Beach Tce; ⏰9am-5pm Mon-Fri, 10am-1pm Sat & Sun) can direct you towards the **Great Ocean Tourist Drive** just north of town – a 10km detour to Anxious Bay via some anxiety-relieving ocean scenery. En route you'll pass Blackfellows, which boasts some of the west coast's best surf. From here you can eyeball the 36-sq-km Flinders Island 35km offshore. Nearby Locks Well has good salmon fishing, and a long, steep stairway called the Staircase to Heaven (283 steps? go on, count 'em...), leads from the car park down to an awesome surf beach, the deep orange sand strewn with seashells.

The Drive ≫ Follow the A1 northwest as it arcs around the eastern reaches of the Great Australian Bight. Some 25km after Port Kenny, a series of narrow back roads heads off the main highway to Baird Bay and Point Labatt.

❽ Point Labatt & Baird Bay

This wild corner of the earth may consist of some of SA's smaller settlements, but attractions come thick and fast out here. Point Labatt overlooks one of the few permanent **sea-lion colonies** on the Australian mainland; ogle them from the clifftops (with binoculars). A few kilometres down the Point Labatt road are the globular **Murphy's Haystacks** (www.streakybay.sa.gov.au; person/family $2/5), an improbable congregation of 'inselbergs' – colourful, weather-sculpted granite outcrops, which are millions of years old. And at Baird Bay, **Baird Bay Ocean Eco Experience** (☏08-8626 5017; www. bairdbay.com; 4hr tours adult/

JOHN WHITE PHOTOS/GETTY IMAGES ©

Greenly Beach Surf beach north of Coffin Bay

child $150/75; ☺Sep-May) sends you out to swim with sea lions and dolphins.

The Drive 》 You could easily spend a most pleasurable hour or two losing yourself in the tiny little back roads that head north to Streaky Bay. It's difficult to get truly lost – head far enough east and you'll hit the main highway, turn west and you're in the Southern Ocean.

- - - - - - - - - -

❾ Streaky Bay

Sheltered from the Southern Ocean by a sturdy headland, there's something almost reassuring about this endearing little seasider, which takes its name from the streaks of seaweed Matt Flinders spied in the bay as he sailed on by. Visible at low tide, the seagrass attracts ocean critters and the bigger critters that eat them – which means first-class fishing. The **Streaky Bay Museum** (www.nationaltrust. org.au/sa; 42 Montgomery Tce; adult/child $6.50/1; ☺1.30-4pm Tue & Fri) is inside a 1901 schoolhouse, and features a fully furnished pug-and-pine hut, an old iron lung and plenty of pioneering history. More recently (1990),

a 5m-long, 1.5-tonne **White Pointer shark** was reeled in off Streaky Bay: check out the unnerving replica inside **Stewarts Roadhouse** (☎08-8626 1222; 15 Alfred Tce; ☺7am-9pm). You may have swum with sharks earlier in the journey, but this is probably about as close as you'll want to get. So sit back, find somewhere to eat the fresh local seafood, and take a moment to reflect on just how far you've come.

✕ ⊨ p249

Eating & Sleeping

Moonta ❸

🛏 Cottage by Cornwall — B&B $$

(📞0438 313 952; www.cottagebycornwall.com.
au; 24 Ryan St; d incl breakfast from $160, extra
adult/child $20/free, 2-night minimum stay; ❄)
The classiest accommodation in Moonta by
a country mile, this tizzied-up 1863 cottage
has three bedrooms (sleeping six), plus fancy
bedding, mod furnishings and a claw-foot
bath. It's just a short stroll to the pub and the
Cornish Kitchen.

Port Lincoln ❺

✖ Fresh Fish Place — Seafood $

(📞08-8682 2166; www.portlincolnseafood.com.
au; 20 Proper Bay Rd; meals $10-14; ⏱8.30am-
5.30pm Mon-Fri, to 12.30pm Sat) Check the
fish-of-the-day on the blackboard out the front
of this fabulous seafood shack. Inside you can
buy fresh local seafood straight off the boats
(King George whiting, tuna, kingfish, flathead
etc), plus Coffin Bay oysters for $12 a dozen
and superb fish and chips. Not to be missed!
Seafood tasting tours and cooking classes also
available.

🛏 Tanonga — B&B $$$

(📞0427 812 013; www.tanonga.com.au;
Charlton Gully; d incl breakfast from $310,
minimum 2-night stay; ❄) Two plush, solar-
powered, architect-designed ecolodges in
the hills behind Port Lincoln. They're both
superprivate and surrounded by native bush,
bird life and walking trails. Roll into town for
dinner, or take advantage of the DIY packs of
local produce available.

Coffin Bay ❻

🛏 Dawes Point Cottage — House $$

(📞0427 844 568; www.coffinbayholidayrentals.
com.au/2_DawesPoint.htm; 5 Heron Ct; per night
$140-200; ❄) This old-fashioned fishing shack
(Aussie author Tim Winton would call it 'fish
deco') was won by the present owners in a card
game! Now a million-dollar property, it maintains
its modesty despite sitting right on the water.
There are three bedrooms and a beaut little deck
above the gin-clear bay. Sleeps six.

Streaky Bay ❾

✖ Mocean — Cafe $$

(📞08-8626 1775; www.moceancafe.com.au;
34b Alfred Tce; mains $17-35; ⏱10am-3pm Tue,
Wed & Sun, 10am-late Thu-Sat; 🍴) It looks like a
big shipping container from the street, but this
jaunty corrugated-iron-clad cafe is the town's
social pacemaker, with murals, Moroccan
lanterns and water views from the wrap-around
balcony. Dishes focus on scrumptious Eyre
Peninsula seafood – try the chilli-and-lime squid
or the abalone. Super coffee and takeaways, too.
Closed in August.

🛏 Streaky Bay Hotel/Motel — Hotel, Motel $

(📞08-8626 1008; www.streakybayhotel.com.au;
33 Alfred Tce; hotel d & tw $50-135, motel d $110;
❄) The upstairs rooms at this 1866 beauty
have ripsnorting views and a balcony from
which to snort them. The downstairs rooms
don't have views, bathrooms, TV or air-con, but
are decent. Motel rooms are unglamorous but
more private. All room tariffs include breakfast.
Meals happen in the **bistro** daily (mains $16 to
$35, serving 7am to 9am, noon to 2pm and 6pm
to 8.30pm).

Coonawarra Wine Region *Rich red soils and irresistable wines*

MILTON WORDLEY/GETTY IMAGES ©

Coonawarra & the Coorong

22

Leave the crowds behind and combine stirring natural phenomena with wines and pretty coastal towns on this quintessentially South Australian road trip.

TRIP HIGHLIGHTS

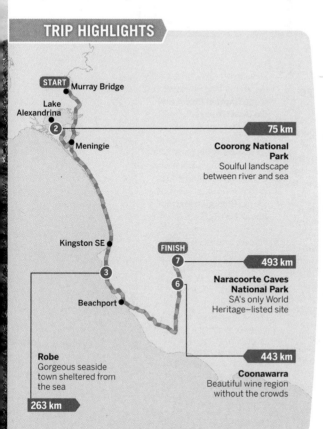

START Murray Bridge

Lake Alexandrina

2

Meningie

75 km

Coorong National Park
Soulful landscape between river and sea

Kingston SE

FINISH

7

493 km

6

Naracoorte Caves National Park
SA's only World Heritage–listed site

Beachport

Robe
Gorgeous seaside town sheltered from the sea

263 km

443 km

Coonawarra
Beautiful wine region without the crowds

3

5–7 DAYS
493KM / 306 MILES

GREAT FOR...

BEST TIME TO GO

Year-round. but can be cold and miserable June to August.

 ### ESSENTIAL PHOTO

The Coorong, where the Murray meets the sea.

 ### BEST FOR FAMILIES

Relive Storm Boy at Coorong National Park.

22 Coonawarra & the Coorong

It wouldn't be a South Australian road trip without wines, but there's so much more to see before you reach the niche wine region of Coonawarra. For a start, there's the Coorong, where the Murray empties into the sea, lovely and historic Robe, and some little-known back roads just in from the sea. And there's South Australia's only World Heritage–listed site to enjoy.

❶ Murray Bridge

There's something about river towns that makes you want to slow down to the pace of sluggish river waters, and Murray Bridge, SA's largest river town, is no exception. It's a rambling regional hub (the fifth-biggest town in SA) where the charms are more subtle than immediately obvious. It's in the older sections closer to the river, in any of the town's many old pubs and out on the water itself, where you'll want to spend most of your time. There are two main options for a river cruise: **MV Barrangul** (📞0407 395 385; www.barrangul. com.au; cruises $25) offers Devonshire-tea cruises departing Sturt Reserve, while **Captain Proud Paddle Boat Cruises** (📞0466 304 092; www.captainproud. com.au; Wharf Rd; lunch/dinner 3hr cruises $59/79) runs lunch or dinner cruises in a refurbished paddleboat. If that's too staid for your liking, **Riverglen Marina Kayak Hire** (📞08-8532 1986; www.riverglen.com.au; Jervois Rd; per hour kayaks/lifejackets $10/2.50) will unleash the DIY explorer in you.

🛏 p257

The Drive >> Drive 24km southwest of Murray Bridge; at Tailem Bend, take the south turn-off towards Meningie. Roll your windows down, smell the salty sea air and enjoy the water views away to the west as you draw near to Coorong National Park.

SOUTHERN OCEAN

TRIP HIGHLIGHT

❷ Coorong National Park

The amazing **Coorong National Park** (www.environment.sa.gov.au) is a fecund lagoon landscape curving along the coast for 145km from Lake Alexandrina towards Kingston SE. A complex series of soaks and salt pans, it's separated from the sea by the chunky dunes of the **Younghusband Peninsula**. More than 200 species of waterbirds live here, and *Storm Boy,* an endearing film about a young boy's friendship with a pelican (based on the novel by Colin Thiele), was filmed here. The Princes Hwy scuttles through the park, but you can't see much from the road. Instead, take the 13km, unsealed Coorong

LINK YOUR TRIP

19 Adelaide Hills & the Barossa

In Murray Bridge, you're only 76km from Adelaide, where Trip 19 begins.

20 McLaren Vale & Kangaroo Island

This journey skirts the west side of the Coorong; to get to McLaren Vale, head west then southwest from Murray Bridge.

253

Scenic Drive. Signed as Seven Mile Rd, it starts 10km southwest of Meningie off the Narrung Rd, and takes you right into the landscape, with its stinky lagoons, sea mists, fishing shanties, pelicans, black swans and wild emus. The road rejoins the Princes Hwy 10km south of Meningie.

🍴 🛏 p257

The Drive » From Kingston SE, at the southeastern end of the Coorong, leave the Princes Hwy and follow the signs towards Robe along the coast road – a detour to Cape Jaffa and its endless Southern Ocean views is well worth making.

SAM VALTENBERGS/GETTY IMAGES ©

TRIP HIGHLIGHT

③ Robe

Poll 100 South Australians for their favourite coastal community and chances are that 90 of them will say Robe; the remaining 10 probably haven't been there. It's a cherubic little fishing port that's become a holiday hotspot for Adelaidians and Melburnians alike. The sign saying 'Drain L Outlet' as you roll into town doesn't promise much, but along the main street you'll find quality eateries and boundless accommodation, there are some magic beaches and lakes around town, and heritage-listed buildings dating from the late 1840s to the 1870s litter the streets. **Little Dip Conservation Park** (www.environment.sa.gov.au) runs along the coast for about 13km south of town. It features a variety of habitats including lakes, wetlands and dunes, and some beaut beaches, Aboriginal middens and walks; access is via Nora Creina Rd.

🍴 🛏 p257

The Drive » Swing southeast along the coast to unpretentious Beachport (46km), then veer inland towards Millicent (32km), from where it's a further 50km southeast into Mt Gambier.

THE MURRAY RIVER

On the lowest gradient of any Australian river, the slow-flowing Murray, Australia's longest river at 2508km, rises in the Australian Alps, demarcates the NSW–Victoria border and then hooks through 650 South Australian kilometres. Here in SA, tamed by weirs and locks, the Murray irrigates the fruit trees and vines of the sandy **Riverland** district to the north, and winds through the dairy country of the **Murraylands** district to the south. Raucous flocks of white corellas and pink galahs launch from cliffs and river red gums, darting across lush vineyards and orchards.

④ Mt Gambier

Strung out along the flatlands below an extinct volcano, Mt Gambier is the Limestone Coast's major town and service hub. 'The Mount' sometimes seems a little short on urban virtues, but it's not what's above the streets that makes Mt Gambier special – it's the deep Blue Lake and the caves that worm their way though the limestone beneath the town. You don't even have to leave town to get a taste – **Cave Gardens** (www.mountgambierpoint. com.au/attractions/cave-

Robe Coastline at nearby Nora Creina

gardens; cnr Bay Rd & Watson Tce; ⏰24hr) is a 50m-deep sinkhole right in the middle of town; you can walk down into it, and watch the nightly Sound & Light Show (from 8.30pm) telling local Aboriginal Dreaming stories. But Mt Gambier's big-ticket item is the luminous, 75m-deep **Blue Lake** (www.mountgambierpoint.com.au/attractions/blue-lake; John Watson Dr; ⏰24hr), which turns an insane hue of blue during summer. Perplexed scientists think it has to do with calcite crystals suspended in the water, which form

at a faster rate during the warmer months. Consequently, if you visit between April and November, the lake will look much like any other – a steely grey. **Aquifer Tours** (☎08-8723 1199; www.aquifertours.com; cnr Bay Rd & John Watson Dr; adult/child/family $9/4/25; ⏰tours hourly 9am-5pm Nov-Jan, 9am-2pm Feb-May & Sep-Oct, 9am-noon Jun-Aug) runs hourly tours, taking you down near the lake shore in a glass-panelled lift.

The Drive ≫ Penola is 51km due north of Mt Gambier along the Riddoch Hwy.

---

⑤ Penola

A rural town on the way up (what a rarity!), Penola (population 1710) is the kind of place where you walk down the main street and three people say 'Hello!' to you before you reach the pub. The town itself has some historic corners – Petticoat Lane is one of Penola's first streets, and although most of the original buildings have been razed, there are still a few old timber-slab houses, red-gum kerbs and gnarly trees to see. Otherwise, Penola is famous for

255

two things: first, for its association with the Sisters of St Joseph of the Sacred Heart, cofounded in 1867 by Australia's first saint, Mary MacKillop; and secondly, for being smack bang in the middle of the **Coonawarra Wine Region**. If you're here for the former, you're here for the **Mary MacKillop Interpretive Centre** (www. mackilloppenola.org.au; cnr Portland St & Petticoat Lane; adult/child $5/free; ⊗10am-4pm).

 p257

The Drive » Tiny Coonawarra township is just 10km north of Penola, but you'll stray wider and more pleasurably from winery to winery on this section of your journey.

TRIP HIGHLIGHT

⑥ Coonawarra

When it comes to spicy cabernet sauvignon, it's just plain foolish to dispute the virtues of the Coonawarra wine region (www.coonawarra. org). The *terra rossa* (red earth) soils here also produce irresistible shiraz and chardonnay and wine-lovers would want to dedicate a couple of days easing from one winery to the next. Where to start? How about **Balnaves of Coonawarra** (www.balnaves.com.

au; Riddoch Hwy; ⊗9am-5pm Mon-Fri, noon-5pm Sat & Sun), where the tasting notes ooze florid wine speak (dark seaweed, anyone?), but even if your nosing skills aren't that subtle, you'll enjoy the cab sav and chardonnay. Nearby, traditional **Zema Estate** (www.zema.com.au; Riddoch Hwy; ⊗9am-5pm Mon-Fri, 10am-4pm Sat & Sun) is ideal for capturing Coonawarra's essence with fine shiraz and cab sav, while **Rymill Coonawarra** (www. rymill.com.au; Riddoch Hwy; ⊗10am-5pm) mixes it up a little with some of the best sauvignon blanc you'll ever taste. Return to Coonawarra's roots at **Wynns Coonawarra Estate** (www.wynns.com.au; 1 Memorial Dr; ⊗10am-5pm), the oldest Coonawarra winery and known for its top-quality shiraz, fragrant riesling and golden chardonnay.

The Drive » It's 50km north then northwest through vineyard country from Penola to Naracoorte town, but it's enough to shift the focus from what lies above the earth to what's below. Access to the national park is 10km before the town.

TRIP HIGHLIGHT

⑦ Naracoorte Caves National Park

About 10km southeast of Naracoorte town-

ship, off the Penola road, Naracoorte Caves National Park is the only Unesco World Heritage–listed site in SA. The discovery of an ancient fossilised marsupial in these limestone caves raised palaeontological eyebrows around the world, and featured in the BBC's David Attenborough series *Life on Earth*. The park visitor centre doubles as the impressive **Wonambi Fossil Centre** (⊿08-8762 2340; www.environment.sa.gov. au/naracoorte; 89 Wonambi Rd; adult/child/family $13/8/36; ⊗9am-5pm), a re-creation of the rainforest (and its inhabitants) that covered this area 200,000 years ago. The 26 limestone caves here, including **Alexandra Cave**, **Cathedral Cave** and **Victoria Fossil Cave**, have bizarre formations of stalactites and stalagmites, while thousands of endangered southern bentwing bats exit en masse at dusk during summer from **Bat Cave**. You can see the **Wet Cave** by self-guided tour, but the others require ranger-guided tours. If you're on your own, stand perfectly still, switch off your torch (flashlight) and listen to the silence – it's a world away from where your journey began.

Eating & Sleeping

Murray Bridge ❶

✖ Murray Bridge Hotel   Pub Food $$

(📞08-8532 2024; www.murraybridgehotel.
com.au; 20 Sixth St; mains $16-31; 🕙noon-2pm
& 6-8pm; 🛜) There are plenty of rambling
old pubs around town, but the stately Murray
Bridge Hotel is your best bet for a feed, with
roasts, sticky BBQ beef ribs and more seafood
than steaks. Savvy wine list, too.

Coorong National Park ❷

✖ Cheese Factory
Restaurant   Pub Food $$

(📞08-8575 1914; www.meningie.com.au; 3
Fiebig Rd, Meningie; mains $15-33; 🕙10.30am-
3pm Tue-Sun & 5.30-late Wed-Sat) Lean on the
front bar with the locals, or munch into steaks,
schnitzels, Coorong mullet or a Coorong wrap
(with mullet!) in the cavernous dining room of
this converted cheese factory (you might have
guessed!). The very lo-fi **Meningie Cheese
Factory Museum** (📞08-8575 1914; www.
meningiecheesefactorymuseum.com; 3 Fiebig
Rd, Meningie; admission $5; 🕙8.30am-5pm)
is here too (butter churns, old typewriters,
domestic knick-knackery).

🛏 Dalton on the Lake   B&B $$

(📞0428 737 161; admason@lm.net.au; 30
Narrung Rd, Meningie; d from $145; ❄)
Generous in spirit and unfailingly clean, this
lakeside B&B goes to great lengths to ensure
your stay is comfortable. There'll be fresh bread
baking when you arrive, jars of homemade
biscuits, and bountiful bacon and eggs for
breakfast. There's a modern self-contained
studio off to one side, and a renovated stone
cottage – book either, or both.

Robe ❸

✖ Robe Providore   Cafe $

(📞08-8768 2891; 4 Victoria St; mains $7-19;
🕙8am-3pm Wed-Mon) A bit of 'big city' comes
to Robe at this polished concrete-and-white
eatery, serving good coffee, big breakfasts
(eggs Benedict, house-baked pastries),
considered lunches (calamari salad) and wood-
oven pizzas. Oh, and Robe Town Amber Ale! Has
communal tables and bench seats; hours are
extended in summer.

🛏 Caledonian Inn   Hotel $

(📞08-8768 2029; www.caledonian.net.au; 1
Victoria St; d from $75; 🛜) This historic inn
(1859) has a half-dozen bright and cosy upstairs
pub rooms with shared bathrooms – great
value. The pub grub is good, too (mains $17 to
$40, serving noon to 2pm and 6pm to 8.30pm).

Penola ❺

✖ Pipers of Penola   Modern Australian $$$

(📞08-8737 3999; www.pipersofpenola.com.
au; 58 Riddoch St; mains $30-37; 🕙6-9pm Tue-
Sat) A classy, intimate dining room tastefully
constructed inside an old Methodist church,
with friendly staff and seasonal fare. The menu
is studded with ingredients like truffled parsnip,
date couscous and mustard 'liaison' – serious
gourmet indicators! The prices are getting up
there, but so is the quality. Superb wine list
with lots of locals (though the beer list could be
craftier).

🛏 Must@Coonawarra   Motel $$

(📞08-8737 3444; www.mustatcoonawarra.
com.au; 126 Church St; r from $160; ❄🛜) Plush
Must has sexy roof curves reminiscent of a
certain opera venue in Sydney. Accommodation
ranges from studios to apartments, with
sustainable features aplenty: rain-water
showers, double glazing and insulation, solar
hot water, natural cleaning products etc. Bike
hire $20 per day.

Burra Historic sites and fine
period architecture

WALTER BIBIKOW/GETTY IMAGES ©

Clare Valley & the Flinders Ranges

23

Rarely is there such a contrast between where a journey begins and ends – start out sipping world-class wines in the lush Clare Valley and finish up beneath the blood-red escarpments of the outback.

TRIP HIGHLIGHTS

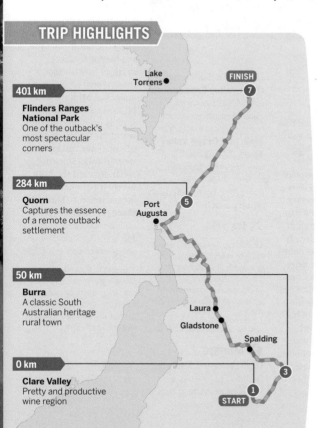

401 km

Flinders Ranges National Park
One of the outback's most spectacular corners

284 km

Quorn
Captures the essence of a remote outback settlement

50 km

Burra
A classic South Australian heritage rural town

0 km

Clare Valley
Pretty and productive wine region

Lake Torrens

FINISH

7

Port Augusta

5

Laura

Gladstone

Spalding

3

START

1

**7–10 DAYS
401KM / 249 MILES**

GREAT FOR...

BEST TIME TO GO

Year-round, but too hot for the outback from December to February.

ESSENTIAL PHOTO

Don't miss Flinders Ranges at sunrise or sunset.

BEST FOR OUTDOORS

Mt Remarkable National Park lives up to its name and is little known.

23 Clare Valley & the Flinders Ranges

Clare Valley has plenty of competition, but is quietly accumulating plaudits as one of South Australia's top wine regions. Vineyards carpet valleys that radiate out from lovely little townships like Mintaro and Burra. Before reaching the outback, there's the aptly named Mt Remarkable, then it's desert and remote settlements all the way into the peerless Flinders Ranges.

TRIP HIGHLIGHT

❶ Clare Valley

A worthy rival to the Barossa and McLaren Vale, the skinny Clare Valley wine region combines the production of world-class rieslings and reds with some really pretty country that makes wine touring an even greater pleasure than it already is. This is gorgeous countryside, with open skies, rounded hills, stands of large gums and wind rippling over wheat fields – the colours speak of both the fertile south and barren north, and you can catch a sense of both, sometimes in a single day. For tours that begin in Clare Valley (rather than in Adelaide), contact **Clare Valley Experiences** (✆08-8842 1880; www.clarevalleyexperiences.com; tours per 2 people incl lunch $430) and **Grape Valley Tours** (✆0418 881 075; www.grapevalleytours.com.au; tours per person incl lunch from $265); both include a winery lunch.

✕ ⊨ p265

The Drive ›› More an adjunct to Clare Valley than anything else, lovely little Mintaro lies a few clicks southeast of Clare; you may even stumble upon it as you explore the wineries of the area.

❷ Mintaro

Heritage-listed Mintaro, founded in 1849, is a lovely stone village that could have been lifted out of the Cotswolds and plonked into the Australian bush – it makes a nice change from the Germanic echoes of the Barossa. There are very few architectural intrusions from the 1900s; let the *Historic Mintaro* pamphlet (you'll find it at various places around the valley) guide your explorations. **Martindale Hall** (✆08-8843 9088; www.martindalehall.com; 1 Manoora Rd; adult/child $10/2.50; ⊙11am-4pm Mon-Fri, noon-4pm Sat & Sun) is an astonishing 1880 manor 3km from Mintaro. Built for young pastoralist Edmund Bowman Jr, who subsequently partied away the family fortune, the manor features original furnishings, a magnificent blackwood staircase, Mintaro-slate billiard table (Mintaro slate is used around the world for the production of same) and an opulent, museum-like smoking room. Reward the kids for their patience with an excursion to **Mintaro Maze** (www.mintaromaze.com; Jacka Rd; adult/child $12/8; ⊙10am-4pm Thu-Mon, daily school holidays, closed Feb).

The Drive ›› Northwest of Mintaro, along a quiet country road fringed with vineyards, follow the signs to Burra, with the last 13km along the much busier A32 into Burra.

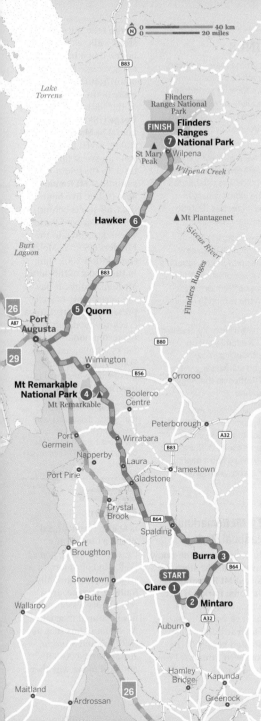

TRIP HIGHLIGHT

③ Burra

Beautiful Burra (population 1110), 40km northeast of Clare, bursts at the seams with historic sites and, unlike in the wine towns down around the Clare Valley, its period architecture dominates the traveller's experience. Burra was a copper-mining boom town between 1847 and 1877, and while it's a lovely town to simply wander at will, **Burra Visitor Information Centre** (📞1300 775 540, 08-8892 2154; www.visitburra.com; 2 Market Sq; ⏰9am-5pm Mon-Fri, 10am-4pm Sat & Sun) sells the self-guided **Burra Heritage Passport** (adult/child $25/ free), providing access to eight historic sights and three museums that will put it all into perspective.

LINK YOUR TRIP

26 Alice Springs to Adelaide

You're heading north to the outback while this trip from the Alice heads south – the routes intersect close to Port Augusta.

29 Across the Nullarbor

Port Augusta, close to Quorn, is at the crossroads for many journeys, including the Nullarbor crossing to Perth.

CLARE VALLEY WINES

The Clare Valley's cool microclimates (around rivers, creeks and gullies) noticeably affect the local wines, enabling whites to be laid down for long periods and still be brilliant. The valley produces some of the world's best riesling, plus grand semillon and shiraz. Many wineries are clustered around Sevenhill, just south of Clare township.

Sevenhill Cellars (☑08-8843 4222; www.sevenhill. com.au; College Rd, Sevenhill; ⊕10am-5pm) Want some religion with your drink? This place was established by Jesuits in 1851, making it the oldest winery in the Clare Valley (check out the incredible 1866 St Aloysius Church). Oh, and the wine is fine too!

Skillogalee (☑08-8843 4311; www.skillogalee.com.au; 23 Trevarrick Rd, Sevenhill; ⊕10am-5pm) Skillogalee is a small family outfit known for its spicy shiraz, fabulous food and top-notch riesling (a glass of which is like kissing a pretty girl on a summer afternoon). Kick back with a long, lazy lunch on the verandah (mains $20 to $35; book ahead).

Pikes (www.pikeswines.com.au; Polish Hill River Rd, Sevenhill; ⊕10am-4pm) The industrious Pike family set up shop in 1984, and have been producing show-stopping riesling ever since (and shiraz, sangiovese, pino grigio, viognier...). It also bottles up the zingy Oakbank Pilsener, if you're parched.

Knappstein (www.knappstein.com.au; 2 Pioneer Ave, Clare; ⊕9am-5pm Mon-Fri, 11am-5pm Sat, 11am-4pm Sun) Taking a minimal-intervention approach to wine making, Knappstein has quite a name for itself. Shiraz and riesling steal the show, but they also make a mighty fine semillon-sauvignon blanc blend (and beer!).

The Drive » A number of routes present themselves but the quickest cuts across rolling wheat country to the B82 via Spalding and Gulnare. At the latter, swing north through Gladstone, Laura (with its long, geranium-adorned main street) and Murray Town, then swing north towards Port Augusta on your way to the well-signed park.

④ Mt Remarkable National Park

Bush-boffins-in-the-know rave about the steep, jagged **Mt Remarkable National Park** (☑08-8634 7068; www.environment. sa.gov.au; person/car $4/10), which straddles the isolated gorges of the Southern Flinders. From the car park at **Alligator Gorge** take the short, steep walk (2km, two hours) down into the craggy gorge (no sign of any 'gators), the ring route (9km, four hours), or the walk to **Hidden Gorge** (18km, seven hours) or **Mambray Creek** (13km, seven hours). Or you can sweat up the track to the 960m-high summit of **Mt Remarkable** (12km, five hours); the trail starts behind Melrose Caravan Park. The oldest town in the Flinders (1853) is Melrose (population 200), snug in the elbow of the 960m Mt Remarkable. It has the perfect mix of well-preserved architecture, a cracking-good pub, quality accommodation and parks with actual grass. You won't see a whole lot of that where you're heading...

The Drive » In this part of the country, most roads head towards Port Augusta. Follow any one of them, but take the Quorn turn-off 10km before Port Augusta.

TRIP HIGHLIGHT

⑤ Quorn

Is Quorn (pronounced 'corn') a film set after the crew has gone home? Well, kind of. Quorn's streetscapes, especially **Railway Terrace**, are a real history lesson, and have featured in iconic Australian films such as *Gallipoli* and *Sunday Too Far Away*. And it's not hard to see why they

RACHEL LEWIS/GETTY IMAGES ©

Parachilna Pub on the outskirts of the Flinders Ranges National Park

chose Quorn – it just looks like we all imagine an outback town would look.

🛏 p265

The Drive » Derelict ruins litter the Quorn–Hawker road. Stop in Kanyaka (1851), a once-thriving sheep station, to take the 20-minute walk to a waterhole loomed over by the massive Death Rock, where local Aboriginal people once placed their dying kinfolk to see out their last hours. It's very dry out here.

⑥ Hawker

Hawker is the last outpost of civilisation before Wilpena Pound, 55km to the north. Much like

Quorn, Hawker has seen better days, most of which were when the old *Ghan* train stopped here – the *Ghan* now runs further east, leaving Hawker marooned in the desert. These days Hawker is a pancake-flat, pit-stop town with an ATM, a general store, a pub and what could be the world's most helpful petrol station. **Bush Pilots Australia** (📞08-8648 4444; www. bushpilots.com.au; 60 Elder Tce; 30min flights per person $180) offers scenic flights out over the Flinders Ranges if you can't wait to get there.

✕ 🛏 p265

The Drive » The drive from Hawker to Wilpena Pound, in the southern Flinders Ranges, is pancake flat, but the early views of the ranges up ahead and to the east will have you tingling with excitement.

TRIP HIGHLIGHT

⑦ Flinders Ranges National Park

One of SA's most treasured parks, **Flinders Ranges National Park** (www.environment.sa.gov. au; per car $10) is laced with craggy gorges, saw-toothed ranges, abandoned homesteads, Aboriginal sites, native wildlife and, after it rains,

Flinders Ranges Rock carvings

carpets of wildflowers. The park's big-ticket drawcard is the 80-sq-km natural basin Ikara (Wilpena Pound) – a sunken elliptical valley ringed by gnarled ridges (don't let anyone tell you it's a meteorite crater!). The only vehicular access to the Pound is via the Wilpena Pound Resort's shuttle bus, which drops you about 1km from the old Hills Homestead, from where you can walk to Wangarra Lookout (another 300m). Pick up the *Bushwalking in Flinders Ranges National Park* brochure from the visitors information centre if you're keen to explore further. To look down on it all, **Central Air Services** (☏08-8648 0040; www.centralairservices.com. au; flights per person $1250, minimum 2 people) offers four-hour scenic flights above Wilpena and Lake Eyre, with lunch at the William Creek Hotel, while **Air Wilpena Scenic Flight Tours** (☏08-8648 0048; www.airwilpena.com. au; 20min/30min/1hr flights $169/199/299) operates shorter excursions from Wilpena Pound Resort.

🛏 p265

Eating & Sleeping

Clare Valley ➊

✖ Artisans Table   Modern Australian $$

(📞08-8842 1796; www.artisanstable.com.au; Lot 3, Wendouree Rd; mains $28-32; ⊘noon-3pm Sat & Sun, 6-9pm Wed-Sat) This mod, airy, hillside bar-restaurant has a broad, sunny balcony – perfect for a bottle of local riesling and some internationally inspired culinary offerings: a bit of Thai, a bit of Indian, a bit of Brazilian... Lots of seasonal and local produce (try the fish curry).

🛏 Riesling Trail & Clare Valley Cottages   B&B $$

(📞0427 842 232; www.rtcvcottages.com.au; 9 Warenda Rd; d incl breakfast from $150, extra person $50; ❄) A well-managed outfit offering seven contemporary cottages, encircled by country gardens and right on the Riesling Trail. **Riesling Trail Bike Hire** (📞0418 777 318; www.rieslingtrailbikehire.com.au; half-/full-day bike hire $25/40, tandems $40/60; ⊘8am-6pm) is across the street. The biggest cottage sleeps six; there are good deals on multinight stays.

Quorn ➎

🛏 Quandong Apartments   Apartments $$

(📞0432 113 473; www.quandongapartments.com; 31 First St; d $160-210; ❄) Next door to the Quandong Café (mains $6 to $15, open 8.30am to 4pm mid-March to mid December), these two self-contained apartments have full kitchens, big TVs, quality linen and chintz-meets-Asian touches. Rates come down for stays of two nights or more.

Hawker ➏

✖ Woolshed Restaurant   Modern Australian $$

(📞08-8648 0126; www.rawnsleypark.com.au; Wilpena Rd, via Hawker; mains $27-36; ⊘noon-2pm Wed-Sun, 5-8.30pm daily) The excellent Woolshed Restaurant does bang-up bush tucker, plus curries, seafood and pizzas.

🛏 Arkaba Station   Boutique Hotel $$$

(📞02-9571 6399, 1300 790 561; www.arkabastation.com; Wilpena Rd via Hawker; d from $1632) Flashy outback station accommodation in an 1850s homestead. 'Wild bush luxury' is the marketing pitch.

Flinders Ranges National Park ➐

🛏 Rawnsley Park Station   Resort $$

(📞caravan park 08-8648 0008, reception 08-8648 0030; www.rawnsleypark.com.au; Wilpena Rd, via Hawker; unpowered/powered sites $25/35, hostel per adult/child $38/28, cabins/units/villas from $98/150/410; ❄ @ 🛜 ☒) This rangy homestead 35km from Hawker offers everything from tent sites to luxe eco-villas, plus caravan-park cabins set up as YHA (www.yha.com.au) dorms. Outback activities include mountain-bike hire ($15 per hour), bushwalks (30 minutes to four hours), 4WD tours and scenic flights. The excellent Woolshed Restaurant is a 20-minute drive away.

🛏 Wilpena Pound Resort   Resort $$

(📞1800 805 802, 08-8648 0004; www.wilpenapound.com.au; Wilpena Rd via Hawker; unpowered/powered sites $23/34, safari tents $180-230, d $236-300; ❄ @ 🛜 ☒) Accommodation at this excellent resort includes motel-style rooms, more upmarket self-contained suites, and a great (although hugely popular) camp site with plush safari tents. Book way in advance over winter (high season). Don't miss a swim in the pool, happy hour at the bar (5pm to 6.30pm) and dinner at the bistro (mains $19 to $32 – try the roo!).

Northern Territory Trips

THE TOP END, THE RED CENTRE, OR SIMPLY 'THE TERRITORY'. Whatever you call it, the Northern Territory has an elemental feel to it. It's here that so many Aussie landmarks of international repute reside, from Uluru, Kata Tjuta (the Olgas) and Kings Canyon in the south to Katherine, Kakadu and Litchfield in the north.

As you'd expect from a predominantly outback region, the roads here can be empty, the distances are immense, and some northern trails may be impassable in the Big Wet (November to March). But the rewards are simply extraordinary, primary among them some of the best opportunities to experience this ancient land alongside its original inhabitants. Stock up on supplies and hit the road.

Devil's Marbles Gigantic granite boulders, believed to be the eggs of the Rainbow Serpent (Trip 25)
NOLAN CALDWELL/GETTY IMAGES ©

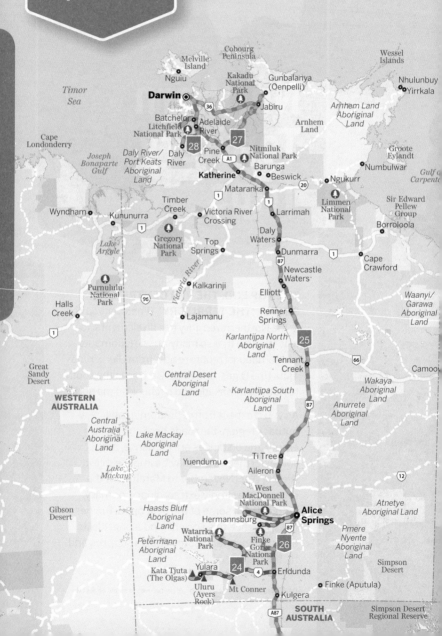

Northern Territory Trips

400 km
200 miles

INDON

Arafura
Sea

*Cobourg
Peninsula*

*Timor
Sea*

Melville
Island

Nguiu

Kakadu
National
Park

Gunbalanya
(Oenpelli)

Nhulunbuy
Yirrkala

Wessel
Islands

Darwin

Jabiru

*Arnhem Land
Aboriginal
Land*

*Cape
Londonderry*

Batchelor
Litchfield
National Park

Adelaide
River

Arnhem
Land

Groote
Eylandt

*Joseph
Bonaparte
Gulf*

28

Pine
Creek

27

Nitmiluk
National Park

Numbulwar

*Gulf o
Carpente*

Daly River/
Port Keats
Aboriginal
Land

Daly
River

Barunga

Beswick

Ngukurr

Katherine

20

Mataranka

*Sir Edward
Pellew
Group*

Wyndham

Kununurra

Timber
Creek

Victoria River
Crossing

Larrimah

Daly
Waters

*Limmen
National
Park*

Borroloola

*Lake
Argyle*

Gregory
National
Park

Top
Springs

Dunmarra

87

Newcastle
Waters

Cape
Crawford

*Waanyi/
Garawa
Aboriginal
Land*

Purnululu
National
Park

96

Kalkarinji

Elliott

Halls
Creek

Lajamanu

Renner
Springs

25

*Great
Sandy
Desert*

*Karlantijpa North
Aboriginal
Land*

Tennant
Creek

66

Camoo

**WESTERN
AUSTRALIA**

*Central
Australia
Aboriginal
Land*

*Central Desert
Aboriginal
Land*

*Karlantijpa South
Aboriginal
Land*

87

*Wakaya
Aboriginal
Land*

*Anurrete
Aboriginal
Land*

*Lake Mackay
Aboriginal
Land*

*Lake
Mackay*

Ti Tree

Yuendumu

Aileron

12

*Gibson
Desert*

*Haasts Bluff
Aboriginal
Land*

West
MacDonnell
National Park

**Alice
Springs**

*Atnetye
Aboriginal Land*

Hermannsburg

*Petermann
Aboriginal
Land*

Watarrka
National
Park

Finke
Gorge
National
Park

87

26

*Pmere
Nyente
Aboriginal
Land*

Yulara

24

4

Erldunda

Finke (Aputula)

*Simpson
Desert*

Kata Tjuta
(The Olgas)

Mt Conner

Uluru
(Ayers
Rock)

Kulgera

A87

**SOUTH
AUSTRALIA**

*Simpson Desert
Regional Reserve*

Classic Trip

24 Uluru & the Red Centre 10–14 Days
Uluru, the Olgas, Kings Canyon and the MacDonnell Ranges. Need we say more? (p271)

25 Alice Springs to Darwin 5–7 Days
Drive from desert to the tropics in one big road trip. (p281)

26 Alice Springs to Adelaide 7 Days
Journey south through the heart of the continent via Coober Pedy. (p291)

27 Darwin & Kakadu 5–7 Days
Set your sights on Kakadu, Australia's premier northern wilderness. (p299)

28 Darwin to Daly River 5 Days
Experience the Territory's other park, marvellous Litchfield. (p307)

DON'T MISS

Standley Chasm
This dramatic defile in the West MacDonnell Ranges is an extraordinary natural wonder. Visit it on Trip 24

Devil's Marbles
This weird-and-wonderful landform sits by the roadside on Trip 25

Henbury Meteorite Craters
Stirring outback country bypassed by the buses. Detour to it on Trip 26

Arnhemlander Cultural & Heritage Tour
Experience northern Kakadu and Arnhem Land art with an Indigenous guide on Trip 27

Tolmer Falls
Among the lesser-known waterfalls of Litchfield National Park, Tolmer Falls is visible on Trip 28

Uluru This unmissable Aussie icon won't disappoint

Classic Trip

Uluru & the Red Centre

24

Welcome to Australia's Red Centre, home to the country's most magnificent and utterly unforgettable outback landmarks – Uluru, the Olgas, Kings Canyon and the MacDonnell Ranges.

TRIP HIGHLIGHTS

406 km

Kings Canyon
Dramatic rocky gorges a long way from anywhere

907 km

Ellery Creek Big Hole
Swim beneath rocky bluffs in the desert

Tyler Pass Lookout
FINISH

West MacDonnell National Park

Meerenie Loop

7

3

Finke Gorge National Park

Yulara

Erldunda

2

START

1

0 km

Mt Conner

Uluru
World-famous icon of the outback

Kata Tjuta
The Rock's rival as a remote and beautiful landform

40 km

10–14 DAYS
1224KM / 761 MILES

GREAT FOR...

BEST TIME TO GO

April to August has cooler temperatures; it's fiercely hot September to March.

ESSENTIAL PHOTO

Sunset at Uluru.

BEST FOR OUTDOORS

Walk through the Valley of the Winds for true outback magic.

271

Classic Trip

24 Uluru & the Red Centre

If you make one trip into the Australian outback, make it this one. Uluru is an extraordinary, soulful place utterly unlike anywhere else on the planet. Nearby, Kata Tjuta (the Olgas) and Kings Canyon leave spellbound all who visit, while the West Macdonnell Ranges capture the essence of the Red Centre — red earth, red rocks and ghostly gums in a spiritually charged landscape.

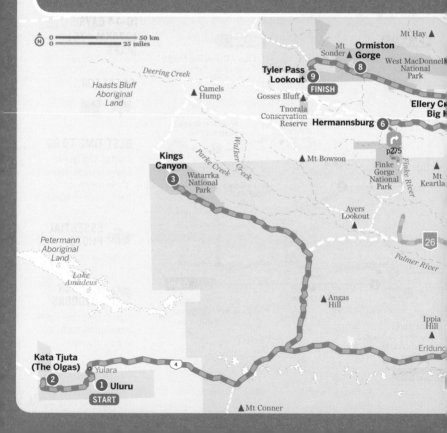

TRIP HIGHLIGHT

❶ Uluru (Ayers Rock)

Uluru: nothing can really prepare you for the immensity, grandeur, changing colour and stillness of 'the Rock'. The first sight of Uluru on the horizon invariably astounds even the most jaded traveller. Before arriving, 1km short of Uluru, visit the **Uluru-Kata Tjuta Cultural Centre** (📞08-8956 1128; www.parksaustralia.gov.au/ uluru/do/cultural-centre.

html; ⏰7am-6pm). **Uluru** itself is 3.6km long and rises a towering 348m from the surrounding sandy scrubland (867m above sea level). Closer inspection reveals a wondrous contoured surface concealing numerous sacred sites of particular significance to the Anangu. If your first sight of Uluru is during the afternoon, it appears as an ochre-brown colour, scored and pitted by dark shadows. As the sun sets, it illuminates the rock in burnished orange, then a series of deeper reds before it fades into charcoal. A performance in reverse, with marginally fewer spectators, is given at dawn. There's plenty to see and do: meandering walks, bike rides, guided tours, desert culture and simply contemplating the many changing colours and moods of the great monolith itself.

 p279

The Drive » The road from Uluru to Kata Tjuta

(40km) is sealed, as is the 20km road between Uluru and Yulara (where all of the accommodation for both places is). There are no other roads out here: you can't get lost.

TRIP HIGHLIGHT

❷ Kata Tjuta (The Olgas)

No journey to Uluru is complete without a visit to Kata Tjuta, part of **Uluru-Kata Tjuta National Park** (www. parksaustralia.gov.au/uluru/ index.html; adult/child $25/ free) and a striking group of domed rocks huddled together about 35km west of Uluru. There are 36 boulders shoulder to shoulder forming deep valleys and steep-sided gorges. Many visitors find them even more captivating than their prominent neighbour. The tallest rock, **Mt Olga** (546m, 1066m above sea level), is approximately 200m higher than Uluru. Kata Tjuta means 'many heads' and is of great *tjukurpa* significance, particularly for men, so stick to the

---

🔗 LINK YOUR TRIP

25 **Alice Springs to Darwin**

Alice Springs is Stop 4 on the Uluru & the Red Centre trip, and it's also where the Alice Springs to Darwin route (1493km) begins.

26 **Alice Springs to Adelaide**

From Alice Springs, the other choice is to head south to Adelaide (1500km).

tracks. The 7.4km **Valley of the Winds** loop (two to four hours) winds through the gorges giving excellent views of the surreal domes. The short signposted track beneath towering rock walls into pretty **Walpa Gorge** (2.6km return, 45 minutes) is especially beautiful in the afternoon. Like Uluru, Kata Tjuta is at its glorious, blood-red best at sunset.

The Drive ›› From Kata Tjuta, return the 40km to Uluru, then 20km more to Yulara, before the long road really begins. The Lasseter Hwy runs east (watch for Mt Conner, the large mesa

(table-top mountain) that looms 350m out of the desert away to the south). Some 137km from Yulara, take the Kings Canyon turn-off, from where you've 169km to go.

- - - - - - - - - - - - - -

TRIP HIGHLIGHT

❸ Kings Canyon

The yawning chasm of Kings Canyon in Watarrka National Park is one of the most spectacular sights in central Australia. This is one place where it pays to get out and walk, and you'll be rewarded with awesome views on the **Kings Canyon Rim Walk** (6km loop, four hours; you must begin before 9am on hot days), which many travellers rate as a highlight of their trip to the Centre. After a

short but steep climb (the only 'difficult' part of the trail), the walk skirts the canyon's rim before descending down wooden stairs to the **Garden of Eden**: a lush pocket of ferns and prehistoric cycads around a tranquil pool. The next section of the trail winds through a swarm of giant beehive domes: weathered sandstone outcrops, which to the Luritja represent the men of the Kuniya Dreaming. If that all sounds like too much hard work, take a scenic helicopter flight with **Professional Helicopter Services** (PHS; ☎08-8956 2003; www.phs.com.au; flights per person $95-275) or **Kings Creek Helicopters** (☎08-8956 7474; www.kingscreekstation.com.au; flights per person $70-480).

📖 p279

The Drive ›› With a 4WD, it's a short hop to Hermannsburg, but for the rest of us, you'll need to return 169km to the Lasseter Hwy, travel 108km east to the Stuart Hwy, then 200km north and then northeast into Alice Springs – a very long day but the scenery has its own rewards.

- - - - - - - - - - - - - -

❹ Alice Springs

Alice Springs is many things to many people – rough-and-tumble frontier town, centre for Indigenous arts, set amid glorious outback scenery. They're all true, and yet sitting as it does in the approximate midpoint of

---

MEREENIE LOOP ROAD

The Red Centre Way is the 'back road' from Alice to the Rock. It incorporates an 'inner loop' comprising Namatjira and Larapinta Drs, plus the rugged Mereenie Loop Rd, the short cut to Kings Canyon. This dusty, heavily corrugated road is not to be taken lightly, and hire car companies won't permit their 2WDs to be driven on it. There can be deep sandy patches and countless corrugations, depending on the time of year and how recently it's been graded. It's best travelled in a high-clearance vehicle, preferably a 4WD. Be aware that 2WD hire vehicles will not be covered by insurance on this road.

To travel along this route, which passes through Aboriginal land, you need a Mereenie Tour Pass ($5), which is valid for one day and includes a booklet with details about local Aboriginal culture and a route map. The pass is issued on the spot (usually only on the day of travel) at the visitor information centre in Alice Springs, Glen Helen Resort, Kings Canyon Resort and Hermannsburg service station.

this journey, its main appeal may lie in the chance to wash off the dust, sleep between clean sheets and keep at bay the great emptiness for a night. To anchor your visit, take in the **Araluen Cultural Precinct** (☎08-8951 1122; http://artsandmuseums.nt.gov.au/araluen-cultural-precinct; cnr Larapinta Dr & Memorial Ave; precinct pass adult/child $15/10), Alice Springs' cultural hub.

 p279

The Drive » Heading west from Alice, 6km short of where the main Larapinta Drive splits, take the turn-off for Standley Chasm.

❺ Standley Chasm

With their stunning beauty and rich diversity of plants and animals, the West MacDonnell Ranges are not to be missed, and nowhere are they more beautiful than here. Spectacular **Standley Chasm** (☎08-8956 7440; adult/concession $10/8; ☉8am-5pm, last chasm entry 4:30pm) is owned and run by the nearby community of Iwupataka. This narrow corridor slices neatly through the rocky range and in places the smooth walls rise to 80m. The rocky path into the gorge (20 minutes, 1.2km) follows a creek bed lined with ghost gums and cycads. You can continue to a second chasm (one hour return) or head up Larapinta Hill (45 minutes return) for a fine view.

The Drive » Six kilometres west of Standley Chasm, the road forks – take the left fork (Larapinta Dr) and follow the signs to Hermannsburg, 126km from the turn-off.

❻ Hermannsburg

The Aboriginal community of Hermannsburg (Ntaria), about 125km from Alice Springs, is famous as the one-time home of artist Albert Namatjira and as the site of the **Hermannsburg Mission** (☎08-8956 7402; www.hermannsburg.com.au; adult/child $10/5; ☉9am-5pm Mon-Sat, 10.30am-5pm Sun),

whose whitewashed walls are shaded by majestic river gums and date palms. This fascinating monument to the Territory's early Lutheran missionaries includes a school building, a church and various outbuildings. The 'Manse' houses an art gallery and a history of the life and times of Albert Namatjira, as well as works of 39 Hermannsburg artists. Just west of Hermannsburg is **Namatjira's House**.

The Drive » Return back to where the road forked, then turn hard left onto Namatjira Dr, which takes you to a whole

DETOUR: FINKE GORGE NATIONAL PARK

Start: ❻ Hermannsburg

With its primordial landscape, the Finke Gorge National Park, south of Hermannsburg, is one of central Australia's premier wilderness reserves. The top attraction is **Palm Valley**, famous for its red cabbage palms, which exist nowhere else in the world. These relics from prehistoric times give the valley the feel of a picture-book oasis. Tracks include the **Arankaia walk** (2km loop, one hour), which traverses the valley, returning via the sandstone plateau; the **Mpulungkinya track** (5km loop, two hours), heading down the gorge before joining the Arankaia walk; and the **Mpaara track** (5km loop, two hours), taking in the Finke River, Palm Bend and a rugged natural amphitheatre (a semicircle of sandstone formations sculpted by a now-extinct meander of Palm Creek).

Access to the park follows the sandy bed of the Finke River and rocky tracks, and so a high-clearance 4WD is essential. If you don't have one, several tour operators go to Palm Valley from Alice Springs. The turn-off to Palm Valley starts about 1km west of the Hermannsburg turn-off on Larapinta Dr.

Classic Trip

RICHARD I'ANSON HOLMES/DESIGN PICS/GETTY IMAGES ©

FRANCES ANDRIJICH/GETTY IMAGES ©

WHY THIS IS A CLASSIC TRIP
ANTHONY HAM, AUTHOR

By the end of this trip you'll have experienced the magic of the outback through its most enduring symbols: Uluru, Kata Tjuta, Kings Canyon and a town called Alice. It's a well-worn trail and one that it's hard not to love, especially if, like me, you find yourself enchanted by desert silences and yearn for its long empty roads.

Top: Kata Tjuta (the Olgas)
Left: Young Indigenous boy nurses a joey (baby kangaroo)
Right: Kings Canyon

276

CREDIT/GETTY IMAGES ©

series of gorges and gaps in the West MacDonnell Ranges. Ellery Creek Big Hole is 51km after you take the turn-off.

- - - - - - - - - - - -

TRIP HIGHLIGHT

❼ Ellery Creek Big Hole

Ellery Creek Big Hole is one of those fabulous outback miracles – a steep-sided rocky waterhole with a small, white-sand beach and hues of Red Centre red, deep waterhole blue and eucalyptus green. The large permanent waterhole is a popular place for a swim on a hot day (the water is usually *freezing*): there are no crocs lurking in the shallows...

The Drive » About 11km further, a rough gravel track leads to narrow, ochre-red Serpentine Gorge, which has a lovely waterhole, a lookout and ancient cycads. The Ochre Pits line a dry creek bed 11km west of Serpentine and were a source of pigment for Aboriginal people. Ormiston Gorge is 25km beyond the Ochre Pits.

- - - - - - - - - - - -

❽ Ormiston Gorge

Majestic Ormiston Gorge is the most impressive chasm in the West Mac-Donnells. There's a waterhole shaded with ghost gums, and the gorge curls around to the enclosed Ormiston Pound. It is a haven for wildlife and you can expect to see some critters among the spinifex slopes and mulga woodland. There are

Classic Trip

walking tracks, including to the **Ghost Gum Look-out** (20 minutes), which affords brilliant views down the gorge, and the excellent, circuitous **Pound Walk** (three hours, 7.5km). There's a visitor centre, a kiosk and an enduring sense of peace whenever the tourist buses move on.

The Drive » About 2km beyond Ormiston Gorge is the turn-off to Glen Helen Gorge, where the Finke River cuts through the MacDonnells. Only 1km past Glen Helen is a good lookout over Mt Sonder. If you continue northwest for 25km you'll reach the turn-off (4WD only) to multihued, cathedral-like Redbank Gorge. The paved road ends at Tyler Pass.

---

⑨ Tyler Pass Lookout

There's something impossibly romantic (in a desert sense, at least) about reaching the end of the paved road, and here you are. Even where your view west is obscured by rolling sand hills, just knowing that the desert stretches out beyond here for thousands of kilometres is enough to produce a delicious sense of vertigo. Tyler Pass Lookout provides a dramatic view of Tnorala (Grosse Bluff), the legacy of an earth-shattering comet impact, but it's the end-of-the-earth, end-of-the-road sense that you'll remember most, long after you've returned home.

Eating & Sleeping

Uluru (Ayers Rock) ①

✖ Bough House — Australian $$$

(Outback Pioneer Hotel & Lodge; mains $30-40; ⏱6.30-10am & 6.30-9.30pm; 🅿) This family-friendly, country-style place overlooks the pool at the Outback Pioneer. Intimate candlelit dining is strangely set in a barnlike dining room. Bough House specialises in native ingredients such as lemon myrtle, Kakadu plums and bush tomatoes. Try the native tasting plate for a selection of Australian wildlife meats, and follow up with the braised wallaby shank for your main. The dessert buffet is free with your main course.

🛏 Sails in the Desert — Hotel $$$

(📞1300 134 044; www.ayersrockresort.com.au/sails; superior d $540, ste $1000; 🌫 @ 🛜 🏊) The rooms still seem overpriced at the resort's flagship hotel. There's a lovely pool and surrounding lawn shaded by sails and trees. There are also tennis courts, a health spa, several restaurants and a piano bar. The best rooms have balcony views of the rock – request one when you make a booking.

Kings Canyon ③

🛏 Kings Canyon Resort — Resort $$$

(📞08-8956 7442, 1300 863 248; www.kingscanyonresort.com.au; Luritja Rd; unpowered/powered sites $39/45, dm $35, d $285/469; 🌫 @ 🛜 🏊) Only 10km from the canyon, this well-designed resort boasts a wide range of accommodation, from a grassy camping area with its own pool and bar to deluxe rooms looking out onto native bushland. Eating and drinking options are as varied, with a bistro, the Thirsty Dingo bar and an outback BBQ for big steaks and live entertainment. There's a general store with fuel and an ATM at reception.

Kings Canyon Wilderness Lodge — Resort $$$

(📞1300 336 932; www.aptouring.com.au; Luritja Rd; tented cabins $640; 🌫) In a secret pocket of Kings Creek Station is this luxury retreat with 10 stylish tents offering private en-suite facilities and decks with relaxing bush views. It's run by APT, so independent travellers may find themselves squeezed in among tour groups. Tariff includes breakfast and dinner.

Alice Springs ④

✖ Hanuman Restaurant — Thai $$

(📞08-8953 7188; www.hanuman.com.au/alice-springs; 82 Barrett Dr, Doubletree by Hilton; mains $25-36; ⏱12.30-2.30pm Mon-Fri, from 6.30pm daily; 🌿) You won't believe you're in the outback when you try the incredible Thai- and Indian-influenced cuisine at this stylish restaurant. The delicate Thai entrees are a real triumph as are the seafood dishes, particularly the Hanuman prawns. Although the menu is ostensibly Thai, there are enough Indian dishes to satisfy a curry craving. There are several vegetarian offerings and a good wine list.

🛏 Alice in the Territory — Resort $$

(📞08-8952 6100; www.alicent.com.au; 46 Stephens Rd; dm $25-35, s & d $110-150; 🌫 @ 🛜 🏊) One of the Alice's best value accommodation options. Sure, it's a large sprawling resort, and the rooms are pretty straight up and down – doubles or four-bed dorms, with tiny bathrooms. But rooms are also bright, spotless and comfortable, and offer two free movie channels. There's a great bar and a multicuisine restaurant, and the big pool sits at the foot of the MacDonnell Ranges.

Devil's Marbles *A traditional site home to precariously piled granite boulders*

MICHAEL RUNKEL/GETTY IMAGES ©

Alice Springs to Darwin

25

One of those great Aussie road trips that cuts through the heart of the continent, Alice Springs to Darwin takes you on a journey to remember.

TRIP HIGHLIGHTS

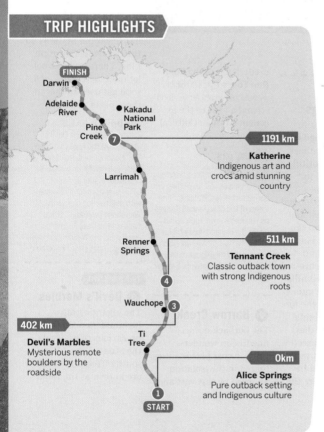

FINISH
Darwin ●

Adelaide ●
River

● Kakadu
National
Park

Pine ●
Creek **7**

1191 km

Katherine
Indigenous art and
crocs amid stunning
country

Larrimah ●

Renner ●
Springs

511 km

Tennant Creek
Classic outback town
with strong Indigenous
roots

4

Wauchope ● **3**

402 km

Devil's Marbles
Mysterious remote
boulders by the
roadside

Ti
Tree ●

0km

Alice Springs
Pure outback setting
and Indigenous culture

1
START

5–7 DAYS
1493KM / 928 MILES

GREAT FOR...

BEST TIME TO GO

April to October – the
Big Wet ruins the
rest of the year in the
north.

 ESSENTIAL PHOTO

Devil's Marbles
for their sacred
connotations and
sheer beauty.

 BEST FOR OUTDOORS

Go looking for crocs by
night at Katherine.

281

25 Alice Springs to Darwin

All the monotony and magnificence of the outback is on show on this long and lonely desert crossing. In Alice Springs, Tennant Creek and all the isolated homesteads and settlements in between, the air is tinder dry and the colours those of the desert. By Katherine, you're in a different world, where the outback meets the tropics, and the latter very much takes hold by the time you pull into Darwin.

TRIP HIGHLIGHT

1 Alice Springs

There's no town quite like Alice, marooned in the heart of the outback this ruggedly beautiful town is shaped by its mythical landscapes. The mesmerising MacDonnell Ranges stretch east and west from the town centre, and you don't have to venture far to find yourself among ochre-red gorges, pastel-hued hills and ghostly white gum trees. As much as the terrain, it's the Aboriginal character of Alice that sets it apart. Two excellent places to start your exploration of local Indigenous culture are the excursions run by **Emu Run Tours** (☏1800 687 220; www.emurun.com.au; 72 Todd St) and a visit to the excellent Araluen Cultural Precinct (p275).

✕ 🛏 p287

The Drive » You've a very long road ahead of you, so getting an early start helps. Watch for fine views of the MacDonnell Ranges as you leave town, then barrel on up the dry and dusty highway for 135km to tiny Aileron – don't blink or you might just miss it – with another 149km into Barrow Creek.

2 Barrow Creek

The outback does a fine line in wonderfully offbeat personalities forged in the isolation afforded by this vast and empty land. Sometimes it's a person, at others a building. But just as often it's the sum total of these and all manner of passing wanderers. One such place is the rustic Barrow Creek Hotel, one of the highway's truly eccentric outback pubs. In the tradition of shearers who'd write their name on a banknote and pin it to the wall to ensure they could afford a drink when next they passed through, travellers continue to leave notes and photos, and the result is a priceless collage of outback life. Food and fuel are available and next door is one of the original Telegraph Stations on the Overland Telegraph Line. There ain't a whole lot more here, but you'll soon get used to that in these parts.

The Drive » It's 118km from Barrow Creek to the Devil's Marbles. At the kooky Wycliffe Well Roadhouse & Holiday Park, you can fill up with fuel and food or stay and spot UFOs that apparently fly over with astonishing regularity. At Wauchope (war-kup), 10km south of the Devil's Marbles, you'll pass the Wauchope Hotel, where you can stay if need be.

TRIP HIGHLIGHT

3 Devil's Marbles

The gigantic granite boulders piled in precarious piles beside the Stuart Hwy, 105km south of Tennant Creek, are known as the Devil's

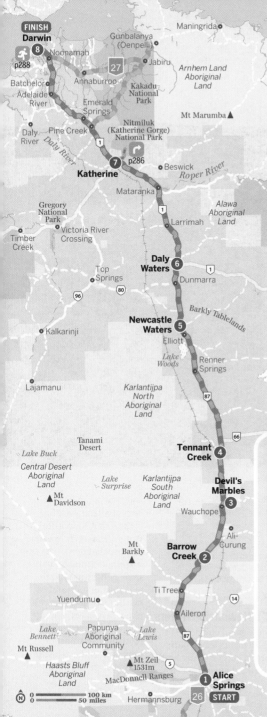

Marbles (or Karlu Karlu in the local Warumungu language) and they're one of the more beautiful sights along this road. The Marbles are a sacred site for the traditional Aboriginal owners of the land, for whom the rocks are, according to one story, believed to be the eggs of the Rainbow Serpent. Such are the extremes of temperature out here that the boulders undergo a constant 24-hour cycle of expansion and contraction, hence the large cracks in many of the boulders.

The Drive » Unless you've slept somewhere along the way, the final 105km into Tennant Creek, 511km north of Alice, can't come quick enough. And after so long on the road, arriving feels even more like paradise thanks to its oasis-like lushness and abundant water.

LINK YOUR TRIP

26 Alice Springs to Adelaide

Instead of heading north, head south. Works especially well if you've done Trip 25 in reverse and began in Darwin.

27 Darwin & Kakadu

After a few days' rest in Darwin, start your next journey there and make for sublime Kakadu.

LOUISE DENTON PHOTOGRAPHY/GETTY IMAGES ©

TRIP HIGHLIGHT

④ Tennant Creek

Tennant Creek is the only town of any size between Katherine, 680km to the north, and Alice Springs, 511km to the south, although it's all relative: just 3061 people lived here the last time the census-takers passed through. Fortunately there's more than just a good meal, petrol and clean sheets to keep you occupied. Tennant Creek is known as Jurnkurakurr to the local Warumungu people (almost half of the town's population is of Aboriginal descent) and the innovative **Nyinkka Nyunyu** (☎08-8962 2699; www.nyinkkanyunyu.com. au; Paterson St; tour guide $15; ☺9am-5pm Mon-Fri & 10am-2pm Sat & Sun Oct-Apr, 8am-6pm Mon-Sat & 10am-2pm Sun May-Sep) **museum** and gallery highlights their dynamic art and culture; learn about bush tucker and Dreaming stories with your personal guide. And to really get a personal experience of the area, take a **Kelly's Ranch** (☎08-8962 2045; www. kellysranch.com.au; 5 Fazaldeen Rd; trail rides per person $150, lesson per person $50) **two-hour horse trail ride with local Warumungu man Jerry Kelly.**

✕ 🛏 p287

The Drive ⟫ Just 26km north of Tennant Creek you'll pass Three Ways, the junction of the Stuart and Barkly Hwys. Banka Banka, 100km north of Tennant Creek, has a mudbrick bar, while Renner Springs is generally accepted as the dividing line between the seasonally wet Top End and the dry Centre; there's a decent roadhouse.

- - - - - - - - - - - -

⑤ Newcastle Waters

Most small outback settlements lead a fairly precarious existence and the line between survival and abandonment can be pretty tenuous. Many make it, but Newcastle Waters is an eerie example of those that don't. The surrounding station of the same name was (and remains) an important cattle station, but the town's role as a drovers' waystation was doomed once road and rail transport took over as the primary means of transport in the

284

Katherine Gorge

1960s. These days it's a veritable ghost town, with atmospheric, historic timber-and-corrugated-iron buildings, including the Junction Hotel, cobbled together from abandoned windmills in 1932.

The Drive » From Newcastle Waters to Daly Waters, it's 132 dry and dusty kilometres. Just before Daly Waters, the sealed Carpentaria Hwy branches off to the east, bound for the Gulf of Carpentaria at Eadangula some 376km away.

- - - - - - - - - - -

6 Daly Waters

Most outback towns of any reasonable size have some unusual claim to fame; Daly Waters, about 3km off the highway, is no exception. Daly Waters was an important staging post in the early days of aviation – Amy Johnson landed here on her epic flight from England to Australia in 1930. Just about everyone stops at the famous **Daly Waters Pub** (☎08-8975 9927; www.dalywaterspub. com; unpowered/powered sites $16/28, d $70-110, cabins $135-175; ❄ ☀). Decorated with business cards, bras, banknotes and memorabilia from passing travellers, the pub claims to be

DETOUR:
NITMILUK (KATHERINE GORGE) NATIONAL PARK

Start: ❼ Katherine

Spectacular **Katherine Gorge** forms the backbone of the 2920-sq-km **Nitmiluk (Katherine Gorge) National Park** (www.parksandwildlife.nt.gov.au/parks/find/nitmiluk), about 30km from Katherine. A series of 13 deep sandstone **gorges** have been carved out by the **Katherine River** on its journey from Arnhem Land to the Timor Sea. It is a hauntingly beautiful place – though it can get crowded in peak season – and a must-do from Katherine. In the Dry the tranquil river is perfect for a paddle, but in the Wet the deep still waters and dividing rapids are engulfed by an awesome torrent that churns through the gorge. Plan to spend at least a full day canoeing or cruising on the river and bushwalking. The traditional owners are the Jawoyn Aboriginal people who jointly manage Nitmiluk with Parks & Wildlife. **Nitmiluk Tours** (☏08-8972 1253, 1300 146 743; www.nitmiluktours.com.au) manages accommodation, cruises and activities within the park.

Sat), a good place to see Aboriginal artists at work, the stunning new **Godinymayin Yijard Rivers Arts & Culture Centre** (☏08-8972 3751; www.gyracc.org.au; Stuart Hwy, Katherine East; ⊘10am-5pm Tue-Fri, to 3pm Sat), and Aboriginal-owned **Djilpin Arts** (☏08-8971 1770; www.djilpinarts.org.au; 27 Katherine Tce; ⊘9am-4pm Mon-Fri). As the sun nears the horizon, change pace entirely by joining the evening croc-spotting cruise of **Crocodile Night Adventure** (☏1800 089 103; www.travelnorth.com.au; adult/child $75/49; ⊘6.30pm May-Oct).

✗ ⬚ p287

The Drive ❯❯ There's not long to go now, at least by outback standards. On the final, steamy 314km into Darwin, name check the tiny settlements of Pine Creek and Adelaide River, before the clamour of wall-to-wall settlements on the Darwin approach will have you longing for the eternal outback horizon.

- - - - - - - - - - - -

❽ Darwin

Australia's only tropical capital city, Darwin gazes out confidently across the Timor Sea. It's closer to Bali than Bondi and can certainly feel far removed from the rest of the country.

the oldest in the Territory (its liquor licence has been valid since 1893).

The Drive ❯❯ Point the car north along the Stuart Hwy and 160km later you'll arrive in Mataranka. En route, watch for tiny Larimah, where the quirky and cheerfully rustic Pink Panther (Larrimah) Hotel serves camel or buffalo pies as well as Devonshire teas – go figure. By Mataranka, you're well and truly in the tropics.

- - - - - - - - - - - -

TRIP HIGHLIGHT

❼ Katherine

Katherine is probably best known for the Nitmiluk (Katherine Gorge)

National Park to the east, and the town makes an obvious base, with plenty of accommodation and good opportunities to immerse yourself in the picturesque surroundings and local Indigenous culture. By day, spend your time exploring the burgeoning world of Aboriginal art at **Top Didj Cultural Experience & Art Gallery** (☏08-8971 2751; www.topdidj.com; cnr Gorge & Jaensch Rds; cultural experience adult/child/family $65/45/200; ⊘cultural experience 9.30am & 2.30pm Sun-Fri, 9.30am & 1.30pm

Eating & Sleeping

Alice Springs ❶

✖ Hanuman Restaurant — Thai $$

(☎08-8953 7188; www.hanuman.com.au/
alice-springs; 82 Barrett Dr, Doubletree by Hilton;
mains $25-36; ⏰12.30-2.30pm Mon-Fri, from
6.30pm daily; 🍴) You won't believe you're in
the outback when you try the incredible Thai-
and Indian-influenced cuisine at this stylish
restaurant. The delicate Thai entrees are a real
triumph as are the seafood dishes, particularly
the Hanuman prawns. Although the menu is
ostensibly Thai, there are enough Indian dishes
to satisfy a curry craving. There are several
vegetarian offerings and a good wine list.

🛏 Alice in the Territory — Resort $$

(☎08-8952 6100; www.alicent.com.au; 46
Stephens Rd; dm $25-35, s & d $110-150;
❋ @ 🛜 🏊) One of the Alice's best value
accommodation options. Sure, it's a large
sprawling resort, and the rooms are pretty
straight up and down – doubles or four-bed
dorms, with tiny bathrooms. But rooms are also
bright, spotless and comfortable, and offer two
free movie channels. There's a great bar and a
multicuisine restaurant, and the big pool sits at
the foot of the MacDonnell Ranges.

Tennant Creek ❹

✖ Woks Up — Chinese $$

(☎08-8962 3888; 108 Paterson St; mains
$14-24; ⏰5pm-late) The clean, modern dining
room, backed by delicious, tasty food with clean
flavours makes Woks Up one of the Territory's

best Chinese diners. Generous portions of stir-
fry in satay, Mongolian or black-bean sauce.

🛏 Safari Lodge Motel — Motel $$

(☎08-8962 2207; http://safari.
budgetmotelchain.com.au; Davidson St; s/d
$110/130; ❋ @ 🛜) You should book ahead to
stay at this family-run motel. Safari Lodge is
centrally located next to the best restaurant in
town and has clean, fairly standard rooms with
phone, fridge and TV.

Katherine ❼

✖ Escarpment Restaurant — Modern Australian $$

(☎08-8971 1600; 50 Giles St; lunch $12, dinner
$25; ⏰11.30am-2.30pm & 5-10pm Mon-Sat)
The exceedingly nice outdoor area, apart from
its view of the carpark, makes outdoor dining
here very tempting. Happily the food backs
the aesthetics. Lunches consist of burgers,
wraps, salads and seafood dishes, with food
preparation and presentation a step above most
other places in town.

🛏 Knott's Crossing Resort — Motel $$

(☎08-8972 2511; www.knottscrossing.com.au;
cnr Cameron & Giles Sts; unpowered/powered
sites $27/43, cabin/motel d from $110/160;
❋ @ 🛜 🏊 🐾) Probably the pick of Katherine's
accommodation options. There is variety to
suit most budgets; a fantastic restaurant; and
the whole place is very professionally run.
Everything is packed pretty tightly into the
tropical gardens at Knott's, but it's easy to
find your own little nook. It's also on the way to
Katherine Gorge, giving you a head start if you
want to get there early.

STRETCH YOUR LEGS
DARWIN

Start/Finish:
Crocosaurus Cove

Distance: 2.5km

Duration: 90 minutes

Darwin can get very humid – start early, stick to the shady side of the street and keep close to the water. Follow these rules and you'll find an engaging city that's proud of its place on Australia's northern frontier.

Take this walk on Trips

Crocosaurus Cove

There's no more appropriate way to begin in the Top End than with the anything-but-humble croc. Right in the middle of Mitchell St, **Crocosaurus Cove** (📞08-8981 7522; www.crocosauruscove. com; 58 Mitchell St; adult/child $32/20; 🕑9am-6pm, last admission 5pm) is as close as you'll ever want to get to these amazing creatures. Six of the largest crocs in captivity can be seen in state-of-the-art aquariums and pools. You can be lowered right into a pool with the crocs in the transparent Cage of Death (one/ two people $160/240).

The Walk » From Crocosaurus Cove, walk 150m southeast along Mitchell St. The next stop is on your left, on the corner with Knuckey St. Along the way, Tap on Mitchell is one of the busiest and best of the area's terrace bars: there are inexpensive meals to complement a great range of beers and wine.

Aboriginal Fine Arts Gallery

Darwin is an important centre for Indigenous art from artists across the Top End, and this excellent **gallery** (www.aaia.com.au; 1st fl, cnr Mitchell & Knuckey Sts; 🕑9am-5pm) displays and sells art from Arnhem Land and the central desert region.

The Walk » Take Knuckey St, heading towards the Esplanade. Lyons Cottage is to your right.

Lyons Cottage

Built in 1925, **Lyons Cottage** (cnr Esplanade & Knuckey St) was Darwin's first stone residence, formerly housing executives from the British Australian Telegraph Company (which laid a submarine cable between Australia and Java). It's one of Darwin's most attractive downtown structures (not many buildings last that long in the tropical heat and humidity).

The Walk » Cross over the Esplanade to the park.

Bicentennial Park

Running the length of Darwin's waterfront **Bicentennial Park** (The Esplanade) is shaded by tropical trees

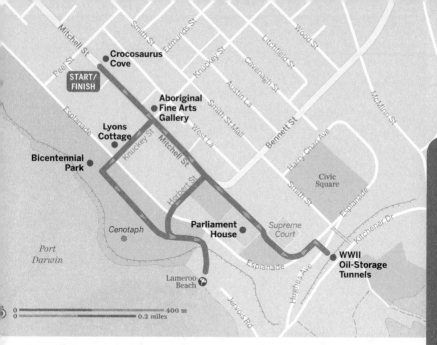

and is an excellent place to stroll. Lameroo Beach is a sheltered cove that was popular in the '20s when it housed the saltwater baths, and traditionally a Larrakia camp area.

The Walk » Stroll through the park to the Cenotaph and down to Lameroo Beach. Then, walk back through the park, cross the Esplanade and walk up Herbert St. Turn right into Mitchell St. Where Mitchell St ends (or loops around to the left), Parliament House lies straight ahead.

Parliament House

At the southern end of Mitchell St is the elegantly box-like **Parliament House** (☎08-8946 1512; www.nt.gov.au/lant; Mitchell St; ⊙8am-4.30pm), which opened in 1994. Reminiscent of Southeast Asian colonial architecture, it's designed to withstand Darwin's monsoonal climate. Attend one of the tours exploring the cavernous interior on Saturday at 9am and 11am (no booking required).

The Walk » Pass the Supreme Court, and the WWII Oil-Storage Tunnels are accessible via a walkway from the Esplanade to Kitchener Dr.

WWII Oil-Storage Tunnels

You can escape from the heat of the day and relive your Hitchcockian fantasies by walking through the **WWII Oil-Storage Tunnels** (☎08-8985 6322; www.darwintours.com.au/ww2tunnels; self-guided tour per person $7; ⊙9am-4pm May-Sep, to 1pm Oct-Apr). They were built in 1942 to store the navy's oil supplies (but never used); now they exhibit wartime photos.

The Walk » Retrace your steps back to Parliament House and then continue along Mitchell St back to Crocosaurus Cove.

Coober Pedy Film set–ready
outback Australia

JOHN WHITE PHOTOS/GETTY IMAGES ©

Alice Springs to Adelaide

26

Alice to Adelaide connects two radically different Aussie belles, from the heart of the outback to the quiet sophistication of the south, along a suitably epic trail.

TRIP HIGHLIGHTS

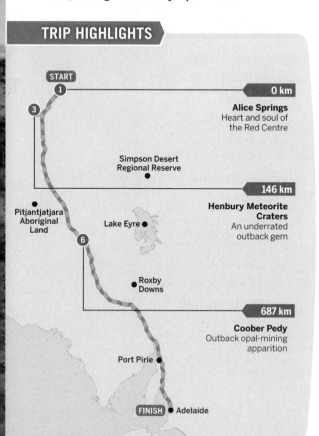

START

1 — **0 km**

Alice Springs
Heart and soul of the Red Centre

3

Simpson Desert Regional Reserve

146 km

Henbury Meteorite Craters
An underrated outback gem

Pitjantjatjara Aboriginal Land

Lake Eyre

6

Roxby Downs

687 km

Coober Pedy
Outback opal-mining apparition

Port Pirie

FINISH ● Adelaide

---

7 DAYS
1500KM / 932 MILES

GREAT FOR...

BEST TIME TO GO

Year-round, although summer (Dec–Feb) can be fiercely hot.

 ESSENTIAL PHOTO

SA–NT border, one of the remotest crossings on earth.

 BEST FOR CULTURE

The underground world of Coober Pedy is a classic outback subculture.

26 Alice Springs to Adelaide

Set the GPS for the south and get on that road – you've a long drive ahead of you. Before you've gone too far, there are a couple of fine local Northern Territory landmarks to enjoy before the long, long road down through the South Australian heartland takes you through Coober Pedy and on to the coast.

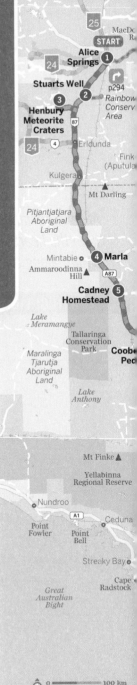

TRIP HIGHLIGHT

❶ Alice Springs

There are many Alices to enjoy, from its role as a cultural capital of Aboriginal Australia to being a base for all that's good about Australia's Red Centre. Begin by taking in the tremendous view, particularly at sunrise and sunset, from the top of Anzac Hill, known as Untyeyetweleye in Arrernte; it's possible to walk (use Lions Walk from Wills Tce) or drive up. From the war memorial there's a 365-degree view over the town down to Heavitree Gap and the Ranges. Outback creatures found nowhere else on the planet are another Central Australian specialty – learn all about reptiles at Alice Springs Reptile Centre, then visit everything from birds of prey to the speckled grunter at the Alice Springs Desert Park.

The Drive ❯❯ The Stuart Hwy that cleaves the Northern Territory in two continues south of Alice; 91km down the road (which you'll share with the tour buses en route to Uluru) you'll come to Stuart's Well.

❷ Stuarts Well

Drivers are urged to 'have a spell' at Stuarts Well. It's worth stopping in for a burger and a beer at **Jim's Place** (☎08-8956 0808; 08-8952

2111; unpowered/powered sites $20/25, budget r with own swag/supplied linen $15/30, cabins s/d $75/95; ❄ @ ☎), run by well-known outback identity Jim Cotterill, who along with his father opened up Kings Canyon to tourism. You might also catch a performance by Dinky the singing and piano-playing dingo...

The Drive » Some 39km southwest of Stuarts Well, watch for the signs to the Henbury Meteorite Craters, 16km off the highway along an unsealed road that's fine for 2WDs if you proceed carefully.

TRIP HIGHLIGHT

❸ Henbury Meteorite Craters

In the rush to the big-ticket attractions of the Red Centre, this cluster of 12 small craters, formed

LINK YOUR TRIP

25 Alice Springs to Darwin

If you've done Trip 26 in reverse (ie from Adelaide to Alice), keep heading north to Darwin to cross the continent.

24 Uluru & the Red Centre

This trip to Uluru, the Olgas, Kings Canyon and the West MacDonnell Ranges passes by Alice en route.

after a meteor fell to earth 4700 years ago, is well worth a detour. These are no mere potholes – the largest of the craters is 180m wide and 15m deep – and the crater floors are, in most cases, sprinkled lightly with green trees, giving the deeper of them a palpable sense of a lost, hidden oasis – they're invisible in some cases from a distance and only reveal themselves when you reach the crater rim. The surrounding country is wildly beautiful in an outback kind of way – red-hued earth, sand dunes and rocky outcrops extend out as far as the eye can see.

The Drive ❭❭ Return 5km to the Ernest Giles Rd, a rough, 4WD-only back route to Kings Canyon, then 11km to the Stuart Hwy. Then it's 162km to the border, with a further 160km into Marla on the South Australian side. The last fuel before Marla is at Kulgera, 20km north of the border and 200km short of Marla.

- - - - - - - - - - - -

④ Marla

Marla may be small (its transient population usually numbers fewer than 250) but it's an important service centre for long-haul drivers and the peoples of the Anangu Pitjantjatjara traditional lands that sweep away in endless plains of mulga scrub to the west. It's also a stop on the Ghan, the Adelaide-to-Darwin railway, and it's here that the legendary, lonesome Oodnadatta Track, one of Australia's most famous 4WD traverses of the outback, begins or ends. The Oodnadatta Track is an unsealed, 615km road between Marla on the Stuart Hwy and Marree in the northern Flinders Ranges. The track traces the route of the old Overland Telegraph Line and the defunct Great Northern Railway. Lake Eyre, the world's sixth-largest lake (usually dry), is just off the road. As such, Marla is a crossroads town whose importance is far out of proportion to its size – treat it as such and you're unlikely to be disappointed.

🛏 p297

The Drive ❭❭ Beyond Marla, the pancake-flat Stuart Hwy goes to Cadney Homestead (82km) and all the way into Coober Pedy.

- - - - - - - - - - - -

⑤ Cadney Homestead

Out here in the South Australian outback, small landmarks and lonely settlements take on singular importance, both in warding off the great emptiness and in orientating and servicing the needs of travellers.

DETOUR:
EAST MACDONNELL RANGES & RAINBOW VALLEY

Start: ① Alice Springs

Although overshadowed by the more popular West Macs, the East MacDonnell Ranges are no less picturesque and, with fewer visitors, can be a more enjoyable outback experience. The sealed Ross Hwy runs 100km east of Alice Springs along the Ranges, which are intersected by a series of scenic gaps and gorges. The gold-mining ghost town of Arltunga is 33km off the Ross Hwy along an unsealed road that is usually OK for 2WD vehicles.

Even better, south of Alice Springs, 24km off the Stuart Hwy along a 4WD track, the Rainbow Valley Conservation Area is a series of freestanding sandstone bluffs and cliffs, in shades ranging from cream to red. It's one of central Australia's more extraordinary sights. A marked walking trail takes you past claypans and in between the multihued outcrops to the aptly named Mushroom Rock. Rainbow Valley is most striking in the early morning or at sunset, but the area's silence will overwhelm you whatever time of day you are here.

KRZYSZTOF DYDYNSKI/GETTY IMAGES ©

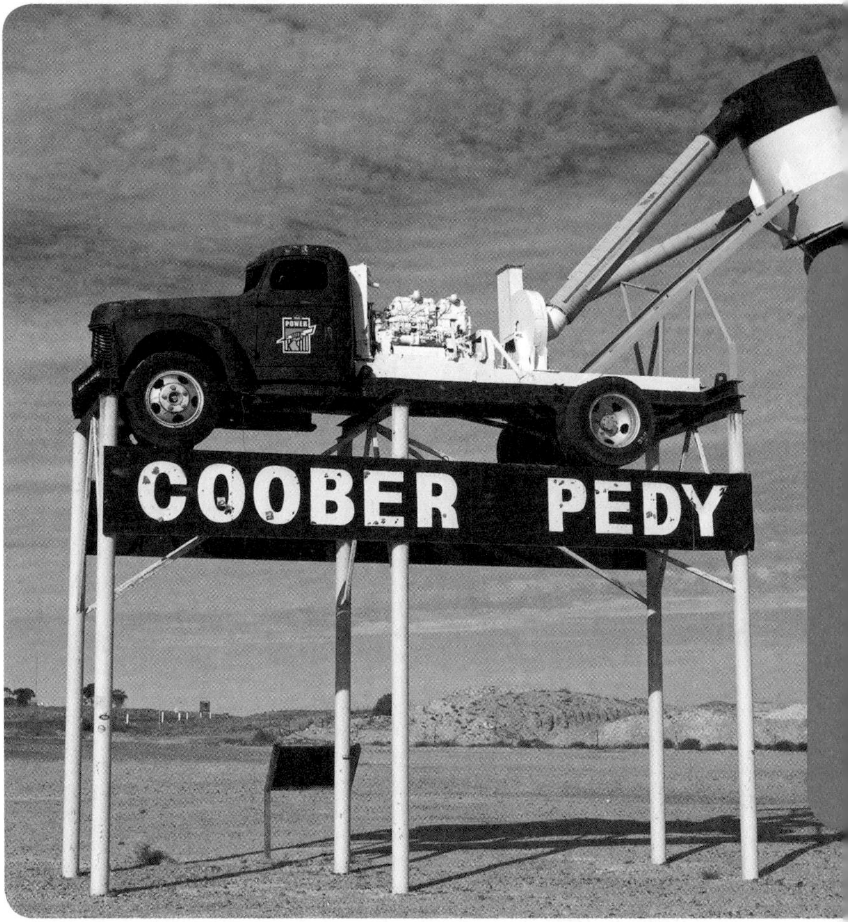

Coober Pedy A mine-blower truck marking the town's entrance

Cadney Homestead (☎08-8670 7994; cadney@bigpond.com; Stuart Hwy; unpowered/powered sites from $16/25, d cabin/motel $85/125; ❄@🏊), 82km southeast of Marla, is one such place with caravan and tent sites, serviceable motel rooms and basic cabins (BYO towel to use the shared caravan park facilities), plus petrol, puncture repairs, takeaways, cold beer, an ATM, a swimming pool... Ask at the homestead about road conditions on the dirt track running west of the settlement – the track is usually passable in a 2WD vehicle, at least as far as the striking and rather aptly named **Painted Desert**. The track runs eventually to Oodnadatta.

The Drive » It's 152km from Cadney to Coober Pedy.

TRIP HIGHLIGHT

6 Coober Pedy

As you pull into the world-famous opal-mining town of Coober Pedy, the dry, barren desert suddenly becomes riddled with holes, literally millions of them, and adjunct piles of dirt – quite suitably, the name derives from local

Aboriginal words *kupa* (white man) and *piti* (hole). When you first get out of the car, you'll be greeted by a post-apocalyptic wasteland – swarms of flies, no trees, 50°C summer days, cave-dwelling locals and rusty car wrecks in front yards. But it somehow all fits the outback's personality and the surrounding desert is jaw-droppingly desolate, a fact not overlooked by international filmmakers who've come here to shoot end-of-the-world epics like *Mad Max III, Red Planet, Ground Zero, Pitch Black* and *Priscilla, Queen of the Desert*. You can't miss the **Big Winch**, from which there are sweeping views over Coober Pedy. Take a tour with **Coober Pedy Tours** (☏08-8672 5223; www.cooberpedytours.com; 2hr tours adult/child from $50/25) and a scenic flight with **Opal Air** (☏08-8670 7997; www.opalair.com.au; flights per person from $470) to really take it all in.

✕ ⊨ p297

The Drive » It's 540km from Coober Pedy to Port Augusta, and it still feels like the outback all the way, with horizonless plains and shimmering salt pans shadowing the road as far as Woomera (366km). Thereafter, the road tracks southeast for 174km into Port Augusta.

----

❼ Port Augusta

Port Augusta proclaims itself to be the 'Crossroads of Australia' and it's not difficult to see why – highways and railways roll west across the Nullarbor into WA, north to the Flinders Ranges or Darwin, south to Adelaide or Port Lincoln, and east to Sydney. Given that you've just come in from the Never Never, there are two places that really speak to the spirit of the whole journey you're on. Just north of town, the excellent Australian Arid Lands Botanic Garden has 250 hectares of sand hills, clay flats and desert flora and fauna. Just as interesting is the Wadlata Outback Centre, a combined museum-visitor centre containing the 'Tunnel of Time', which traces local Aboriginal and European histories using audiovisual displays, interactive exhibits and a distressingly big snake.

✕ ⊨ p297

The Drive » The final stretch from Port Augusta to Adelaide is the antithesis of where you've been so far – busy roadside towns at regular intervals, frequent glimpses of water, constant traffic and even a dual-carriage motorway for the last 95km into Adelaide.

----

❽ Adelaide

Sophisticated, cultured, neat-casual – this is the self-image Adelaide projects and in this it bears little resemblance to the frontier charms of the outback. For decades this 'City of Churches' had a slightly staid reputation, but these days things are different. Multicultural flavours infuse Adelaide's restaurants; there's a pumping arts and live-music scene; and the city's festival calendar has vanquished dull Saturday nights. There are still plenty of church spires here, but they're hopelessly outnumbered by pubs and a growing number of hip bars tucked away in lanes. You're also on the cusp of some of Australia's most celebrated wine regions, but that's a whole other story...

Eating & Sleeping

Marla ④

🛏 Marla Travellers Rest Caravan Park **$**
(📞08-8670 7001; www.marla.com.au; Stuart Hwy; unpowered/powered sites/cabins $20/30/40, d from $120; ❄ @ 🏊) Has fuel, motel rooms, camp sites, a pool, a cafe and a supermarket.

Coober Pedy ⑥

🍴 John's Pizza Bar & Restaurant Italian **$$**
(📞08-8672 5561; www.johnspizzabarand-restaurant.com.au; Shop 24, 1 Hutchison St; mains $13-32; ⏱10am-10pm) Serving up table-sized pizzas, hearty pastas and heat-beating gelato, you can't go past John's. Grills, salads, burgers, yiros, and fish and chips also available. Sit inside, order some takeaways, or pull up a seat with the bedraggled pot plants by the street.

🍴 Tom & Mary's Greek Taverna Greek **$$**
(📞08-8672 5622; Shop 4/2 Hutchison St; mains $17-32; ⏱6-9pm Mon-Sat) This busy Greek diner does everything from a superb moussaka to yiros, seafood, Greek salads and pastas with Hellenic zing. Sit back with a cold retsina as the red sun sets on another dusty day in Coober Pedy.

🛏 Desert Cave Hotel Hotel **$$**
(📞08-8672 5688; www.desertcave.com.au; Lot 1 Hutchison St; d/tr from $170/200, extra person $35; ❄ @ 🛜 🏊) Top of the CP price tree, the Desert Cave brings a much-needed shot of desert luxury – plus a beaut pool, a daytime cafe, airport transfers and the excellent **Umberto's** restaurant. Staff are supercourteous and there are tours on offer. Above-ground rooms also available (huge, but there are more soulful places to stay in town).

🛏 Down to Erth B&B B&B **$$**
(📞08-8672 5762; www.downtoerth.com.au; Lot 1785 Monument Rd; d incl breakfast $165, extra person $25; 🛜 🏊) A real dugout gem about 3km from town: your own subterranean two-bedroom bunker (sleeps five – perfect for a family) with a kitchen/lounge area, a shady plunge pool for cooling off after a day exploring the Earth, wood-fuelled BBQ and complimentary chocolates.

Port Augusta ⑦

🍴 Cooinda Club Pub Food **$**
(📞8641 0166; Commercial Rd; mains $7.50-17; ⏱lunch & dinner Mon-Sat) Specialising in pub-style dishes, the Cooinda loves a good theme night (schnitzel, seafood etc). But there's also a few gourmet surprises including the feral mixed grill with venison, emu and 'roo fillet.

🛏 Crossroads Ecomotel Motel **$$**
(📞08-8642 2540; www.ecomotel.com.au; 45 Eyre Hwy; d from $120; ❄ 🛜) Brand new when we visited, this is one cool motel (literally). Built using rammed earth, double glazing and 'sips' (structural insulated panels), the aim is to provide a thermally stable environment for guests, plus 100% more architectural style than anything else in Port Augusta. Desert hues, nice linen and free wi-fi seal the deal. A pool is on the cards.

Nourlangie *An exemplary pocket of Kakadu*

PETER WALTON PHOTOGRAPHY/GETTY IMAGES ©

Darwin & Kakadu

27

Kakadu is one of the world's greatest national parks – it's as simple as that – and this itinerary spends a healthy proportion of its time within park boundaries.

TRIP HIGHLIGHTS

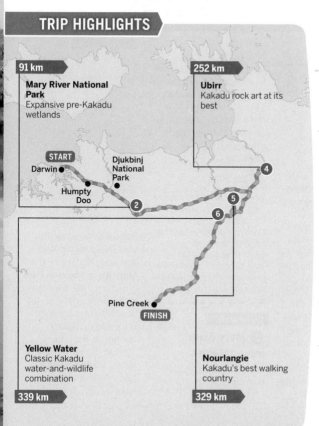

91 km

Mary River National Park
Expansive pre-Kakadu wetlands

252 km

Ubirr
Kakadu rock art at its best

START
Darwin

Djukbinj National Park

Humpty Doo

2

4

5

6

Pine Creek
FINISH

Yellow Water
Classic Kakadu water-and-wildlife combination

339 km

Nourlangie
Kakadu's best walking country

329 km

5–7 DAYS
459KM / 285 MILES

GREAT FOR...

BEST TIME TO GO

April to October; much of the park is impassable the rest of the year.

ESSENTIAL PHOTO

Sunset in Kakadu is a classic image of Australia.

BEST FOR FAMILIES

Crocs and kangaroos bring Kakadu to life.

27 | Darwin & Kakadu

For lovers of wilderness, it's hard to beat this circular loop through the best Kakakdu National Park has to offer. Steamy Darwin and the watery world of Mary River National Park are mere preludes to this extraordinary park that's as rich in wildlife as it is in dramatic landforms, soulful and ancient rock art and a blissful sense of a wild and untamed landscape.

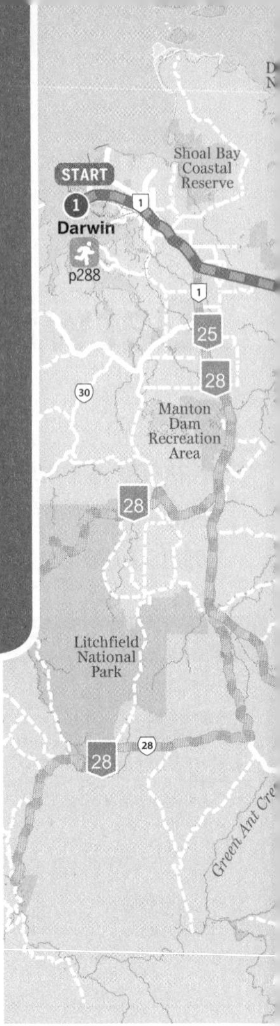

- START
- ① Darwin p288
- Shoal Bay Coastal Reserve
- 25
- 28
- 30
- Manton Dam Recreation Area
- 28
- Litchfield National Park
- 28
- 28
- Green Ant Creek

① Darwin

This trip is all about dramatic, wildlife-rich country inhabited by its traditional owners for millennia, so what better way to begin than getting a taste for such things before even leaving Darwin. Begin at the superb Museum & Art Gallery of the Northern Territory, which boasts an exceptional collection of carvings from the Tiwi Islands, bark paintings from Arnhem Land and dot paintings from the desert. Right in the middle of Mitchell St, Crocosaurus Cove (p288) is as close as you'll ever want to get to these amazing creatures, with six of the largest crocs in captivity in state-of-the-art aquariums and pools. And for a slice of nature, enjoy the wetlands of Charles Darwin National Park that sneak right inside city limits.

✕ 🛏 p305

The Drive » There's only one main road out of Darwin. Follow it for 35km, then take the left-(east-) branching Arnhem Hwy, ignoring the signs to Humpty Doo (yes, we just wanted to write it once...). From where the highway starts, it's around 80km to the Mary River turn-off.

TRIP HIGHLIGHT

② Mary River National Park

The Mary River region is one of the Top End's richest collections of wetlands and wildlife, and it all centres on the **Mary River National Park** (www.parksandwildlife.nt.gov.au/parks/find/maryriver) that begins by the Arnhem Hwy and extends to the north. For a taste of what the park is all about, **Bird Billabong**, just off the highway a

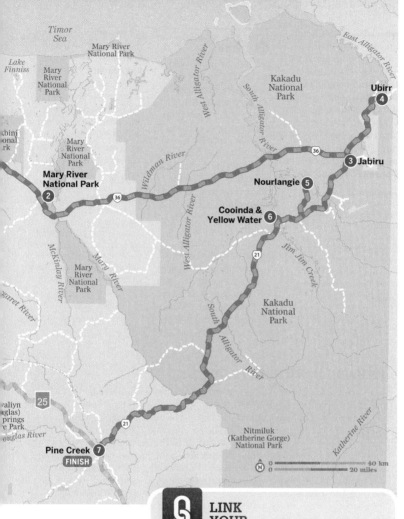

few kilometres before
Mary River Crossing, is
a back-flow billabong,
filled by creeks flowing
off the nearby Mt Bundy
Hill during the Wet. It's
4km off the highway
and accessible by 2WD
year-round. The scenic
loop walk (4.5km, two
hours) passes through
tropical woodlands, with

LINK YOUR TRIP

25 Alice Springs to Darwin

This journey from the
Red Centre to the high
tropics ends in Darwin
but it could just as easily
turn around and begin
here.

28 Darwin to Daly River

This trip through Litchfield
National Par begins
in Darwin; from Pine
Creek, drive northwest to
Adelaide Hills (112km) and
join it there.

a backdrop of Mt Bundy granite rocks. Back in the car, about another 2km along the same road is the emerald-green **Mary River Billabong**, with a BBQ area. From here the 4WD-only Hardies Track leads deeper into the national park to **Corroboree Billabong** (25km) and **Couzens Lookout** (37km).

The Drive » Back on the Arnhem Hwy, you'll enter Kakadu National Park and all the joys that brings. For much of the way, the road passes hardy woodland growing from low red-sand hills and fine escarpments. You'll want to pause for photos where the road crosses South Alligator River.

3 Jabiru

You may be in the wilderness but Jabiru serves as a reminder that Kakadu is a fragile paradise. The town, with a population of 1129 people, exists solely because of the nearby Ranger uranium mine, but for the purposes of this trip, it's more noteworthy as a base for explorations out into the park – this is Kakadu's major service centre, with a bank, a newsagent, a medical centre, a supermarket, a bakery and a service station. You can even play a round of golf here! To get a sense of what all the fuss is about,

we recommended taking a scenic (fixed-wing or helicopter) flight with **Kakadu Air** (1800 089 113, 08-8941 9611; www.kakaduair.com.au); note that flights are only available over Jim Jim Falls in the wet season – traditional owners request that the 'skies are rested' in the Dry.

✕ ⊨ p305

The Drive » North of Jabiru, the paved road battles on bravely for 39km towards Arnhem Land before petering out at East Alligator River, where you'll find Ubirr and, on the river's far bank, Arnhem Land in all its 4WD-accessible glory.

KAKADU NATIONAL PARK

Kakadu is a whole lot more than a national park. It's also a vibrant, living acknowledgement of the elemental link between the Aboriginal custodians and the country they have nurtured, endured and respected for thousands of generations. Encompassing almost 20,000 sq km (about 200km north–south and 100km east–west), it holds in its boundaries a spectacular ecosystem and a mind-blowing concentration of ancient **rock art**. The landscape is an ever-changing tapestry – periodically scorched and flooded, apparently desolate or obviously abundant depending on the season. In just a few days you can cruise on billabongs bursting with **wildlife**, examine 25,000-year-old rock paintings with the help of an Indigenous guide, swim in pools at the foot of tumbling **waterfalls** and hike through ancient sandstone escarpment country.

Creeks cut across the rocky plateau formed by the circuitous Arnhem Land escarpment, a dramatic 30m- to 200m-high sandstone cliff line. They then flow across the lowlands to swamp Kakadu's vast northern flood plains. The coastal zone has long stretches of mangrove swamp, important for halting erosion and as a breeding ground for bird and marine life. More than 80% of Kakadu is savannah woodland. It has more than 1000 plant species, many still used by Aboriginal people for food and medicinal purposes.

Kakadu has more than 60 species of mammals, more than 280 bird species, 120 recorded species of reptile, 25 species of frog, 55 freshwater fish species and at least 10,000 different kinds of insect. Most visitors see only a fraction of these creatures (except the insects), since many of them are shy, nocturnal or scarce.

ANDREW WATSON/GETTY IMAGES ©

Ubirr Rock art

❹ Ubirr

It may get busy with busloads of visitors in the Dry, but even then they can do little to disturb Ubirr's inherent majesty and grace. Layers of **rock-art paintings**, in various styles and from various centuries, command a mesmerising stillness. The main gallery is astonishingly rich with images of kangaroos, tortoises and fish painted in x-ray, which became the dominant style about 8000 years ago. Pre-dating these are the paintings of mimi spirits: cheeky, dynamic figures who, it's believed, were the first of the Creation Ancestors to paint on rock. The magnificent **Nardab Lookout** is a 250m scramble from the main gallery. Surveying the billiard-table-green floodplain and watching the sun set and the moon rise, like they're on an invisible set of scales, is glorious, to say the least. If you're tempted to venture beyond, Aboriginal-owned and -operated **Arnhemlander Cultural & Heritage Tour** (☏08-8979 2548; www.kakadutours.com. au; adult/child $258/205) can take you out into northern Kakadu and to meet local artists at Injalak Arts Centre in Oenpelli, while **Guluyambi Cultural Cruise** (www.aptouring.com. au/KCT; adult/child $72/48; ◷9am, 11am, 1pm & 3pm May-Nov) offers an Aboriginal-led river cruise from the upstream boat ramp on the East Alligator River near Cahills Crossing.

The Drive » With a longing look over your shoulder at Arnhem Land, return back down the road to Jabiru. Pass right on through, travelling southwest along the Kakadu Hwy to a turn-off that says Nourlangie Rock. The unsealed road should be passable in a 2WD but check in Jabiru before setting out.

⑤ Nourlangie

This little corner of Kakadu is one of the most accessible places in the park for those who want to get out there on their own and under their own steam. The **Barrk Sandstone Bushwalk** is often rated as the park's best walk and is an exemplary way to appreciate Kakadu's extraordinary diversity; it starts from Anbangbang Gallery at Nourlangie. Another option is **Nawurlandja Lookout Walk**, which begins 1km north of Nourlangie car park – the 600m, 30-minute walk takes you up to a fine vantage point overlooking the woodlands. Yet another possibility is the **Anbangbang Billabong Walk**, a 2.5km loop around a picturesque, lily-filled billabong and through paperbark swamp. And don't miss **Nanguluwur Gallery**, an outstanding rock gallery that sees far fewer visitors than Nourlangie simply because it's further to walk (3.5km return, 1½ hours, easy).

The Drive » Return to the Kakadu Hwy, then continue

southwest for around 10km to Cooinda. If you're coming directly from Jabiru, the turn-off to the Cooinda accommodation complex and Yellow Water wetlands is 47km down the Kakadu Hwy from the Arnhem Hwy intersection.

⑥ Cooinda & Yellow Water

Tiny Cooinda is the gateway to all that's good about the central Kakadu region. Before setting out on one of the tours that are the main reasons to come to these parts, the **Warradjan Aboriginal Cultural Centre** (www.gagudju-dreaming.com; Yellow Water Area; ◷9am-5pm), around 1km from the resort, depicts Creation stories and has a great permanent exhibition that includes clap sticks, sugarbag holders and rock-art samples, and there's a mini theatre with a huge selection of films from which to choose. As soon as you can, get out onto the waters of the South Alligator River and Yellow Water Billabong with **Yellow Water Cruises** (☎1800 500 401; www.gagudju-dreaming.com) – a fabulous wildlife-watching experience. For something a

little different, **Kakadu Animal Tracks** (☎0409 350 842; www.animaltracks.com.au; adult/child $205/135) runs seven-hour tours with an Indigenous guide combining a wildlife safari and Aboriginal cultural tour. You'll see thousands of birds, get to hunt, gather, prepare and consume bush tucker, and crunch on some green ants.

 p305

The Drive » Red Kakadu sand and scrubby woodland lap at the road verges all along the Kakadu Hwy as it meanders southwest through the park. Traffic is light, although becomes less so as you near Pine Creek (158km from Cooinda) and the main Stuart Hwy.

⑦ Pine Creek

Pine Creek, where the Kakadu and Stuart Hwys meet, is a small, dusty settlement and an anticlimax at the best of times, although it was once the scene of a frantic gold rush. If nothing else, this is where you reconnect with the main road and start dreaming of where your next adventure may take you.

Eating & Sleeping

Darwin ❶

✕ Darwin Ski Club   Modern Australian $$

(☎08-8981 6630; www.darwinskiclub.com.
au; Conacher St, Fannie Bay; mains $18-24;
🕒1-9pm) This place just keeps getting better.
Already Darwin's finest location for a sunset
beer, it now does seriously good tucker too.
The dishes are well prepared, and the menu is
thoughtful and enticing. We had the pork belly
and were astonished with the quality of the dish,
while the chorizo and barramundi linguine also
gets the thumbs up. Highly recommended by
locals.

🛏 Argus   Apartments $$$

(☎08-8925 5000; www.argusdarwin.com.
au; 6 Cardona Ct; 1-/2-/3-bedroom apt from
$350/450/550; [P] [❄] [@] [⛵]) Apartments are
very spacious at Argus, and the whole place
rings with quality. There are lovely bathrooms,
generous expanses of cool floor tiles, simple
balcony living/dining spaces and snazzy
kitchens with all the requisite appliances. The
pool is shady and welcoming on a sticky Top End
afternoon.

Jabiru ❸

✕ Jabiru Sports & Social Club   Pub Food $$

(☎08-8979 2326; Lakeside Dr; mains $16-35;
🕒noon-2pm Thu-Sun, 6-8.30pm Tue-Sat) Along
with the golf club, this low-slung hangar is the
place to meet locals over a beer or glass of
wine. The bistro meals such as steak, chicken
parma or fish and chips are honest, and there's
an outdoor deck overlooking the lake, a kids'
playground, and sport on TV.

🛏 Anbinik (Lakeview) Resort   Cabins $$

(☎08-8979 3144; www.lakeviewkakadu.com.
au; 27 Lakeside Dr; en-suite powered sites $40,
bungalows/d/cabins $130/140/245; [❄] [⛵]) This
Aboriginal-owned park is one of Kakadu's best
with a range of tropical-design bungalows set
in lush gardens. The doubles share a communal
kitchen, bathroom and lounge, and also come
equipped with their own TV and fridge. The
'bush bungalows' are stylish, elevated safari
designs (no air-con) with private external
bathroom. Bungalows sleep up to four. By far
the best value in Jabiru.

Cooinda & Yellow Water ❻

✕ Barra Bar & Bistro   Bistro $$

(☎1800 500 401; www.gagudju-dreaming.com;
Cooinda; mains $15-36; 🕒all day) The casual
open-air Barra Bar & Bistro, within Gagudju
Lodge & Camping Cooinda, serves cafe-style
fare.

🛏 Gagudju Lodge & Camping Cooinda   Resort $

(☎1800 500 401; www.gagudju-dreaming.com;
Cooinda; unpowered/powered sites $38/50,
budget/lodge r from $75/310; [❄] [@] [⛵])
This sprawling place has a good variety of
accommodation options and is Kakadu's most
popular resort. Even with 380 camp sites,
facilities can get very stretched. The budget
air-con units share camping ground facilities
and are compact and comfy enough. The lodge
rooms are spacious and more comfortable,
sleeping up to four people. There's a grocery
shop, tour desk, fuel pump and the excellent
open-air Barra Bar & Bistro here too.

Litchfield National Park
*Swimming holes, bushwalks and
giant termite mounds*

Darwin to Daly River

28

While most travellers rush to Kakadu, discerning travellers leave the crowds behind and head for Litchfield before taking on its better-known cousin.

TRIP HIGHLIGHTS

Darwin START

140 km

Magnetic Termite Mounds
Otherworldly introduction to the wonders of Litchfield

3

168 km

6

Wangi Falls
One of the most beautiful waterfalls in the Top End

Litchfield National Park

275 km

Daly River
Barramundi fishing and Indigenous culture

8
FINISH

**5 DAYS
275KM / 171 MILES**

GREAT FOR...

BEST TIME TO GO
April to October
(the dry season).

ESSENTIAL PHOTO
Magnetic Termite Mounds look for all the world like outback apparitions.

BEST FOR OUTDOORS
Enjoy the croc-free swimming at beautiful Buley Rockholes.

MARCO SARACCO/GETTY IMAGES ©

28 Darwin to Daly River

Only a fraction of the Top End's visitors know about Litchfield, and even fewer visit. Like Kakadu, there are picturesque waterfalls and strange landforms in abundance, not to mention a palpable sense of passing through a remote, red-earthed wilderness. But here you're unlikely to be photo-bombed by a single other traveller or tour bus.

➊ Darwin

Darwin, where so many journeys in the Top End begin, stands on the cusp of some pretty spectacular country, but it's also the last place before you set out where you can get a choice of meals, a glass of fine wine and have all the attractions and comforts of the big city near at hand. Stock up, soak up the closest you'll get to sophistication in these parts and get ready to head south. To get your taste of croc legends, Crocodylus Park showcases hundreds of crocs and has a mini-zoo comprising lions, tigers and other big cats, spider monkeys, marmosets, cassowaries and large birds. The park is about 15km from the city centre; take bus 5 from Darwin. Downtown, Crocosaurus Cove (p288) is another option.

✗ ⏘ p313

The Drive » Loop north, then east, then south, following the main highway past the turn-offs to Palmerston and Virginia, before resisting the temptations of Kakadu as you veer right onto the Stuart Hwy. Some 86km after leaving Darwin, take the right (west) turn-off to Litchfield National Park. Batchelor is 12km southwest.

➋ Batchelor & Litchfield National Park

Batchelor, home to the well-stocked **Batchelor General Store** (cnr Tarkarri & Nurndina Rds; ⏘6am-6pm), is the gateway town for a park that many Territory locals rate even higher than Kakadu. While we think such comparisons pointless – don't miss either if you've time – Litchfield is certainly one of the best places in the Top End for bushwalking, camping and especially swimming, with waterfalls plunging into gorgeous, *safe* swimming holes. What gives this 1500-sq-km national park its drama is that the park boundaries enclose much of the spectacular Tabletop Range, a wide sandstone plateau mostly surrounded by cliffs. The waterfalls that pour off the edge of this plateau are a highlight of the park, feeding crystal-clear cascades and croc-free plunge pools.

✗ ⏘ p313

The Drive » It's around 25km from Batchelor to the park entrance, and a further 17km to the Magnetic Termite Mounds. It's a paved road all the way.

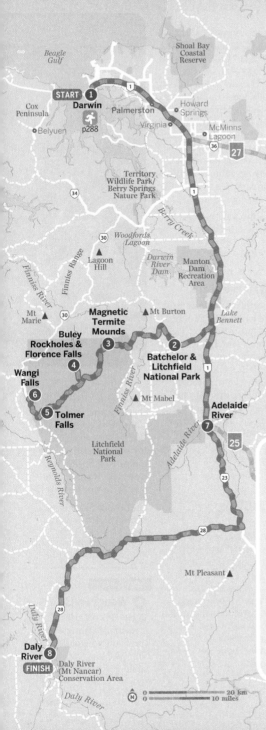

TRIP HIGHLIGHT

❸ Magnetic Termite Mounds

Looking for all the world like a cross between an abandoned cemetery and a Top End Stonehenge, the otherworldly and entirely **natural magnetic termite mounds** are one of the Top End's more curious apparitions. They may resemble tombstones, but only the very tip of these magnetic termite mounds is used to bury the dead; at the bottom are the king and queen termites, with workers in between. They're perfectly aligned to regulate temperature, catching the morning sun, then allowing the residents to dodge the midday heat. Nearby are some giant, red-hued mounds made by the aptly named cathedral

LINK YOUR TRIP

25 Alice Springs to Darwin

This trip shares the Stuart Hwy; if you're coming from the south, skip Darwin and join at Batchelor.

27 Darwin & Kakadu

Both trips begin in Darwin. If you don't wish to backtrack, drive north from Pine Creek to Batchelor and begin this trip there.

termites – they're impressive and tower impossibly high, but their structure looks more like you'd expect a termite mound to.

The Drive » The paved road continues on through the park and another 6km beyond the termite mounds is the turn-off to Buley Rockholes (2km) and Florence Falls (5km).

---

❹ Buley Rockholes & Florence Falls

At Buley Rockholes, the water cascades through a series of rock pools big enough to swim in. Anywhere else in this part of the world and you'd be keeping a careful eye out for crocs, but here it's just crystalline-clear water funnelling through a forest of green, and it couldn't be more tempting. If you find the right spot, the waters crashing over the rocks have a massaging, pummelling effect without being strong enough to dislodge you

from your perch. From the Rockholes, a walking track (1.7km, 45 minutes) follows Florence Creek all the way to Florence Falls, where a 15-minute, 135-step descent leads to a deep, beautiful pool surrounded by monsoon forest. Alternatively, you can see the falls from a lookout, 120m from the car park. Either way, it's a gorgeous spot.

The Drive » Return to the main route through the park and turn right. After about 18km, take the turn-off to Tolmer Falls.

---

❺ Tolmer Falls

Spectacular Tolmer Falls are for looking at only, but my goodness it's a lovely view! The trickle of water that approaches the falls from above is barely visible through the dense greenery and rocky landscape of the plateau until it emerges to settle ever-so briefly in a pool just above the rim before plunging down

off the cliff. Down below, there's a hint of partially submerged caves, and the whole scene looks for all the world like the quintessential Top End waterfall, worthy of the Kimberleys or Kakadu.

The Drive » Back on the main (and very much still paved) Litchfield road, it's 7km further on to the Wangi Falls turn-off. The falls are 1.6km beyond the turn.

TRIP HIGHLIGHT

❻ Wangi Falls

Litchfield's big-ticket attraction is Wangi Falls (pronounced Wong-guy). The falls flow year-round, spilling either side of a

---

EXPLORING LITCHFIELD ON FOOT

If you've been beguiled by Litchfield and have the kind of schedule (and equipment) that allows for an extended walk through the bush, consider the **Tabletop Track** (39km) to really see all that Litchfield has to offer. This circuit of the park takes three to five days to complete, depending on how many side tracks you follow. You can access the track at Florence Falls, Wangi Falls and Walker Creek. You must carry a topographic map of the area, available from tourist and retail outlets in Batchelor. The track is closed late September to March.

MANFRED GOTTSCHALK/GETTY IMAGES ©

Florence Falls Litchfield National Park

huge orange-rock outcrop and filling an enormous swimming hole bordered by rainforest and palm trees. It's particularly spectacular in the wet season, when the falls thunder and the waters at the base are wonderfully deep, but it can be dangerous as a result. There may not be enough water here for swimming and the falls may be rather modest if you come near the end of the Dry. Then again, it's at its most popular during the Dry (when there's a portable refreshment kiosk here; and, in a Territory first, free public wi-fi...who'd have thought?).

The Drive » You've gone as far as you can on a paved road in Litchfield (a rough 4WD track runs 59km north to connect to roads back into Darwin or Mandorah), so there's nothing for it but to retrace your steps. It's 87km back to the Stuart Hwy, then a further 28km south to Adelaide River.

- - - - - - - - - -

⑦ Adelaide River

With its broad tree-lined streets and riverside setting, Adelaide River could be any Australian country town were it not for the crocs in the river and the knowledge that this is one of the last settlements on the long, lonely road to Katherine and beyond. Other than the roadhouse and petrol station (obligatory in these parts), don't miss the **Adelaide River War Cemetery** (Memorial Tce), a poignant and important legacy with a sea of little brass plaques commemorating those killed in the 1942–43 air raids on northern Australia.

🛏 p313

The Drive » Leave the Stuart Hwy and head south of town along Rte 23 for 32km. A hard right (to the west) takes you onto narrow Rte 28 that skirts along the southern boundary of Litchfield National Park, before swinging south to Daly River, which you reach after 77km.

311

TRIP HIGHLIGHT

❽ Daly River

One of the most remote settlements that you can reach in the Territory by paved road, tiny Daly River (population 512 souls) sits on the river of the same name and is known for some of the best **barramundi fishing** in the Territory. The town itself has an appealing end-of-the-road charm but it's the river that's the real draw – even if you're not into fishing, it's a pretty place and even a little exploring by boat will take you within sight of some choice spots. There's a shop and fuel here and visitors are welcome without a fishing permit, but note that this is a dry community (no alcohol). Other than fishing, the main attraction here is **Merrepen Arts** (📞08-8978 2533; www.merrepenarts. com.au; ⏰9am-5pm Mon-Fri, Sat Jun-Sep), a gallery displaying locally made arts and crafts including etchings, screen prints, acrylic paintings, carvings, weaving and textiles – the quality varies, but it lacks the 'scene' of other Territory arts complexes. The **Merrepen Arts Festival** (www.merrepenfestival. com.au; adult/child $20/10) at the end of May celebrates arts and music from communities around the district, including Nauiyu, Wadeye and Peppimenarti, with displays, art auctions, workshops and dancing. The festival is held in Nauiyu, about 5km northwest of Daly River.

🛏 p313

Eating & Sleeping

Darwin ❶

✗ Char Restaurant · Steak $$$

(☏08-8981 4544; www.charrestaurant.com.au; cnr The Esplanade & Knuckey St; mains $30-60; ⏱noon-3pm Wed-Fri, 6-11pm daily) Housed in the grounds of the historic Admiralty House is Char, a carnivore's paradise. The speciality here is chargrilled steaks – aged, grain-fed and cooked to perfection – but there's also a range of clever seafood creations such as banana prawn and crab tian, with avocado puree and tobiko caviar.

🛏 Darwin Central Hotel · Hotel $$

(☏08-8944 9000, 1300 364 263; www.darwincentral.com.au; 21 Knuckey St; d from $180; [P][❄][@][📶][🏊][🐾]; [🚌]4, 5, 8, 10) Right in the centre of town, this plush independent oozes contemporary style and impeccable facilities. There are a range of stylish rooms with excellent accessibility for disabled travellers. Rack rates are steep, but internet, weekend, and three-night-stay discounts make it great value. The excellent breakfast caps things off nicely.

Batchelor ❷

✗ Pandanus · Australian $

(☏08-8976 0242; www.pandanuslitchfield.com.au; 275 Litchfield Park Rd; budget r $50, cabin $115, mains $10-15) This handy little place has some great value accommodation but the real reason to stay, or at least stop in, is the food. The restaurant here specialises in Australian indigenous ingredients and puts an Aussie twist on most dishes. Wattleseed damper anyone? The menu uses the language of the local Koongurrukun people. It's a real gem and great value too. Pandanus is 2.5km past the Litchfield Park Road turn-off.

🛏 Batchelor Butterfly Farm · Resort $$

(☏08-8976 0199; 8 Meneling Rd; d $120-170; [❄][@][📶][🏊]) This compact retreat divides itself between a low-key tourist attraction and friendly tropical-style resort. The kids will love the butterfly farm (adult/child $10/5) and mini zoo, which is free for staying guests. There are en-suite cabins, a large homestay, and a busy all-day cafe/restaurant (mains $20 to $30) featuring Asian-inspired dishes. It's all a bit Zen with Buddha statues, chill music and wicker chairs on the shaded deck.

Adelaide River ❼

🛏 Adelaide River Inn · Pub $

(☏08-8976 7047; www.adelaideriverinn.com.au; 106 Stuart Hwy; unpowered/powered sites $20/28, budget/motel/cabin d $95/120/160; [❄][🏊]) An affable little pub (mains $12 to $30, open all day) hiding behind the BP petrol station. On the corner of the bar stands Charlie the water buffalo, who lived here in relative obscurity until shooting to fame in *Crocodile Dundee*. When he died, the owner had him stuffed for posterity. There is a range of en-suite accommodation including neat cabins across the road.

Daly River ❽

🛏 Daly River Mango Farm · Campground $

(☏08-8978 2464; www.mangofarm.com.au; unpowered/powered sites $30/35, d $130-200; [❄][🏊]) The camping ground here, on the Daly River 9km from the crossing, is shaded by a magnificent grove of near-century-old mango trees. Other accommodation includes budget and self-contained cabins. Guided fishing trips and boat hire available.

Western Australia Trips

WESTERN AUSTRALIA HAS MORE ATTRACTIONS THAN MANY LARGE countries, and our road trips connect them like interlocking strands in a spider's web. The outback desert looms large as you cross the Nullabor, traverse the southern Kimberley and even as you travel the coast, with the Pinnacles within a sea-breeze's journey inland.

Wines of the Margaret River wine region dominate the southwest, which also just happens to be one of the best places to see whales if you're anywhere near Albany. Go a little further and Cape Le Grand and Fitzgerald River national parks have some of the best beaches in the country. Ningaloo Reef, Monkey Mia, the Dampier Peninsula and the Bungle Bungles are simply and utterly magnificent as well.

The Kimberley Cruising the Dampier Peninsula by 4WD (Trip 33)
SAM VALTENBERGS/GETTY IMAGES ©

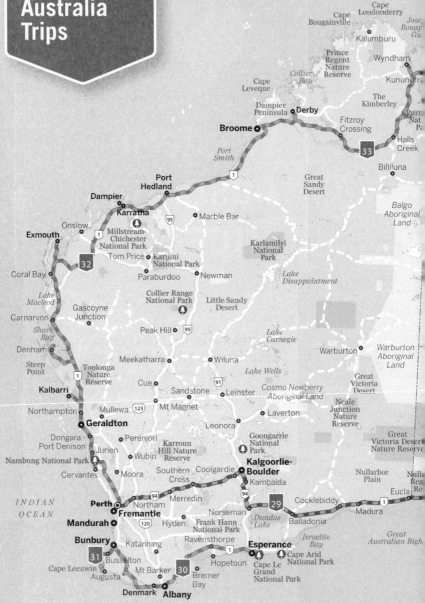

Western Australia Trips

Timor Sea

Cape Londonderry

Cape Bougainville

Kalumburu

Prince Regent Nature Reserve

Wyndham

Jose Bonap Gu

Cape Leveque

Collier Bay

Kununurra

The Kimberley

Dampier Peninsula

Derby

Fitzroy Crossing

Purn Nat Pa

Broome

Halls Creek

33

Port Smith

Bililuna

Great Sandy Desert

Port Hedland

Balgo Aboriginal Land

Dampier

Karratha

Onslow

Marble Bar

95

Exmouth

Millstream-Chichester National Park

Karlamilyi National Park

Lake Disappointment

Tom Price

Karijini National Park

Paraburdoo

Newman

Coral Bay

32

Gascoyne Junction

Collier Range National Park

Little Sandy Desert

Lake Carnegie

Peak Hill

95

Carnarvon

Shark Bay

Lake Macleod

Denham

Steep Point

Meekatharra

Wiluna

Lake Wells

Warburton

Warburton Aboriginal Land

Great Victoria Desert

Toolonga Nature Reserve

Cue

Sandstone

91

Leinster

Cosmo Newberry Aboriginal Land

Neale Junction Nature Reserve

Kalbarri

Mt Magnet

Northampton

Mullewa

123

Laverton

Great Victoria Desert Nature Reserve

Geraldton

Leonora

Dongara Port Denison

Perenjori

Karroun Hill Nature Reserve

Goongarrie National Park

Jurien

Wubin

Kalgoorlie-Boulder

Nambung National Park

Moora

Southern Cross

Coolgardie

Nullarbor Plain

Null Reg Re

Cervantes

Kambalda

Eucla

Perth

94

Merredin

Fremantle

Northam

Cocklebiddy

29

Mandurah

Hyden

Norseman

94

Madura

INDIAN OCEAN

120

Frank Hann National Park

Dundas Lake

Balladonia

Nulla Reg Re

Bunbury

Katanning

Ravensthorpe

Israelite Bay

Great Australian Bigh

31

Busselton

Esperance

Cape Leeuwin

Augusta

Mt Barker

30

Bremer Bay

Hopetoun

Cape Le Grand National Park

Cape Arid National Park

Denmark

Albany

SOUTHERN OCEAN

0   500 km
0   250 miles

Margaret River Visitors head for the beach

DON'T MISS

Eyre Highway

Drive Australia's longest stretch of straight road, a mere 145km without a curve, as part of Trip **29**

Valley of the Giants

Walk amid the treetops close to where the forest meets the sea as part of Trip **30**

Vasse Felix

Combine fine art, fine wines and fine foods as you tour the Margaret River area on Trip **31**

Dolphin-feeding

Feed wild dolphins at Monkey Mia before snorkelling and taking an Indigenous tour on Trip **32**

Mimbi Caves

Be led underground by an Aboriginal guide where the Kimberley meets the desert on Trip **33**

Classic Trip

29 Across the Nullarbor 5–7 Days
This epic Australian drive crosses the country like no other. (p319)

30 Western Australia's Southwest Coast 7 Days
Travel one of the country's most underrated coastlines, with whales and forests. (p331)

31 Margaret River Wine Region 3–4 Days
Sophistication oozes from every pore of this Tuscan-style wine region. (p339)

32 Coral Coast 10–14 Days
One of the country's most rewarding journeys, from Perth to Broome. (p351)

33 Kimberley Crossing 14 Days
Experience the outback and the Kimberleys without going off-road. (p363)

The Nullarbor Take the long drive past tiny roadhouses and the odd 'roo

Classic Trip

Across the Nullarbor

29

Truly an epic, this crossing of Australia from Port Augusta to Perth is long and either rich in interest or utterly monotonous, depending on your perspective. We prefer the former.

TRIP HIGHLIGHTS

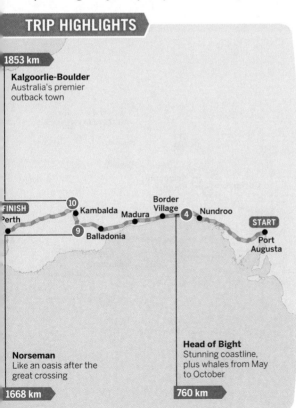

1853 km

Kalgoorlie-Boulder
Australia's premier outback town

FINISH
Perth

10 Kambalda Madura **Border Village** 4 Nundroo

9 Balladonia

START
Port Augusta

Norseman
Like an oasis after the great crossing

1668 km

Head of Bight
Stunning coastline, plus whales from May to October

760 km

5–7 DAYS
2493KM / 1549 MILES

GREAT FOR...

BEST TIME TO GO

Apr–Oct is best for the mildest temperatures, but this route is possible year-round.

ESSENTIAL PHOTO

The sign '90 Mile Straight: Australia's Longest Straight Road (146.6km)'.

BEST FOR OUTDOORS

Watch for whales at Head of Bight.

29 Across the Nullarbor

'Crossing the Nullarbor' is absolutely about the journey as much as the destination, so relax and enjoy the big skies and forever horizons. With so few towns along the way, the Nullarbor is vast, inhabited by roadhouses and roadsides speckled with spinifex. The full effect begins after Ceduna, while Head of Bight and Kalgoorlie are first-rate attractions, and not only because it will take you so long to reach them.

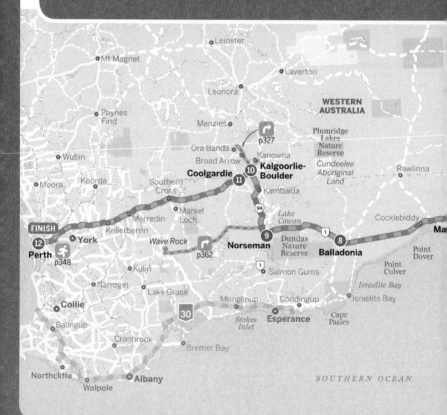

① Port Augusta

Port Augusta is where the journey begins and it's the last place of any size before you reach Perth. There are some pretty spots close to the water, and the Homestead Park Pioneer Museum features an original pine-log homestead (1850s) furnished in period style. If the mere thought of what lies ahead leaves you longing for water, Gulf Getaways offers a 2½-hour eco-cruise on the Spencer Gulf, checking out mangroves, dolphins and birdlife, while Port Augusta Aquatic & Outdoor Adventure Centre provides lessons and gear rental for kayaking, windsurfing, rock climbing, abseiling, snorkelling, bushwalking, sailing... Enjoy such choice while you can.

✕ 🏠 p328

The Drive » The Eyre Hwy, the A1, loops down to the

LINK YOUR TRIP

26 Alice Springs to Adelaide

Port Augusta is Stop 6 on the Alice to Adelaide trip (1500km), and the start/end point of the Nullarbor crossing.

30 Western Australia's Southwest Coast

There are three ways to plug into Trip 30 – Perth to Bunbury (173km), Wave Rock to Ravensthorpe (195km) or Norseman to Esperance (202km).

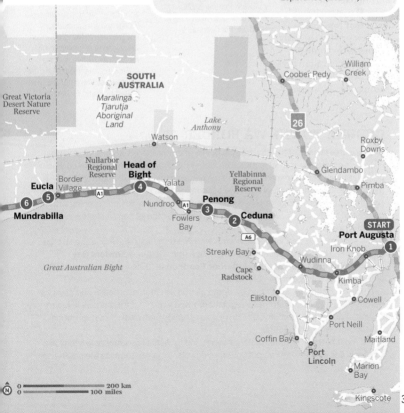

SOUTH AUSTRALIA

Maralinga Tjarutja Aboriginal Land

Great Victoria Desert Nature Reserve

Watson

Lake Anthony

Coober Pedy

William Creek

Roxby Downs

Nullarbor Regional Reserve

Head of Bight ④

Border Village

Eucla ⑤

Mundrabilla

A1

⑥

Yalata

Nundroo

Penong

A1 ③

Yellabinna Regional Reserve

Fowlers Bay

② **Ceduna**

A6

Streaky Bay

Cape Radstock

Elliston

Coffin Bay

Port Lincoln

Glendambo

Pimba

START

Port Augusta

Iron Knob ①

Wudinna

Kimba

Cowell

Port Neill

Maitland

Marion Bay

Kingscote

Great Australian Bight

Ⓝ 0 ——— 200 km
    0 ——— 100 miles

Classic Trip

southwest, then northwest, shadowing the coastline of the Great Australian Bight, whose shores the road finally reaches at Ceduna, 497km after leaving Port Augusta.

❷ Ceduna

Despite the locals' best intentions, Ceduna remains a raggedy fishing town that just can't shake its tag as a blow-through pit stop en route to WA (there are *five* caravan parks here). But the local oysters love it! **Oysterfest** (www.ceduna. sa.gov.au/oysterfest) in early October is the undisputed king of Australian oyster parties. And if you're heading west in whale season (May to October), Ceduna is the place for updates on sightings at Head of Bight. Beyond that, the sea-inspired works of local Indigenous artists from along the coast steal the show at the casual **Ceduna Aboriginal Arts & Culture Centre** (2 Eyre Hwy; ⏲9am-5pm Mon-Fri), and make a nice break from the desert colours and themes that dominate so much Australian Indigenous art.

✕ 🛏 p328

The Drive » Take the highway and revel in the fact that there's the odd settlement by the roadside. Penong is 72km (the mere blink of a Nullarbor eye...) northwest of Ceduna.

❸ Penong

Turn off the highway at Penong (population 200) and follow the 21km dirt road to **Point Sinclair** and **Cactus Beach**, which has three of Australia's most famous surf breaks. Caves is a wicked right-hand break for experienced surfers (locals don't take too kindly to tourists dropping in). There's bush camping on private property close to the breaks; BYO drinking water.

🛏 p328

The Drive » Return 21km to the main highway, turn left and charge straight on through. Wheat and sheep paddocks line the road to Nundroo, after which you're in mallee scrub for another 100km. Around 20km later, the trees thin to low bluebush as you enter the true Nullarbor (Latin for 'no trees').

CEDUNA TO THE WA BORDER

Crossing this stretch of the Nullarbor is not for the ill-prepared. Ensure your vehicle is up to the distance and carry more drinking water than you think you'll need. Fuel prices are high and there can be a distance between fuel stops of about 200km. All roadhouses sell food and fuel and have accommodation ranging from often barren camp sites to basic budget rooms and motels. There's free roadside camping with toilets and tables about every 250km. See www.nullarbornet.com.au for touring information.

It's 480km from Ceduna to the border with Western Australia. Along the stretch you can get a bed and a beer at **Penong** (72km from Ceduna), **Fowlers Bay** (141km), **Nundroo** (151km), the **Nullarbor Roadhouse** (295km) near Head of Bight, and at **Border Village** on the border itself.

If you're continuing west into WA, dump all fruit, vegetables, cheese and plants at Border Village (as per quarantine regulations), and watch out for animals if you're driving at night. Note that if you're driving east rather than west, SA's quarantine checkpoint isn't until Ceduna.

For most of the way, road trains, caravans and cyclists of questionable sanity are your only companions as you put your foot down and career towards the setting sun.

4 Head of Bight

The viewing platforms at **Head of Bight** (📞0407 832 297; www.yalata.org; adult $20, child under/over 15 free/$15; ⏱8am-5pm) overlook a major southern-right-whale breeding ground. Whales migrate here from Antarctica, and you can see them cavorting from May to October. The breeding area is protected by the **Great Australian Bight Commonwealth Marine Reserve** (www.environment. gov.au), the world's second-largest marine park after the Great Barrier Reef. Head of Bight is a part of the Yalata Indigenous Protected Area. Pay your entry fee and get the latest whale information from the White Well Ranger Station on the way in to the viewing area. The signposted turn-off is 14km east of the Nullarbor Roadhouse. While you're in the Head of Bight area, you can also check out **Murrawijinie Cave**, a large overhang behind the Nullarbor Roadhouse, and have a look at the signposted coastal lookouts along the top of the 80m-high Bunda Cliffs.

🛏 p328

The Drive ≫ It's 11km up to the main highway, then 15km to the Nullarbor Roadhouse, then you'll start to lose track along the 197km to Eucla.

5 Eucla

Just 13km into Western Australia, Eucla is a suitably impressive place, surrounded as it is by stunning sand dunes and pristine beaches. Visit the atmospheric ruins of the 1877 telegraph station, 5km south of town and gradually being engulfed by the dunes; the remains of the old jetty are a 15-minute walk beyond.

🛏 p329

The Drive ≫ It's 101km from Eucla to Mundrabilla. That's about as exciting as we can make it sound...

6 Mundrabilla

After waving goodbye to Eucla, the first stop of any note (and yes, it is all relative out here) is Mundrabilla. You'll like this tiny place even more when you learn that the **Mundrabilla Motel Hotel** (📞08-9039 3465; mundrabilla@bigpond.com. au; unpowered/powered sites $20/25, r $80-110; ❄) has cheaper fuel prices than roadhouses further west. There's not a whole lot more we can say about this place other than that out here, such things matter!

The Drive ≫ Count on 116km from Mundrabilla to Madura

7 Madura

A little bit larger than Mundrabilla, Madura sits astride the spectacular Hampton Tablelands. The best of the scenery – semi-arid woodland sloping down off the escarpment and into eternity – is visible from along the road which rises up and over the Madura Pass, and it's a stretch of road you'll remember, not least because so much of the rest of this road is flat, flat, flat... The **Madura Pass Oasis Inn** (📞08-9039 3464; maduraoasis@bigpond. com; unpowered/powered sites $15/25, r $105-125; ❄🖳) has a very welcome pool.

The Drive ≫ From Madura, there's a mere 91km into gloriously named Cocklebiddy, with a further 210km into Balladonia. The last 160km from Caiguna includes Australia's longest stretch of straight road (146.6km) – it's arguably the Nullarbor's most famous stretch of tarmac.

8 Balladonia

At Balladonia, the **Balladonia Hotel Motel** (📞08-9039 3453; www.balladoniahotelmotel. com.au; unpowered/powered sites $19/28, dm $50, r from $130; ❄@🖳) has a small museum including debris from Skylab's 1979 nearby return to earth. When Skylab was due to return to earth, there was much fear-mongering about the devastation it would cause. With all due deference to the good folk of Balladonia,

Classic Trip

WHY THIS IS A CLASSIC TRIP
ANTHONY HAM, AUTHOR

Out here, it's about the little things – a rough-and-ready roadhouse in the middle of nowhere can seem like paradise. It's the whales frolicking offshore at Head of Bight, it's driving the straightest road on the planet, it's Wave Rock. By the time you reach Norseman and Kalgoorlie-Boulder, you've crossed the Nullarbor, and the trip's epic sense of a vast crossing is all but completed.

Top: Gums line the road on the way to Coolgardie
Right: Road sign in outback WA
Left: Gold mine tailings heap near Norseman

300 m
ON RIGHT

JOHN W BANAGAN/GETTY IMAGES ©

it is difficult to imagine that it caused anything more than a ripple in the heat haze out here...

The Drive » It's 193km from Balladonia to Norseman. Close to the halfway mark is Fraser Range Station with heritage buildings and a camping ground.

TRIP HIGHLIGHT

❾ Norseman

You'll be almost dizzy with relief (or regret if the Nullarbor has you in its thrall) and with choice when you arrive in Norseman. From the crossroads township of Norseman you could head south to Esperance, north to Kalgoorlie, westwards to Hyden and Wave Rock, or east across the Nullarbor. Stretch your legs at the **Beacon Hill Mararoa Lookout**, where there's a walking trail, and stop at the **Historical Museum** (Battery Rd; adult/child $3/1; ☉10am-1pm Mon-Sat). Pick up the **Dundas Coach Road Heritage Trail** brochure, for a 50km loop drive with interpretive panels.

🛏 p329

The Drive » After the distances you've crossed, the 187km trip into Kalgoorlie (via Kambalda) will seem very short indeed. Take the Coolgardie Esperance Hwy north for 111km, then take the Kalgoorlie-Boulder turn-off.

Classic Trip

TRIP HIGHLIGHT

⑩ Kalgoorlie-Boulder

With well-preserved historic buildings, Kalgoorlie-Boulder is an outback success story, and is still the centre for mining in this part of the state. Historically, mine workers would come straight to town to spend up at Kalgoorlie's infamous brothels, or at pubs staffed by 'skimp-ies' (scantily clad female bar staff). Today 'Kal' is definitely more family-friendly – mine workers must reside in town and cannot be transient 'fly-in, fly-out' labour. It still feels a bit like the Wild West though, and the heritage pubs and 'skimpy' bar staff are reminders of a more rambunctious past. Mine tours by **Kalgoorlie Tours & Charters** (☎08-9021 2211; www.kalgoorlietours.com.au; 250 Hannan St; adult/child $70/45; ☻9.30am & 1.30pm Mon-Sat), town tours with **Goldrush Tours** (☎1800 620 440; www.goldrushtours.com.au; adult/child $150/75) and even brothel tours by **Questa Casa** (☎08-9021 4897; www.questacasa.com; 133 Hay St; tours $25; ☻tours 3pm) all take you behind the facade. Don't miss the **Royal Flying Doctor Service** (www.flyingdoctor.org.au; Kalgoorlie-Boulder Airport; admission by donation; ☻10am-3pm Mon-Fri), **Super Pit lookout** (www.superpit.com.au; Outram St; ☻7am-7pm) or the outstanding **Western Australian Museum** (www.museum.wa.gov.au; 17 Hannan St; suggested donation $5; ☻10am-4.30pm).

 p329

The Drive » It's just 39km down the road to Coolgardie – so short you could almost walk.

DETOUR: WAVE ROCK

Start: ⑨ Norseman

Only in the Nullarbor would a 600km round trip be called a detour...

Large granite outcrops dot the central and southern wheat belts, and the most famous of these is the multicoloured cresting swell of **Wave Rock**, 350km from Perth and 300km from Norseman. Formed some 60 million years ago by weathering and water erosion, Wave Rock is streaked with colours created by run-off from local mineral springs. To get the most out of Wave Rock, obtain the *Walk Trails at Wave Rock and The Humps* brochure from the **visitor centre** (☎08-9880 5182; www.waverock.com.au; Wave Rock; ☻9am-5pm). Park at Hippos Yawn (no fee) and follow the shady track back along the rock base to Wave Rock (1km).

The road to Wave Rock from Norseman is unsealed, but suitable for 2WD vehicles in dry conditions. Check at Norseman before setting out.

The superb **Mulkas Cave and the Humps** are a further 16km from Wave Rock. Mulkas Cave, an easy stroll from the car park, is an important rock-art site with over 450 stencils and hand prints. The more adventurous can choose from two walking tracks. The **Kalari Trail** (1.6km return) climbs up onto a huge granite outcrop (one of the Humps) with excellent views, somehow wilder and more impressive than Wave Rock, while the **Gnamma Trail** (1.2km return) stays low and investigates natural waterholes with panels explaining Noongar culture.

⑪ Coolgardie

In 1898 sleepy Coolgardie was the third-biggest town in WA, with a population of 15,000, six newspapers, two stock exchanges, more than 20 hotels and three breweries. It all took off just hours after Arthur Bayley rode into Southern Cross in 1892 and dumped 554oz of Coolgardie gold on the mining warden's counter. The only echoes that remain are stately historic buildings lining the uncharacteristically wide main road. The **Goldfields Museum & Visitor Centre** (☎08-9026 6090; www.coolgardie.wa.gov.au; Bayley St, Warden's Court; adult/child $4/2; ☻8.30am-4.20pm Mon-Fri, 10am-3pm Sat & Sun) showcases goldfields memorabilia, including information about former US president Herbert Hoover's days on the goldfields in Gwalia, as well as the fascinating story of Modesto Varischetti, the 'Entombed Miner'. There are also camel rides at the **Camel Farm** (☎08-9026 6159; Great Eastern Hwy; adult/ child $7/3; ☻10am-4pm school & public holidays, or by appointment) 4km west of town; book ahead.

🛏 p329

The Drive » There's an accumulating sense of approaching civilisation as you head west to Perth. It's still 555km into Perth, but the true Nullarbor is well and truly behind you by the time you leave Coolgardie.

DETOUR: GOLD GHOST TOWNS

Start: ⑩ **Kalgoorlie-Boulder**

Easy day trips north from Kalgoorlie include the gold ghost towns of **Kanowna** (18km northeast), **Broad Arrow** (38km north) and **Ora Banda** (65km northwest). Little remains of Kanowna apart from the foundations of its 16 hotels (!), but its pioneer cemetery is interesting. Broad Arrow was featured in *The Nickel Queen* (1971), the first full-length feature film made in WA. At the beginning of the 20th century it had a population of 2400. Now there's just one pub, popular with Kal locals at weekends. The 1911 **Ora Banda Historical Inn** (☎08-9024 2444; www.orabanda.com.au; sites per 2 people $20-30, r $75-120) has a beer garden, simple accommodation and dusty camping.

⑫ Perth

Perth is, by some estimates, the most remote city on earth, and having crossed the Nullarbor, you'll need no convincing of this fact. With its sunny optimism, sea breeze and fine places to stay, eat and drink, it's the perfect place to end this journey along one of the emptiest roads on the planet.

🍴 🛏 p329

Eating & Sleeping

Port Augusta ❶

✖ Hot Peppers Cafe · · · · · · Cafe $

(34 Commercial Rd; mains $6-14; ⊘8.30am-5pm Mon-Fri, to 1.30pm Sat) There's a dazzling dearth of quality places to eat in Port Augusta. This little cafe on the main street is nothing flash, but it's a stable bet for a burger, baked potato or steak sandwich.

✖ Gottabe Fish · · · · · · Fish & Chips $

(☎08-8641 3777; 6 Marryatt St; meals $7-14; ⊘lunch & dinner) Here at the top of Spencer Gulf, you expect quality seafood. This sweaty takeaway joint serves fresh king fish, snapper, King George whiting, prawns, butterfish and Smoky Bay oysters, plus burgers, yiros and steak sandwiches.

⊨ Crossroads Ecomotel · · · · · · Motel $$

(☎08-8642 2540; www.ecomotel.com.au; 45 Eyre Hwy; d from $120; ❄ 🤖) Brand new when we visited, this is one cool motel (literally). Built using rammed earth, double glazing and 'sips' (structural insulated panels), the aim is to provide a thermally stable environment for guests, plus 100% more architectural style than anything else in Port Augusta. Desert hues, nice linen and free wi-fi seal the deal. A pool is on the cards.

⊨ Oasis Apartments · · · · · · Apartments $$

(☎08-8648 9000, 1800 008 648; www.majestichotels.com.au; Marryatt St; apt $153-219; ❄ 🤖 🏊) Catering largely to conventioneers, this group of 75 luxury units (from studios to two-bedroom) with jaunty designs is right by the water. All rooms have washing machines, dryers, TVs, fridges, microwaves, fortresslike security and flashy interior design. Free wi-fi too.

Ceduna ❷

✖ Ceduna Oyster Bar · · · · · · Seafood $$

(☎08-8626 9086; www.facebook.com/oysterbarceduna; Eyre Hwy; 12 oysters $12, meals $14-22; ⊘9.30am-7.30pm) Pick up a box of freshly shucked molluscs and head for the foreshore, or sit up on the rooftop here (are the renovations finished yet?) and watch the road trains rumble in from WA. Fresh as can be.

⊨ Ceduna Foreshore Hotel/Motel · · · · · · Motel $$

(☎08-8625 2008; www.cedunahotel.com.au; 32 O'Loughlin Tce; d $125-195, f $160-180; ❄ 🤖) The renovated 54-room Foreshore is the most luxurious option in town, with water views and a **bistro** focused on west-coast seafood (mains $17 to $38, serving 6.30am to 9am, noon to 2pm and 6pm to 8.30pm). The view from the outdoor terrace extends through Norfolk Island pines and out across the bay.

Penong ❸

⊨ Penong Caravan Park · · · Caravan Park $

(☎08-8625 1111; www.nullarbornet.com.au/towns/penong.html; 3 Stiggants Rd, Penong; unpowered/powered sites from $22/25, on-site vans/cabins from $45/75; ❄) A short hop from Ceduna, this well-kept park is rated by some travellers as the best on the Nullarbor. The cabins are in good shape, and the camping area has a laundry and barbecues. Extra charge for linen.

Head of Bight ❹

⊨ Nullarbor Roadhouse · · · · · · Motel $

(☎08-8625 6271; www.nullarbornet.com.au/towns/nullarbor.html; Eyre Hwy, Nullarbor; unpowered/powered sites $20/25, budget rooms s/d/tr $47/57/67, motel s/d/tr from

$125/145/165; ❋) Close to the Head of Bight whale-watching area, this roadhouse is a real oasis for weary road-warriors. The on-site bar/restaurant is open from 7am to 10pm (meals $15 to $30).

Eucla ⑤

🛏 Eucla Motor Hotel　　Motel $
(☏08-9039 3468; euclamotel@bigpond.com; unpowered/powered sites $10/20, r $45-110; ❋) Camp sites and spacious rooms are available at the Eucla Motor Hotel.

Norseman ⑨

🛏 Great Western Motel　　Motel $
(☏08-9039 1633; www.norsemangreat westernmotel.com.au; Prinsep St; r $120; ❋ ☒) 'Budget' and 'lodge' rooms in an older block are perfectly adequate, but the rammed-earth 'motel' rooms are much nicer. There's a cafe-restaurant on site.

Kalgoorlie-Boulder ⑩

🍴 Hoover's Cafe　　Pub Food $$
(www.palacehotelkalgoorlie.com/hoovers-cafe/; 137 Hannan St; mains $11-26; ◷8am-5pm; 🛜) At the Palace Hotel, this pub dining room serves good-value, tasty food. Upstairs is the flash **Balcony Bar & Restaurant** (mains $36-47; ◷from 5pm) serving steak and seafood.

🍴 Larcombe's Bar & Grill　Restaurant $$
(☏08-9080 0800; 21 Davidson St, Rydges; mains $28-38) Very much a hotel restaurant, Larcombe's is just a tad too brightly lit to be truly intimate, but it's still the place of choice for spruced-up locals on a romantic date. The menu has a Mod Oz sensibility, gainfully plundering French, Italian and Chinese styles.

🛏 Rydges Kalgoorlie　　Hotel $$
(☏08-9080 0800; www.rydges.com; 21 Davidson St; r from $209; ❋ @ 🛜 ☒) Kalgoorlie's best accommodation is located in a residential area between Kalgoorlie and Boulder. In an oasis of lush native bush, the rooms are spacious and very comfortable.

🛏 Langtrees　　Boutique Hotel $$$
(☏08-9026 2181; www.langtreeshotel.com; 181 Hay St; d $300) Formerly a famous brothel, Langtrees has 10 themed rooms including an Afghan boudoir or the Holden-On room that's perfect for recovering petrolheads. Less ostentatious rooms are also available.

Coolgardie ⑪

🛏 Coolgardie Goldrush Motel　Motel $
(☏08-9026 6080; www.coolgardiemotels. com.au; 49-53 Bayley St; r $125-150; ❋ 🛜 ☒) With bright linen, spotless bathrooms and flat-screen televisions, the Goldrush's compact but colourful rooms are very comfortable. The attached restaurant serves excellent homemade pies.

Perth ⑫

🍴 Restaurant
Amusé　　Modern Australian $$$
(☏08-9325 4900; www.restaurantamuse.com.au; 64 Bronte St; degustation without/with wine pairing $130/210; ◷6.30pm-late Tue-Sat) The critics have certainly been amused by this degustation-only establishment, regularly rated as one of Australia's finest. Ongoing accolades include being dubbed WA's number one eatery by *Gourmet Traveller* magazine every year since 2010. Book well ahead and come prepared for a culinary adventure. Look forward to a stellar WA-focused wine list, too.

🛏 Durack House　　B&B $$
(☏08-9370 4305; www.durackhouse.com.au; 7 Almondbury Rd; r $195-215; 🛜) It's hard to avoid words like 'delightful' when describing this cottage, set on a peaceful suburban street behind a rose-adorned white picket fence. The three rooms have plenty of old-world charm, paired with thoroughly modern bathrooms. It's only 250m from Mt Lawley station; turn left onto Railway Pde and then take the first right onto Almondbury Rd.

Cape Le Grand National Park
Dazzling beaches and scenery

Western Australia's Southwest Coast

30

A road trip down to and then along Western Australia's southwest coast is one of the continent's most rewarding drives, with wineries, gorgeous national parks and postcard-perfect beaches en route.

TRIP HIGHLIGHTS

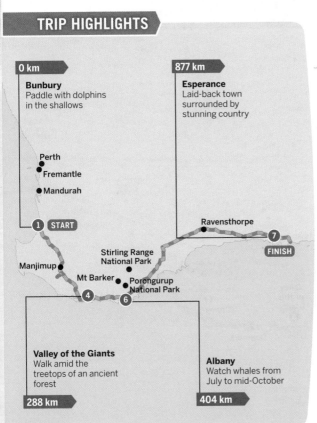

0 km

Bunbury
Paddle with dolphins in the shallows

877 km

Esperance
Laid-back town surrounded by stunning country

Perth

Fremantle

Mandurah

1 START

Ravensthorpe

7

FINISH

Manjimup

Stirling Range National Park

Mt Barker

Porongurup National Park

4

6

Valley of the Giants
Walk amid the treetops of an ancient forest

Albany
Watch whales from July to mid-October

288 km

404 km

7 DAYS
933KM / 580 MILES

GREAT FOR...

BEST TIME TO GO

December to February; July to September is best for whales.

 ESSENTIAL PHOTO

Walk through the tree tops of really tall trees at the Valley of the Giants.

 BEST FOR FAMILIES

Wade in alongside the dolphins at the Dolphin Discovery Centre, Bunbury.

331

ANDREW WATSON/GETTY IMAGES ©

30 Western Australia's Southwest Coast

Most visitors to Western Australia's southwest make a beeline for Margaret River, but there's so much more to explore. Whale-watching is one of the more memorable highlights of this wild and dramatic shore where beaches stretch to eternity and dolphins draw near in the shallows. Best of all, the further you go, the quieter the roads become and the more the thrilling sense of this vast continent takes hold.

TRIP HIGHLIGHT

❶ Bunbury

Once purely industrial Bunbury is on the up. The port area has been redeveloped (especially just north of the compact city centre where you'll find numerous waterside restaurants) and the city now draws a growing crowd of nature-lovers. The real stars are the roughly 60 bottlenose dolphins that live in Bunbury's Koombana Bay; their numbers swell to more than 250 in

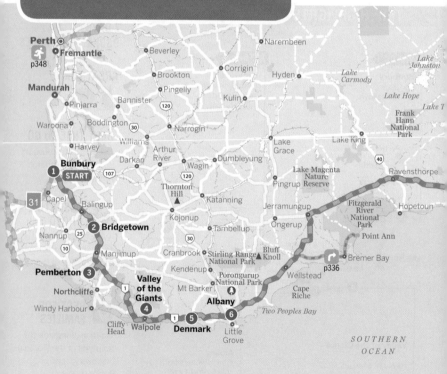

SOUTHERN OCEAN

summer. The Dolphin Discovery Centre has a beachside zone where dolphins regularly come to interact with people in the shallows, and you can wade in alongside them, under the supervision of trained volunteers. A close encounter is more likely in the early mornings between November and April – you may find yourself giggling in childish delight as the dolphins nuzzle up to your toes.

 p337

The Drive » From Bunbury, the main route south branches to the Bussell Hwy (for Margaret River), and the South Western Hwy (to the southern forests and south coast). Take the latter, passing through Donnybrook and Greenbushes in the 96km run into Bridgetown.

- - - - - - - - - - - - - -

❷ Bridgetown

Lovely little Bridgetown is a quintessential rural Aussie town, surrounded by karri forests and rolling farmland with some lovely Blackwood River frontage that turns yellow, red and orange in autumn. It's garnering something of a reputation as a popular weekender and the town comes alive from Friday evening to Sunday lunch. Wander its historic main street and watch in particular for **Bridgedale House** (Hampton St; admission by gold-coin donation; ⏱10am-2pm Sat & Sun), built of mud and clay by the area's first settler in 1862, and since restored by the National Trust.

The Drive » Thick forest crowds the roadside south of Bridgetown, particularly around the truffle-and-timber town of Manjimup (36km). Around 15km south of Manjimup, take the turn-off right (southwest) for the last 19km into Pemberton.

- - - - - - - - - - - - - -

❸ Pemberton

It's hard not to fall in love with drowsy little Pemberton, hidden deep in the karri forests that are such a feature of this corner of the country. To get out among the tall timbers, aim to spend a day or two driving the well-marked **Karri Forest Explorer tracks**, walking the trails and picnicking in the green depths; check in at the **visitor centre** (📞08-9776 1133; www.pembertonvisitor.com. au; Brockman St; ⏱9am-4pm) in town for maps and advice. Wineries, too, are a big part of Pemberton's star appeal. If Margaret River is WA's Bordeaux, Pemberton is its Burgundy, producing excellent chardonnay and

LINK YOUR TRIP

29 Across the Nullarbor

You could join this route either in Perth, or by driving 202km north from Esperance to Norseman.

31 Margaret River Wine Region

Bunbury is a feature of both itineraries and you could easily loop through the Margaret River area and return to the southwest coast.

pinot noir, among other varietals. One option is to visit **Mountford** (www. mountfordwines.com.au; Bamess Rd; ☻10am-4pm), where the wines and ciders produced are all certified organic, plus there's a gallery on site. **Pemberton Wine Centre** (www.marima.com.au; 388 Old Vasse Rd; ☻noon-4pm Mon-Fri), in the heart of Warren National Park, is another appealing option.

The Drive » Return 19km northeast through the forests to the South Western Hwy, where you turn right. From here, the road angles southeast through more wonderfully dense forests. From the turn-off, it's 103km into the tiny seaside hamlet of Walpole; watch for big ocean views opening up on the final approach.

ANDREW WATSON/GETTY IMAGES ©

TRIP HIGHLIGHT

④ Valley of the Giants

Peaceful little Walpole (pop 320) makes a good base from which to explore the heavily forested Walpole Wilderness Area, which covers a whopping 3630 sq km. The undoubted (and most accessible) highlight of this fabulously wild corner is the **Valley of the Giants** (www.valleyofthegiants.com. au; Tree Top Walk adult/child $15/7.50; ☻9am-5pm, free guided tours 10.15am, 11.30am & 2pm) and its irresistible Tree Top Walk. Here, a 600m-long ramp rises from the valley, allowing visitors access high

into the canopy of the giant tingle trees. Good walking tracks include a section of the **Bibbulmun Track**, which passes through Walpole to Coalmine Beach. Scenic drives include the **Knoll Drive**, 3km east of Walpole.

The Drive » At Walpole, the South Western Hwy (Rte 1) becomes the South Coast Hwy. It occasionally emerges from the forests soon after passing the turn-off to Peaceful Bay, with some wonderful ocean views away to the south as you near Denmark, 66km from Walpole.

⑤ Denmark

The first of the medium-sized towns you come to along WA's south coast, Denmark has a truly lovely setting with long sandy beaches and sheltered inlets to the south and forests hard up against its back on the inland side. It's slowly earning a reputation as something of a sustainable and artsy place, and the result is a community, both permanent and transitory, of farmers, fishers and families. Denmark is located in the cool-climate Great Southern wine region, with **Howard Park** (www. burchfamilywines.com.au; Scotsdale Rd; ☻10am-4pm) and **Forest Hill** (www. foresthillwines.com.au; cnr South Coast Hwy & Myers Rd; ☻10am-4pm) among the better wineries nearby. To really get the most

of these wineries and Denmark's natural hinterland, book ahead with **Denmark Wine Lovers Tour** (☏0410 423 262; www. denmarkwinelovers.com.au), which offers all-day tours to the wineries or further afield to Porongurup National Park or Mt Barker.

✕ ⎯ p337

The Drive » It's just 50km from Denmark to Albany and you know the deal – forests to the left of you, ocean to the right, and it's all really rather beautiful.

Valley of the Giants Tree Top Walk

TRIP HIGHLIGHT

6 Albany

Established in 1826, Albany is Western Australia's oldest town, a bustling commercial centre with a stately and genteel decaying colonial quarter and a waterfront in the midst of redevelopment. Take a stroll down Stirling Tce and up York St for fine Victorian-era architecture. But it's Albany's waters where we recommend you spend most of your time. Southern right and humpback whales gather near the bays and coves of King George Sound from July to mid-October. You can sometimes spot them from the beach, but going with **Albany Whale Tours** (☎08-9845 1068; www.albanywhaletours.com. au; Albany Waterfront Marina, cnr Princess Royal Dr & Toll Pl; adult/child $90/55; ☻Jun-Oct) or **Albany Ocean Adventures** (☎0428 429 876; www. whales.com.au; adult/child $88/50; ☻Jun-Oct) will increase your chances. Diving and snorkelling is another Albany specialty, thanks to the 2001 scuttling of the warship HMAS *Perth* to create an artificial reef for divers; contact **Southcoast Diving Supplies** (☎08-9841 7176; www.divealbany.com. au; 84b Serpentine Rd). East of the town centre, the beautiful **Middleton** and **Emu Beaches** face King George Sound.

✗ ☷ p337

The Drive » The road and the coastline turns northeast, arcing up and over the Great Australian Bight. It's 292km to the Hopetoun turn-off, from where it's another 49km down to the coast.

TRIP HIGHLIGHT

7 Esperance

Framed by turquoise waters and utterly pristine white beaches,

DETOUR:
BREMER BAY & FITZGERALD RIVER NATIONAL PARK

Start: ❻ Albany

Far enough off the main road to remain a secret, sleepy **Bremer Bay** is fringed with brilliant white sand and translucent green waters. It's quiet and very beautiful. From July to November the bay is a cetacean maternity ward for southern right whales, while the town also serves as a gateway to **Fitzgerald River National Park**. Walkers will discover beautiful coastline, sand plains, rugged coastal hills (known as 'the Barrens') and deep, wide river valleys. In season, you'll almost certainly see whales and their calves from the shore at Point Ann, where there's a lookout and a heritage walk that follows a short stretch of the 1164km No 2 rabbit-proof fence, one of the longest fences on earth. Entry to the park from Bremer Bay is via Swamp and Murray Rds, and all roads are gravel and passable in 2WD vehicle except after rains – check locally before you set out.

To get here, drive 117km northwest of Albany along Rte 1 to Boxwood Hill. Bremer Bay lies 62km due east of Boxwood Hill.

Esperance sits in solitary splendour on the Bay of Isles. It's such an appealing place that families still travel from Perth or Kalgoorlie just to plug into the easygoing vibe and great beach life. Picture-perfect beaches dot the even more remote national parks to the town's southeast, and the pristine environment of the 105 islands of the offshore Recherche Archipelago are home to fur seals, penguins and sea birds; a tour to Woody Island is highly recommended, ask at the **visitor centre** (☏08-9083 1555; www.visitesperance.com; cnr Kemp & Dempster Sts; ☉9am-5pm Mon-Fri, to 2pm Sat, to noon Sun) in Esperance for details. Wreck-diving is also possible with **Esperance Diving & Fishing** (☏08-9071 5111; www.esperancedivingandfishing.com.au; 72 The Esplanade).

The Drive ❯❯ Take the Condingup road that runs northeast, then follow the signs along sealed roads first to Gerbryn, then Cape Le Grand National Park.

- - - - - - - - - - -

❽ Cape Le Grand National Park

Starting 60km east of Esperance, Cape Le Grand National Park boasts spectacular coastal scenery, dazzling beaches and excellent walking tracks. There's good fishing, swimming and camping at Lucky Bay and Le Grand Beach, and day-use facilities at gorgeous Hellfire Bay. Make the effort to climb Frenchman Peak (a steep 3km return, allow two hours), as the views from the top and through the rocky 'eye', especially during the late afternoon, are superb. To explore further, your best bet is a 4WD tour along the sand and two-hour circuits of Great Ocean Dr with **Eco-Discovery Tours** (☏0407 737 261; www.esperancetours.com.au).

Eating & Sleeping

Bunbury ❶

✕ Happy Wife   Cafe $$

(www.thehappywife.com.au; 98 Stirling St; mains
$11-24; ⏱6.30am-3.30pm Mon-Fri, 7.30am-
2.30pm Sat) Grab a spot in the garden of this
Cape Cod–style cottage just a short drive
from the centre of town. Excellent home-style
baking and regular lunch specials make it
worth seeking out. Try the Asian-style sticky
pork salad with nashi pear, cabbage salad and
toasted peanuts.

⊨ The Clifton   Motel $$

(☎08-9721 4300; www.theclifton.com.au; 2
Molloy St; r $150-275; 🕾) For luxurious heritage
accommodation, go for the top-of-the-range
rooms in the Clifton's historic Grittleton Lodge
(1885). Good-value motel rooms are also
available.

Denmark ❺

✕ Mrs Jones   Cafe $$

(☎0467 481 878; www.mrsjonescafe.com; 12
Mt Shadforth Rd; mains $9-18; ⏱7am-4pm)
Denmark's best coffee is at this spacious spot
with high ceilings and exposed beams. Settle
in with locals and tourists for interesting cafe
fare, often with an Asian or Mediterranean spin.
The mixed platter ($42) with prawns, squid and
salmon makes a great lunch for two.

✕ Pepper &
Salt   Modern Australian, Asian $$$

(☎08-9848 3053; www.pepperandsalt.com.
au; 1564 South Coast Hwy, Forest Hill Vineyard;
mains $38-42; ⏱noon-3pm Thu-Sun, from
6pm Fri) With his Fijian-Indian heritage, chef
Silas Masih's knowledge of spices and herbs is
wonderfully showcased in his fresh and vibrant
food. Highlights include king prawns with chilli
popcorn and lime mayonnaise, or the excellent

tapas platter ($62), which effortlessly detours
from Asia to the Middle East. Bookings essential.

⊨ Sensational Heights   B&B $$

(☎08-9840 9000; www.sensational-
heightsbandb.com.au; 159 Suttons Rd;
r $200-260; ✳🕾) Yep, it's on top of a hill
(off Scotsdale Rd) and, yes, the views are
sensational. Expect contemporary decor,
luxurious linen and very comfy beds. The
pricier rooms have spa baths.

⊨ Cape Howe Cottages   Cottage $$$

(☎08-9845 1295; www.capehowe.com.au; 322
Tennessee Rd S; cottages $180-290; ✳) For a
remote getaway, these five cottages in bushland
southeast of Denmark really make the grade.
They're all different, but the best is only 1.5km
from dolphin-favoured Lowlands Beach and
is properly plush – with a BBQ on the deck, a
dishwasher in the kitchen and laundry facilities.

Albany ❻

✕ York Street Cafe   Cafe $$

(www.184york.com; 184 York St; breakfast &
lunch $13-23, dinner $24-27; ⏱7.30am-3pm
Sun-Tue, to late Wed-Sat; 🕾) The food is
excellent at this cosmopolitan and versatile cafe
on the main strip. Lunch includes Asian-style
pork belly with spiced apple chutney on Turkish
bread, while at dinner the attention turns
to bistro items such as prosciutto-wrapped
chicken on couscous. BYO wine.

⊨ Beach House
at Bayside   Boutique Hotel $$$

(☎08-9844 8844; www.thebeachhouse-
atbayside.com.au; 33 Barry Ct, Collingwood
Park; r $280-375; ✳) Positioned right by the
beach and the golf course in a quiet cul-de-sac,
midway between Middleton Beach and Emu
Point, this modern accommodation offers
wonderful service. Rates include breakfast,
afternoon tea, and evening port and chocolates.

Margaret River Epicurean delights among the vines

Margaret River Wine Region

31

Wines and wild country are a wonderful combination in Margaret River, one of Australia's most celebrated wine regions, with a foothold on the extreme southwestern corner of the Australian continent.

TRIP HIGHLIGHTS

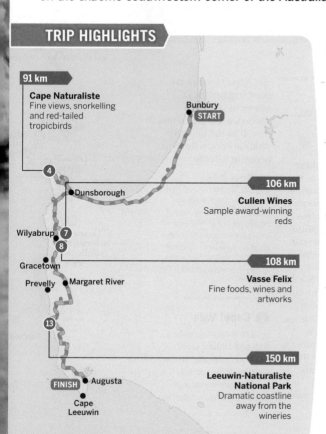

91 km

Cape Naturaliste
Fine views, snorkelling and red-tailed tropicbirds

Bunbury
START

4

Dunsborough

Wilyabrup 7

8

Gracetown

Prevelly Margaret River

13

FINISH Augusta

Cape Leeuwin

106 km

Cullen Wines
Sample award-winning reds

108 km

Vasse Felix
Fine foods, wines and artworks

150 km

Leeuwin-Naturaliste National Park
Dramatic coastline away from the wineries

**3–4 DAYS
195KM / 120 MILES**

GREAT FOR...

BEST TIME TO GO

Spring for wildflowers in Leeuwin-Naturaliste National Park.

ESSENTIAL PHOTO

Wine-glass selfie at any winery.

BEST FOR FOOD

Vasse Felix is a wonderful all-round package of food, wine and fine art.

KEVEN OSBORNE/FOX FOTOS/GETTY IMAGES ©

Margaret River Wine Region

The farmland, forests, rivers and coast of the lush, green southwestern corner of Western Australia contrast vividly with the stark, sunburnt terrain of much of the state. On land, world-class wineries and craft breweries beckon, while offshore, bottlenose dolphins and whales frolic, and devoted surfers search for their perfect break. And, unusually for WA, distances between the many attractions are short, making it a fantastic area to explore for a few days.

❶ Bunbury

With long beaches that leave all hint of the town's post-industrial heritage behind, and the chance to see dolphins really close to town, Bunbury is a destination that appeals to kids and lovers of wildlife alike. For bottlenose dolphins swimming around your legs, head to Koombana Bay and the Dolphin Discovery Centre. For the memorable opportunity to swim with dolphins, Swim Encounter Cruises has three-hour excursions when the weather's warm. There's also the **Mangrove Boardwalk**, which you enter off Koombana Dr and which meanders through the most southerly mangroves in WA and a 2500-year-old ecosystem, as well as the Bunbury Wildlife Park, with loads of native wildlife.

The Drive » Take the Bussell Hwy (for Margaret River) that follows the coast south of Bunbury. You'll barely have time to get out of third gear before finding yourself in the small town of Capel. Ignore the town, and head for the winery by taking Mallokup Rd near the centre of the town.

❷ Capel Vale

Where the Geographe Bay and Indian Ocean coast arcs around to the southwest in a near-perfect moon-curve, **Capel Vale** (www.capelvale.

com.au; Mallokup Rd; ⊙ cellar door 10am-4.30pm, restaurant 11.30am-3pm Thu-Mon) carpets the green coastal hinterland with vines that produce some of Western Australia's most respected wines; you'll find them in restaurants and bottle-shops across the country. It offers free tastings from its cellar door and its well-regarded restaurant overlooks the vines. It has a wonderfully diverse portfolio, from cabernet sauvignon and merlot to riesling and sauv blanc.

The Drive » Ease back onto the main highway at Capel, then cruise on into Busselton, just a few clicks up the road.

③ Busselton

Unpretentious and uncomplicated, Busselton is what passes for the big smoke in these parts. Surrounded by calm

LINK YOUR TRIP

30 Western Australia's Southwest Coast

Both trips begin in Bunbury, so joining them up couldn't be easier.

32 Coral Coast

It's a two-hour, 175km drive north from Bunbury to Perth where this wonderful Perth-to-Broome road trip begins.

waters and white-sand beaches, the outlandishly long **Busselton Jetty** (☎08-9754 0900; www.busseltonjetty.com.au; adult/child $2.50/free, return train adult/child $11/6, Interpretive Centre admission free; ⊙Interpretive Centre 9am-5pm) is its most famous attraction – the 1865 timber-piled jetty is the longest in the southern hemisphere (1841m). A little **train** chugs along to the **Underwater Observatory** (adult/child incl train $29.50/14; ⊙9am-4.25pm), where tours take place 8m below the surface; bookings are essential. There's also an Interpretive Centre, in an attractive building in the style of 1930s bathing sheds, about 50m along the jetty. During school holidays the population increases fourfold and accommodation prices soar, but for all that Busselton makes a good base for the northern half of the Margaret River region.

✕ ⛺ p347

The Drive » You're within sight of the shimmering blue of the Indian Ocean almost all the way from Busselton to Cape Naturaliste, an easy, pretty drive where you may be tempted to park and go for a quick swim. Unless you do, you'll probably be at the cape in less than an hour.

PHILLIP HAYSON/GETTY IMAGES ©

TRIP HIGHLIGHT

➍ Cape Naturaliste

Northwest of Dunsborough, a beach-worshipping town that gets inundated with schoolies around the end of November – avoid this time at all costs – Cape Naturaliste Rd leads to the excellent beaches of **Meelup**, **Eagle Bay** and **Bunker Bay**. Whales and hammerhead sharks like to hang out on the edge of Bunker Bay, where the continental shelf drops 75m. There's also excellent snorkelling on the edge of the shelf at **Shelley Cove**. The cape itself is marked with the **Cape Naturaliste Lighthouse** (adult/child $14/7; ⊙tours every 30min 9.30am-4pm), built in 1903. Standing in the lighthouse's shadow, protected from burning sun and buffeting Indian Ocean winds alike, it's difficult to escape the feeling that one is standing upon Australia's final headland, contemplating eternity. From September to May, take the 3.5km boardwalk that runs south from the Cape Naturaliste lighthouse to a viewpoint overlooking Sugarloaf Rock and Australia's most southerly breeding colony of the really rather splendid red-tailed tropicbird (*Phaethon rubricauda*).

The Drive » Return to Dunsborough, then take the small side road that trickles down towards the coast at Yallingup.

➎ Yallingup

You're permitted to let a 'wow' escape when the surf-battered coastline first comes into view around Yallingup – from here the ocean stretches all the way to Africa. Beautiful walking trails follow the coast between here and **Smiths Beach**. Just a little inland, between Dunsborough and Yallingup, the

Busselton Busselton Jetty

500,000-year-old **Ngilgi Cave** (☎08-9755 2152; www.geographebay.com; Yallingup Caves Rd; adult/child $22/12; ⊙9am-5pm) has fabulous formations; tours depart every half-hour. But magnificent as these attractions are, that's not, for the most part, why people come. Instead, two of the grand passions of West Australian life converge on the beach at Yallingup: here are surf beaches par excellence, while beer aficionados just can't resist its lure. If you plan on pursuing these passions, it is possible to take a surf lesson with the **Yallingup Surf School** (☎08-9755 2755; www.yallingupsurfschool.com) in the morning, then pay a visit to the **Wicked Ale Brewery** (☎08-9755 2848; www.wickedalebrewery.com.au; Caves Rd; ⊙10am-5pm) in the afternoon. Speaking of passions, romantics may also love the fact that Yallingup means 'place of love' in the Wardandi Noongar tongue.

🛏 p347

The Drive ≫ A quiet back road runs south from Yallingup and within sight of the coast, with even quieter tracks running right down to the coast away to the right at regular intervals. Vineyards increasingly carpet the rolling hills here, especially east of the road. Around 2km short of tiny Wilyabrup, turn left (east) at the sign for Bootleg Brewery; it's 2km along on the right.

- - - - - - - - - - -

❻ Bootleg Brewery

In a reminder of just how far the Margaret River region has evolved from its exclusively wine-producing roots, **Bootleg Brewery** (www.bootlegbrewery.com.au; off Yelverton Rd, Wilyabrup; ⊙11am-6pm) is deliberately more rustic than some of the area's flashier breweries, but lots of fun with a pint in the sun – especially with live bands on Saturday.

343

The Drive » Return the 2km to the main north–south road and turn left (south). Blink and you could easily miss Wilyabrup, a tiny hamlet. A few clicks south of the last house, there'll you'll find Cullen Wines.

TRIP HIGHLIGHT

❼ Cullen Wines

The area around Wilyabrup is where the Margaret River wine story began way back in the 1960s; one of the pioneers, **Cullen Wines** (☎08-9755 5277; www.cullenwines.com.au; 4323 Caves Rd, Cowaramup; mains $25-38; ⊙10am-4pm), is still very much around. Grapes were first planted here in 1966 and Cullen has an ongoing commitment to organic and biodynamic principles in both food and wine. Celebrating a relaxed ambience, Cullen's food is excellent, with many of the fruits and vegetables sourced from its own gardens. But it's the wines it's best known for: Cullen's 2009 Diana Madeline cabernet sauvignon merlot won Wine of the Year in the Australian Wine Annual 2012.

The Drive » Around 2km south of Cullen Wines, look for Vasse Felix on the left.

TASTING TIMES & WINERY TOURS

Most of the wineries offer tastings between 10am and 5pm daily. At busy times (this includes every weekend), consider booking ahead for lunch before you set out.

Harvest Tours (☎0429 728 687; www.harvesttours.com.au; adult/child $155/55) Food and wine tour with an emphasis on organic, sustainable and ethical producers. Lunch is included at **Cullen Wines**.

Taste the South (☎0438 210 373; www.tastethesouth.com.au; per person from $95) Wine and craft beer tours. Up to five breweries can be visited, and the special Hits with Kids tour combines children-friendly vineyards with activities including lamb feeding, sheep shearing and a chocolate factory.

Wine for Dudes (☎0427 774 994; www.winefordudes.com; tours $95) Includes a brewery, a chocolate factory, four wineries, a wine-blending experience and lunch.

Margies Big Day Out (☎0416 180 493; www.margaretrivertourswa.com.au; tours $95) Three wineries, two breweries, cheese, chocolate and lunch.

TRIP HIGHLIGHT

❽ Vasse Felix

Visiting wineries may be pleasurable for its own sake but a number of these fine establishments make sure you don't do it entirely on an empty stomach. One of the best examples of this holistic approach is **Vasse Felix** (☎08-9756 5050; www.vassefelix.com.au; cnr Caves Rd & Harmans Rd S, Cowaramup; mains $32-39, 3-course menu $65, mains $32-39; ⊙cellar door 10am-5pm, restaurant to 3pm), one of the oldest Margaret River vineyards and a good all-round winery with a fabulous art collection: the grounds are peppered with sculptures, while the gallery displays works from the Holmes à Court collection. Many also consider this to be the best fine-dining restaurant in the region. Here, in classic winery style, the big wooden dining room evokes an extremely flash barn, while the sophisticated flavours are, as you'd expect, perfectly matched to the right Vasse Felix wines, such as its Heytesbury cabernet blend and Heytesbury chardonnay.

The Drive » From Vasse Felix, head south and almost immediately, take the track turning left (northeast). After around 2.5km, you'll see the sign for Ashbrook on the left side of the road.

⑨ Ashbrook

If you're not quite done before taking a breather in Margaret River, consider a short detour on to **Ashbrook** (www.ashbrookwines.com.au; 448 Tom Cullity Dr, Wilyabrup; ⊙10am-5pm). Ashbrook grows all of its grapes on site and its award-winning rieslings are rightly lauded, with the cabernet merlot also worthy of closer inspection.

The Drive » If you're the designated driver, and hopefully with your car boot (trunk) filled with cases of wine to enjoy when everyone else has fallen asleep in a deliciously drunken haze, guide the car south to Margaret River – you can't miss it.

⑩ Margaret River

Although tourists usually outnumber locals, Margaret River still feels like a country town. The advantage of basing yourself here is that after 5pm, once the wineries shut up shop, it's one of the few places with any vital signs. Plus it's close to the incredible surf of **Margaret River Mouth** and **Southside**, and the swimming beaches at **Prevelly** and **Gracetown**. Margaret River spills over with tourists every weekend and gets very, very busy at Easter and Christmas (when you should book weeks, if not months, ahead). And yes, beyond the town's limits, vineyards producing

---

MARGARET RIVER GOURMET ESCAPE

From Rick Stein and Heston Blumenthal to *MasterChef*'s George Calombaris, the **Gourmet Escape** (www.gourmetescape.com.au; ⊙late Nov) food and wine festival attracts the big names in global and Australian cuisine. Look forward to three days of food workshops, tastings, vineyard events and demonstrations.

---

excellent chardonnays and Bordeaux-style reds segue into rural back roads punctuated with craft breweries, provedores, cheese shops, chocolate shops and art galleries.

✗ 🛏 p347

The Drive » Take the Bussel Hwy south of Margaret River, and around 5km south of town you'll see the sign for Watershed on your left.

⑪ Watershed Premium Wines

After a long lie-in, a light breakfast and some morning fresh air down by the coast, plan to arrive at **Watershed Premium Wines** (www.watershedwines.com.au; cnr Bussell Hwy & Darch Rd; cafe $16-29, restaurant $38-44; ⊙10am-5pm) around lunchtime. We just love the combination of tasting some fine wines, choosing your favourite to take home and then sitting down to an equally fine meal – isn't that, after all, what this is all about? Watershed does

---

that combination wonderfully well, with one of Western Australia's best vineyard restaurants and a portfolio that includes its highly respected Awakening cabernet sauvignon.

The Drive » Continue south along the Bussel Hwy for 3km. At Witchcliffe, turn right (west), then take the first right – an unsealed but passable gravel road leads straight to Leeuwin Estate.

⑫ Leeuwin Estate

One of Margaret River's most celebrated icons, **Leeuwin Estate** (☎08-9759 0000; www.leeuwinestate.com.au; Stevens Rd; mains $31-39; ⊙10am-5pm daily, dinner Sat) revels in the finer things in life – the much-lauded Art Series chardonnay and cabernet merlot, the monthly concerts that occasionally feature the Perth Symphony Orchestra, and an impressive estate with tall trees and lawns gently rolling down to the bush. Behind-the-scenes wine tours and tastings take place at 11am (adult/child $12.50/4).

The Drive » Return to the sealed road, but instead of turning left back towards Witchcliffe, turn right (west) and head for the coast. Once there, follow any and all of the little tracks that meander west in search of the sea.

TRIP HIGHLIGHT

⑬ Leeuwin-Naturaliste National Park

Stretching from Gracetown all the way down south to Cape Leeuwin, **Leeuwin-Naturaliste National Park** (Caves Rd) is wildly beautiful, known for its forests, sand dunes and a startling variety of endemic wildflowers. The 155-sq-km park explodes with colour in the spring months. The demanding environment of buffeting winds and complicated soil system prevents any one species predominating, leaving instead a gorgeous array of fantastically evolved orchids, sundews, kangaroo paws and the like to flourish in their exclusive niches. Walking in the park in spring (September to November), it's possible to see orchids, banksias, clematis, cowslips, and many other species, including the improbably named prickly moses. When the sun's out, the flowers are in bloom and the deep blues of sea and sky provide a backdrop, you'll wonder if you've stumbled onto one of Australia's prettiest corners.

The Drive » Take any north–south road from anywhere along the eastern fringe of the national park and you'll end up in Augusta, right down at the region's southern end.

⑭ Augusta

At the mouth of the Blackwood River, and 5km north of end-of-the-earth-like Cape Leeuwin, Augusta can appear to be quite separate from the main wine region. The vibe here is a little less epicurean, and more languid, more focused on other aspects of nature's bounty. Take a couple of close-by excursions and you'll soon see what we mean. Begin with wild and windy **Cape Leeuwin Lighthouse** (www. margaretriver.com; adult/child $8/5; ⊙9am-4.30pm), where the Indian and Southern Oceans meet – it's the most southwesterly point in Australia. The lighthouse (1896), WA's tallest, offers magnificent views of the coastline. Then, if it's September to December, go whale-watching with **Naturaliste Charters** (☏08-9750 5500; www.whales-australia. com.au; adult/child $80/$50; ⊙whale watching Jun-Dec, fishing charters Jan-Mar); from January to March its emphasis switches to beaches, limestone caves with Indigenous art, and wildlife including dolphins and New Zealand fur seals. And then there's **Jewel Cave** (www. margaretriver.com; Caves Rd; adult/child $22/10; ⊙tours hourly 9.30am-3.30pm), 8km northwest of Augusta at the south end of Caves Rd. The most spectacular of the region's caves, Jewel Cave has an impressive 5.9m straw stalactite, so far the longest seen in a tourist cave. Fossil remains of a Tasmanian tiger (thylacine), believed to be 3500 years old, were discovered here. It's a mysterious, soulful place to end your journey.

✕ ⨋ p347

Eating & Sleeping

Busselton ❸

✗ Laundry 43   Cafe $$

(www.laundry43.com.au; 43 Prince St; shared plates $14-29; ☺9am-late Tue-Sat) Brick walls and a honey-coloured jarrah bar form the backdrop for Margaret River beers and wines, great cocktails, and classy shared plates and bigger dishes. Definitely get ready to linger longer than you planned. Wednesday nights offer live music from 7.30pm.

⊫ Observatory Guesthouse   B&B $$

(☎08-9751 3336; www.observatoryguesthouse. com; 7 Brown St; d $145-155; ❋) A five-minute walk from the jetty, this friendly B&B has four bright, cheerful rooms. They're not overly big, but you can spread out on the communal sea-facing balcony and front courtyard.

Yallingup ❺

⊫ Wildwood Valley Cottages & Cooking School   Cottage $$$

(☎08-9755 2120; www.wildwoodvalley.com. au; 1481 Wildwood Rd; cottages from $250; ☎) Luxury cottages trimmed by native bush are arrayed across 48 hectares, and the property's main house also hosts the Mad About Food Cooking School with Sioban and Carlo Baldini. Sioban's CV includes cooking at Longrain and living in Tuscany, so the culinary emphasis is Thai or Italian. Cooking classes are $135 per person and usually run on a Wednesday.

Margaret River ❿

✗ Blue Ginger   Cafe, Deli $

(www.bluegingerfinefoods.com; 31 Station Rd; mains $12-20; ☺8am-6pm Mon-Fri, 9am-3pm Sat & Sun; ✐) Ease into the colourful, mismatched furniture on the enclosed terrace and tuck into hearty cafe fare with some adventurous twists. It's very local, crammed with regulars easing into their first of coffee of the day. Lots of organic and natural wholefoods are available for virtuous travellers.

✗ Larder   Deli $$

(www.thelarder.biz; 2/99 Bussell Hwy; ☺9.30am-6pm Mon-Sat, 10.30am-4pm Sun) Showcasing local Margaret River produce and gourmet foods, The Larder also sells takeaway meals ($15 to $17) – a good option for dinner – and comprehensive breakfast packs, picnic hampers and barbecue fixings ($50 to $95). Occasional cooking classes complete the tasty menu.

⊫ Burnside Organic Farm   Bungalows $$$

(☎08-9757 2139; www.burnsideorganicfarm. com.au; 287 Burnside Rd; d $280-325; ❋) Welcome to the perfect private retreat after a day cruising the region's wine, beer and food highlights. Rammed-earth and limestone bungalows have spacious decks and designer kitchens, and the surrounding farm hosts a menagerie of animals and organic orchards. Guests can pick vegetables from the garden. Minimum two-night stay.

Augusta ⓲

✗ Deckchair Gourmet   Cafe $

(Blackwood Ave; mains $10-25; ☺8am-3pm Mon-Sat, to noon Sun; ☎) Excellent coffee and good food. Try the bacon and egg wrap for breakfast.

⊫ Best Western Georgiana Molloy   Motel $$

(☎08-9758 1255; www.augustaaccommodation. com.au; 84 Blackwood Ave; r $110-180) The decor's a little dated, but the spacious, self-contained units are stand-out value, each with a small garden area.

STRETCH YOUR LEGS
PERTH

Start/Finish: Art Gallery of Western Australia

Distance: 4.5km

Duration: 3 hours

Perth is a sunny seaside city with a distinguished arts heritage, some fine old buildings, plenty of green parklands, fabulous places to drink and a sense that the water is never far away. This walk takes you into that world.

Take this walk on Trips

Art Gallery of Western Australia

Begin at the **Art Gallery of Western Australia** (www.artgallery.wa.gov.au; Perth Cultural Centre; ⊙10am-5pm Wed-Mon) Founded in 1895, this excellent gallery houses the state's pre-eminent art collection, including important post-WWII works by Australian luminaries such as Arthur Boyd, Albert Tucker, Grace Cossington Smith, Russell Drysdale, Arthur Streeton and Sidney Nolan. The gallery's Indigenous galleries are also very well regarded.

The Walk » It couldn't be easier getting to your next stop – the Perth Institute of Contemporary Arts is in the same complex at the Perth Cultural Centre.

Perth Institute of Contemporary Arts

The **Perth Institute of Contemporary Arts** (PICA; www.pica.org.au; Perth Cultural Centre; ⊙10am-5pm), known almost universally as PICA (pee-kah), may look traditional – it's housed in an 1896 red-brick former school – but inside it's one of Australia's more innovative platforms for contemporary art including installations, performance, sculpture and video. From 10am Tuesday to Sunday, the PICA Bar is a top spot for a coffee or cocktail, and has occasional live music.

The Walk » Walk southeast along James St. Stop 3 is not far along on your left, on the corner with Beaufort St.

Western Australian Museum – Perth

This fine **museum** (www.museum.wa.gov.au; Perth Cultural Centre; ⊙9.30am-5pm) includes dinosaur, mammal, butterfly and bird galleries, a children's discovery centre, and excellent displays covering Indigenous and colonial history. In the courtyard, set in its own preservative bath, is Megamouth, a curious-looking species of shark with a soft, rounded head. Only about five of these

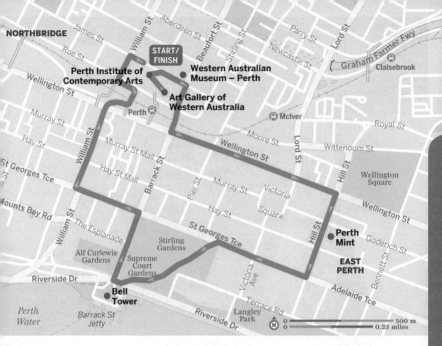

benign creatures have ever been found; this one beached itself near Mandurah, south of Perth. The museum complex includes Perth's original gaol, built in 1856 and used until 1888 – the site of many hangings.

The Walk » Take Beaufort St south, turn left on Wellington St then walk for around 750m, before turning right onto Hill St. The Perth Mint is around 200m along on your left.

Perth Mint

Dating from 1899, the compelling **Perth Mint** (www.perthmint.com.au; 310 Hay St; adult/child $25/8; ⊙9am-5pm) displays a collection of coins, nuggets and gold bars. You can fondle a bar worth over $200,000 – it's worth coming here just for this strangely thrilling experience – mint your own coins and watch gold pours (on the half-hour, from 9.30am to 3.30pm). The Mint's Gold Exhibition features a massive 1-tonne gold coin worth a staggering $50 million. No, you can't touch it.

The Walk » From the Mint, take Hill St south and then take the second right along St Georges Tce. When you see the greenery open up to your left, cross Stirling Gardens and Supreme Court Gardens to Bell Tower, south of Riverside Drive.

Bell Tower

The pointy glass spire known as **Bell Tower** (www.thebelltower.com.au; adult/child $14/9; ⊙10am-4pm, ringing noon-1pm Sat-Mon & Thu) is fronted by copper sails and contains the royal bells of London's St Martin's-in-the-Fields, the oldest of which dates to 1550. They were given to WA by the British government in 1988, and are the only set known to have left England. Clamber to the top for 360-degree views of Perth by the river.

The Walk » To return to your car, walk up Barrack St, turn left on St Georges Tce, then right on William St, cross the railway tracks then turn right on James St.

Pinnacles Desert *A vast alien landscape of natural sculptures*

SARA WINTER/GETTY IMAGES ©

Coral Coast | 32

Australia's western shore is simply magnificent, a road-tripper's playground of good driving country with regular, spectacular, utterly gorgeous stops all along the way.

TRIP HIGHLIGHTS

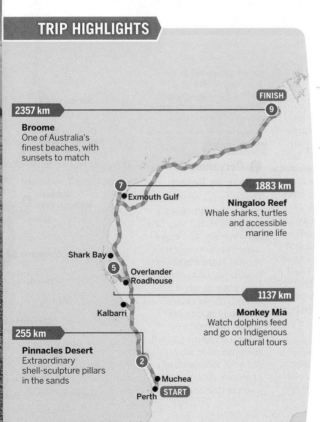

2357 km

Broome
One of Australia's finest beaches, with sunsets to match

7 Exmouth Gulf

1883 km

Ningaloo Reef
Whale sharks, turtles and accessible marine life

Shark Bay

5 Overlander Roadhouse

1137 km

Monkey Mia
Watch dolphins feed and go on Indigenous cultural tours

Kalbarri

255 km

Pinnacles Desert
Extraordinary shell-sculpture pillars in the sands

2

Muchea

Perth **START**

10–14 DAYS
2357KM / 1465 MILES

GREAT FOR...

BEST TIME TO GO

April to October. It's impossibly humid from November onwards; cyclones possible January to March.

ESSENTIAL PHOTO

Underwater at Ningaloo Reef.

BEST FOR OUTDOORS

Dolphins at Monkey Mia.

351

32 Coral Coast

The road from Perth to Broome connects two entirely different worlds, one busy and sophisticated, the other remote, tropical and located on the cusp of the true outback, with the vast Indian Ocean keeping you company all the way. There are some fabulous places to break up the journey, including many that highlight the intersection of desert and wild coast that is such a feature of this route, from the Pinnacles Desert to Ningaloo Reef.

INDIAN OCEAN

Macker
Islands
Exmouth & Onslo
Ningaloo Reef
⑦ Peedan
Learmonth *Exmouth Gulf*

Coral Bay
Gnaraloo *Minilya Roadhou*
Lake Macleod
Quobba
Carnavon ⑥
Shark Bay Gas
Jur
Denham &
Monkey Mia ⑤ ①
Useless Loop

Overlander Roadhouse To
N
Re
Kalbarri
National Park ④
Kalbarri
Northampton Bi
M
Geraldton ③
Dongara-
Port Denison

Jurien Bay
Cervantes &
Pinnacles Desert
Lance
Two R
Rottnest Is
INDIAN OCEAN **Mand**

① Perth

By some estimates, Perth is one of the most isolated cities on earth (it all depends on your definition of a city), but that's nothing compared to where you're heading. With so many miles ahead of you, soak up the choice of big-city restaurants, the cool breeze of the south and the easy communications of the big smoke. You'll find all of these along the way, but not like here. For more about Perth, see p348.

The Drive » Head northeast out of Perth as if heading for the Nullabor, but after 18km swing north, following the signs for Geraldton. At Muchea, take the left highway fork for the Brand Hwy. At 206km out of Perth, at the small settlement of Badgingarra, take the Cervantes turn-off for the final 49km.

TRIP HIGHLIGHT

② Cervantes & Pinnacles Desert

The laid-back crayfishing town of Cervantes is a fine place to end your first day's journey. The major attraction here, and it's a big one, is the Pinnacles Desert, one of Australia's most photographed land-forms. This singularly eye-catching stand of weird-and-wonderful natural sculptures, a vast, alien-like plain stud-ded with thousands of limestone pillars, is 19km south of Cervantes in

Nambung National Park
(per car $12). Rising eerily
from the desert floor, the
pillars are remnants of
compacted seashells that
once covered the plain
and, over millennia,
subsequently eroded. A
loop road runs through
the formations, but it's
more fun to wander on
foot. In Cervantes itself,
walkways wend along
the coastline and provide
access to some lovely
beaches.

✕ 🛏 p358

The Drive » Instead of
returning to the Brand Hwy,
head north out of Cervantes
along Indian Ocean Dr. Aside
from having far less traffic,
panoramic ocean views open up
at regular intervals and you'll
pull over often to take it all in. At
124km from Cervantes, the road
rejoins the Brand Hwy, from
where it's 94km to Geraldton.

LINK YOUR TRIP

29 Across the Nullarbor

Where one epic ends
(crossing the Nullarbor
begins or ends in Perth),
another begins.

33 Kimberley Crossing

The drive to Kununurra
(1045km) begins where this
foray up the Coral Coast
ends – joining up the two
couldn't be easier.

➌ Geraldton

Capital of the midwest and the largest town between Perth and Darwin, sun-drenched 'Gero' is surrounded by excellent beaches. Still a work in progress, Gero blends big-city sophistication with small-town friendliness, offering a strong arts culture, a blossoming foodie scene and some great local music. Most activities are water-based, but there is also an excellent network of bike paths, including the 10km-long coastal route from Tarcoola Beach to Chapman River; **Revolutions** (☎08-9964 1399; www.revolutionsgeraldton. com.au; 2c Jensen St; bike hire per day $20; ◷9am-5.30pm Mon-Fri, to noon Sat) rents out bikes. **Midwest Surf School** (☎0419 988 756; http://surf2skool.com; lessons from $60, board hire $30) runs surf lessons at Geraldton's back beach while **KiteWest** (☎0449 021 784; www.kitewest.com. au; coaching per hr from $50) do all sorts of things on water and on land, among them kiteboarding courses, surfing lessons and paddleboarding tuition, as well as fishing, scenic and wildflower daytrips. And amid such adventurous pursuits, save time for the **Western Australian Museum – Geraldton** (☎08-9921 5080; www.museum.wa.gov. au; 1 Museum Pl; admission by donation; ◷9.30am-4pm), one of the state's best museums.

✕ ⛏ p358

The Drive » Unless you plan to camp overnight in Kalbarri National Park, get an early start out of Geraldton. At exactly 100km north of town, take the Kalbarri turn-off – it's 54km into Kalbarri.

➍ Kalbarri National Park

With its magnificent river red gums and Tumblagooda sandstone, the rugged **Kalbarri National Park** (per car $12) contains almost 2000 sq km of wild bushland, stunning river gorges and savagely eroded coastal cliffs. There's abundant wildlife, including 200 species of birds, and spectacular wildflowers between July and November. A string of lookouts dot the impressive coast south of town and the easy **Bigurda Trail** (8km one way) follows the cliff tops between **Natural Bridge** and **Eagle Gorge**; from July to November you may spot migrating whales. The river gorges are east of Kalbarri, 11km down Ajana Kalbarri Rd to the turn-off, and then 20km unsealed to a T-intersection. Turn left for lookouts over the **Loop** and the superb **Nature's Window** (1km return). Turning right at the T leads to **Z-Bend**, with a breathtaking

MICHAEL RUNKEL/GETTY IMAGES ©

lookout (1.2km return), or you can continue steeply down to the gorge bottom (2.6km return).

The Drive » Take the 54km from Kalbarri back to the main highway, where you turn left (north). At 158km north of the turn-off, at the Overlander Roadhouse, turn left (west) and from here it's 128km across some narrow spits of land into Denham.

> **TRIP HIGHLIGHT**

➎ Denham & Monkey Mia

Beautiful, laid-back Denham, Australia's westernmost town, is, with its turquoise sea

Broome Camel safari along Cable Beach

and palm-fringed beachfront, a terrific base for trips to some fine surrounding national and marine parks. **Shark Bay Scenic Flights** (0417 919 059; www.sharkbayair.com.au) offers a brilliant perspective on the area, while watching the wild dolphins turning up for a feed each morning in the shallow waters of Monkey Mia, 26km beyond Denham, is a highlight of every traveller's trip to the region. The pier makes a good vantage point; the first feed is around 7.45am although the dolphins arrive earlier. To see more wildlife, take the 2½-hour wildlife cruise with **Wildsights** (1800 241 481; www.monkeymiawildsights.com.au). Back on land, learn 'how to let Country talk to you' on the excellent bushwalks run by **Wula Guda Nyinda Aboriginal Cultural Tours** (0429 708 847; www.wulaguda.com.au; 90min tours adult/child from $60/30).

 p358

The Drive » Return to the main highway (128km). At the Overlander Roadhouse, turn left (north) and it's 193km into Carnavon – watch for fine Shark Bay views en route.

6 Carnavon

On Yinggarda country at the mouth of the Gascoyne River, fertile Carnarvon, with its fruit and vegetable plantations and thriving fishing industry, makes a pleasant stopover between Denham and Exmouth. It's a friendly, vibrant place with a growing reputation in foodie circles – Carnarvon's luxuriant plantations along North and South River Rds provide a large proportion of WA's fruit and veg; grab the *Gascoyne Food Trail* (www.gascoynefood.com.au) brochure from the **visitor**

SHARK BAY

The World Heritage–listed area of Shark Bay, stretching from Kalbarri to Carnarvon, consists of more than 1500km of spectacular coastline, containing turquoise lagoons, barren finger-like peninsulas, hidden bays, white-sand beaches, towering limestone cliffs and numerous islands. It's the westernmost part of the Australian mainland, and one of WA's most biologically rich habitats, with an array of plant and animal life found nowhere else on earth. Lush beds of sea-grass and sheltered bays nourish dugongs, sea turtles, humpback whales, dolphins, stingrays, sharks and other aquatic life. On land, Shark Bay's biodiversity has benefited from Project Eden, an ambitious ecosystem-regeneration program that has sought to eradicate feral animals and reintroduce endemic species. Shark Bay is also home to the amazing stromatolites of Hamelin Pool. The Malgana, Nhanda and Inggarda peoples originally inhabited the area, and visitors can take Indigenous cultural tours to learn about Country.

centre (☑08-9941 1146; www.carnarvon.org.au; Civic Centre, 21 Robinson St; ⊙9am-5pm Mon-Fri, to noon Sat).

The tree-lined CBD exudes a tropical feel – it's the first real hint that you're on your way to WA's far north – and the palm-fringed waterfront is a relaxing place to amble. You can also walk or ride 2.5km along the old tramway to the Heritage Precinct on Babbage Island (www.carnarvonheritage.com.au), once the city's port.

 p358

The Drive ≫ It's 140 flat and rather uneventful kilometres from Carnarvon north to the Minilya Roadhouse. There, the North West Coastal Hwy (as it's called north of Carnarvon) veers northeast. Instead, take the Minilya Exmouth Rd 215km into Exmouth; the prettiest stretch is along the Exmouth Gulf, along the final approach to town.

- - - - - - - - - -

TRIP HIGHLIGHT

❼ Exmouth & Ningaloo Reef

Once a WWII submarine base, Exmouth is a flat, hot and sprawling town of modest appeal, where emus wander footpaths, galahs screech overhead and roos lounge in the shade. But you didn't come all this way to see Exmouth. Instead, out here it's all about World Heritage–listed and exquisite Ningaloo Reef. **Ningaloo Marine Park** is home to a staggering array of marine life – sharks, manta rays, humpback whales, turtles, dugongs, dolphins and more than 500 species of fish. Australia's largest fringing reef is also easily accessible, in places only 100m offshore. Swim with whale sharks (April to July), spot wildlife, dive, snorkel (try the **Bay Snorkel Area**), kayak, surf and fish to your heart's content – the **visitor centre** (☑08-9949 1176; www.visitningaloo.com. au; Murat Rd; ⊙9am-5pm) has the full list of tours available, but our favourites include **Three Islands** (Whaleshark Dive; ☑1800 138 501; www.whalesharkdive.com; whale shark swim/observation $385/225; ⊙tours Mar-Aug) and **Kings Ningaloo Reef Tours** (☑08-9949 1764; www. kingsningalooreeftours.com.au; snorkeller/observer $385/285). Outside whale-shark season, marine tours focus on manta rays, while **DPaW Turtle Interaction Tour** (☑08-9947 8000; Jurabi Turtle Centre, Yardie Creek Rd; adult/child $20/10; ⊙6.30pm Nov-Mar) is the best and most ecologically safe way to encounter nesting turtles (November to March).

✕ 🛏 p359

The Drive ≫ It's a long road back and you've a very long day ahead of you, but we can't imagine it hasn't been worth it. Take the road 86km south of Exmouth (watch for goannas ambling across the highway), and turn left on the Burkett Rd, from where it's 79km back to the main highway. After rejoining the highway, it's 599km into Port Hedland.

8 Port Hedland

Port Hedland ain't the prettiest place. A high-visibility dystopia of railway yards, iron-ore stockpiles, salt mountains, furnaces and a massive deep-water port confront the passing traveller. Yet under that red dust lurks a colourful 130-year history of mining booms and busts, cyclones, pearling and WWII action. Several pleasant hours may be spent exploring Hedland's thriving art and cafe (real coffee!) scene, historic CBD and scenic foreshore. From the **visitor centre** (☎08-9173 1711; www.visitporthedland.com; 13 Wedge St; ☺9am-5pm Mon-Fri, to 2pm Sat-Sun; ☎), popular **BHP Billiton** (adult/child $45/30; ☺vary) iron-ore plant tours depart. And when Port Hedland's muscular personality gets the better of you, there are two fine escapes. **Courthouse Gallery** (☎08-9173 1064; www.courthousegallery.com.au; 16 Edgar St; ☺9am-4.30pm Mon-Fri, to 2pm Sat & Sun) is the town's leafy arts HQ and the centre of all goodness in Hedland, with stunning local contemporary and Indigenous exhibitions and sporadic craft markets. And if you're here between November and February, **flatback turtles** nest on nearby beaches.

 p359

The Drive ›› The Big Empty stretches from Port Hedland to Broome, as the Great Northern Hwy skirts the Great Sandy Desert. It's 609km of willy-willies and dust and not much else. There are only two roadhouses, Pardoo (148km) and Sandfire (288km), so keep the tank full. The coast, wild and unspoilt, is never far away.

TRIP HIGHLIGHT

9 Broome

Like a paste jewel set in a tiara of natural splendours, Broome clings to a narrow strip of red pindan on the Kimberley's far western edge, at the base of the pristine Dampier Peninsula. Surrounded by the aquamarine waters of the Indian Ocean and the creeks, mangroves and mudflats of Roebuck Bay, this Yawuru country is a good 2000km from the nearest capital city, and it will feel like paradise after the long drive to reach it. Magnificent Cable Beach, with its luxury resorts, hauls in the tourists during high (dry) season (April to October), with romantic notions of camels and surf. Each evening, the whole town pauses, collective drinks in mid-air, while the sun slips slowly seawards. For more on Broome, see p360.

✕ ⨯ p359

STAIRCASE TO THE MOON

You might hear them talk in these parts of a strange attraction known as the Staircase to the Moon. No, it's not the WA version of Led Zeppelin's classic, but instead an appealing natural phenomenon whereby, when seen from an easterly facing beach, the full moon rising above the sea (and/or mudflats) resembles a staircase to the moon. Port Hedland, Broome and Dampier are three places where you might see it from March to October.

Eating & Sleeping

Cervantes & Pinnacles Desert ❷

✖ Lobster Shack   Seafood $$

([☎]08-9652 7010; www.lobstershack.com.au; 11
Madrid St; [⊙]shop 9am-5pm, lunch 11.30am-
2.30pm, tours 12.30-2pm) Craving crayfish?
They don't come much fresher than at this
lobster factory-turned-lunch spot, where a
delicious grilled cray, chips and salad will set
you back $40. Lobster rolls are good value at
$18. Tours (adult/child $15/7.50) and takeaway frozen seafood are also available.

🛏 Cervantes Lodge & Pinnacles
Beach Backpackers   Hostel $

([☎]1800 245 232; www.cervanteslodge.com.au;
91 Seville St, www.pinnaclesholidaypark.com.
au; dm $33, d with/without bathroom $130/90;
[@]) In a great location behind the dunes, this
relaxing hostel has a wide verandah, small and
tidy dorms, a nice communal kitchen and a cosy
lounge area. Bright, spacious en-suite rooms,
some with views, are next door in the lodge.

Geraldton ❸

✖ Saltdish   Cafe $$

([☎]08-9964 6030; 35 Marine Tce; breakfast
$8-20, lunch $16-32; [⊙]7.30am-4pm Mon-Fri;
[🛜]) The hippest cafe in town serves innovative,
contemporary brekkies, light lunches and
industrial-strength coffee, and screens films
in its courtyard on summer evenings. Try the
sweetcorn and coriander fritters. BYO wine or
beer.

🛏 Ospreys Beach Chalet   Cottage $$

([☎]0447 647 994; enerhkalm@gmail.com;
40 Bosuns Cr, Point Moore; 2 persons from
$155) Both ospreys and beach are nearby this
sustainably restored cottage, which began
life as a proof-of-concept project. Rainwater
tanks and solar panels complement recycled
materials in a restoration that doesn't skimp on
comfort. There are plenty of outdoor areas and
the rear native garden is a gem.

Denham & Monkey Mia ❺

✖ Ocean Restaurant   Cafe $$

(www.oceanpark.com.au; Shark Bay Rd; mains
$26-32; [⊙]9am-5pm; [🛜]) The most refined
lunch in Shark Bay also comes with the best
view. Inside Ocean Park, overlooking turquoise
waters, you can partner beer and wine with
tapas, all-day brekkies and local seafood. The
platter for two people ($42) is excellent value.
Fully licensed.

🛏 Monkey Mia
Dolphin Resort   Resort $$

([☎]1800 653 611; www.monkeymia.com.au; tent
sites per person $16, van sites from $44, dm/d
$30/109, garden units $229, beachfront villas
$329; [❄][@][🛜][🏊]) With a stunning location
the only accommodation option in Monkey Mia
caters to campers, backpackers, package and
top-end tourists. The staff are friendly, and
the backpacker 'shared en-suites' are good
value, but the top-end rooms are expensive.
It can also get very crowded. The restaurant
has sensational water views but meals are
overpriced, while the backpacker bar has
cheaper food and excitable backpackers.

Carnavon ❻

✖ Harbourside Café   Seafood $$

([☎]08-9941 4111; Small Boat Harbour; mains
$11-32; [⊙]11am-3pm & 5-8pm Tue-Sun) Fresh
seafood and imaginative recipes make for a
rewarding dining experience at this casual,
sunny restaurant near the water. The Eastern-
accented menu includes Asian-spiced calamari,
Thai shrimp salad and Carnarvon snapper.

🛏 Carnarvon Central
Apartments   Apartment $

([☎]08-9941 1317; www.carnarvonholidays.
com; 120 Robinson St; 2-bedroom apt $140; [❄])
These neat, fully self-contained apartments are
popular with business travellers.

Exmouth & Ningaloo Reef ❼

✖ Whalers Restaurant   Seafood $$

(📞08-9949 2416; whalersrestaurant.com.au;
27 Murat Rd, inside Exmouth Escape; mains
$29-40; 🕒6pm-late) Recently relocated, this
Exmouth institution is famous for its delicious
Creole-influenced seafood. Don't miss the
signature New Orleans gumbo, complemented
by a seafood tasting starter of soft-shell crab,
local prawns and oyster shooters. Die-hard
bug aficionados need look no further than the
towering seafood medley.

🛏 Novotel Ningaloo Resort   Resort $$$

(📞08-9949 0000; www.novotelningaloo.
com.au; Madaffari Dr; d/apt from $275/355;
❄🛜🏊) In the marina, the Novotel Ningaloo
is at the pointy end of sophistication (and
expense) in Exmouth. The tastefully designed
rooms are spacious and well-equipped and all
have balconies.

Port Hedland ❽

✖ Silver Star   Cafe $$

(📞0411 143 663; Edgar St; breakfast $10-20,
lunch $18-24; 🕒7am-3pm) Possibly the coolest
cafe in the Pilbara, this 1930s American Silver
Star railcar serves up decent coffee, brekkies
and sophisticated lunches in the original
observation lounge and outside on a shady
deck.

🛏 Esplanade Hotel   Resort $$$

(📞08-9173 9700; www.theesplanade-
porthedland.com.au; 2-4 Anderson St; d from
$255; 🕒12pm-late; ❄@🛜) Previously one of
the roughest pubs in Port Hedland, the 'Nard'
is now an exclusive 4.5-star resort with fully
clothed staff, sumptuous though expensive
doubles, à la carte dining (dinner $32 to $45),
bar pizzas ($25) and popular all-you-can-eat
buffets ($55).

Broome ❾

✖ 18 Degrees   International $$

(📞08-9192 7915; www.18degrees.com.au; Shop
4, 63 Robinson St, Seaview Centre; mains $20-
33) Broome's new and very contemporary spot
whips up some great share plates, delicious
mains (for example, barramundi parcels and
lamb tenderloin) and boasts a wine and cocktail
list as large as a crocodile smile.

✖ Cable Beach General
Store & Cafe   Cafe $

(📞08-9192 5572; www.cablebeachstore.com.
au; cnr Cable Beach & Murray Rds; snacks
$10-20; 🕒6am-8.30pm daily; 🛜) Cable Beach
unplugged – a typical Aussie corner shop with
egg breakfasts, barra burgers, pies, internet
and no hidden charges. You can even play a
round of minigolf.

🛏 McAlpine House   B&B $$$

(📞08-9192 0588; www.pinctada.com.au; 55
Herbert St; d $185-420; P❄🛜🏊) A former
pearl master's cottage (built in 1910), Lord
McAlpine made this stunning house his Broome
residence during the '80s, renovating it to its
former glory. Rooms vary in size (some are
squeezy), but a library, airy eating patio, pool
and verandahs add to its charm. A canopy of
trees, from mangos to frangipanis, provide cool
relief from the heat.

🛏 Cable Beach Club Resort   Hotel $$$

(📞08-9192 0400; www.cablebeachclub.
com; Cable Beach Rd; d/bungalows/villas from
$395/745/1200; P❄❄🛜🏊) Cable Beach's
original resort helped put Broome on the tourist
map. This lovely spot – featuring Broome
architecture plus touches of Eastern exoticism –
is still an idyllic retreat behind Cable Beach.
Lush gardens, serene swimming pools, fine
restaurants, a spa and numerous other facilities
add to the appeal.

STRETCH YOUR LEGS
BROOME

Start/Finish:
Short Street Gallery

Distance: 5.5km

Duration: 4-5 hours

You can't spend all your time on Cable Beach, and Broome has some fine attractions that point to its somewhat turbulent past, from the rigours of pearl fishing to WWII. Late afternoon is the best time to do this walk.

Take this walk on Trips

Short Street Gallery

Whichever journey you've completed or are about to take, Indigenous culture is sure to be a big part of the experience. The original building that houses the **Short Street Gallery** (☎08-9192 6118; www.shortstgallery.com.au; 7 Short St; ⊙10am-3pm Mon-Fri, 11am-3pm Sat) runs back-to-back exhibitions of contemporary Indigenous artworks. It's an agent for Yulparija artists plus art centres in the Kimberley and beyond.

The Walk ≫ Walk east along Short St and take the first right (Carnavon St). Sun Pictures is around 50m along on your right.

Sun Pictures

Sink back in a canvas deck chair at **Sun Pictures** (☎08-9192 1077; www.sunpictures. com.au; 27 Carnarvon St; adult/child $17/12), the world's oldest operating picture gardens – it opened in 1916. These days, it still shows evening movies. The history of the Sun building is the history of Broome itself – different racial groups were assigned to different seats, floods were frequent and planes flew directly overhead (the cinema is still under the approach flight path).

The Walk ≫ You don't have to walk far south along Carnavon St to transition into Chinatown.

Chinatown

Broome's pearl-fishing industry was a magnet for treasure-seekers from across the world, and the Chinese community in particular made up one of the largest and more enduring groups. Tin shanties are still visible lining Carnarvon St, Short St, Dampier Tce and Napier Tce.

The Walk ≫ From Carnavon St, take Johnny Chi Lane, then turn right on Dampier Tce. Pearl Luggers is not far along on your left.

Pearl Luggers

Broome's history centres around its pearling industry and pearls are still exported around the world. The compact Pearl Luggers museum provides an interesting talk on Broome's tragic pearling past, evoking the diver experience with genuine artefacts. You can also wander over two of the last surviving (and restored) luggers, *Sam Male* and *DMcD*.

The Walk » Return to Carnarvon St and walk south for around 500m – Matso's brewery is around 500m on your left.

Matso's Broome Brewery

In Broome's climate it can feel as if any time is a good time for a beer, and no doubt you're ready for one now. At the excellent **Matso's Broome Brewery** ([☎]08-9193 5811; www.matsos.com. au; 60 Hamersley St; ☺7am-midnight), which prides itself on its handcrafted beers, order a Pearler's pale ale (or another home brew). Warning: you may not finish your walk if you stay too long.

The Walk » Follow Carnarvon St as it loops around to the west, then head southwest on Hammersley St. You're now in Old Broome, the town's original settlement. Follow Hammersley St, then turn left on Robinson St. Continue south until you reach Town Beach.

Town Beach

Cable Beach it ain't, but tiny Town Beach is fine for a dip when the tide is in (as long as it's not stinger season). If it's not, there are fine views out across the flats to Roebuck Bay.

The Walk » Start walking an hour before low tide, and head roughly southeast for 1.5km (about 30 minutes). Check with the visitor centre for tide times.

WWII Flying Boat Wrecks

On a very low tide it's possible to walk out across the mudflats from Town Beach to the wrecks of *Catalina* and *Dornier* flying boats attacked by Japanese 'Zeroes' during WWII. Over 60 people and 15 flying boats (mostly Dutch and British) were lost. Only six wrecks are visible, with the rest in deep water. Don't linger too long – plan to get going before the tide turns and heads for the shore.

The Walk » To get back to your car at the gallery, retrace your steps, although we strongly recommend a second pause at Matso's Broome Brewery for some liquid sustenance en route.

Derby Gateway to traditional lands and culture

Kimberley Crossing

33

Red earth, blue skies and a ribbon of tarmac unfurling out across the void... This expedition through the Kimberley outback is one of the great Aussie road trips.

KERRY LORIMER/GETTY IMAGES ©

TRIP HIGHLIGHTS

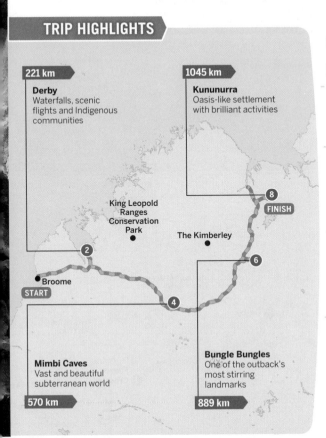

221 km

Derby
Waterfalls, scenic flights and Indigenous communities

1045 km

Kununurra
Oasis-like settlement with brilliant activities

King Leopold Ranges Conservation Park

The Kimberley

8 FINISH

6

2

Broome
START

4

Mimbi Caves
Vast and beautiful subterranean world

570 km

Bungle Bungles
One of the outback's most stirring landmarks

889 km

14 DAYS
1045KM / 649 MILES

GREAT FOR...

BEST TIME TO GO

April to September. Wet season rest of the year and cyclones possible January to March.

 ESSENTIAL PHOTO

The Bungle Bungles have a lonely outback charm and beauty.

 BEST FOR CULTURE

Explore Country with an Indigenous guide at Mimbi Caves.

363

33 Kimberley Crossing

What a trip! This significant chunk of the Savannah Way (www.savannahway.com.au) from Broome to Kununurra will show you why people fall in love with the outback. There will be times when you're longing for the next town or roadhouse, but these will fade from the memory, crowded out with so many images of isolated places of outback lore, among them Fitzroy Crossing, Halls Creek, the Bungle Bungles and Kununurra.

❶ Broome

The former pearl-fishing town of Broome is the most accessible of all the Kimberley gateway towns, although its focus is very much on the sea – camel safaris along seemingly endless **Cable Beach** are an iconic Aussie experience, and Broome sunsets are simply unforgettable. For a primer on the sort of wildlife you may just see along the way, head out to Malcolm Douglas Wilderness Park, a 30-hectare animal refuge 16km northeast of Broome.

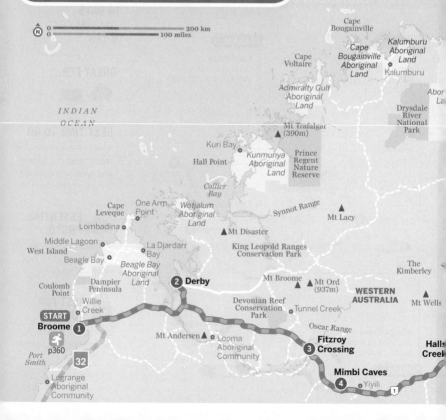

The Drive ›› As long as you stay on the paved road, it's difficult to go wrong as there aren't that many of them out here. It's 221 flat and fairly unremarkable kilometres from Broome to Derby – you pass the turn-off for the Dampier Peninsula after 10km, and the coast road heading south after a further 24km.

TRIP HIGHLIGHT

❷ Derby

In Derby, boabs line the main street; its setting is strategically important, and the town's expanse of green amid the mudflats, mangroves and surrounding desert has a peculiar kind of drama. The main attraction in town is Norval Gallery, an exciting gallery-cafe in an old tin shed on the edge of town, while the Kimberley School of the Air offers a fascinating look at how school is conducted over the radio for children on remote stations. Otherwise, Derby is the departure point for tours out to see one of the most intriguing features of the Kimberley coastline, the phenomenon known as **horizontal waterfalls**. Despite the name, the falls are simply tides gushing through narrow coastal gorges in the Buccaneer Archipelago, north of Derby. Scenic flights with Horizontal Falls Seaplane Adventures or North West Bush Pilots are the best option. Aboriginal cultural tours are also excellent – consider Uptuyu and Windjana Tours.

🛏 p369

The Drive ›› Return 41km along the road from Derby, then turn left (east) onto the Great Northern Hwy. Vast deserts sweep away south of the road, Kimberley rock formations loom to the north and tempting tracks disappear off into the sands.

❸ Fitzroy Crossing

Where the Great Northern Hwy crosses the mighty Fitzroy River, Fitzroy is a small, predominantly Indigenous settlement. Although there are some fabulous national parks not far north of the road – among them **Windjana Gorge**, **Tunnel Creek** and **Geikie Gorge** – you'll need a 4WD for most of them. In the town itself, check out **Mangkaja Arts** (📞08-9191 5833; www.mangkaja.com; 8 Bell Rd; ⏰noon-4pm Mon-Fri), where desert and river tribes interact producing unique acrylics, prints and baskets, and the exquisite glass and ceramics at **Dr Sawfish** (📞0419 908 586; www.drsawfish.com; ⏰8am-4pm Mon-Fri, shorter hrs Sat & Sun), which is next to the tyre guy, whom you may well need. There's also a new, well-stocked supermarket – out here, such places take on the quality of a major attraction.

🛏 p369

Joseph Bonaparte Gulf

pe St
mbert

Lacrosse Island

ombulgurri

❼ **Wyndham**

460kms to

❽ (FINISH) 25

Kununurra

Lake Argyle

Warmun

Purnululu National Park

❻ **Bungle Bungles**

NORTHERN TERRITORY

96

Kundat Djaru

LINK YOUR TRIP

25 Alice Springs to Darwin

To connect with this trip, you'd need to drive from Kununurra to Katherine, a mere 513km.

32 Coral Coast

This trip from Perth to Broome connects with Trip 33, and could just as easily be done in reverse.

The Drive » As the Great Northern Hwy continues a southward loop, you'll pass salt pans, dry riverbeds and endless tufts of spinifex grasses to the south, and more fissured Kimberley outcrops on your left. Watch for the sign 1km before the Mimbi Caves turn-off.

FEARGUS COONEY/GETTY IMAGES ©

TRIP HIGHLIGHT

❹ Mimbi Caves

One of the Kimberley's best-kept secrets is the vast subterranean labyrinth of **Mimbi Caves** (Mt Pierre Station), **90km** southeast of Fitzroy Crossing. Located within Mt Pierre Station, on Gooniyandi land, the caves house a significant collection of Aboriginal rock art and some of the most impressive fish fossils in the southern hemisphere. Aboriginal-owned **Girloorloo Tours** (www.mimbicaves.com.au; 3hr tour adult/child $80/40; ⏰10am Tue-Sat Apr-Sep) runs trips including an

introduction to local Dreaming stories, bush tucker and traditional medicines. Book through the visitor centres in **Fitzroy Crossing** (☏08-9191 5355; www.sdwk.wa.gov. au; ⏰8.30am-4pm Mon-Fri) or **Halls Creek** (☏08-9168 6262; www.hallscreektourism. com.au; Great Northern Hwy; ⏰7am-5pm).

🛏 p369

The Drive » Return to the main Great Northern Hwy and on the roughly 200km into Halls Creek you'll see turn-offs to numerous cattle stations, encounter the occasional roadhouse and then pass through Yiyili some 125km before arriving.

❺ Halls Creek

On the edge of the Great Sandy Desert, Halls Creek is a small town which is home to Indigenous communities of Kija, Jaru and Gooniyandi people. Like

most outback towns, Halls Creek is more necessary than desirable but it stands on the cusp of some extraordinary country. One of the best things to do here is take a 70-minute scenic flight with **Northwest Regional Airlines** (☏08-9168 5211; www.northwestregional.com. au; Halls Creek Airport; per person from $512) out to the **Wolfe Creek Meteorite Crater** (880m across and 60m deep), 137km south of Halls Creek along the rough, 4WD-only Tanami Track. According to the local Jaru people, Kandi-malal, as the crater is tra-ditionally known, marks

GIBB RIVER ROAD

The epic Gibb River Road (GRR) runs for 647km from Derby to the Kununurra–Wyndham Rd, an utterly magnificent 4WD journey through the heart of the Kimberley. The first 100-odd kilometres (and the final few kilometres) of the GRR are now sealed. In between, you'll cross croc-infested rivers, camp in the shade of red-rock gorges, enjoy the hospitality of remote roadhouses, traverse vast cattle stations and be spellbound by the beauty of the King Leopold Ranges. Driving the GRR is a major undertaking that requires careful planning – vehicles can be rented in Broome, which is also a good place to get a feel for road conditions and potential pitfalls. The road is only passable from April or May to September.

Bungle Bungles Purnululu National Park

the spot where a huge rainbow serpent emerged from the ground.

✕ ⌷ p369

The Drive ≫ To reach the Bungle Bungles, you'll probably end up taking a tour from Halls Creek. Otherwise, rugged rocky outcrops line the road all the way north to Wyndham.

- - - - - - - - - -

TRIP HIGHLIGHT

❻ Bungle Bungles

Looking like a packet of half-melted Jaffas, the World Heritage **Purnululu National Park** (per car $12; ☺Apr-Nov) is home to the incredible ochre-and-black-striped 'beehive' domes of the Bungle Bungle Range. The distinctive rounded rock towers are made of sandstone and conglomerates moulded by rainfall over millions of years. It's so remote out here that whitefellas only 'discovered' the range during the mid-1980s. Rangers are based here from April to November and the park is closed outside this time. Although most Kimberley tour operators can get you to Purnululu and back – try **Bungle Bungle Expeditions** (☎08-9169 1995; www.bunglebungleexpeditions.com.au; bus day/overnight $285/695, helicopter from $295) – you can also pick up tours at Warmun Roadhouse, Halls Creek and Mabel Downs.

The Drive ≫ Purnululu National Park lies just east of the Great Northern Hwy. Once back on the highway, head north, passing between the O'Donnell and Carr Boyd Ranges just before the turn-off to Wyndham, where a giant 20m croc greets visitors entering town.

- - - - - - - - - -

❼ Wyndham

A gold-rush town that has fallen on leaner times, Wyndham is scenically nestled between rugged hills and the Cambridge Gulf, some

100km northwest of Kununurra. Sunsets are superb from the spectacular **Five Rivers Lookout** on Mt Bastion (325m) overlooking the King, Pentecost, Durack, Forrest and Ord Rivers entering Cambridge Gulf. The historic port precinct is 5km beyond the croc sign. Birdwatchers won't want to miss **Parry Lagoons Nature Reserve**, a beautiful RAMSAR-listed wetland, 25km from Wyndham, that teems in the Wet with migratory birds arriving from as far away as Siberia. There's an excellent view from **Telegraph Hill**.

 p369

The Drive ❯❯ It's 56 paved kilometres back down the road to the main highway. At the T-junction, turn left (east) and from there it's a further 46km into Kununurra. You may be on the outback fringe, but there's a tropical hue to the landscape; Kununurra is an irrigated oasis of lush farmland and tropical fruit and sandalwood plantations.

TRIP HIGHLIGHT

❽ Kununurra

Kununurra, in Miriwoong country, is a relaxed town, and with good transport and communications, excellent services and well-stocked supermarkets, it's every traveller's favourite slice of civilisation between Broome and Darwin. Across the highway from the township, **Lily Creek Lagoon** is a miniwetlands with amazing birdlife, boating and freshwater crocs. And don't miss the excellent **Waringarri Aboriginal Arts Centre** (☏08-9168 2212; www.waringarriarts. com.au; 16 Speargrass Rd; ⏰8.30am-4.30pm Mon-Fri, 10am-2pm Sat dry season, weekdays only wet season; 🅿), opposite the road to **Kelly's Knob**, a popular sunset viewpoint. On the eastern edge of town, **Mirima National Park** is like a mini-Bungle Bungles – the eroded

gorges of Hidden Valley are home to brittle red peaks, spinifex, boab trees and abundant wildlife. A scenic flight out over the Bungle Bungles, Cambridge Gulf and other dramatic landforms of the East Kimberley region are possible with **Kingfisher Tours** (☏08-9168 1333; www.kingfishertours.net; per person from $290) and **East Kimberley** (☏08-9168 2213; www.eastkimberleytours. com.au; 1-/2-/3-day tours $720/1593/1831, safari tents from $225). For a more leisurely exploration closer to town, try the popular sunset 'BBQ Dinner' cruises on Lily Creek Lagoon and the Ord River with **Kimberley Sunset Cruises** (☏08-9169 1995; www.kimberleysunsetcruises. com.au; adult/child $85/35).

🍴 🛏 p369

Eating & Sleeping

Derby ❷

🛏 Desert Rose   B&B $$

(☎08-9193 2813; 4 Marmion St; d $225; ❄) It's worth booking ahead for the best sleep in town; spacious, individually styled rooms with a nice shady pool, lead-light windows and a sumptuous breakfast. Host Anne is a font of local information.

Fitzroy Crossing ❸

🛏 Fitzroy River Lodge   Resort $$

(☎08-9191 5141; www.fitzroyriverlodge.com.au; Great Northern Hwy; camping per person $15, tent d $160, motel d $220; ❄@🌐❄) Across the river from town, Fitzroy River Lodge has comfortable motel rooms, exclusive Riverview studios and grassy camp sites. The friendly bar has decent counter meals ($22 to $36).

Mimbi Caves ❹

🛏 Larrawa Station   Campground $

(☎08-9191 7025; www.larrawabushcamp.com; Great Northern Hwy; sites $20, s with/without meals $120/70; @) Halfway between Fitzroy Crossing and Halls Creek, Larrawa makes a good overnight stop, with hot showers, basic camp sites, a couple of shearers' rooms, and meals (when available). There's also a three-room cottage.

Halls Creek ❺

✕ Russian Jack's   Motel $$$

(mains $28-42) Probably the best food in Halls Creek with legendary helpings of bistro-fare.

🛏 Kimberley Hotel   Hotel $$

(☎08-9168 6101; www.kimberleyhotel.com.au; Roberta Ave; r from $172, restaurant mains $22-46; ❄🌐❄) Comfortable rooms are complemented

by a lovely pool, shady terrace bar and a kitchen open for breakfast, lunch and dinner.

Wyndham ❼

✕ Five Rivers Cafe   Cafe $

(☎08-9161 2271; www.facebook.com/ FiveRiversCafe; 12 Great Northern Hwy; meals $6-16; ⏱7.30am-2pm Mon-Fri, 8am-1pm Sat, to 1pm & 5-8pm Sun) Enjoy an honest barra burger under the mango tree at this early opener. Excellent coffee, smoothies and breakfasts, as well as pizza on Sunday nights.

🛏 Rusty Wheelbarrow   B&B $$

(☎0408 902 887; www.facebook.com/pages/ The-Rusty-Wheelbarrow-Bed-Breakfast; 1293 Great Northern Hwy; d $160; ❄) Wyndham's newest accommodation is set on a 4-hectare block 5km from town. Beautiful elevated rooms, all with en-suites, open onto a common airy 'breezeway'. Both continental and cooked breakfasts are available, there's plenty of fresh fruit and you can even purchase a 'BBQ pack' should you feel like dining in.

Kununurra ❽

✕ PumpHouse   Modern Australian $$$

(☎08-9169 3222; www.thepumphouse-restaurant.com; Lakeview Dr; lunches $19-36, dinners $32-45; ⏱4.30pm-late Tue-Thu, 11.30am-late Fri, 8am-late Sat & Sun; P🌐) Idyllically situated on Lake Kununurra, the PumpHouse creates succulent dishes featuring quality local ingredients. Watch the catfish swarm should a morsel slip off the verandah. Or just have a beer and watch the sunset. There's an excellent wine list and free wi-fi.

🛏 Wunan House   B&B $

(☎08-9168 2436; www.wunanhouse.com; 167 Coolibah Dr; r from $90; P❄❄🌐) Indigenous owned and run, this immaculate B&B offers light, airy rooms, all with en-suites and TVs. There's free wi-fi, off-street parking and an ample continental breakfast.

Tasmania Trips

IF YOU LOOK AT A MAP OF TASMANIA, you could be forgiven for thinking that it has barely any roads at all. Think again. Thinly populated and yet home to some of Australia's earliest settlements, Tasmania combines the human and natural worlds exceptionally well, and our road trips take you there. Hobart is the starting point for some fine journeys, not least to the sea cliffs and Port Arthur penal colony on the Tasman Peninsula, and the Heritage Trail that connects some fine old towns in the island's heart. Elsewhere, our drives connect the dramatic east coast and the thickly forested west coast, with Cradle Mountain and the Tamar Valley Gourmet Region in between. Little wonder that Tassie ends up being many visitors' favourite corner of the country.

Cradle Mountain Walled Mountain and bushland (Trip 38)
SHANE PEDERSEN/GETTY IMAGES ©

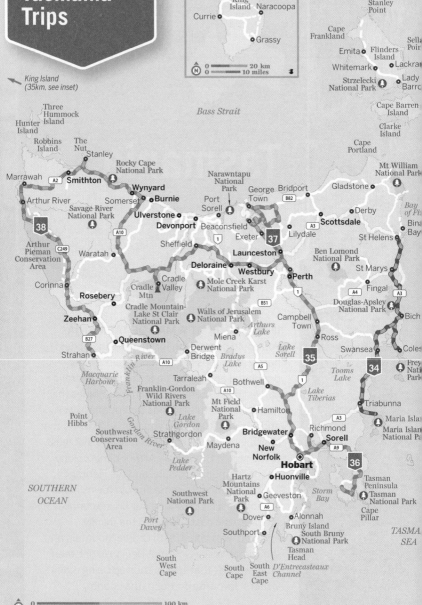

Tasmania
Trips

King Island
(35km, see inset)

King Island

Yambacoona

King
Island   Naracoopa

Currie

Grassy

0 ___ 20 km
0 ___ 10 miles

Bass Strait

Three
Hummock
Island

Hunter
Island

Robbins
Island   The
Nut   Stanley

Marrawah   **38**   **Smithton**   Rocky Cape
National Park

Arthur River   Somerset   **Wynyard**
Savage River   **Burnie**
National Park   **Ulverstone**

38   **Devonport**

Arthur
Pieman   **A10**   Sheffield
Conservation   C249   Waratah
Area

Corinna

Rosebery   Cradle
Valley

Zeehan   Cradle
Mtn   **Deloraine**

Cradle Mountain-
Lake St Clair
National Park

Queenstown

Strahan   Derwent
Bridge   Miena

Bradus
Lake

Macquarie
Harbour   Tarraleah   Bothwell

Franklin-Gordon
Wild Rivers
National Park   **A10**
Mt Field
National
Park   Hamilton

Point
Hibbs

Southwest   Strathgordon
Conservation
Area   Maydena

Lake
Pedder   **New
Norfolk**

SOUTHERN
OCEAN   Hartz
Mountains
National
Park   Geeveston

Southwest   **A6**
National Park   Dover   Alonnah

Port
Davey   Southport   **Bruny Island**
South Bruny
National Park

Tasman
Head

South
West
Cape   South
Cape   South
East
Cape   D'Entrecasteaux
Channel

Stanley
Point

Cape
Frankland   Sella
Poir

Emita   Flinders
Island   Lackrar

Whitemark   Lady
Barro
Strzelecki
National Park

Cape Barren
Island

Clarke
Island

Cape
Portland

Narawntapu
National
Park   George   Bridport   Gladstone
Town

Port   **B82**
Sorell   Derby
Beaconsfield   **A3**   **Scottsdale**   Bina
Exeter   Lilydale   St Helens   Bay
37   **Launceston**   Ben Lomond
National Park   St Marys
Westbury   Fingal   **A3**
Perth   **A4**   Bich
Mole Creek Karst
National Park   Douglas-Apsley
B51   National Park
Walls of Jerusalem   Campbell   Bich
National Park   Town
Arthurs   Ross   Swansea   Coles
Lake

Lake
Sorell   **35**   **34**   Frey
Nat
Park
Lake
Tiberias   Triabunna   Maria
Island

Lake
Tiberias   **A3**   Maria Islan
National Pa

Richmond   **Bridgewater**   Maria Islan
National Pa
Sorell
Hobart   **A9**
Huonville   **36**
Tasman
Peninsula
Tasman
National Park
Storm   Cape
Bay   Pillar

TASMA
SEA

0 ___ 100 km
0 ___ 50 miles

34 **East Coast Tasmania 3–5 Days**
Think of Tasmania and there's a fair chance you're thinking of the storied east coast. (p375)

35 **Heritage Trail 3 Days**
This short drive stops regularly in some of Australia's best-preserved towns. (p385)

36 **Tasman Peninsula 3–4 Days**
The incredible sea cliffs of the southeast and poignant Port Arthur – the rest is just window dressing. (p395)

37 **Tamar Valley Gourmet Trail 4–5 Days**
Wines, berry farms and even penguins make this a fine escape from Launceston. (p403)

38 **West Coast Wilderness Way 14 Days**
The rainforests of the far west make for a fine dirt-road adventure, with Cradle Mountain thrown in. (p413)

 DON'T MISS

Wineglass Bay

Walk up to the Wineglass Bay Lookout and marvel at nature's perfection as part of Trip **34**

Evandale

This heritage-listed town is a model of 19th-century Australia. See it on Trip **35**

Fortescue Bay

Detour off the main trail to see the famous sea cliffs of the southeast. You'll find the details in Trip **36**

Pipers River

This respected wine region is far enough from the Tamar Valley for many travellers to miss it. Visit as part of Trip **37**

Corinna

A fabulous rainforest immersion experience, yet many Taswegians don't even know it exists. Visit on Trip **38**

Bay of Fires One of the most beautiful beaches in the world

Classic Trip

East Coast Tasmania

34

Tasmania's east coast is the undisputed jewel in the island's crown, a beguiling combination of pretty seaside settlements, magnificent coastline and some of the best wildlife-watching.

TRIP HIGHLIGHTS

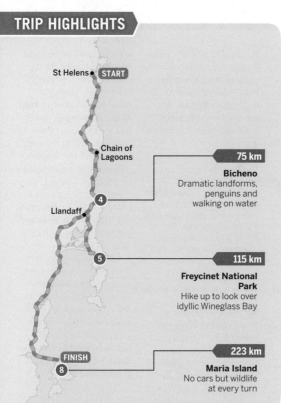

3–5 DAYS
223KM / 139 MILES

GREAT FOR...

BEST TIME TO GO

October to April; in March and April the sea is at its warmest.

 ESSENTIAL PHOTO

Wineglass Bay is best shot from above.

BEST FOR OUTDOORS

Maria Island is one of the best places to watch wildlife in Australia.

St Helens • START

Chain of Lagoons

4 — 75 km

Bicheno
Dramatic landforms, penguins and walking on water

Llandaff •

5 — 115 km

Freycinet National Park
Hike up to look over idyllic Wineglass Bay

FINISH — 223 km

8

Maria Island
No cars but wildlife at every turn

34 East Coast Tasmania

This journey from St Helens to Maria Island takes in two of Tasmania's most stirring natural attractions – perfectly formed Wineglass Bay (arguably Tasmania's most famous image) and wildlife-rich Maria Island. A detour to the peerless Bay of Fires, fine beaches at Scamander, impressive landforms at Bicheno and St Marys, and a slew of wineries further south all add up to Tasmania at its best.

❶ St Helens

On the broad, protected sweep of Georges Bay, St Helens has always made the best of what it has – it was born as a whaling and sealing settlement in the 1830s, it soon learned to harvest the local black swan population for its feathers, and it now makes a tidy living as a fishing town par excellence – this is Tasmania's ocean-fishing capital, both for amateur anglers and the state's largest fishing fleet – and as a gateway town for the east coast. Charter boats will take you out to where the big game fish play – try **Keen Angler** (☎03-6376 3119) and **Gone Fishing Charters** (☎0419 353 041, 03-6376 1553; www. breamfishing.com.au). For the nonanglers among you, both sides of the entrance to Georges Bay are state reserves and are laced with easy walking tracks.

✕ p383

The Drive » The road cuts inland to the southeast then rejoins the coast at Dianas Beach, whereafter the road remains largely within sight of the sea until arriving in Scamander, 37km after leaving St Helens. Just short of Scamander, take a short detour to Shelley Point, with rock pools and fine views.

❷ Scamander

You wouldn't cross the state to see Scamander, but its beaches – beautiful, long white-sand beaches where the surf rolls in and you feel like you can wander forever – are another matter altogether. There's reliable surf around **Four Mile Creek**, while fisherfolk can toss in a line for bream from the old bridge over the Scamander River, or catch trout further upstream. If your reason for being here is more about the end product, **Iron House Brewery** (☎0409 308 824, 03-6372 2228; www.ironhouse.com. au; 21554 Tasman Hwy, White Sands Estate, Four Mile Creek; tastings $5, refundable with purchase; ⏰11.30am-7.30pm, reduced winter hours), 16km south of Scamander, is a craft brewery producing flavoursome pale ale, lager, wheat beer, stout, pilsner and porter.

The Drive » Leave the coast behind for a time on the 19km run into St Marys, as the roadside transitions from coastal views to rolling farm country and green mountains away to the west.

---

③ St Marys

Set back from the coast, St Marys is an unhurried little village in the Mt Nicholas range encircled by forests and cattle farms. Visit for the small-town vibes and the craggy heights around town, which you can climb for memorable views over the area. The top of **South Sister** (832m), towering over German Town Rd 6km north of town, is a 10-minute walk from the car park. To get to **St Patricks Head** (683m), turn down Irishtown Rd,

LINK YOUR TRIP

36 Tasman Peninsula
From where our classic East Coast Tasmania trip ends its mainland section, at Triabunna, it's just 57km southwest to Sorell (Stop 3 on Trip 36).

38 West Coast Wilderness Way
Trip 38 begins in Strahan and ends in Launceston, 655km later. Launceston is 163km from St Helens along the Tasman Hwy.

Classic Trip

just east of town. This long, steep, 90-minute (one-way) climb, with some cables and a ladder, is a real challenge, but at the top there's a stellar vista along the coast.

🍴 🛏 p383

The Drive » On the first 17km of this drive, the road searches for the sea, passing the densely forested Elephant Pass en route. From Chain of Lagoons, the road (A3) plays hide and seek with the sea for 28km into Bicheno.

- - - - - - - - - - -

TRIP HIGHLIGHT

④ Bicheno

Bicheno (bish-uh-no) has brilliant ocean views and lovely beaches, and it's madly popular with

holidaymakers, but it has an appealing lack of polish. Off the northern end of Redbill Beach, **Diamond Island** (off Gordon St) is a photogenic granite outcrop, connected to the mainland via a short, semisubmerged, sandy isthmus, which you can wade across – watch the tides! Otherwise, there are long walking tracks along the coast, and 4km north of Bicheno is the turn-off to **Douglas-Apsley National Park** (☎03-6359 2217; www. parks.tas.gov.au; person/ vehicle per day $12/24), protecting undisturbed dry eucalypt forest, waterfalls, gorges and an abundance of birds and animals. To get out on the water, try **Bicheno's Glass Bottom Boat** (☎03-6375 1294, 0407 812 217; bichenoglassbottomboat@ activ8.net.au; Esplanade, the Gulch; adult/child $20/5; ☺10am, noon & 2pm). Bicheno is one of the top spots in Tasmania to see penguins – take a dusk tour with **Bicheno Penguin Tours** (☎03-6375 1333; www. bichenopenguintours.com. au; Tasman Hwy; adult/child $30/15; ☺ dusk nightly).

🛏 p383

The Drive » Take the road south from Bicheno along the main highway as far as the tiny hamlet of Llandaff, then turn south onto the quiet, pretty road to Coles Bay, which is 27km after the turn-off. Along the way, the road skirts around the estuary of the Swan River and

---

↱ DETOUR: BAY OF FIRES

Start: ① St Helens

The Bay of Fires is a 29km-long sweep of powder-white sand and crystal-clear seas that's been called one of the most beautiful beaches in the world. To refer to the Bay of Fires as a single beach, though, is a mistake: it's actually a string of superb beaches, punctuated by lagoons and rocky headlands, backed by coastal heath and bush.

Curling around a sheltered sandy inlet 11km north of St Helens, gorgeous Binalong Bay (reached along the paved C850) is the only permanent settlement in the Bay of Fires. There's not much here – the beach, a restaurant and a hillside dotted with pricey holiday houses – but this is precisely why everyone loves it. There's good surf in and around the bay, and great swimming on calm days. This is also one of the best spots in Tasmania for diving: the elusive weedy sea dragon often hangs out here. **Bay of Fires Dive** (☎03-6376 8335, 0419 372 342; www.bayoffiresdive. com.au; 291 Gardens Rd, Binalong Bay) rents out scuba equipment, snorkelling gear and wetsuits, and runs boat dives and sub-aqua training.

The bay's northern end is reached via the gravel C843, which leads to **Ansons Bay** and then **Mt William National Park** (☎03-6376 1550; www.parks. tas.gov.au; person/vehicle per day $12/24, camping s/d/f $13/13/16, extra adult/child $5/2.50). **Eddystone Point**, just north of Ansons Bay, within Mt William National Park, marks the Bay of Fires' northern extremity.

Moulting Lagoon, an important breeding ground for waterbirds.

❺ Coles Bay

Coles Bay township sits on a sweep of sand at the foot of the dramatic pink-granite peaks of the Hazards. For all the drama of its location, Coles Bay is appealing for its convenience as a base for visiting the Freycinet Peninsula.

Freycinet Adventures (☎03-6257 0500; www.freycinetadventures.com.au; 2 Freycinet Dr, Coles Bay; tour per person $95; ⊙tours 8.30am Oct-Apr, 9am May-Sep) offers three-hour kayaking outings onto the sheltered waters of Coles Bay. Even better, **Wineglass Bay Cruises** (☎03-6257 0355; www.wineglassbaycruises.com; Jetty Rd, Coles Bay; adult/child $130/85; ⊙tours 10am Sep-May) runs sedate, four-hour cruises from Coles Bay to Wineglass Bay, including champagne, oysters and nibbles. The boat chugs around the southern end of the peninsula, passing Hazards Beach and Schouten Island en route. You're likely to see dolphins, sea eagles, seals, penguins and perhaps even migrating whales in the right season.

 p383

The Drive » Return 27km back up the road to the A3, then turn left (southwest). You'll see wineries in abundance the closer you get to Swansea, especially climbing the slopes of

DETOUR: FREYCINET NATIONAL PARK

Start: ❺ Coles Bay

The sublime **Freycinet National Park** (www.parks.tas.gov.au) is the reason everyone is here: a wild domain of sugar-white beaches and gin-clear water. In the coastal heath and forests, wildflowers and native critters hold sway. The park's big-ticket sight is the gorgeous goblet of **Wineglass Bay**. This route is deservedly one of the most popular walks in Tasmania. You can make the steep climb to the **Wineglass Bay Lookout** (1½ hours return) for a super view over the bay and peninsula, but if you want to hear the beach squeak beneath your feet, you're in for a longer walk. The steep descent from the lookout to the bay takes another 30 minutes, making the out-and-back trip from the car park 2½ to three hours. Alternatively, the 500m wheelchair-friendly boardwalk at **Cape Tourville** affords sweeping coastal panoramas and a less-strenuous glimpse of Wineglass Bay.

the Grange Hills east of the road on the final run into town.

❻ Swansea

Unhurried Swansea dapples the western shore of sheltered Great Oyster Bay, with sweeping views across the water to the peaks of the Freycinet Peninsula. Founded in 1820 as 'Great Swanport', Swansea also delivers some interesting historic buildings such as the 1871 **Anglican Church** (Noyes St), the 1838 **Morris' General Store** (13 Franklin St) and, about 7km south of town, the rather amazing **Spiky Bridge**, built by convicts in the early 1840s using thousands of local fieldstones. Nearby

Kelvedon Beach and **Cressy Beach** have deep golden sand and rarely a footprint. The **Loontitetermairrelehoiner Walk** skirts the headland between Waterloo Beach and the Esplanade, passing a mutton bird (short-tailed shearwater) rookery. During breeding season (September to April) the adult birds return at dusk after feeding at sea.

🛏 p383

The Drive » It's just 50km down the Tasman Hwy (A3) from Swansea to Triabunna, with some stirring views across the water towards the Freycinet Peninsula on the first half of the trip.

TIM PHILLIPS PHOTOS/GETTY IMAGES ©

ANDREW BAIN /GETTY IMAGES ©

WHY THIS IS A CLASSIC TRIP
ANTHONY HAM, AUTHOR

Any road that leads to Wineglass Bay just has to be a classic. Throw in the Bay of Fires detour, Bicheno, and the wildlife of Maria Island and you'll soon discover that this is the best Tasmania has to offer. And there's nowhere else on earth where Tasmanian devils are so easy to see in the wild.

Top: Wineglass Bay, Freycinet National Park
Right: Bushwalkers, Maria Island
Left: Painted Cliffs, Maria Island

HOLGER LEUE/GETTY IMAGES ©

⑦ Triabunna

Triabunna sits on an inlet of Spring Bay and shelters a small cray- and scallop-fishing fleet. There's an old pub here and the **Triabunna Visitor information Centre** (☎03-6257 4772; www.tasmaniaseastcoast.com.au; Charles St; ⊙9am-5pm Oct-Apr, 10am-4pm May-Sep), but not much else of interest to tourists...other than the fact that this is the jumping-off point for magical Maria Island.
East Coast Cruises (☎03-6257 1300; www.eastcoastcruises.com.au; tours adult/child from $175/65) runs full-day ecotours to the island, visiting the Ile des Phoques seal colony, the island's Painted Cliffs and the old convict settlement at Darlington. Otherwise, take the **Maria Island Ferry** (☎0419 746 668; www.mariaislandferry.com.au; adult/child return $35/25, bike/kayak $10/20).

The Drive » No real driving – just head down to the Maria Island Ferry and walk aboard (no vehicles allowed).

TRIP HIGHLIGHT

⑧ Maria Island

Captivating Maria Island (ma-*rye*-ah), with its jagged peaks, rises up like a fairy-tale castle across Mercury Passage, which separates it from the mainland. A former 19th-century penal colony,

381

it's a carefree, car-free haven, laced with impressive scenery: curious cliffs, fern-draped forests, squeaky-sand beaches and azure seas. Forester kangaroos, wombats and wallabies wander around and an insurance population of Tasmanian devils has been released and is thriving. Below the water there's also lots to see, with good snorkelling and diving in the clear, shallow marine reserve. It all adds up to one of our favourite places in Tasmania and the perfect place to end your journey. But one last thing before you leave the mainland (and your car): Maria Island doesn't have any shops, so BYO food and gear.

EAST COAST WINERIES

Along the Tasman Hwy between Bicheno and Swansea you'll encounter a string of terrific wineries where the producers are making the most of sunny east-coast days and cool nights.

Freycinet Vineyard (☎03-6257 8574; www.freycinetvineyard.com.au; 15919 Tasman Hwy, Apslawn; ◷10am-5pm) The Bull family has been growing grapes 'neath the east-coast sun since 1980 – it was the first vineyard on the coast. The vibe at the cellar door is agricultural, not flashy – we like it! Super sauvignon blanc.

Devil's Corner (☎03-6257 8881; www.brownbrothers.com.au; Sherbourne Rd, Apslawn; ◷10am-5pm) Just past the Great Oyster Bay lookout, Devil's Corner is one of Tasmania's largest vineyards, run by the estimable Brown Brothers company.

Gala Estate Vineyard (☎0408 681 014; www.galaestate.com.au; 14891 Tasman Hwy, Cranbrook; ◷10am-4pm Sep-May) A funky little cellar door right on the main road through Cranbrook. Stop by for some pinot gris, a few walnuts and a ploughman's lunch.

Spring Vale Wines (☎03-6257 8208; www.springvalewines.com; 130 Spring Vale Rd, Cranbrook; ◷11am-4pm) Down a long driveway in Cranbrook, 15km north of Swansea, this winery is on land owned by the same family since 1875. The cellar door is housed in an 1842 stable. Don't miss the pinot gris.

Eating & Sleeping

St Helens ①

✕ Binalong Bay Cafe
Modern Australian $$$

(☎03-6376 8116; 64a Main Rd, Binalong Bay; breakfast & dinner $12-24, dinner $30-38; ⊙9am-8pm) With Bay of Fires views, the Binalong Bay Cafe has one of the best locations in Tasmania. Thankfully, the food is also well up to scratch with interesting and vibrant spins on classic dishes. We especially enjoyed a lazy brunch of the sand crab omelette with Asian slaw and chilli jam. It's a 15-minute drive from St Helens.

St Marys ③

✕ Purple Possum Wholefoods
Cafe $

(☎03-6372 2655; www.purplepossum.com.au; 5 Story St; mains $7-13; ⊙to 2.30pm Sat; 🛜🖊) An unexpected find in a little country town, this chipper wholefoods cafe serves excellent homemade soups, vegetarian wraps, fabulous coffee, cakes and slices. There are also vats of nuts, chocolates and spices, and a DIY peanut butter grinder. You'll regret it forever if you don't try the rhubarb cake.

🛏 Addlestone House
B&B $$

(☎03-6372 2783, 0412 425 666; www. addlestonehouse.com.au; 19 Gray Rd; s/d incl breakfast $140/165; @🛜) This immaculate, 100-year-old B&B (transported here a while ago from nearby Mathinna) is as good as they get. The rooms are beautifully decorated, there's a snug guest lounge and the host is a charming gent. Highly recommended: the best place to stay in this neck of the woods.

Bicheno ④

🛏 Diamond Island Resort
Resort $$$

(☎03-6375 0100; www.diamondisland.com.au; 69 Tasman Hwy; d $250-510; 🛜🏊) About 2km north of Bicheno, this complex of 27 sun-soaked apartments is surrounded by lawns and has winning views north along the coast. There's private beach access, or a swimming pool if you'd rather have chlorine than salt in your hair. Wander over to namesake Diamond Island itself when the tide is low. There's an on-site restaurant, **Facets** (☎03-6375 0100; www. diamondisland.com.au; 69 Tasman Hwy; mains from $24; ⊙5.30-8.30pm), and free penguin tours for guests.

Coles Bay ⑤

✕ Freycinet Marine Farm
Seafood $$

(☎03-6257 0140; www.freycinetmarinefarm. com; 1784 Coles Bay Rd; plates $15-25; ⊙9am-5pm Sep-May, 10am-4pm Jun, 11am-4pm Jul & Aug) Super-popular Freycinet Marine Farm grows huge, succulent oysters ($15 a dozen) in the tidal waters of Moulting Lagoon. Also for your consideration are mussels, rock lobsters, scallops and abalone. Sit on the deck, sip some chardonnay and dig into your seafood picnic, as fresh as Freycinet.

Swansea ⑥

🛏 Schouten House
B&B $$

(☎03-6257 8564; www.schoutenhouse.com. au; 1 Waterloo Rd; d incl breakfast $160-200) This brick-and-sandstone 1844 mansion was built by convicts, and was the centre of Great Swanport before the action shifted a little to the north. Decorated in simple, masculine Georgian style (no frills), its huge rooms now house antique beds and bathrooms. The history-buff owners do a mean pancake breakfast, and have perfected the art of making shortbread.

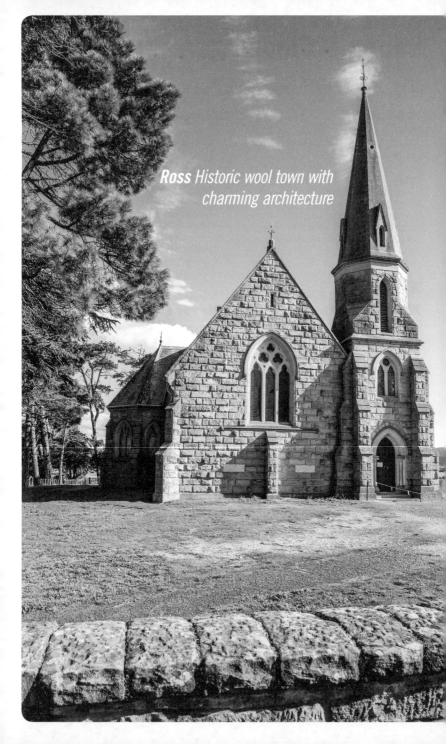

Ross Historic wool town with charming architecture

JOHN WHITE PHOTOS/GETTY IMAGES ©

Heritage Trail

35

This journey from south to north connects Tasmania's two premier cities and cuts a swath through the historic towns of Tasmania's heartland.

TRIP HIGHLIGHTS

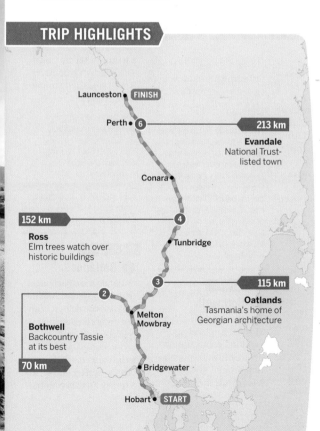

Launceston • **FINISH**

Perth • **6**

213 km

Evandale
National Trust-listed town

Conara •

152 km

4

Ross
Elm trees watch over historic buildings

• Tunbridge

3

115 km

Oatlands
Tasmania's home of Georgian architecture

2

• Melton
Mowbray

Bothwell
Backcountry Tassie at its best

70 km

• Bridgewater

Hobart • **START**

---

3 DAYS
230KM / 143 MILES

GREAT FOR...

BEST TIME TO GO

October to April; Ross elm trees are best in autumn.

ESSENTIAL PHOTO

Evandale's main street is lined with heritage architecture like nowhere else in the state.

BEST FOR HISTORY

The Georgian architecture of Oatlands tells a fine historical tale.

35 Heritage Trail

Hobart to Launceston may lack the natural drama of many Tasmanian drives, but it more than compensates with its open-air galleries of colonial-era architecture. The town names, building facades and landscapes (though not the colours) resemble a jaunt through the rolling farmlands of southern England. And all but one of these towns lie just off the main highway and receive far fewer visitors than you might expect.

1 Hobart

Hobart is one of the more agreeable of Australia's state capitals, inhabiting as it does the leafy lands that lie between high hills and the expansive waters of the Derwent River. A comfortable base with good eateries and places to stay, it's also a worthy destination in its own right, from the buzzing appeal of the sandstone Salamanca zone just back from the water to the more sedate charms of Battery Point nearby. This downtown area is easily navigable on foot, while the world-class MONA (p393) is worth a day on its own and is best reached by ferry; the museum is closed on a Tuesday.

🛏 p391

The Drive ›〉 Follow the signs to Launceston east and then north out of Hobart. The road hugs the Derwent River; watch for MONA on your right 5km north of the city. Turn right (north) at the iron bridge 21km north of Hobart, watching for swans and other birdlife nearby. Thirty-five kilometres north of the bridge, at Melton Mowbray, turn northwest to Bothwell (21km).

TRIP HIGHLIGHT

2 Bothwell

The journey's first echoes of rural England and Scotland come at quiet little Bothwell (population around 400). Far enough off the main highway to keep visitors to a trickle and not really on the road to anywhere, Bothwell is becalmed, backcountry Tasmania at its best. The town encircles a village green where the broad Clyde River Valley meets the road. It has some lovely historic buildings, among them the **Bootmaker's Shop**, the **Castle Hotel**, first licensed in 1821, and the endearing 1831 **St Luke's Church**. Bothwell's Scottish heritage makes itself felt in numerous ways, from the excellent Nant Distillery to Australia's oldest golf course at Ratho Farm; in case you missed the point, Bothwell's street signs have a winning tartan motif. The nearby Clyde River is well regarded among trout fishers.

The Drive ›〉 Retrace your steps to Melton Mowbray (21km), where you rejoin Tasmania's Rte 1, heading northeast through rolling farm country (with that unmistakeably Australian brown tinge in summer) to Oatlands, 38km from Melton Mowbray and just east of the highway.

TRIP HIGHLIGHT

3 Oatlands

Oatlands is so much more than your average Australian roadside detour. With Australia's largest single collection of Georgian architecture, Oatlands feels like a cross between a picture-perfect film set and a stately English country

town harking back to the days of the rural nobility; along the main street alone there are 87 historic buildings. It was one of Tasmania's earliest settlements, first conceived in 1821 as one of four military posts on the Hobart–George Town road. The architecture suits the grand dreams of its early settlers – in 1832 an optimistic town surveyor marked out 80km of streets on the assumption Oatlands would become the Midlands' capital. Its heyday was the 1830s, when settlers began erecting solid buildings with the help of former convicts and soldiers who were skilled carpenters and stonemasons. With the architecture in place, Oatlands settled back into quiet obscurity and thus it blissfully remains.

p391

LINK YOUR TRIP

36 Tasman Peninsula

A 142km foray east of Hobart and then down towards Port Arthur and the stunning sea cliffs of Tasmania's far southeast.

37 Tamar Valley Gourmet Trail

A 178km round-trip loop through the wineries, berry farms and wildlife-rich corners of the Tamar River Valley.

JODIE GRIGGS/GETTY IMAGES ©

The Drive » Return to the main Rte 1 (also known as the Midland Hwy) and a mere (and really rather flat) 37km north of Oatlands, take the turn-off for Ross.

TRIP HIGHLIGHT

④ Ross

Immaculate little Ross feels like a world away from the clamour and sophistication of city life. Begun in 1812 to protect Hobart–Launceston travellers from bushrangers, Ross quickly became an important coach-staging post at the centre of Tasmania's burgeoning wool industry; the **Tasmanian Wool Centre** (☎03-6381 5466; www.taswoolcentre.com. au; 48 Church St; ⊗9.30am-4.30pm Mon-Fri, 10am-4pm Sat & Sun) is a fascinating insight to the town's woolly past. Not surprisingly, this refuge from the busy road has 19th-century architecture at every turn. The crossroads in the middle of town, known as the Four Corners of Ross, could lead your soul in one of four directions: temptation (represented by the **Man O'Ross Hotel**), salvation (the **Catholic Church**), recreation (the **town hall**) or damnation (the **old jail**). Other notable historic edifices include the 1832 **Scotch Thistle Inn**; the 1830 **barracks**; the **Uniting Church** (1885); **St John's Anglican Church**, (1868); and the **post office**, opened in 1896 and

still going strong. With all of this architectural splendour sheltering beneath the beautiful elms (visit in autumn for the full effect), Ross is the perfect place to overnight.

✖ ⤒ p391

The Drive » There's barely time to get going once you're back on the main highway – Campbell Town is just 12km north of Ross and the main road passes right through the centre of town.

⑤ Campbell Town

One minute you're speeding along the Midland Hwy, the next you're surrounded by the considerable charm of Campbell Town. With far more through traffic than the other old-world towns along this route, Campbell Town wears its history a little more lightly. Even so, there's no mistaking its august heritage: this was another former garrison and convict settlement and has a slew of mid-19th-century public and private buildings on show. Also, all along High St, rows of red bricks set into the footpath detail the crimes, sentences and arrival dates of convicts sent here for crimes as various as stealing potatoes, bigamy and murder. After convict transportation ended, Campbell Town's first white settlers were Irish timber workers who spoke Gaelic and had

a particularly debauched reputation. Today, Campbell Town is ground zero for Tasmania's cattle- and sheep-farming industries. The annual **Campbell Town Show** (www. campbelltownshow.com.au), held in May, is the oldest country show in Australia (since 1839).

✖ p391

The Drive » The drive to Evandale (50km) is mostly along the Midland Hwy, with undulating farmland interspersed with low hills and light woodland all the way to the Evandale turn-off (B41). It's an easy drive, but if you reach Perth, you've gone too far.

Hobart Fishing boats moored on the city's waterfront

TRIP HIGHLIGHT

⑥ Evandale

The most northerly of the towns that line the Midland Hwy (Heritage Hwy) like a string of pearls, Evandale is arguably the prettiest of them all. Walk down the main street here and you'll feel like you've time-warped back a century, which is, of course, precisely why the entire town is National Trust listed. It's a ridiculously photogenic place, and a few hours spent wandering the quiet streets, browsing the galleries and hanging out at the cafes is time well spent. The highlight of the year is February's **National Penny Farthing Championships** (www.evandalevillagefair. com), when two-wheel warriors race around the town's streets at alarming velocities. There's also an agreeable Sunday morning market, the usual portfolio of stunning old-style churches, and, south of town via Nile Rd, two-storey, neo-classical **Clarendon** (☎03-6398 6220; www.nationaltrust.org.au/tas/clarendon; 234 Clarendon Station Rd; adult/child $15/free; ◷10am-4pm Sep-Jun), which looks like it's stepped straight out of *Gone with the Wind*. Built in 1938, Clarendon is, perhaps incongruously, home to the **Australian Fly Fishing Museum** (☎03-6398 6220; www.affm.net.au; Clarendon, 234 Clarendon Station Rd; admission $5; ◷10am-4pm Mon-Sat, noon-4pm Sun). Evandale is within striking distance of Launceston Airport: it's an option for accommodation if you've got an early flight.

🛏 p391

The Drive » If you're headed north, pretty much all roads here lead to Launceston (or its airport, which lies closer to Evandale than it does to the city that bears its name). Follow the signs to the city centre.

THE HERITAGE HIGHWAY

The Heritage Hwy is Tasmania's oldest road. Hobart was founded in 1804 and Launceston in 1805. By 1807 the need for a land link between the two settlements prompted surveyor Charles Grimes to map an appropriate route. The road was constructed by convict gangs, and by 1821 was suitable for horses and carriages. Two years later a mail cart operated between the two towns, which became Tasmania's first coach service. The main towns on this road were established in the 1820s as garrisons for prisoners and guards, protecting travellers from the menace of bushrangers. Online, see www.heritagehighway.com.au.

❼ Launceston

Launceston, Tasmania's second-largest city, is a modern Aussie town with a real foodie culture. For beer lovers, the highlight is likely to be a tour of **Boag's Brewery** (✆03-6332 6300; www.boags. com.au; 39 William St; tours adult/child $30/15; ⊙tours 11am, 1pm & 3pm), home of the famous James Boag's beer, while just about every visitor raves about **Cataract Gorge**. A mere 10-minute wander west of the city centre, magnificent Cataract Gorge has bushland, cliffs and the ice-cold South Esk River – it all feels a million miles from town. At **First Basin** there's a free outdoor swimming pool (November to March), the world's longest single-span chairlift (9am to 5.30pm), summer concerts, huge European trees and sociable peacocks. Eating options include a cafe, a kiosk and the sassy **Gorge Restaurant** (✆03-6331 3330; www.launcestoncataractgorge. com.au/gorgerestaurant. html; Cataract Gorge; lunch mains from $22, dinner $30-39; ⊙noon-2.30pm daily, 6.30pm-late Tue-Sat). The whole shebang is impressively floodlit at night and it's a magical place to end your journey.

Eating & Sleeping

Hobart ❶

🛏 Islington   Boutique Hotel $$$

(📞03-6220 2123; www.islingtonhotel.com;
321 Davey St, South Hobart; d from $395;
🅿🛜) At the top of Hobart's accommodation
tree, the classy Islington effortlessly merges
heritage architecture with antique furniture,
contemporary art and a glorious garden.
Service is attentive but understated, with
breakfast served in an expansive conservatory.
In the evening, wind down with a wine in the
guest library, study and music room or drawing
room. Exquisite private dinners are also
available. Superb.

Oatlands ❸

🛏 Oatlands Lodge   B&B $$

(📞03-6254 1444; www.oatlandslodge.com; 92
High St; s/d incl breakfast $100/120) Warm and
welcoming in two-storey, hen-pecked sandstone
splendour, Oatlands Lodge (1837) is a classy
B&B option. Rates include a huge breakfast
spread and lots of chat with the affable owners.

Ross ❹

✕ Ross General Store,
Bakery & Tearooms   Cafe $

(31 Church St; light meals $4-10; 🕐breakfast
& lunch) This jack-of-all-trades store has an
olden-days vibe, an open fire and a fuss-free
menu of breakfast, soups, homemade cakes
and sandwiches. The scallop pies are among
Tassie's best.

🛏 Ross B&B   B&B $$

(📞0417 522 354, 03-6381 5354; www.
rossaccommodation.com.au; 12 Church St; B&B
d $110-140, cottage d $170-180; 🛜) Choose
from two en-suite rooms in a 1927 abode, or a
two-bedroom retreat in a separate wing, among
plenty of peachy colours and a garden setting
with warbling birds. This organisation also
manages a few other carefully restored, self-
contained cottages dotted around Ross: see the
website for details.

Campbell Town ❺

✕ Red Bridge Cafe & Providore   Cafe $

(📞03-6381 1169; 137 High St; snacks $4-13;
🕐7.30am-4pm Mon, Wed & Thu, to 5pm Fri,
8am-5pm Sat & Sun; 🛜) At the southern end
of town, near the eponymous Red Bridge, a
former brewery has been transformed into a
funky dining room with shared wooden tables
and a providore packed with beaut Tasmanian
food, wine and beer. Fab cakes, quiches, tarts
and gourmet pies make this an essential stop
heading either north or south.

Evandale ❻

🛏 Arendon Cottage   Cottage $$

(📞0428 353 430, 03-6391 8520; www.
evandaletasmania.com/arendon-cottage-
boutique-accommodation.html; 30 Russell St;
d incl breakfast $130-160, extra person $25;
❄🛜) A lovely little self-contained 1840s
cottage at the quiet end of the main street. Its
pure Georgian proportions were redeemed
after the owners rebuilt the original roof shape
a few years ago. Two bedrooms; sleeps four.
Full kitchen and laundry. The owners live in the
house out the back, so no parties now, y'hear?

STRETCH
YOUR LEGS
HOBART

Start/Finish: Tasmanian Museum & Art Gallery

Distance 3.5km

Duration 2 to 3 hours

Hobart life (and this walk through the city) revolves around the water. There are some first-rate sights to focus on, such as Salamanca, Battery Point and MONA (reached via ferry), but it's the location as much as anything that you'll remember.

Take this walk on Trips

x

Tasmanian Museum & Art Gallery

Incorporating Hobart's oldest building, the Commissariat Store (1808), the revamped **Tasmanian Museum & Art Gallery** (www.tmag.tas.gov.au; Dunn Pl; 10am-4pm Tue-Sun) features colonial relics and excellent Aboriginal and wildlife displays. There's a cool cafe, too.

The Walk » Cross Argyle St to admire the 1864-built Town Hall, then turn left, pass the Lark Distillery to Mawson's Hut Replica Museum by Constitution Dock (where the yachts arrive at the end of the annual Sydney–Hobart yacht race).

Mawson's Hut Replica Museum

The excellent new waterfront installation at the **Mawson's Hut Replica Museum** (www.mawsons-huts-replica.org.au; cnr Morrison & Argyle Sts; adult/child/family $12/4/26; 9am-6pm Oct-Apr, 10am-5pm May-Sep) is an exact model of the hut in which Sir Douglas Mawson hunkered down on his 1911–14 Australasian Antarctic Expedition, which set sail from right here in Hobart. Inside it's 100% authentic, right down to the matches, the stove and the bunks. Entry fees go towards the upkeep of the original hut at Cape Denison in the Antarctic.

The Walk » If it's time for lunch, do like a local and sit in the sun, eat some fish and chips and watch the harbour hubbub. Wander across to the northeastern side of the Dock to Hunter St, then return southwest to Parliament House.

Parliament House

Presiding over an oak-studded park adjacent to Salamanca Pl, Tasmania's sandstone 1840-built **Parliament House** (03-6212 2248; www.parliament.tas.gov.au; Salamanca Pl; tours 10am & 2pm Mon-Fri on nonsitting days) was originally a customs house. There's a tunnel under Murray St from Parliament House to the Customs House pub opposite: the official line is that no one knows what it was used for...

The Walk » Assuming the tunnel's not working, just walk out the door and Salamanca Place is visible just a short stroll away.

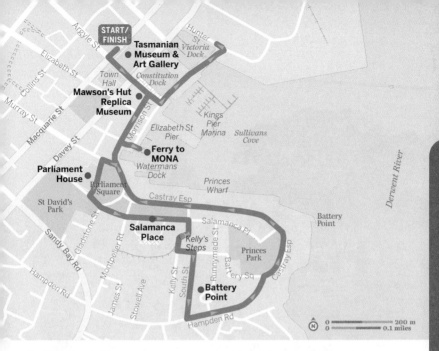

Salamanca Place

Salamanca Place's picturesque row of four-storey sandstone warehouses is a classic example of Australian colonial architecture. Dating back to the whaling days of the 1830s, Salamanca was the hub of Hobart's trade and commerce; restoration began in the 1970s. These days Salamanca hosts myriad restaurants, cafes, bars and shops, and the unmissable Saturday morning **Salamanca Market** (www.salamanca.com.au; ⏰8am-3pm Sat).

The Walk » To reach Battery Point from Salamanca, climb the well-weathered Kelly's Steps (1839), wedged between warehouses halfway along the main block of buildings.

Battery Point

The old maritime village of Battery Point is a tight nest of lanes and 19th-century cottages, packed together like shanghaied landlubbers in a ship's belly. Spend an afternoon exploring: after stumbling up Kelly's Steps from Salamanca Pl, dogleg into South St, where the red lights once burned night and day. Spin around picturesque **Arthur Circus**, refuel in the cafes on **Hampden Rd**, then ogle **St George's Anglican Church** on Cromwell St.

The Walk » Loop around Castray Esplanade. The well-signposted ferry for MONA leaves around 150m north of Salamanca Place.

MONA

Twelve kilometres north of Hobart's city centre, **MONA** (Museum of Old & New Art; ☎03-6277 9900; www.mona.net. au; 655 Main Rd, Berriedale; adult/child $20/ free, Tasmanian residents free; ⏰10am-6pm Wed-Mon Dec & Feb-Apr, 10am-6pm daily Jan, 10am-5pm Wed-Mon May-Nov) occupies a saucepan-shaped peninsula jutting into the Derwent River. Arrayed across three underground levels, abutting a sheer rock face, the $75-million museum has been described by philanthropist owner David Walsh as 'a subversive adult Disneyland'.

The Walk » Upon your return by ferry, it's a short walk to Argyle St and the Tasmanian Museum & Art Gallery.

AD
1823

GLENN VAN DER KNIJFF/GETTY IMAGES ©

Tasman Peninsula

36

Staggering coastal landscapes, sandy beaches and one of Australia's most celebrated historic locations, all within striking distance of Hobart — need we say more?

TRIP HIGHLIGHTS

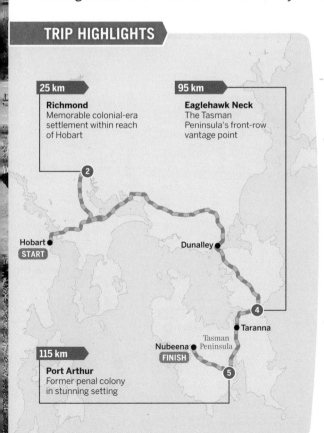

25 km

Richmond
Memorable colonial-era settlement within reach of Hobart

95 km

Eaglehawk Neck
The Tasman Peninsula's front-row vantage point

2

Hobart •
START

Dunalley •

4

• Taranna

Tasman Peninsula

Nubeena •
FINISH

5

115 km

Port Arthur
Former penal colony in stunning setting

3–4 DAYS
142KM / 88 MILES

GREAT FOR...

BEST TIME TO GO

There's more chance of fine weather and less chance of rain from October to April.

📷 ESSENTIAL PHOTO

Port Arthur combines ghostly architecture with a fine natural setting.

☑ BEST FOR OUTDOORS

Walk from Fortescue Bay for extraordinary sea-cliff views.

36 | Tasman Peninsula

The Tasman Peninsula packs a lot into a small space. On the one hand, there's Port Arthur, a hauntingly beautiful former penal colony on a once-lonely stretch of coast – it's one of Australia's most memorable historic sites. But there's also the peninsula's legendary 300m-high sea cliffs – the tallest in the southern hemisphere – which will dose you up on natural awe.

❶ Hobart

Long derided as a provincial Tasmanian backwater without the class and energy of Australia's other state capitals, Hobart has been gaining plaudits of late for its burgeoning foodie and cultural scene, while still retaining its appealing small-town feel.

The Drive › Head east and then north along the shores of the Derwent River, then cross the Tasman Bridge, following the signs for Sorell. Before reaching Sorell, take the turn-off for Richmond. From here, the road

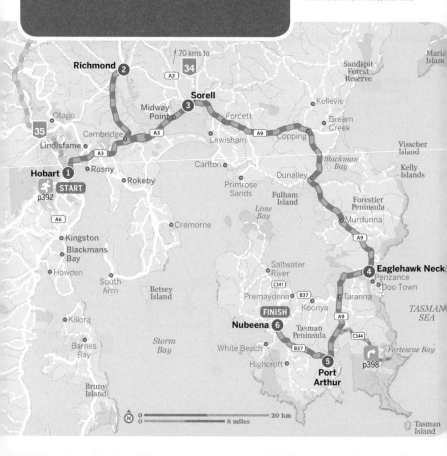

runs through verdant green hills, with wineries and dairy farms lining the roadside. Richmond is just 27km from Hobart.

- - - - - - - - - - -

TRIP HIGHLIGHT

❷ Richmond

You've barely left Hobart, and yet Richmond is at least two centuries distant. Straddling the Coal River, this engaging historic town was once a strategic military post and convict station on the road to Port Arthur. Riddled with 19th-century buildings, it's one of Tasmania's premier historic townships and is undergoing something of a tourism-led revival that has assured the protection of the town's historic architecture. Interesting historic buildings abound around the old town: check out St John's Church, the

LINK YOUR TRIP

34 **East Coast Tasmania**

The Classic east coast road trip (223km) ends (or it could begin) in Maria Island, 57km northeast of Sorell.

35 **Heritage Trail**
The drive through Tassie's historic inland towns begins in Hobart and goes all the way north to Launceston (198km).

first **Catholic church** in Australia (1836); the castellated St Luke's Church of England, built 1834; the 1825 courthouse; the 1826 post office; and the solid Richmond Arms Hotel, a mere youngster dating from 1888. Kids (and quite a few adults) will love Old Hobart Town, an impressive re-creation of historic Hobart in miniature, while more mature tastes should consider the Puddleduck Vineyard, a niche, boutique winery. If you've time, consider a 34km round-trip detour to the Bonorong Wildlife Centre for a fairly full complement of native animal species.

✕ ⛏ p401

The Drive ⟫ Although there are shorter routes, return via the B31 to the main A3 highway, where you'll turn east and cross two long causeways with some pretty scenery out across Pitt Water. Sorell is just after the second causeway, 26km after leaving Richmond.

- - - - - - - - - - -

❸ Sorell

What we're about to tell you may not initially ring true when you look out your vehicle's window: Sorell is one of Tasmania's oldest towns. It was settled and built in 1808, primarily to supply locally processed wheat and flour to the rest of the colony. But unlike other, younger towns in the vicinity, Sorell's historic

aura has tarnished with the march of time. These days it's a T-junction service town with more petrol stations and fast-food joints than anything else. If you're not in need of any of these, stay long enough to check out the handful of 19th-century buildings: the 1841 **Scots Uniting Church** (Arthur St, Sorell); the **Sorell Barracks** (www.sorellbarracks. com; 31 Walker St, Sorell); the 1829 **Blue Bell Inn** (26 Somerville St, Sorell); and, along the main drag, the 1884 **St George's Anglican Church** (www. srtanglican.org.au; 16 Gordon St, Sorell). The *Let's Talk About Sorell* brochure from the visitor information centre has a map. That done, drive right on through, because Sorell remains the gateway to the Tasman Peninsula.

The Drive ⟫ It's after Sorell, along the Arthur Hwy, that the journey really gets interesting, bucking and weaving through open country and increasing stands of eucalyptus woodland. Cross the narrow isthmus at Dunalley, then climb up through the trees. Just before Eaglehawk Neck, take the sign for the Pirates Bay Lookout just 1km down the road – this is your utterly splendid first glimpse of the sea cliffs.

- - - - - - - - - - -

TRIP HIGHLIGHT

❹ Eaglehawk Neck

The thickly timbered Forestier Peninsula – the precursor peninsula you'll cross en route to the Tasman Peninsula – is a fine prelude to so much beauty further south. The town of Eaglehawk Neck has little obvious charm, but here, location is everything. The isthmus is all that stops the Tasman Peninsula from being an island, and therein lies the town's historical claim to fame: in convict days, the 100m-wide Neck had a row of ornery dogs chained across it to prevent escape – the infamous Dogline. Timber platforms were also built in narrow Eaglehawk Bay to the west, and stocked with yet more ferocious dogs to prevent convicts from wading around the Dogline. These days, it's just a really pretty spot and a gateway to more. For a close-up look at the spectacular coastline south of the Neck, follow the signs to the **Blowhole**, **Tasman Arch** (a cavern-like natural bridge) and **Devil's Kitchen** (a rugged 60m-deep cleft). On the road to the Blowhole, look for the signposted 4km gravel road leading to **Waterfall Bay**, which has further camera-conducive views.

🛏 p401

The Drive » The road from Eaglehawk Neck follows a narrow arm of Eaglehawk Bay west, then veers south through the same attractive mix of eucalypts and open rangelands, bound for Port Arthur.

- - - - - - - - - - -

TRIP HIGHLIGHT

❺ Port Arthur

The juxtaposition of natural beauty and an unsettling human history is nowhere as profound as it is in **Port Arthur** (📞03-6251 2310; www.portarthur.org.au; Arthur Hwy; adult/child/family from $37/17/90; ⊙tours & buildings 9am-5pm, grounds

---

DETOUR: FORTESCUE BAY

Start: ❹ Eaglehawk Neck

To get the best out of the Tasman Peninsula, resist, if you, can the urge to hurry on to Port Arthur and take a detour beyond the paved road. Just before the small hamlet of Oakwood, halfway between Taranna and Port Arthur, a decent gravel road runs 12km from the Arthur Hwy down to blissfully becalmed Fortescue Bay, with a sweeping sandy arc backed by thickly forested slopes.

Fortescue Bay is one of the main access points for **Tasman National Park** (📞03-6250 3497; www.parks.tas.gov.au; person/vehicle per day $12/24). Offshore, dolphins, seals, penguins and whales are regular passersby. Apart from swimming and bumming around on the beach, most people come here to launch fishing boats or do some bushwalking.

Several walking tracks kick off at Fortescue Bay. Heading north, a solid track traces the shoreline to **Canoe Bay** (two hours return) and **Bivouac Bay** (four hours return), continuing all the way to the **Devil's Kitchen** car park at Eaglehawk Neck (10 hours one way). To the east, a track meanders out to **Cape Hauy** (four to five hours return) – a well-used path leading out to sea cliffs with sensational views of the famous **Candlestick** and **Totem Pole** sea stacks. To get into some rainforest, follow the same track towards Cape Hauy, then take the steep side track to **Mt Fortescue** (six to seven hours return). Another track extends all the way to **Cape Pillar** near Tasman Island, where the sea cliffs are 300m high – the highest in the southern hemisphere. You'll need two to three days return to knock off the Cape Pillar track.

The new **Three Capes Track**, linking Cape Raoul, Cape Pillar and Cape Hauy, was being built at the time of writing: check the park's website for updates.

CREDIT/GETTY IMAGES ©

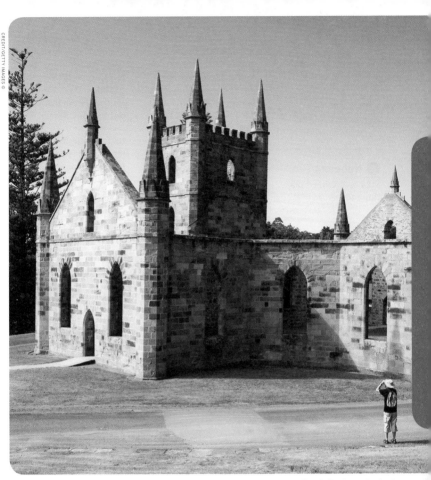

Port Arthur Ruins of a church

9am-dusk), Tasmania's premier historic site. In 1830 Governor Arthur chose the beautiful site to confine prisoners who had committed further crimes in the colony. It was a 'natural penitentiary' – escape was nearly impossible – and between 1830 and 1877, 12,500 convicts did hard, brutal prison time here. Port Arthur became the hub of a network of penal stations on the peninsula, its fine buildings sustaining thriving convict-labour industries, including timber milling, shipbuilding, coal mining, shoemaking and brick and nail production. Many of these buildings remain, and wandering the expansive grounds is a stirring, soulful experience. Despite its redemption as a major tourist site, Port Arthur is a sombre place. There's a sadness here that's undeniable, and a Gothic pall of woe that can cloud your senses on the sunniest of days. Add to that the 1996 massacre in which 35 people were gunned down here, and it's the sort of place that will leave you deeply affected.

✕ 🛏 p401

The Drive » It's just 13km from Port Arthur to Nubeena and, except in the height of summer, it's a quiet road forsaken by day-trippers rushing back to Hobart. As you drive, imagine what it must have been like to have escaped Port Arthur and be on the run here...

- - - - - - - - - - -

❻ Nubeena

Nubeena, fanned out along the shore of Wedge Bay, is the largest town on the Tasman Peninsula, but that's not saying much – barely 500 souls call it home. It's much more low-key than Port Arthur – it's really just an easygoing holiday destination for locals, with some holiday accommodation sprinkled around. The main things to do around town are swimming and chilling out on nearby White Beach (population 280),

or fishing from the jetty or foreshore. Down a side road 3km south of town is some energetic walking to **Tunnel Bay** (five hours return), **Raoul Bay Lookout** (two hours return) and the exquisitely named **Cape Raoul** (five hours return). To the north is **Roaring Beach**, which gets wicked surf but isn't safe for swimming.

Eating & Sleeping

Richmond ❷

✕ Richmond Wine Centre   Modern Australian $$

(✆03-6260 2619; www.richmondwinecentre.com.au; 27 Bridge St; mains $22-30; ⊙10am-4pm daily, 6-9pm Fri & Sat) Don't be duped by the name: this place dedicates itself to fine food as well as 100% Tasmanian wine. Slink over the daisy-studded lawn to one of the dinky outdoor tables and peruse the menu. Tassie produce reigns supreme.

⌂ Daisy Bank Cottages   B&B $$

(✆03-6260 2390; www.daisybankcottages.com.au; 78 Middle Tea Tree Rd; d $150-190) This place is a rural delight: two spotless, stylish self-contained units (one with spa) in a converted 1840s sandstone barn on a working sheep farm. There are loft bedrooms, views of the Richmond rooftops and plenty of bucolic distractions for the kids. The surrounding farmland has interpretative walks and soaring birds of prey. Breakfast provisions daily. Hard to beat.

Eaglehawk Neck ❹

⌂ Eaglehawk Café & Guesthouse   B&B

(✆03-6250 3331; 5131 Arthur Hwy; mains $10-23; ⊙breakfast & lunch year-round, dinner Fri-Sun Dec-Feb) Above this groovy cafe (c 1929) are three lovely B&B rooms (doubles including breakfast $110 to $130) that were once the refuge of sleeping shipwrights. Two of the rooms have French doors opening onto a balcony overlooking Eaglehawk Bay. Downstairs the stylish cafe-cum-restaurant offers a fine day-turns-to-night menu (try the Doo Town venison kebabs) as well as great coffee and cakes.

Port Arthur ❺

✕ Gabriel's on the Bay   Modern Australian $$

(✆03-6250 2771; www.stewartsbaylodge.com.au; Stewarts Bay Lodge, 6955 Arthur Hwy; lunch mains $18-35, dinner $28-35; ⊙8-10am & noon-2pm daily, 5.30-8.30pm Thu-Mon ; 🖥) Housed in a modern glass-and-wood pavilion with water views, Gabe's showcases local produce with Eaglehawk Neck oysters, Tasman Peninsula salmon burgers and Tasmanian scotch fillet with sweet-potato mash, braised leeks and red wine jus. Definitely worth a detour if you're overnighting anywhere nearby. Bookings recommended.

⌂ Comfort Inn Port Arthur   Motel $$

(✆1800 030 747, 03-6250 2101; www.portarthur-inn.com.au; 29 Safety Cove Rd; d $145-185) The superb views over the historic site from the Comfort Inn rooms are more remarkable than the rooms themselves, but the Commandant's Table Restaurant is noteworthy. Ask about packages including accommodation, dinner, breakfast and a Port Arthur ghost tour (from $270 for two).

⌂ Sea Change Safety Cove   B&B $$

(✆0438 502 719, 03-6250 2719; www.safetycove.com; 425 Safety Cove Rd, Safety Cove; d $180-240, extra adult/child $40/20; 🖥) Whichever way you look from this guest house, 4km south of Port Arthur, there are fantastic views – misty cliffs, sea-wracked Safety Cove Beach or scrubby bushland. There are a couple of B&B rooms inside the house plus a self-contained unit downstairs that sleeps five. Outside, camellia-filled gardens roll down to a beaut deck overlooking the beach (G&Ts anyone?).

Tamar River Valley *Serene countryside and celebrated wines*

PETER WALTON PHOTOGRAPHY/GETTY IMAGES ©

Tamar Valley Gourmet Trail

37

Funnelling 64km north from Launceston, the Tamar River Valley is fringed with emerald hills and cool-climate wineries that add up to one of Australia's finest wine-touring areas.

TRIP HIGHLIGHTS

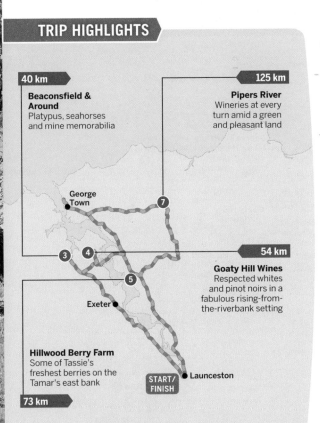

40 km

Beaconsfield & Around
Platypus, seahorses and mine memorabilia

125 km

Pipers River
Wineries at every turn amid a green and pleasant land

George Town

7

3 **4**

54 km

Goaty Hill Wines
Respected whites and pinot noirs in a fabulous rising-from-the-riverbank setting

5

Exeter

Hillwood Berry Farm
Some of Tassie's freshest berries on the Tamar's east bank

START/FINISH • Launceston

73 km

4–5 DAYS
232KM / 144 MILES

GREAT FOR...

BEST TIME TO GO

October to May is northern Tassie's best chance for fine, mild weather.

ESSENTIAL PHOTO

Low Head Lighthouse overlooking Bass Strait.

BEST FOR FOOD & WINE

Pipers River is one of Australia's most underrated wine regions.

Tamar Valley Gourmet Trail

You could make this up-and-back journey in a single day, but that would be to miss the point. It's the sort of route where you'll meander along a riverbank, go off on a tangent to a winery or two and plan your day around the comings and goings of wildlife. The western bank of the valley is the prettier of the two. The Batman Bridge unites the Tamar's two shores near Deviot.

① Launceston

Laid-back Launceston is a fine starting point for a foodie's exploration of Tasmania's north, with Cataract Gorge providing a dramatic counterpoint within walking distance of the city centre.

🛏 p409

The Drive » From downtown Launceston, take the West Tamar Hwy (A7) 22km northwest to Exeter. The road stays close to the Tamar's west riverbank, and en route you'll catch glimpses of the river, with the best views from well-signposted Brady's Lookout around 5km southeast of Exeter.

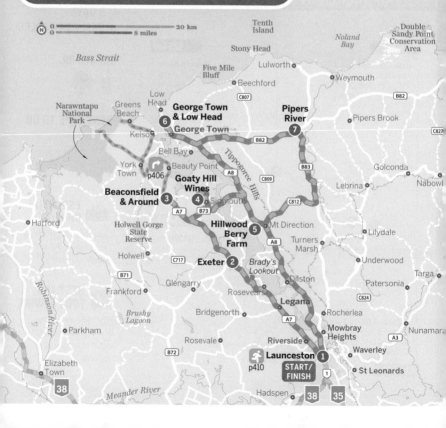

② Exeter

Sleepy little Exeter, close to a bend in the Tamar's increasingly tortuous path, is an important part of the Tamar Valley story – set in the heart of orchard and farming country, it's from here that so much of Tasmania's fresh produce derives. There's not much to see in the town itself, but with a great place to stay and the legendary Exeter bakery still going strong, it's the sort of place where you may just be tempted to stop for the night. If you do, a nice little excursion south of town along Gravelly Beach Rd will take you to Robigana (derived

LINK YOUR TRIP

35 **Heritage Trail**
From Hobart to Launceston (or in reverse, but 230km either way) via the historic towns of the Tasmanian interior.

38 **West Coast Wilderness Way**
This 655km journey ends (but could just as easily begin) in Launceston, taking in the great forests, remote rivers, high mountains and historic towns of the Tassie interior.

from the Aboriginal word for swans), where the road crosses the Supply River. From here there's a marked walking track (one hour return) beside the Tamar River to Paper Beach.

The premium cool-climate wines of the Tamar Valley have been swilled at the tables of royalty and to make sure you don't miss the best the region has to offer, check out the **Tamar Valley Wine Route** (www.tamarvalleywineroute.com.au), pick up a self-drive guide from the Tamar Visitor Information Centre in Exeter, or take a guided tour with Valleybrook Wine Tours.

 p409

The Drive » The road northwest from Exeter to Beaconsfield (16km) crosses the pancake-flat river flats, which are a deep shade of green for most of the year. Branching away to the east, Batman Bridge crosses the Tamar, but simply make a note of it for now, as you've some essential business still to transact on the western shore first.

TRIP HIGHLIGHT

③ Beaconsfield & Around

The international spotlight briefly shone on little Beaconsfield (population 1200) during a mine collapse in 2006, but these days it's a quiet, slightly shabby gold-mining town in the heart of the Tamar's

apple-growing country. Pause long enough to visit the **Beaconsfield Mine & Heritage Centre** (☏03-6383 1473; www.beaconsfieldheritage.com.au; West St, Beaconsfield; adult/child/family $12/4/30; ☺9.30am-4.30pm), which has hands-on interactive exhibits. Six kilometres to the north of Beaconsfield, Beauty Point has two further winning attractions. **Platypus House** (☏03-6383 4884; www.platypushouse.com.au; 200 Flinders St, Inspection Head Wharf, Beauty Point; adult/child/family $23/9/55; ☺9.30am-3.30pm) is a fine chance to see everyone's favourite monotreme, while **Seahorse World** (☏03-6383 4111; www.seahorseworld.com.au; 200 Flinders St, Inspection Head Wharf, Beauty Point; adult/child/family $22/9/54; ☺9.30am-4pm Dec-Apr, 10am-3pm May-Nov) has to be one of the world's more unusual aquariums, with a pot-bellied seahorse the main drawcard...

If you plan on visiting the Beaconsfield Mine & Heritage Centre, Platypus House and Seahorse World, consider buying the three-attraction Tamar Triple Pass (adult/family $49/135) from any of the visitor information centres in the Tamar Valley area.

 ⎘ p409

The Drive » The A7 north of Beaconsfield snakes around the inlets of the Tamar River.

It's a beautiful drive through increasingly rough country. The paved road ends at windy Greens Beach. On your way south, take the turn-off west towards Batman Bridge, then follow the signs to Kayena just before crossing the bridge.

TRIP HIGHLIGHT

 Goaty Hill Wines

Before leaving the Tamar's west bank, detour north to the tiny hamlet of Kayena. Here you'll find a real gem, the family-friendly **Goaty Hill Wines** (🖉1300 819 997; www.goatyhill. com; 530 Auburn Rd, Kayena; ⏲10am-5pm Aug-May, by appointment Jun & Jul). This well-regarded winery has cellar-door sales and tastings (you'll need to

ring ahead in the depths of winter) and is best known for its top-notch riesling and pinots gris and noir. Acoustic troubadors strum on the deck in summer; impromptu cricket matches happen on the lawns. Bliss.

The Drive » From Kayena, return south to the B73 and Batman Bridge, cross over to the Tamar's east bank, then turn south along the East Tamar Hwy (A8). Almost immediately, watch for signs to Hillwood, which overlooks the river just down off the main road.

TRIP HIGHLIGHT

⑤ Hillwood Berry Farm

Tamar Valley wines may steal all the plaudits, but

the valley is also much-loved for the fresh fruits that emerge from its numerous orchards. One of these is the **Hillwood Berry Farm** (🖉03-6394 8180; www.hillwoodberryfarm. com.au; 105 Hillwood Rd, Hillwood; ⏲9am-5pm daily late Oct-Feb, 10am-5pm Wed-Sun Mar), which is at its best in summer when the hillsides are almost universally under berry. Pick your own strawberries, raspberries, loganberries, blackcurrants, redcurrants and blueberries and then make a beeline for the cafe (mains $8 to $16) for a berry sundae, a slice of berry-swirl cheesecake or a coffee.

The Drive » Return to the A8, then follow it for 22km north amid the fruit-growing hills above the Tamar's eastern riverbank. Almost as far as you can go in Tasmania without falling off into Bass Strait, you'll hit George Town, with Low Head – the two are barely divided and you won't notice leaving one before arriving in the other – a mere 5km further on.

⑥ George Town & Low Head

George Town stands sentinel on the Tamar River's eastern shore, close to where it empties into Bass Strait, and believe it or not, it owes its existence to a fear of foreign invasion. The town was founded in 1804 as part of the British attempt to stave off settlement by the French, who had

---

DETOUR: NARAWNTAPU NATIONAL PARK

Start: ❸ Beaconsfield

Tasmania is one of Australia's most underrated wildlife-watching destinations and that can be the only reason why Narawntapu National Park is barely known beyond these shores. So prolific is this reserve of coastal heath, dunes and bushland that it has been called Tasmania's Serengeti. Visit just on dusk and you'll see Forester kangaroos, foraging wombats, wallabies and pademelons. It used to be called Asbestos Range National Park, but park management thought the name was deterring people from visiting. Go figure...

The park can be accessed at two points near the small coastal settlement of Greens Beach (via the C721), or via the main entrance at Springlawn off the B71 near Port Sorell, where there's a ranger station. Rangers run guided walks and activities from here in summer. If you're entering the park from the Greens Beach side, self-register on entry.

ANDREW WATSON/GETTY IMAGES ©

Hillwood Berry Farm Summer strawberry picking

been reconnoitring the area. Aside from a few mid-19th-century buildings, George Town is best visited as a prelude to salty and historic Low Head, with its glorious setting looking out over the swirling – and treacherous – waters. There's good surf at **East Beach** on Bass Strait, and safe swimming away from the river mouth at beaches around the head. The main attraction in these parts is **Low Head Lighthouse** (☎03-6382 2826; www. lowheadpilotstation.com; end of Low Head Rd; ☺grounds 9am-6pm Sep-May, to 5pm Jun-Aug); built in 1888, it's a terrific spot to watch the torrent of the Tamar spilling into Bass Strait. **Low Head Penguin Tours** (☎0418 361 860; http:// penguintours.lowhead.com; end of Low Head Rd; adult/ child $18/10; ☺dusk) leave nightly at dusk from a signposted spot beside Low Head Rd, just south of the lighthouse.

✕ ⊨ p409

The Drive » Some 7km south of George Town (or 12km from Low Head), the B82 veers east out over the low and verdant Tippogoree Hills and passes through the Den Ranges Forest

Reserve before emerging amid the vineyards of Pipers River, just 27km after leaving George Town.

- - - - - - - - - - -

❼ Pipers River

In the eastern Tamar Valley hinterland, the Pipers River Wine Region (www.tamarvalleywine-route.com.au) is a lovely adjunct to the Tamar's charms. **Pipers Brook** (☏03-6382 7527; www.pipersbrook.com.au; 1216 Pipers Brook Rd, Pipers Brook; tastings free, cafe mains $14-25; ⊙10am-5pm, cafe 10am-3pm) is the region's most famous vineyard. Next door to Pipers Brook, savvy **Jansz Wine Room** (☏03-6382 7066; www.jansz.com.au; 1216b Pipers Brook Rd, Pipers Brook; ⊙10am-4.30pm) makes fine sparkling wine, aka 'Méthode Tasmanoise'. About 3km south of the main Pipers River T-intersection, **Bay of Fires Wines** (☏03-6382 7622; www.bayoffireswines.com.au; 40 Baxters Rd, Pipers River; ⊙10am-5pm Sep-May, 11am-4pm Jun-Aug) is the home of prestigious Arras sparkling and easy-drinking whites and pinots. There's a touch of Cape Cod about the cellar-door design. On a smaller scale, affable, family-run **Delamere Vineyards** (☏03-6382 7190; www.delamerevineyards.com.au; 4238 Bridport Rd, Pipers Brook; ⊙10am-5pm) is the antithesis of the big-ticket wineries around here.

The Drive » Drive south from Pipers River along the B83 to Lower Turners Marsh (14km), turn right (west) along the C812 to Mt Direction (13km), then rejoin the main Tamar Valley route (A8) all the way into Launceston.

Eating & Sleeping

Launceston ❶

🛏 Two Four Two   Apartment $$$

(☎03-6331 9242; www.twofourtwo.com.au; 242 Charles St; d incl breakfast from $250; 🛜) Now this is a cool renovation! Furniture maker Alan has channelled his craft into four self-contained town houses, each with blackwood, myrtle or Tasmanian-oak detailing. Stainless-steel kitchens, coffee machines, private courtyards and spa baths complete the experience. The Charles St restaurants are on tap.

Exeter ❷

✖ Exeter Bakery   Bakery $

(☎03-6394 4069; 104 Main Rd; snacks $3-9; ⏰7am-5pm Mon-Fri, 8am-3pm Sat, 9am-3pm Sun) The century-old wood-fired oven here produces all manner of pies – from seafood to egg and bacon to tender wallaby and glistening custard. Also on offer are cakes, breads, slices, tarts, ham-and-cheese croissants and filled rolls to go.

Beaconsfield & Around ❸

✖ River Cafe   Cafe, Modern Australian $$

(☎03-6383 4099; www.therivercafe.com.au; 225 Flinders St; mains $8-30; ⏰11am-late; 🛜) On sunny days at the River Cafe, the windows fold right back and the water feels so close you could touch it. The menu tempts with fresh local fare – the Tasmanian eye fillet is sublime – and the coffe is just about perfect, too. Takeaway pizzas, free wi-fi and Tamar Valley wines all the way.

🛏 Tamar Cove   Motel $$

(☎03-6383 4375; www.tamarcove.com; 4421 Main Rd; d $119-150, 2-bedroom apt $149; 🛜🏊) What a winning little hillside enclave!

Nine stylishly done-up motel rooms front well-manicured gardens with a solar-heated pool. The **restaurant** (mains $15 to $30, serving 8am until late) gets rave reviews, too – don't go past the house-special seafood chowder. Free wi-fi. Good one!

George Town & Low Head ❻

✖ Coxwain's Cottage Café   Cafe $$

(☎03-6382 2826; www.lowheadpilotstation. com; 399 Low Head Rd, Low Head Pilot Station; mains $6-20; ⏰10am-5pm Jun-Nov, 9am-5pm Dec-May) The best (only) place to eat in Low Head is this excellent cafe in an 1847 cottage at the Low Head Pilot Station. Offerings include homemade pies (try the lamb-and-veggie version), quiches, toasted sandwiches and hearty soups in winter – plus Pipers River wines and fine espresso.

🛏 Peppers
York Cove   Hotel, Apartment $$

(☎03-6382 9900; www.peppers.com.au/york-cove; 2 Ferry Blvd; d $170-250, 2-/3-bedroom apt from $270/300; ⏰restaurant 7-10am daily, noon-3pm Tue-Sun, 6-8pm Mon-Sat; 🛜🏊) This corporate waterfront resort is making waves on the Tamar. There are upmarket hotel rooms and apartments, and the funky bar-restaurant (lunch and dinner mains $24 to $35) does contemporary cafe food and excellent coffee.

🛏 Low Head Pilot Station   Cottage $$

(☎03-6382 2826; www.lowheadpilotstation. com; 399 Low Head Rd; 2-/5-/6-/8-/9-person cottages $180/210/210/250/300) Low Head's historic pilot station precinct offers a range of nine very smartly refurbished, self-contained, waterfront cottages for up to nine people. Great for families, the kids will get into the maritime mood and wait with flapping ears for the foghorn boom from the lighthouse (midday on Sundays).

STRETCH YOUR LEGS
LAUNCESTON

Start/Finish: Queen Victoria Museum & Art Gallery

Distance: 4km

Duration: 2 hours

Launceston is an appealing city that's large enough to have a handful of artistic and architectural attractions, and its compact town centre has an intimate feel with soothing river frontage and parkland never far away.

Take this walk on Trips

Queen Victoria Museum & Art Gallery (Part 1)

Launceston's air of quiet provinciality is dispelled almost immediately upon entering the brilliant **Queen Victoria Museum & Art Gallery** (QVMAG; ☎03-6323 3777; www.qvmag.tas.gov.au; 2 Wellington St; ⏰10am-4pm). This is the first of two locations at the Inveresk Railyards, and it houses the natural, social and technology-focused collections at the museum.

The Walk » Cross the parkland to Invermay Rd, turn left and then cross the North Esk River. After crossing the bridge, take the second left and the National Automobile Museum is around 250m along on your left. Cross the road into City Park.

City Park

Expansive **City Park** (www.launceston.tas. gov.au; cnr Tamar & Cimtiere Sts; ⏰daylight hours) has enormous oak and plane trees, an elegant fountain, a glass conservatory, a Victorian bandstand and a playground and mini-train for kids. Peer into your gene pool at the glass-walled **Japanese macaque enclosure**, a gift from Japanese sister city Ikeda.

The Walk » Your next stop lies in the southwestern corner of City Park. If you're unsure about finding it, head to the park's western edge along Tamar St, turn left and you'll be there in no time.

Design Centre Tasmania

The deconsecrated heritage church hall of **Design Centre Tasmania** (☎03-6331 5506; www.designtasmania.com.au; cnr Brisbane & Tamar Sts; ⏰9.30am-5.30pm Mon-Fri, 10am-4pm Sat & Sun) has a lovely exhibition selling beautiful handmade Tasmanian crafts. Next door is the excellent **Design Tasmania Wood Collection** (entry by donation), showcasing local timber furniture design.

The Walk » With your back to the Design Centre, turn right (northwest) on Tamar St, then first left along Cameron St. At George St, turn left again, with the Old Umbrella Shop just along on your right at No 60.

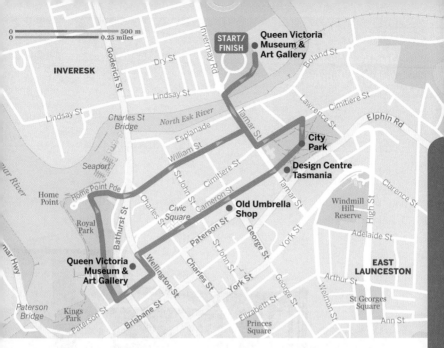

Old Umbrella Shop

Launcestonians once kept dry under the umbrellas made here at the **Old Umbrella Shop** (☎03-6331 9248; www. nationaltrust.org.au; 60 George St; ⊘9am-5pm Mon-Fri, to noon Sat) by R Shott & Sons. Now the shop stands as a rare example of an intact early-20th-century store, complete with its original till and blackwood display cases. Visiting here is one of those intimate, still-in-touch-with-its-roots experiences that Launceston excels at.

The Walk » Return to Cameron St. A couple of blocks along you come to Civic Sq. On your left, watch for the beautifully ugly Henty House, Tasmania's finest example of raw concrete brutalist architecture. The museum is opposite where Cameron St ends.

Queen Victoria Museum & Art Gallery (Part 2)

The second part of the **Queen Victoria Museum & Art Gallery**, on the edge of Royal Park, is a meticulously restored art gallery with the gallery's storehouse of colonial painting and decorative arts.

The Walk » Walk north through Royal Park to Home Point, admire Old Launceston Seaport on your left as walk east along Seaport Blvd. Continue northeast along William St to Invermay St, turn left, cross the river and return to where you started.

Stanley *Picturesque village on a rugged, windswept coast*

West Coast Wilderness Way

38

This journey is one of Australia's premier rainforest and wilderness drives, with historic villages, lonely beaches and amazing wildlife-watching opportunities.

TRIP HIGHLIGHTS

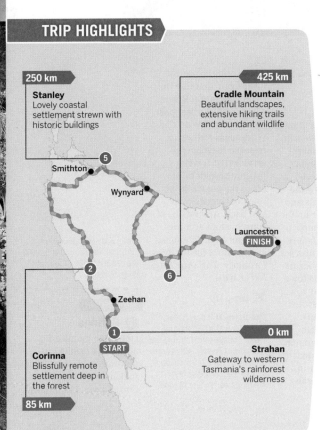

250 km

Stanley
Lovely coastal settlement strewn with historic buildings

425 km

Cradle Mountain
Beautiful landscapes, extensive hiking trails and abundant wildlife

Smithton

⑤

Wynyard

Launceston
FINISH

②

⑥

Zeehan

0 km

①
START

Strahan
Gateway to western Tasmania's rainforest wilderness

Corinna
Blissfully remote settlement deep in the forest

85 km

**14 DAYS
655KM / 407 MILES**

GREAT FOR...

BEST TIME TO GO

October to April; avoid the depths of winter (June to August).

 **ESSENTIAL
PHOTO**

Wombats at Cradle Mountain.

 **BEST FOR
OUTDOORS**

Take the Pieman River cruise through the rainforest from Corinna.

413

PETER WALTON PHOTOGRAPHY/GETTY IMAGES ©

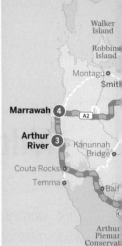

38 West Coast Wilderness Way

Northwestern Tasmania has it all. There's tall-timbered rainforest at Strahan, Corinna and Arthur River, the immense beaches of the west coast as far north as Marrawah, and the historic towns of Stanley, Sheffield and Deloraine, with the peerless natural world of Cradle Mountain in between. In other words, just about everything good about Tasmania lines up along this route.

TRIP HIGHLIGHT

1 Strahan

With its perfect location, nestled between the wild waters of the Southern Ocean and the rainforest, and with restored pioneer buildings – the cutesy shops, hotels and cottages crowding up the slope from the compact waterfront – Strahan resembles a Disney film set. The unbelievable beauty that surrounds the town makes it a gateway town par excellence. Devote a day to a boat cruise with World Heritage Cruises, a fine excursion that explores Macquarie Harbour, the haunting penal colony of **Sarah Island** and the soulful rainforests that line the remote Franklin River. Also worth the best part of a day is the West Coast Wilderness Railway, a restored heritage rail service that travels inland through rainforest to the eerie mining town of Queenstown and back. And on one of your Strahan evenings, don't miss the fabulously entertaining theatre performance, *The Ship That Never Was*.

 p419

The Drive » It doesn't take long after leaving Strahan on the B27 before forests crowd the roadside. At Zeehan, 43km north of Strahan, the C249 meanders off into the forest (the first 40km sealed, the last 12 good gravel and easily passable in a 2WD). Where the road ends, ring the bell and wait for the river barge to come.

TRIP HIGHLIGHT

2 Corinna

Out in the middle of nowhere, Corinna is a first-rate wilderness destination. In gold-rush days Corinna was a humming

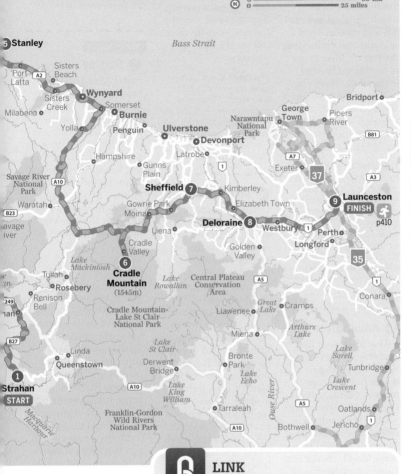

REGION **38** WEST COAST WILDERNESS WAY

town with a population that numbered 2500 souls. That's hard to believe now when you pull up on the forested edge of the Pieman, turn off your car's engine and absorb the unbelievable forest peace. Now a comfortable yet rustic rainforest resort, Corinna offers comfy cabins,

LINK YOUR TRIP

35 Heritage Trail

The road between Hobart and Launceston (230km) takes you through some of Tasmania's best-preserved historic towns.

37 Tamar Valley Gourmet Trail

This 178km round-trip loop is foodie heaven thanks to its wineries and berry farms, with some excellent wildlife watching en route.

magnificent bushwalks, fine wildlife-watching (think wallabies, pademelons and wombats) and a splendid boat cruise along the Pieman River to one of the wildest beaches in Australia. There's no mobile-phone reception and no TVs (the most prevalent sound is birdsong), but there is a fine pub and restaurant.

The Drive » Leaving Corinna, the Tarkine rainforest crowds above the gravel track and, despite breaks in the forest canopy, it's a sensation that may not leave you until you arrive in Arthur River, 109km later. Check on road conditions in Corinna, but the unpaved road, known aptly as the Western Explorer Rd (C249), is fine in a 2WD for most of the year.

❸ Arthur River

Arthur River feels like (and may just be) the end of the earth and it even has a sign to prove it. Gardiner Point, signposted off the main road on the southern side of Arthur River, is Tasmania's official Edge of the World: the sea here stretches uninterrupted all the way to Argentina. There's a plaque at the point – a great place to take those leaning-into-the-wind, world's-end photos. And therein lies the appeal of this small, otherwise nondescript settlement, which is home to only a few hardy souls: deliciously remote, Arthur River is where the

paved road begins once again (if you're coming from the south) but the frontiers of civilisation still seem a long, long way away.

The Drive » Just 14km of paved road connects Arthur River with Marrawah to the north. En route, you'll pass wild, windswept fields and isolated farmsteads, with distant glimpses of the seemingly endless Southern Ocean.

❹ Marrawah

Untamed, unspoilt Marrawah is a domain of vast ocean beaches, mind-blowing sunsets and, by some estimates, the cleanest air on the planet. The power of the ocean here is astounding, and the wild beaches, rocky coves and headlands have changed little since they were the homeland of Tasmania's first people; at every turn, there's a feeling of lonely emptiness, as if the Aboriginal custodians have only just left the land. It's vast ocean waves that Marrawah is best known for today. Experienced surfers and windsurfers come for the challenging breaks. There's a general store here, but very little else.

The Drive » It's 73km from Marrawah to Stanley along the Bass Hwy (A2). The first half of the journey burrows through the northern reaches of the Tarkine rainforest, before opening up into the dairy farmlands that sustain Smithton. Stanley lies

7km north of the main road, and this last stretch is the prettiest section.

TRIP HIGHLIGHT

❺ Stanley

Stanley could just be Tasmania's prettiest coastal town. The town is a scatter of brightly painted timber cottages, sheltering in the lee of an ancient volcano, the Nut, and historic structures dominate the town's facades. *Under the Nut – Stanley Heritage Walk*, available from the **visitor information centre** (📞 03-6458 1330, 1300 138 229; www.stanley.com.au; 45 Main Rd; ⏰ 9.30am-5pm Oct-May, 10am-4pm Jun-Sep), takes you on a self-guided tour of 14 of Stanley's more beautiful and/or interesting historic buildings. Stroll through town on a fine day and you may not feel that underlying edginess that comes from being on the world's rim, but when the Roaring Forties blast through, you'll feel it sure enough, and that's part of the excitement of being here. Highlights include the 19th-century homestead **Highfield** (📞 03-6458 1100; www.historic-highfield.com.au; Green Hills Rd; adult/child/family $12/6/30; ⏰ 9.30am-4.30pm daily Sep-May, Mon-Fri Jun-Aug), the **chairlift** (adult one-way/return $9/15, child $6/10; ⏰ 9.30am-5pm Oct-May, 10am-4pm Jun-Sep) and views from the summit of the Nut, and the

PETER WALTON PHOTOGRAPHY/GETTY IMAGES ©

Pieman River Boating in the Tarkine Wilderness Area, near Corinna

chance to see Australian fur seals with **Stanley Seal Cruises** (📞0419 550 134, 03-6458 1294; www.stanleysealcruises.com.au; Fisherman's Dock; adult/over 5yr/under 5yr $55/18/10; ⏲Sep–mid-Jun).

🍴 🛏 p419

The Drive » Return to the main A2 Bass Hwy. The further west you go, the greater the sense of the accumulating clamour and traffic of civilisation. Just past Wynyard, 73km after leaving Stanley, take the Murchison Hwy (A10). It's 88km to the C132 turn-off that leads to Cradle Mountain, but plan on a couple of hours thanks to the dramatic descent into Hellyer Gorge.

TRIP HIGHLIGHT
6 Cradle Mountain

Cradle Mountain is one of Australia's premier national parks, a stirring landscape of glacier-sculpted mountain ramparts, remote lakes and wild alpine moorlands. This is prime bushwalking country, from the week-long Overland Track that begins here to shorter boardwalk hikes that are ideal for families. Dove Lake, where the paved road ends, is the starting point for so many hikes both leisurely and seriously

challenging. The lake also offers the best views of the mountain and it's connected to hidden Crater Lake via a glorious three-hour-return hike. And these are just the beginning, with well-marked trails fanning out into the wilderness. Even close to the vehicle access points, Cradle Mountain is a fabulous wildlife-watching destination as well – wombats, Bennett's wallabies and pademelons are almost guaranteed, with echidnas, Tassie devils and platypuses also possible.

🍴 🛏 p419

WATCHING WILDLIFE IN CRADLE MOUNTAIN

Cradle Mountain is one of the easiest places in Australia to see wildlife in abundance. In addition to the following, it's possible to see Tasmanian devils, echidnas, spotted-tailed quolls and eastern quolls.

Common wombat Seen regularly throughout the park, but best found along the Ronny Creek valley before dusk.

Tasmanian pademelon This small, plump, wallaby-like creature is commonly seen throughout the park, especially around accommodation such as Cradle Mountain Hotel.

Bennett's wallaby Not as common as the pademelon, but still seen regularly, including around Ronny Creek.

Platypus Present in most of the park's rivers, but try Ronny Creek close to dawn or dusk.

The Drive >> It's an easy 65km drive from Cradle Mountain to Sheffield. At first, the route crosses a high, lightly forested plateau, with denser forest around the middle section of the road before the more open country around Sheffield; watch out for wombats and echidnas by the roadside, especially close to sunrise or sunset.

⑦ Sheffield

Sheffield would be a typical work-a-day inland, provincial Tasmanian town were it not for the remarkable profusion of murals that have adorned the town's facades since the 1980s. Based on an idea from Chemainus in Canada, the large murals depict scenes from the district's pioneer days, and Sheffield is now a veritable outdoor art gallery, with over 50 fantastic large-scale murals and the annual **Muralfest** (www.muralfest. com.au; ⊙ late Mar-early Apr) to produce more. To see Sheffield's best, grab a headset ($9) from the **visitor centre** (☎03-6491 1036; www.sheffieldcradleinfo. com.au; 5 Pioneer Cres; ⊙9am-5pm) and take a thoroughly informative **Mural Audio Tour** of Sheffield's outdoor art.

The Drive >> Rolling hill country dominates the journey along the B14 then B13 to the main Rte 1; take the turn-off to Deloraine 7km southeast of Elizabeth Town.

⑧ Deloraine

At the foot of the Great Western Tiers, a long line of hills that separates the northern coastal hinterland from the island's more rugged interior, Deloraine feels like a perfectly sited English country town. That has as much to do with the setting as it does with the architecture: Georgian and Victorian buildings, ornate with wrought-iron tracery, crowd the main street, which leads to green parkland on the banks of the Meander River. The town has an artsy, vibrant feel, with several cool little eateries, some bohemian boutiques and secondhand shops.

The Drive >> Sadly, the prettiest part of your journey now lies behind you, and the best things that can be said about the final 50km along Rte 1 to Launceston are the distant views of Bass Strait and the high hills away to the south. Otherwise, there's little reason to linger.

⑨ Launceston

Launceston may be Tasmania's second city, but its inhabitants argue that their architecture is more elegant, their parks more beautiful and their surrounding hills more verdant. Art and design are big here, and there's a new respect for the city's fabulous cache of heritage buildings. Launceston has also become a sporty, outdoorsy city of late, much of it revolving around gorgeous Cataract Gorge.

🛏 p419

Eating & Sleeping

Strahan ❶

✗ Risby Cove   Modern Australian $$

(☏03-6471 7572; www.risbycove.com.au; Esplanade; mains $22-38; ☺6-9pm) People come from all over to dine at the Cove, a quietly sophisticated place just across the water from the town centre. The menu features fancy dishes such as roast Tamar Valley duck, and there's always fresh Macquarie Harbour ocean trout. There's a good kids menu, too. The views over the water are sensational.

🛏 Gordon Gateway   Apartment $$

(☏03-6471 7165, 1300 134 425; www. gordongateway.com.au; Grining St; d $79-140) On the hillside on the way to Regatta Point, this place has motel-like studio units and larger A-frame chalets, most with sweeping water and township views.

Stanley ❺

✗ Xanders   Modern Australian $$$

(☏03-6458 1111; 25 Church St; mains $28-42; ☺6-9pm Wed-Sun) Stanley's best fine-dining restaurant is set in an old house on the main street with views back and front. The menu has an accent on fish and seafood, but Xanders also serves the area's excellent beef and specials such as duck and tandoori-rubbed rack of lamb. There's a good kids menu, too.

🛏 Ark Stanley   Boutique Hotel $$

(☏0421 695 224; www.thearkstanley.com.au; 18 Wharf Rd; d $140-300) Polished wooden floors, wrought-iron furnishings, luxury linens, goose-down duvets...this place, with its individually styled rooms, takes attention to detail to a whole new level. Fine views are to be had from some of the rooms and the service is discreet but attentive.

Cradle Mountain ❻

✗ Tavern Bar & Bistro   Bistro $$

(☏03-6492 2100; www.cradlemountainlodge. com.au; mains $16-29; ☺noon-8.30pm) Hearty mountain fare and a roaring open fire give this unpretentious place at Cradle Mountain Lodge its charm. It's all about pasta, burgers, steaks and salmon and it has a good kids' menu. There's also live music some Wednesdays at 8.30pm.

🛏 Cradle Mountain Lodge   Lodge $$$

(☏1300 806 192, 03-6492 2103; www. cradlemountainlodge.com.au; Cradle Mountain Rd; d $189-870; P ❄ @ 🛜) When this mountain resort of wooden cabins emerges from the swirling mist on a winter's day, you can't help but be charmed by its ambience. Most rooms wear a contemporary feel and some have open fires, the lodge puts on dozens of activities and guided walks, and the Waldheim Alpine Spa offers relaxing massages and beauty treatments.

Launceston ❾

🛏 Fresh on Charles   Apartment $$

(☏03-6331 4299; www.freshoncharles.com. au; 178 Charles St; d $120-150; 🛜) Take the stairs up from vegetarian cafe **Fresh on Charles** (☏03-6331 4299; mains $10-22, shared plates $35-65; ☺8.30am-3pm Sat-Thu, 8.30am-late Fri; 🛜 🍴) to these two excellent self-contained apartments with polished concrete floors. They're retro, minimal, brilliantly central and great value for money. The pricier unit faces off with the boughs of Princes Sq across the road. Free street parking out the front after dark.

Driving in Australia

With more than 350,000km of paved roads criss-crossing the country, Australia is an infinitely fascinating road movie come to life.

Driving Fast Facts

→ **Right or left?** Drive on the left
→ **Legal driving age** 18
→ **Top speed limit** 110km/h
→ **Signature car** Holden Commodore

DRIVING LICENCE & DOCUMENTS

To drive in Australia you'll need to hold a current driving licence issued in English from your home country. If the licence isn't in English, you'll also need to carry an International Driving Permit, issued in your home country.

INSURANCE

Third-party insurance With the exception of NSW and Queensland, third-party personal-injury insurance is included in the vehicle registration cost, ensuring that every registered vehicle carries at least minimum insurance (if registering your own car in NSW or Queensland, you'll need to arrange this privately). We recommend extending that minimum to at least third-party property insurance – minor collisions can be amazingly expensive.

Rental vehicles When it comes to hire cars, understand your liability in the event of an accident. Rather than risk paying out thousands of dollars, consider taking out comprehensive car insurance or paying an additional daily amount to the rental company for excess reduction (this reduces the excess payable in the event of an accident from between $2000 and $5000 to a few hundred dollars).

Exclusions Be aware that if travelling on dirt roads, you usually will not be covered by insurance unless you have a 4WD (read the fine print). Also, many companies' insurance won't cover the cost of damage to glass (including the windscreen) or tyres.

HIRING A CAR

Larger car-rental companies have drop-offs in major cities and towns. Most companies require drivers to be over the age of 21, though in some cases it's 18 and in others 25.

Suggestions to assist in the process:

→ Read the contract from cover to cover.

→ Some companies may require a signed credit-card slip as a bond, others may actually charge your credit card; if this is the case, find out when you'll get a refund.

→ Ask if unlimited kilometres are included and, if not, what the extra charge per kilometre is.

Road Trip Websites

Australian Bureau of Meteorology (www.bom.gov.au) Weather information.

Department of Planning, Transport & Infrastructure (☎1300 361 033; www.transport.sa.gov.au) SA road conditions.

Green Vehicle Guide (www.greenvehicleguide.gov.au) Rates Australian vehicles based on greenhouse and air-pollution emissions.

Live Traffic NSW (☎1300 131 122; www.livetraffic.com) NSW road conditions.

Main Roads Western Australia (☎13 81 38; www.mainroads.wa.gov.au) WA road conditions.

Motorcycle Council of NSW (☎1300 679 622; www.mccofnsw.org.au) One of many such organisations around Australia.

Road Report (☎1800 246 199; www.roadreport.nt.gov.au) NT road conditions.

Traffic & Travel Information (☎13 19 40; www.transport.sa.gov.au) Queensland road conditions.

➡ Find out what excess you'll have to pay if you have a prang, and if it can be lowered by an extra charge per day (this option will usually be offered to you whether you ask or not). Check if your personal travel insurance covers you for vehicle accidents and excess.

➡ Check for exclusions (hitting a kangaroo, damage on unsealed roads etc) and whether you're covered on unavoidable unsealed roads (eg accessing camp sites). Some companies also exclude parts of the car from cover, such as the underbelly, tyres and windscreen.

➡ At pick-up inspect the vehicle for any damage. Make a note of anything on the contract before you sign.

➡ Ask about breakdown and accident procedures.

➡ If you can, return the vehicle during business hours and insist on an inspection in your presence.

The usual big international companies operate in Australia (Avis, Budget, Europcar, Hertz, Thrifty). The following websites offer last-minute discounts and the opportunity to compare rates between the big operators:

➡ www.carhire.com.au
➡ www.drivenow.com.au
➡ www.webjet.com.au

MAPS

Good-quality road and topographical maps are plentiful and readily available around Australia. State motoring organisations are a dependable source of road maps, including road atlases with comprehensive coverage of road networks.

Hema's *Australia Road Atlas* is a good general road atlas covering the entire country, and it also offers a range of smaller fold-out maps on specific destinations.

ROADS & CONDITIONS

Australia's roads are generally in excellent condition, but never discount the possibility of potholes, especially in rural areas that receive heavy truck traffic.

Overtaking Lanes

If you've spent any time in Europe, you'll be underwhelmed by Australia's dearth of dual carriageway roads. Apart from the Hume Fwy connecting Sydney and Melbourne (the inland route, not the coast road), most motorways are restricted to a 100km (or less) radius around major cities. Although there are regular overtaking lanes on many roads and traffic flows generally maintain a reasonable speed, there are times when you'll become frustrated as you wait to pass a slow caravan, truck or old man in a hat out for a Sunday drive. The only sensible response in such circumstances is patience.

Unsealed Roads

At last count, Australia was so vast that it had 466,874km of unsealed roads – that's significantly more than the distance from earth to the moon! While many of these are suitable for 2WD vehicles when conditions are dry, many more are not, and most become treacherous or impassable after even a little rain. Others peter out into the sand. The simple rule is this – never leave the paved road unless you know the road, have checked recent weather conditions and asked locals for their advice.

Toll Roads

Toll roads are restricted to freeways within major cities such as Melbourne and Sydney. If you're travelling in a rental vehicle, it should have the necessary electronic reader and any tolls will be charged when you return your vehicle. Either way, take note of any numbers to call at the tollpoints to make sure you don't get hit with a fine for late payment – you usually have between one and three days to make any payment.

ROAD RULES

Give way An important road rule is 'give way to the right' – if an intersection is unmarked (unusual) and at roundabouts, you must give way to vehicles entering the intersection from your right.

Speed limits The general speed limit in built-up and residential areas is 50km/h. Near schools, the limit is usually 25km/h (sometimes 40km/h) in the morning and afternoon. On the highway it's usually 100km/h or 110km/h; in the NT it's either 110km/h or 130km/h. Police have speed radar guns and cameras and are fond of using them in strategic locations.

Seatbelts and car seats It's the law to wear seatbelts in the front and back seats; you're likely to get a fine if you don't. Small children must be belted into an approved safety seat.

Drink-driving Random breath-tests are common. If you're caught with a blood-alcohol level of more than 0.05% expect a fine and the loss of your licence. Police can randomly pull any driver over for a breathalyser or drug test.

Mobile phones Using a mobile phone while driving is illegal in Australia (excluding hands-free technology).

FUEL

Fuel types Unleaded and diesel fuel is available from service stations sporting well-known international brand names. LPG (liquefied petroleum gas) is not always stocked at more remote roadhouses; if you're on gas it's safer to have dual-fuel capacity.

Costs Prices vary from place to place, but at the time of writing unleaded was hovering

---

Driving Problem-Buster

What should I do if my car breaks down? Call the service number of your car-hire company and a local garage will be contacted.

What if I have an accident? Your first call should be to the insurance company and you should make sure that you have the contact details (at the very least) of the drivers of all other vehicles involved. Never admit fault unless instructed to do so by your insurance company. For minor accidents you'll need to fill out an accident statement when you return the vehicle. If problems crop up, go to the nearest police station.

What should I do if I get stopped by the police? The police will want to see your driving licence, passport (if you're from overseas) and proof of insurance.

What if I can't find anywhere to stay? If you're travelling during summer and/or holiday periods, always book accommodation in advance as beds fill up fast. If you're stuck and it's getting late, motels and motor inns line the roadside in even small Australian towns, while in outback areas the nearest roadhouse (a one-stop shop for accommodation, food and fuel) is likely to be your only option.

Road Distances (km)

	Adelaide	Albany	Alice Springs	Birdsville	Brisbane	Broome	Cairns	Canberra	Cape York	Darwin	Kalgoorlie	Melbourne	Perth	Sydney	Townsville
Albany	2649														
Alice Springs	1512	3573													
Birdsville	1183	3244	1176												
Brisbane	1942	4178	1849	1573											
Broome	4043	2865	2571	3564	5065										
Cairns	3079	5601	2396	1919	1705	4111									
Canberra	1372	4021	2725	2038	1287	5296	2923								
Cape York	4444	6566	3361	2884	2601	5076	965	3888							
Darwin	3006	5067	1494	2273	3774	1844	2820	3948	3785						
Kalgoorlie	2168	885	3092	2763	3697	3052	5234	3540	6199	4896					
Melbourne	728	3377	2240	1911	1860	4811	3496	637	4461	3734	2896				
Perth	2624	411	3548	3219	4153	2454	6565	3996	7530	4298	598	3352			
Sydney	1597	4246	3109	2007	940	5208	2634	289	3599	3917	3765	862	3869		
Townsville	3237	5374	2055	1578	1295	3770	341	2582	1306	2479	4893	3155	5349	2293	
Uluru	1559	3620	441	1617	2290	3012	2837	2931	3802	1935	3139	2287	3595	2804	2496

	Bicheno	Cradle Mountain	Devonport	Hobart	Launceston
Cradle Mountain	383				
Devonport	283	100			
Hobart	186	296	334		
Launceston	178	205	105	209	
Queenston	443	69	168	257	273

These are the shortest distances by road; other routes may be considerably longer.
For distances by coach, check the companies' leaflets.

between \$1.20 and \$1.50 in the cities. Out in the country, prices soar – in outback NT, SA, WA and Queensland you can pay as much as \$2.20 per litre.

Availability In cities and towns petrol stations proliferate, but distances between fill-ups can be long in the outback. That said, there are only a handful of tracks where you'll require a long-range fuel tank. On main roads there'll be a small town or roadhouse roughly every 150km to 200km. Many petrol stations, but not all, are open 24 hours.

SAFETY

Theft from vehicles can be an issue in large cities or tourist areas, but the risk is unlikely to be any higher than you'd encounter back home.

Animal Hazards

➜ Roadkill is a huge problem in Australia and many Australians avoid travelling once the sun drops because of the risks posed by nocturnal animals on the roads.

➜ Kangaroos are common on country roads, as are cows and sheep in the unfenced outback. Kangaroos are most active around dawn and dusk and often travel in groups: if you see one hopping across the road, slow right down, as its friends may be just behind it.

➜ If you hit and kill an animal while driving, pull it off the road, preventing the next car from having a potential accident. If the animal is only injured and is small, or perhaps an orphaned joey (baby kangaroo), wrap it in a towel or blanket and call the relevant wildlife rescue line:

Department of Environment & Heritage Protection (☏1300 264 625; www.ehp.qld.gov.au) Queensland.

Department of Parks & Wildlife (Wildcare Helpline ☏08-9474 9055; www.parks.dpaw.wa.gov.au) WA.

Fauna Rescue of South Australia (☏08-7226 0017; www.faunarescue.org.au) SA.

NSW Wildlife Information, Rescue & Education Service (WIRES; ☏1300 094 737; www.wires.org.au) NSW.

Parks & Wildlife Service (after hours ☏03-6165 4305, 1300 827 727; www.parks.tas.gov.au) Tasmania.

Wildcare Inc NT (☏0408 885 341, 08-8988 6121; www.wildcarent.org.au) NT.

Wildlife Victoria (☏1300 094 535; www.wildlifevictoria.org.au) Victoria.

Behind the Wheel

Fatigue Be wary of driver fatigue; driving long distances (particularly in hot weather) can be utterly exhausting. Falling asleep at the wheel is not uncommon. On a long haul, stop and rest every two hours or so – do some exercise, change drivers or have a coffee.

Road trains Be careful overtaking road trains (trucks with two or three trailers stretching for as long as 50m); you'll need distance and plenty of speed. On single-lane roads get right off the road when one approaches.

Unsealed roads Unsealed road conditions vary wildly and cars perform differently when braking and turning on dirt. Don't exceed 80km/h on dirt roads; if you go faster, you won't have time to respond to a sharp turn, stock on the road or an unmarked gate or cattle grid.

OUTBACK DRIVING

In 'Power & the Passion', Midnight Oil's damning ode to the Australian suburban condition, Peter Garrett sings, 'And no one goes outback that's that.' It really is amazing how few Australians have explored the outback. To many, it's either a mythical place inhabited by tourists and Indigenous Australians, or something for the too-hard basket – too hot, too far to drive, too expensive to fly, too many sand dunes and flies... But for those who make the effort, a strange awakening occurs – a quiet comprehension of the primal terrain and profound size of Australia that you simply can't fathom while sitting on Bondi Beach.

About the Outback

The Australian outback is vast, blanketing the centre of the continent. While most Australians live on the coast, that thin green fringe of the continent is hardly typical of this enormous land mass. Inland is the desert soul of Australia.

Weather patterns vary from region to region – from sandy arid deserts to semi-arid scrublands to tropical savannah – but you can generally rely on hot sunny days, starry night skies and mile after mile of unbroken horizon.

Australia Playlist

Flame Trees (Cold Chisel; 1984) Small town, big song.

Back In Black (AC/DC; 1980) The greatest guitar riff ever?

Wide Open Road (The Triffids; 1986) Road-tripping melancholia.

Beds Are Burning (Midnight Oil; 1987) Aboriginal land rights anthem. Any Midnight Oil would be a fine thing to have in your glove box.

Under The Milky Way (The Church; 1988) Arty haircuts, pointy shoes, jangly guitars.

Nullarbor (Kasey Chambers; 2010) Poignant understatement from Australia's first lady of alt-country.

Great albums to have on hand are:
➡ *Diesel & Dust* (Midnight Oil)
➡ *Circus Animals* (Cold Chisel)
➡ *Neon Ballroom* (Silverchair)
➡ *Kick* (INXS)
➡ *Woodface* (Crowded House)
➡ *The Boatman's Call* (Nick Cave & the Bad Seeds)
➡ *Songs From the South: Paul Kelly's Greatest Hits* (Paul Kelly)

Type of Vehicle

2WD Depending on where you want to travel, a regulation 2WD vehicle might suffice. They're cheaper to hire, buy and run than 4WDs and are more readily available. Most are fuel efficient, and easy to repair and sell. Downsides: no off-road capability and no room to sleep!

4WD Four-wheel drives are good for outback travel as they can access almost any track you get a hankering for. And there might even be space to sleep in the back. Downsides: poor fuel economy, awkward to park and more expensive to hire or buy.

Campervan Creature comforts at your fingertips: sink, fridge, cupboards, beds, kitchen and space to relax. Downsides: slow and often not fuel-efficient, not great on dirt roads and too big for nipping around the city.

Motorcycle The Australian climate is great for riding, and bikes are handy in city traffic. Downsides: Australia isn't particularly bike-friendly in terms of driver awareness, there's limited luggage capacity, and exposure to the elements.

Outback Driving & Safety Checklist

You need to be particularly organised and vigilant when travelling in the outback, especially on remote sandy tracks, due to the scorching temperatures, long distances between fuel stops and isolation. Following are a few tips.

Communication

➡ Report your route and schedule to the police, a friend or relative.

➡ Mobile phones are practically useless in the outback. A safety net is to hire a satellite phone, high-frequency (HF) radio transceiver equipped to pick up the Royal Flying Doctor Service bases, or emergency position-indicating radio beacon (EPIRB).

➡ In an emergency, stay with your vehicle; it's easier to spot than you are, and you won't be able to carry a heavy load of water very far. Don't sit inside your vehicle as it will become an oven in hot weather.

➡ If you do become stranded, set fire to a spare tyre (let the air out first). The pall of smoke will be visible for miles.

Dirt-Road Driving

➡ Inflate your tyres to the recommended levels for the terrain you're travelling on; on desert dirt, deflate your tyres to 25psi to avoid punctures.

➡ Reduce speed on unsealed roads, as traction is decreased and braking distances increase.

Road Trains

On many outback highways you'll see thundering road trains: huge trucks (a prime mover plus two or three trailers) up to 50m long. These things don't move over for anyone, and it's like a scene out of *Mad Max* having one bear down on you at 120km/h. When you see a road train approaching on a narrow bitumen road, slow down and pull over – if the truck has to put its wheels off the road to pass you, the resulting barrage of stones will almost certainly smash your windscreen. When trying to overtake one, allow plenty of room (about a kilometre) to complete the manoeuvre. Road trains throw up a lot of dust on dirt roads, so if you see one coming it's best to just pull over and stop until it's gone past.
And while you're on outback roads, don't forget to give the standard bush wave to oncoming drivers – it's simply a matter of lifting the index finger off the steering wheel to acknowledge your fellow motorist.

Automobile Associations

Under the auspices of the **Australian Automobile Association** (☎02-6247 7311; www.aaa.asn.au) are automobile clubs in each state, handy when it comes to insurance, regulations, maps and roadside assistance. Club membership (around $100 to $150) can save you a lot of trouble if things go wrong mechanically. If you're a member of an auto club in your home country, check if reciprocal rights are offered in Australia. The major Australian auto clubs generally offer reciprocal rights in other states and territories.

AANT (Automobile Association of the Northern Territory; ☎13 11 11; www.aant. com.au)

NRMA (National Roads & Motorists' Association; ☎13 11 22; www.mynrma.com. au) NSW and the ACT.

RAC (Royal Automobile Club of Western Australia; ☎13 17 03; www.rac.com.au)

RACQ (Royal Automobile Club of Queensland; ☎13 19 05; www.racq.com.au)

RACT (Royal Automobile Club of Tasmania; ☎13 27 22; www.ract.com.au)

RACV (Royal Automobile Club of Victoria; ☎13 72 28; www.racv.com.au)

➡ Dirt roads are often corrugated: keeping an even speed is the best approach.

➡ Dust on outback roads can obscure your vision, so always stop and wait for it to settle.

➡ If your vehicle is struggling through deep sand, deflating your tyres a bit will help. If you do get stuck, don't attempt to get out by revving the engine; this just causes wheels to dig in deeper.

Road Hazards

➡ Outback highways are usually long, flat ribbons of tarmac stretching across the red desert flats. The temptation is to get it over with quickly, but try to keep a lid on your speed.

➡ Take a rest every few hours: driver fatigue is a real problem.

➡ Wandering cattle, sheep, emus, kangaroos, camels, etc make driving fast a dangerous prospect. Take care and avoid nocturnal driving, as this is often when native animals come out. Many car-hire companies prohibit nighttime driving.

➡ Road trains are an ever-present menace on the main highways. Give them a wide berth, they're much bigger than you!

Supplies & Equipment

➡ Always carry plenty of water: in warm weather allow 5L per person per day and an extra amount for the radiator, carried in several containers.

➡ Bring plenty of food in case of a breakdown.

➡ Carry a first-aid kit, a good set of maps, a torch and spare batteries, a compass, and a shovel for digging if you get bogged.

Weather & Road Conditions

➡ Check road conditions before travelling: roads that are passable in the Dry (March to October) can disappear beneath water during the Wet.

➡ Check weather forecasts daily.

➡ Keep an eye out for potholes, rough sections, roads changing surfaces without notice, soft and broken verges, and single-lane bridges.

➡ Take note of the water-level markers at creek crossings to gauge the water's depth before you proceed.

➡ Don't attempt to cross flooded bridges or causeways unless you're sure of the depth, and of any road damage hidden underwater.

Your Vehicle

➡ Have your vehicle serviced and checked before you leave.

➡ Load your vehicle evenly, with heavy items inside and light items on the roof rack.

➡ Check locations and opening times of service stations, and carry spare fuel and provisions; opportunities for fill-ups can be infrequent.

➡ Carry essential tools: a spare tyre (two if possible), a fan belt and a radiator hose, as well as a tyre-pressure gauge and an air pump.

➡ An off-road jack might come in handy, as will a snatchem strap or tow rope for quick extraction when you're stuck (useful if there's another vehicle to pull you out).

➡ A set of cheap, high-profile tyres (around $80 each) will give your car a little more ground clearance.

BEHIND THE SCENES

SEND US YOUR FEEDBACK

We love to hear from travellers – your comments help make our books better. We read every word, and we guarantee that your feedback goes straight to the authors. Visit **lonelyplanet. com/contact** to submit your updates and suggestions.

Note: We may edit, reproduce and incorporate your comments in Lonely Planet products such as guidebooks, websites and digital products, so let us know if you don't want your comments reproduced or your name acknowledged. For a copy of our privacy policy visit lonelyplanet.com/privacy.

ACKNOWLEDGMENTS

Climate map data adapted from Peel MC, Finlayson BL & McMahon TA (2007) 'Updated World Map of the Köppen-Geiger Climate Classification', *Hydrology and Earth System Sciences*, 11, 163344.

Front cover photographs: (top) Eyre Highway, Nullarbor National Park, Peter Walton Photography/Getty; (left) Palm Beach, Queensland, David Hancock/Alamy; (right) Mt Field National Park, Andrew Watson/Alamy

Back cover photograph: Devil's Marbles, Northern Territory, Australian Scenics/Getty

AUTHOR THANKS

Heartfelt thanks to Tasmin Waby, Julie Sheridan and Katie O'Connell whose wisdom and insights contributed so much to this book. Thanks also to my talented fellow Lonely Planet authors Kate Armstrong, Brett Atkinson, Carolyn Bain, Peter Dragicevich, Paul Harding, Miriam Raphael, Charles Rawlings-Way, Steve Waters and Meg Worby, without whom this book would never have been possible. And to countless locals who shared their passion for and expertise on this wonderful corner of the earth. To Ron, Jan, Lisa, Greg, Alex, Greta, Damien, Ron, Elaine and all the Pumpas – you represent all that I love about this country. To Marina, Carlota and Valentina – *os quiero* and I can't wait to revisit the road trips in this book with you.

THIS BOOK

This 1st edition of *Australia's Best Trips* was researched and written by Anthony Ham. This guidebook was produced by the following:

Destination Editor Tasmin Waby

Product Editors Anne Mason, Katie O'Connell

Senior Cartographer Julie Sheridan

Book Designer Katherine Marsh

Assisting Editors Imogen Bannister, Andrea Dobbin, Victoria Harrison, Kate James, Vicky Smith, Ross Taylor

Assisting Cartographers Julie Dodkins, Rachel Imeson, Diana Von Holdt

Cover Researcher Campbell McKenzie

Thanks to Andi Jones, Catherine Naghten, Karyn Noble, Jessica Rose, Tony Wheeler

OUR STORY

A beat-up old car, a few dollars in the pocket and a sense of adventure. In 1972 that's all Tony and Maureen Wheeler needed for the trip of a lifetime – across Europe and Asia overland to Australia. It took several months, and at the end – broke but inspired – they sat at their kitchen table writing and stapling together their first travel guide, *Across Asia on the Cheap*. Within a week they'd sold 1500 copies. Lonely Planet was born.

Today, Lonely Planet has offices in Melbourne, London and Oakland, with more than 600 staff and writers. We share Tony's belief that 'a great guidebook should do three things: inform, educate and amuse'.

INDEX

OUR WRITER

ANTHONY HAM

Anthony (www.anthonyham.com) was born in Melbourne, grew up in Sydney and spent much of his adult life travelling the world. He recently returned to Australia after ten years living in Madrid and brings to this guide more than fifteen years' experience as a travel writer. As a recently returned expat, Anthony is loving the opportunity to rediscover his country and indulge his passion for the wilderness. He brings to the book the unique perspective of knowing the land intimately and yet seeing it anew as if through the eyes of an outsider.

My Favourite Trip 33 **Kimberley Crossing** for the soulful and dramatic desert scenery, and the solitude of this beguiling corner of the country.

Published by Lonely Planet Publications Pty Ltd
ABN 36 005 607 983
1st edition – Nov 2015
ISBN 978 1 74360 517 2
© Lonely Planet 2015   Photographs © as indicated 2015
10 9 8 7 6 5 4 3 2 1
Printed in China

Although the authors and Lonely Planet have taken all reasonable care in preparing this book, we make no warranty about the accuracy or completeness of its content and, to the maximum extent permitted, disclaim all liability arising from its use.

All rights reserved. No part of this publication may be copied, stored in a retrieval system, or transmitted in any form by any means, electronic, mechanical, recording or otherwise, except brief extracts for the purpose of review, and no part of this publication may be sold or hired, without the written permission of the publisher. Lonely Planet and the Lonely Planet logo are trademarks of Lonely Planet and are registered in the US Patent and Trademark Office and in other countries. Lonely Planet does not allow its name or logo to be appropriated by commercial establishments, such as retailers, restaurants or hotels. Please let us know of any misuses: lonelyplanet.com/ip.